*Chaucer and
the Country of the Stars*

Frontispiece: Late Gothic Astrolabe (front and back)

This book has been composed in Linotype Caslon Old Face

Publication of this book has been aided by
the Whitney Darrow Publication Reserve Fund of
Princeton University Press

Printed in the United States of America
by Princeton University Press,
Princeton, New Jersey

TO SARAH

Penelope and Marcia Catoun,
Mak of youre wyfhod no comparisoun

"*And thus maketh Love entrechaungeable the perdurable courses; and thus is discordable bataile yput out of the contre of the sterres.*"

"*For the erthe overcomen yeveth the sterres.*"

BOETHIUS

Preface

IN THE Middle Ages astrology was closely linked with mythology, with the problems of free will and determinism, and with the understanding of character and personality. Because of these associations it was fundamental to Chaucer's epoch in a way difficult to imagine today. Thus, while astrology is neither the cornerstone, the keystone, nor the touchstone of Chaucer's art, it is featured prominently among his materials, and we should not downgrade the importance of astrological imagery in a poet who both opened and closed his *Canterbury Tales* with references to the zodiac. It follows that this book is not as narrow a study as one might think from the title, for astrology was once not as narrow as today's newspaper horoscopes and weighing machine fortunes. Moreover, it has not been my intention to write a book about astrology, but rather about Chaucer. I have tried to write essays of historical criticism in which an analysis of certain incidental astrological images based on mediaeval source materials would lead to a reconsideration of the poetry in which those images occurred.

In this respect I have departed from the mainstream of Chaucerian scholarship, which has been confined to analyzing the astrological imagery in Chaucer solely from the technical point of view. The rare attempts to probe the poetic function of Chaucer's astrological images, notably those of Professor Curry, have made a profitable start by studying the horoscopes of some of Chaucer's literary characters. However, recent work in art history suggests that the sense of mediaeval artistic uses of astrological images should be studied in a wider context that would include, among other things, mythology and mythography. There is, then, much that has not been done, and although the immensity of the subject and its not infrequent obscurity have caused it to be neglected by scholars, there is as a consequence an excellent and rarely assumed vantage point here for a fresh look at many of Chaucer's poems.[1]

[1] When one considers the writings debating the merits of astrology as well as the writings of the astrologers themselves, the resulting corpus is impressively large. No less a scholar than Don Cameron Allen has remarked on this: "The literature of astrology is as vast as the history of man. No one scholar can possibly hope to untangle all of its intricately woven strands . . ." (*The Star-crossed Renaissance*

Because this book's orientation is toward poetic and not astrological explication, I have made little attempt to adjust the length of different chapters, and have tried to say as much about the poetry as was warranted in each case and no more. For the same reason I have not made any effort to analyze every astrological image in Chaucer's extant work, but have pursued those that preliminary investigation suggested would be the most fruitful. This has resulted in a somewhat cursory treatment of the *Troilus*, but the major astrological imagery there has already been treated in detail by Professor O'Connor, and any further study should properly take up the astrological references in their relation to the abundant mythological imagery in the poem. This will be more appropriate after the appearance of Professor Mc-Call's work on classical mythology in the *Troilus*.[2]

As for astrology per se, I have not given a history of the subject nor have I tried to find presumed "sources" for passages in Chaucer, nor have I attempted to document the astrologers' opinions in strict chronological order. I have devoted a chapter to the vexed issue of Chaucer's attitude toward astrology, but I have not always made an effort to separate the astrologers one from another. There were two phenomena before Chaucer's era that caused many astrological writings to be disjoined from their original authors: the first was the encyclopedic activity in Arabian astrology from the tenth to the twelfth centuries, which saw much compiling of earlier writings, and the second was the vigorous work of translation from Arabic into Latin in the twelfth century. The latter also tended to erase any chronological sense, and was accompanied by new compilations by translators themselves, such as the famous one of John of Seville.[3]

[Durham, 1941], p. v). For Curry's work see the revised edition of his book: Walter Clyde Curry, *Chaucer and the Mediaeval Sciences* (New York, 1960).

[2] See John J. O'Connor, "The Astronomical Dating of Chaucer's *Troilus*," *JEGP*, LV (1956), 556-62; and John P. McCall's unpublished dissertation, "Classical Myth in Chaucer's *Troilus and Criseyde*" (Princeton, 1955).

[3] The classification of Arabian astrology into various periods is taken from Carmody's invaluable bibliography: Francis J. Carmody, *Arabic Astronomical and Astrological Sciences in Latin Translation: A Critical Bibliography* (Berkeley and Los Angeles, 1956). On the history of translations see George Sarton, *Introduction to the History of Science*, 3 vols. in 5 (Washington, 1927-48), II, Part 1, pp. 20-21, 114, 167-75. Sarton points out that the Moorish occupation of Spain from 712-1085

Thus, by the fourteenth century there were a great number of astrological manuscripts available to Chaucer, and many of them borrowed from one another either openly or tacitly. This situation is further complicated by the mediaeval predilection for *florilegia,* epitomes, and *centiloquia,* which often show heavy editing and make the identification of particular ideas even more difficult.[4] Chaucer mentions very few astrologers by name—Ptolemy, Alchabitius, and Al-Kindi being the only ones—and while I have consulted the works of these men, it would be foolish to think that Chaucer knew only their writings or knew them better than those of other astrologers, for his specific references are too meager.[5] In the case of an author like Boccaccio, who was in the habit of referring his astrological remarks in the *Genealogy of the Pagan Gods* to their respective sources—Dorotheus Sidonius, Andalo da Negri, Haly, etc.—one could make out a plausible case for sources of astrological imagery in his other works, but this will not work for Chaucer.

Chaucer's creations, like the works of other fine artists, are always greater than the sum of their parts, but we must perceive and understand these contributory elements if we are to appreciate fully the

provided a center of learning in Toledo. After the reconquest, this learning was tapped heavily and abruptly, accounting for the chronological concentration of the translations.

[4] For example, there are many more extant manuscripts of a *florilegium* based on Albumasar than there are of his major work, the *Introductorium.* (See Carmody, *Sciences,* pp. 88-94.) In the same vein we should not forget that the Wife of Bath's proverbs from "Ptolemy" are in fact taken from a list of apothegms prefixed to an edition of Ptolemy by a twelfth-century translator. See Ewald Flügel, "Ueber Einige Stellen aus dem Almagestum Cl. Ptolemei Bei Chaucer Und Im Rosenroman," *Anglia,* XVIII (1895-96), 133-40; and R. Steele, "Chaucer and the 'Almagest,'" *Library,* Ser. 3, X (1919), 243-47.

[5] Chaucer refers to Ptolemy in the Wife of Bath's Prologue, discussed in the note previous, and in the *Treatise on the Astrolabe,* wherein occurs his only reference to Alchabitius. The reference to Al-Kindi is to be found only in the Paris Manuscript, wherein Nicholas, the clerk and roué of the *Miller's Tale,* is said to prize, in addition to his "augrym stones" his "Grayel, Myssal, and Holy Euangel / Of Marke alkyndys wryten fayre and wel, / The Book that hight *Non est iudicium.*" See the review by Roland M. Smith of Derek Price's edition of *The Equatorie of the Planetis,* *JEGP,* LVII (1958), 537. It is also worth mentioning that Chaucer's contemporary, John Gower, refers to the Arabian astrologer Albumasar by name in *Confessio Amantis* VII, 1239, in *The English Works of John Gower,* ed. G. C. Macaulay, EETS, Extra Series No. 82 (London, 1901), II, 266.

precise nature of the greatness of the whole. I hope that this investigation will contribute to this first level of perception, and perhaps to other levels as well. I do not expect that every interpretation of the various astrological cruxes offered here will find universal acceptance, but hopefully some attention will be drawn to a series of important and intriguing Chaucerian problems.

ALL QUOTATIONS from Chaucer are from *The Works of Geoffrey Chaucer*, ed. F. N. Robinson (Boston, 1957), and are specified by an abbreviated title and a line number or by line numbers only, when a single work is under consideration. The abbreviations used are Robinson's with a few exceptions, and the italics used for emphasis in some Chaucerian passages, although not always so indicated, are mine. I am grateful to the Houghton Mifflin Company for permission to cite from the Robinson edition, and to the editors and publishers of *Modern Language Quarterly*, *Philological Quarterly*, and *Traditio* for permission to use slightly revised versions of articles of mine that originally appeared in these journals. The research for this volume and the writing of it were carried out at several institutions and under various auspices. Of these I am particularly indebted to the National Endowment for the Humanities for a grant to complete the writing of the book, and to the Graduate School of the University of Wisconsin for a summer research grant and other research funds. I also wish to thank the University of Cincinnati Graduate School and the Hollins College Faculty Committee on Travel and Research for their support of my work. Thanks are also due to the Graduate School of McMaster University for funds for the acquisition and payment of reproduction fees for the photographs and diagrams in this book.

My debts to persons are both more numerous and more profound than my debts to institutions. Professors Urban Tigner Holmes and Francis Lee Utley read the entire manuscript and offered many cogent suggestions for its improvement, for which I am most grateful. Thomas Roche helped me with my earliest forays into this field with his characteristic erudition and generosity. I am indebted to Leeds Barroll for his continuing encouragement, both personal and professional. My thanks go also to my friend and sometime colleague, Eric

Rothstein, who has been both enthusiastic advocate and impartial critic of my ventures into Chaucerian scholarship for a decade. My parents have always applauded my scholarly interests, and my gratitude to them is matched by my admiration of them. My thanks to my wife are expressed in the dedication of this book.

My greatest debt with regard to this book is to D. W. Robertson, Jr., who first kindled my enthusiasm for Chaucer. He suggested the topic of the doctoral dissertation on which this book is based, and has advised and encouraged my study ever since. The scholarly debt I owe him will be obvious from my approach to Chaucer through historical criticism. I wish, however, to acknowledge my further indebtedness to him for his inspiring classroom teaching. To read Chaucer with him is, as Dante said of his own reading of Boethius and Cicero, to seek silver and find gold.

Contents

Contents

List of Illustrations
Following index

Frontispiece. Late Gothic Astrolabe (two views). Oxford, Museum of the History of Science, Lewis Evans Collection.

1. Horoscope of Agostino Chigi for December 1, 1466 (Baldassare Peruzzi). Rome, Palazzo Farnesina, Sala della Galatea. Foto Sciamanna, Rome—Art Reference Bureau.

2. God and the Planets (Raphael). Rome, Santa Maria del Popolo, Cappella Chigi, Cupola. Photo Alinari—Art Reference Bureau.

3. Night Sky of Florence, July 8-9, 1422. Florence, San Lorenzo, Sagrestia Vecchia, Cupola. Photo Brogi—Art Reference Bureau.

4. Influence of the Zodiac on the Body (Pol de Limbourg). *Les très riches heures de Jean de France, Duc de Berry*. Chantilly, Musée de Condé, MS 65, folio 14ᵛ. Photo Giraudon.

5. The Zodiac and the Labors of the Months. Amiens, West Portal. Photo Marburg—Art Reference Bureau.
   a. Virgo/August and Libra/September.
   b. Scorpio/October and Sagittarius/November.

6. The Zodiac and the Labors of the Months: Taurus/April (Pol de Limbourg). *Les très riches heures de Jean de France, Duc de Berry*. Chantilly, Musée de Condé, MS 65, folio 4ᵛ. Photo Giraudon.

7. The Zodiac and the Labors of the Months: Libra/September (Pol de Limbourg). *Les très riches heures de Jean de France, Duc de Berry*. Chantilly, Musée de Condé, MS 65, folio 9ᵛ. Photo Giraudon.

8. The Zodiac and the Labors of the Months: Scorpio/October (Pol de Limbourg). *Les très riches heures de Jean de France, Duc de Berry*. Chantilly, Musée de Condé, MS 65, folio 10ᵛ. Photo Giraudon.

9. The Zodiac and the Labors of the Months. Chartres, Royal Portal, Left Door, Tympanum and Archivolts. Photo Marburg—Art Reference Bureau.

xvii

*Chaucer and
the Country of the Stars*

CHAPTER I

Chaucer's Attitude Toward Astrology

I. THE NATURE OF BELIEF

To ARGUE, as Professor Curry has done, that it is "both a futile and a useless procedure" to attempt to reconstruct Chaucer's personal attitude toward astrology is short-sighted.[1] While this observation might hold true for some other artist in some other age, there are certain presuppositions made in connection with it that many Chaucerian scholars would be reluctant to accept. The heart of the matter is that this opinion presumes that the genius of Chaucer's art begins and ends with the creation of self-determining characters who are free to work out their own destinies. As Professor Curry puts it:

> His primary purpose was evidently to create characters acting in stories before a specific audience whose beliefs and prejudices were known; and as artist, with his personal attitudes carefully concealed, he permitted his people to discuss whatever subjects they liked and to express whatever conclusions they pleased.[2]

Such an approach denies the existence in the Middle Ages of any pattern of normative values against which literary characters were to be measured, a view more appropriate to modern than to mediaeval letters. Thus, when Professor Curry goes on to argue that the Franklin's "strictures on natural magic cannot be said to reflect Chaucer's opinion," we must perforce agree, but in fact the issue is not whether or not the characters speak for Chaucer but rather what it means when they speak for themselves. We do not expect that whatever one of Chaucer's characters says will automatically express Chaucer's personal view on the matter—although there was once a tendency to think this—so it is important that we attempt to determine the attitude of Chaucer and of his society toward these various matters by means of analysis of non-literary statements. When this is done we shall have a norm against which we can measure the characters as they are presented. For example, it makes a great deal of difference

---

[1] Curry, *Chaucer and the Mediaeval Sciences*, p. xv.
[2] *Ibid.*, pp. xv-xvi.

what Chaucer and his society thought of the "natural magic" that the Franklin said was "nat worth a flye" (*FranklT*, 1132), for if the subject was scorned by all, then the Franklin is wise, and if Chaucer and others prized astrological magic, then the Franklin is being satirized.

This is, of course, an oversimplification of the problems facing the critic of Chaucer, since our judgment of the Franklin and of the *Franklin's Tale* will depend not only on what is said, but how it is said, and in what intrinsic literary context as well as in what sort of extrinsic conceptual context it is said. The fact remains, however, that we cannot avoid coming to grips with the problem of Chaucer's personal attitude toward astrology and the attitude of those in his audience, for if we assume that Chaucer had goals in mind in his poetry other than the presentation of character for its own sake, then we must assume that all of his own attitudes are important. Once again if we make allowances for tone, the Wife of Bath's plangent cry, "Allas! allas! that evere love was synne!" (*WB Prol*, 614), which follows on the heels of her statement of her horoscope, produces one impression of her character if we assume that Chaucer believed that the configuration of stars at her birth inevitably and unalterably determined that she would be lustful beyond her control. Yet we should draw quite a different conclusion about her predicament if we were reasonably sure that Chaucer thought that horoscopes were nonsense. It is not easy to reduce a subject as complicated and as latitudinous as astrology to such pure blacks and whites of opinion, but it should be possible to obtain some idea of Chaucer's attitudes toward various facets of the science.

This fragmentation of astrology is of great importance, for one of the problems plaguing the study of mediaeval attitudes toward astrology has been a certain tendency toward monolithism: a tendency to survey a writer's remarks on the subject, made at various times and in various contexts, and then to conclude that the author in question was or was not a "believer" in astrology. The subject of the mediaeval attitude toward astrology demands and has received a book length treatment, as has the problem of the Renaissance atti-

tude toward astrology;[3] but although a thorough investigation of the problem is not possible here, some consideration of the nature of the problem and an analysis of the work done on the subject is better than no statement at all. Essentially the situation is that while a great many people believed in astrology in the Middle Ages, there were also many who did not believe at all, while among the "believers" only a very few believed in unalterable astral determinism. However, two issues have tended to cloud the discussions on the subject: how does one define astrology, and how does one define belief?

Part of the difficulty lies in the fact that the words astrology and astronomy were sometimes interchanged in the Middle Ages. This does not mean that the two subjects were necessarily "confused" or that people saw no significant differences between them, but it does mean that there exists an area in which mistakes can be made. Isidore of Seville gives a definition that is interesting because it both distinguishes between astronomy and astrology and shows what we would find to be a common ground between them. Astronomy, according to Isidore, deals only with the motion of the heavens and the causes thereof, while the motions of the sun, moon, and stars are a part of the science of astrology. The other part of astrology, concerning predictions, is merely a superstition.[4] Thus, even when a distinction is drawn between astronomy and astrology there remains a part of astrology that does not concern divination, and this study

[3] Theodore Otto Wedel, *The Mediaeval Attitude Toward Astrology*, Yale Studies in English, No. 60 (New Haven, 1920); and Allen, *Star-crossed Renaissance*.

[4] "Inter astronomiam et astrologiam aliquid differt. Nam astronomia conversionem coeli, ortus, obitus motusque siderum continet, vel qua ex causa ita vocentur. Astrologia vero partim naturalis, partim superstitiosa est. Naturalis, dum exsequitur solis et lunae cursus, vel stellarum, certasque temporum stationes. Superstitiosa vero est illa quam mathematici sequuntur, qui in stellis augurantur, quique etiam duodecim signa per singula animae vel corporis membra disponunt, siderumque cursu nativitates hominum et mores praedicere conantur" (Isidore of Seville, *Etymologiae*, *PL*, 82, col. 170). The term "superstition" carried the sense of theological rather than rational error in the Middle Ages. A distinction virtually the same as the modern one is made by Gower in *Confessio Amantis* VII, 670-84, in *The English Works of John Gower*, II, 251-52.

of celestial motions is not something that requires or does not require "belief." It is rather something to be studied or ignored.

In a similar fashion, a distinction was sometimes drawn between astrology as it pertained to the study of the stars and planets and their motions, and judicial astrology, which had to do with the computation of horoscopes and so on. Chaucer commented on judicial astrology, and we shall investigate his remarks in due course. Professor D. C. Allen, writing on the Renaissance attitude toward astrology, points out that while there were many opponents of judicial astrology—that is, people who claimed that the nature or extent of astral influence could not be precisely calculated, much less predicted —still no one disputed *astrologia naturalis,* the concept that the stars did indeed influence at least some kinds of terrestrial phenomena.[5] Thus, while today we can easily say that such-and-such a person believes in astrology and another does not believe in it, similar distinctions are much less valid in the discussion of earlier ages; there are some very real semantic problems to be faced.

If we conjure up a mental image of a present-day believer in astrology, we tend to think of someone mildly eccentric who frequents quacks and charlatans for advice on his or her business and personal life based on the presumed influence of planetary movements on terrestrial affairs. We hasten to add that *we* don't "believe" in "astrology," but in fact we do believe in some kinds of stellar influences on terrestrial events; the difference is that most of us would deny that there are any demonstrable celestial influences on people. No one would deny, of course, that the sun's varying altitude in the course of the year is the direct cause of the summer's heat and the winter's cold, and we could scarcely take exception if someone wanted to argue that the sun's presence in one sign or another of the zodiac caused cold or hot weather. So far we are only concerned with a difference of expression. If we move on to lunar periodicity the distinction becomes more subtle. We know today that some sea urchins, land crabs, and palolo worms display certain forms of behavior depending upon the phase of the moon.[6] In fact, the palolo worm sends its tail section to the surface of the water on a given day,

---

[5] Allen, *Star-crossed Renaissance,* p. 148.

[6] Louis MacNeice, *Astrology* (London and New York, 1964), p. 46.

at a given hour, when the moon is in its last quarter.[7] We have, then, situations where we can point to the influence of the moon in its monthly course of the zodiac, the sun in its yearly course of the zodiac, and the sun in its daily movement around the earth (which could be expressed as its passage through the twelve "houses" of the judicial astrologers).

In all of this we are still concerned with differences in kind rather than degree, for we would reject the influence of astral bodies other than the sun and the moon on terrestrial affairs, and we would also deny that human beings could be affected in the way that palolo worms are. Part of the difficulty in discussing mediaeval as opposed to modern ideas about astrology is that in the Middle Ages virtually everyone granted a little more celestial influence than would the great majority today: mediaeval people believed that all the "planets" (we shall, as they did, have to consider the sun a planet) had sub-lunar influences, and they believed that people as well as other animals were affected.

On the other hand, there is a further complication of the issue in the fact that while in the Middle Ages almost everyone believed in astrology to a greater extent than do people today, not only what one believed but how one believed was important. We have noted that there were areas of overlap between astronomy and astrology, and that once within the realm of astrology it makes a great deal of difference whether one believes that the stars compel or merely incline. Similarly, how one believed in stellar influence could vary considerably; for while astrology was often the instrument of profiteering charlatans, no less an event than the birth of Christ had been foretold if not foreordained by a star. At the same time that diviners were condemned, prophets were exalted. Thus, the wise man might use even judicial astrology well, even though the subject was widely abused. St. Augustine's distinction about use is therefore essential: "A wise man may use the most precious food without any vice. . . . We are to be commended or reprimanded not because of the things we use, but because of the motive in using them."[8] With this in

[7] *Ecology*, ed. Peter Farb, et al., in *Life Nature Series* (New York, 1963), p. 80.
[8] St. Augustine, *On Christian Doctrine*, trans. D. W. Robertson, Jr., Library of Liberal Arts (New York, 1958), p. 91.

mind we shall have to note that there are believers and believers, who may be distinguished both in kind and in degree.

Probably the most sobering way in which to approach the kind and degree of mediaeval belief in astrology is to examine the position of its very famous opponent, the French contemporary of Chaucer, Nicole Oresme.[9] In the first two chapters of his *Livre de divinacions*, Oresme divides astrology into six parts and makes a judgment as to how much we can know about each. The first part, which we would call astronomy today, is concerned with "the movements, the signs, and the measurements of the heavenly bodies, so that by means of tables, constellations, eclipses and suchlike things in the future can be known." This part, Oresme assures us, is "speculative and mathematical, a very noble and excellent science," and it can be "adequately known but it cannot be known precisely." The second part is concerned with the "qualities, the influences, and physical powers of the stars, with the signs of the zodiac, with degrees, with the heavenly signs, and so on." Here there is a basic variance with what a modern man would believe, for Oresme accepts this study of general stellar influence as a legitimate area of inquiry practiced wrongly in his day. "The second part is a part of natural science and is a great science and it too can be known as far as its nature is concerned but we know too little about it." Furthermore, he says, "the rules in the books are false . . . for the fixed stars . . . are not now in the position they were in then."

The definition of the second part of astrology is rather precise. When Oresme speaks well of the general stellar influences of this part, he is concerned with influences on things terrestrial that are physical and very general, as we may see by his example. "As, for instance, that a star in one quarter of the sky signifies or has power to cause heat or cold, dryness or moisture, and similarly with other physical effects." It is not clear in whom or in what the stars will cause dryness or cold, but it is important to note that these are physical

---

[9] No direct influence of Oresme on Chaucer can be posited, nor are there a great many extant manuscripts of his *Livre de divinacions*. However, Eustache Deschamps, Chaucer's literary if not personal acquaintance, transcribed the bulk of the eighth and ninth chapters of the work, with a few additions, as *Demoustracions contre sortilèges*. See G. W. Coopland, *Nicole Oresme and the Astrologers* (Cambridge, Mass., 1952), pp. 8-9. The citations from Oresme are from this work, pp. 53-57.

changes of the same kind as those produced by the sun's and the moon's revolutions. Another important distinction of Oresme's is that the stars either signify or cause events. This is a common statement and one that makes it very difficult to determine who believed what about astrology. There is all the difference in the world between causing and signifying events, yet one commonly encounters statements about signification being accepted as evidence of belief in astrology. It is belief, to be sure, but belief of a very different order from the belief in the deterministic power of the stars.

For his third category of astrology Oresme is once again concerned with physical influences of the planets and stars, but here with their predictive possibilities. He subdivides his category into three kinds of predictions. "The third part deals with the revolutions of the stars and with the conjunctions of the planets, and is applied to three kinds of predictions; first, that we may know from the major conjunctions the great events of the world, as plagues, mortalities, famine, floods, great wars, the rise and fall of kingdoms, the appearance of prophets, new religions, and similar changes; next, that we may know the state of the atmosphere, the changes in the weather, from hot to cold, from dry to wet, winds, storms, and such movements in nature; third, that we may judge as to the humours of the body and as to taking medicine and so on." Of course, Oresme's second subdivision is of great interest, because we ourselves ascribe certain macrophenomena of the weather to the sun, and we should expect that Oresme would assent to this branch of the science. However, he once again argues that while the field is a legitimate branch of inquiry, present study is misdirected. "Secondly, as regards change in the weather, this part by its nature permits of knowledge being acquired therein but it is very difficult and is not now, nor has it ever been to any one who has studied it, more than worthless, for the rules of the second part are mostly false, as I have said, and are assumed in this branch." By this Oresme refers to the influences of the fixed stars on terrestrial things, which he regarded as existent but as wrongly understood, because, as he correctly observed, the fixed stars have shifted their positions with regard to the zodiac since the time of the ancient writings on the subject. Insofar as any detailed knowledge is concerned, Oresme had nothing but scorn for astrolo-

gers, for, he says, "we see every day that sailors and husbandmen can prophesy changes in the weather better than the astronomers."

Even more surprising than Oresme's disbelief in the ability of astrologers to know anything about the weather is his admission that the relationship of astrology to great events of the world not only is a legitimate area of inquiry, but also is better known than the relationship between the stars and the weather. Of the predictions of great events, he says that the subject "can be and is sufficiently well known but only in general terms. Especially we cannot know in what country, in what month, through what persons, or under what conditions, such things will happen." As for the last part of the third category, that concerning the prediction of proper times for taking medicine and the like, Oresme says "we can know a certain amount as regards the effects which ensue from the course of the sun and moon but beyond this little or nothing." Here again, while Oresme indicates much less belief in astrological medicine than is usually ascribed to the men of the Middle Ages, he does not dismiss the subject out of hand.

Oresme distinguishes the next three categories as having to do with fortune, whereas the first three were concerned with physical influence. While it is hard to see how the appearance of a new religion constitutes a physical phenomenon, the distinction is in general between influences on natural phenomena, mass human phenomena, or on the physical bodies of individual people, and influences on intangible events in the lives of individual persons. At all events, Oresme promptly throws out the arts of "interrogations" and "elections" as totally false, as we should expect from an opponent of astrology. The practices of electing favorable times to get married, declare war, and the like, and inquiring of the stars about the advisability of business transactions or the moral probity of one's neighbor were among those most abused by astrologers. However, the subject of nativities, which is nowadays thought of as the whole science of astrology, is not completely condemned by Oresme. Rather, he says that the fourth part of astrology, concerning nativities, is not in itself beyond knowledge so far as the complexion and inclination of the person born at a given time are concerned, but this part "cannot be known when it comes to fortune and things which can be

hindered by the human will, and this section has to do with those things rather than with physical effects." Thus, while Oresme would deny that the stars could predetermine that a man would be rich or that he would choose one career rather than another, he would not deny that the stars might influence someone to have an imbalance of humours or to be wrathful or lecherous.

If someone like Nicole Oresme had read the Wife of Bath's plaint, what would his reaction have been? Certainly her association of an ascendant in Taurus with an inclination toward what she calls "love" he would believe to be possible. "Myn ascendent was Taur, and Mars therinne," she says, and then, assuming that the audience knows that this configuration was said to incline a person toward lechery, she complains, "Allas! allas! that evere love was synne!" There is more to it, however, which becomes evident when the Wife of Bath proceeds to elaborate the relationships between her horoscope and her behavior:

> I folwed ay myn *inclinacioun*
> By vertu of my constellacioun;
> That made me I koude noght withdrawe
> My chambre of Venus from a good felawe.
>
> (*WB Prol*, 615-18)

Now depending upon what he thought of the Wife's sincerity, Nicole Oresme might have made several judgments about her character, but as to the astrological situation there is no doubt what his judgment would have been. That the configuration or "constellation" of stars at her birth might have inclined the Wife toward lechery he would not deny, for he admitted that inclination and complexion can be influenced by the celestial bodies; but the Wife's following her "inclinacioun" is her own responsibility, for "things which can be hindered by the human will" cannot be determined by astrological phenomena. Whether the Wife's outcry is poignant or defiant will be discussed later.

When we consider that Oresme, who draws the line only at complete determinism, was actually a vigorous opponent of astrological practice, we see the hopelessness of dividing up mediaeval people into "believers" and "non-believers" with reference to modern definitions.

On the other hand, we can say that someone who allowed astral influence on human inclinations might or might not have considered himself a "believer" according to mediaeval theories, depending on just how binding he considered those inclinations to be. Thus, it would seem that the Wife of Bath was deterministic to the extent that she believed or at least professed that the stellar inclinations "made" her unable to withdraw her chamber of Venus from a "good felawe." Having considered the Wife's attitude toward her horoscope, and what Nicole Oresme might have thought about her attitude toward her horoscope, let us now consider what Chaucer thought about nativities, leaving his feelings about the Wife herself for a later discussion.

2. CHAUCER'S COMMENTS IN THE *TREATISE ON THE ASTROLABE*

BECAUSE most scholars have chosen to let Chaucer's characters speak for Chaucer the man, they have regarded his poetic statements about astrology as being of more importance than his two statements *in propria persona*. These statements, occurring in the middle of the *Treatise on the Astrolabe*, have never been fully studied in context. They should be perused, however, in some detail, for here is one of those rare and happy instances in which a prolific author writes in an expository fashion on a vexed issue that might otherwise be known only in a possibly ambiguous literary context.

The first of Chaucer's statements has to do with the general effects of celestial bodies on earthly affairs, and is part of his description of the astrolabe itself. An astrolabe is an instrument for measuring the altitudes of stars and planets and performing other astronomical tasks, and Chaucer's treatise, which is heavily derivative, treats the device in two parts. The first is a description of the instrument, and the second a series of "conclusions" or operations that can be performed with it. In his description of the astrolabe Chaucer has occasion to describe the zodiac inscribed on the astrolabe, which leads him to discuss the heavenly zodiac, which in turn leads him to comment on celestial influences:

And this forseide hevenysshe zodiak is clepid the cercle of the signes, or the cercle of the bestes, for "zodia" in langage of Grek

sowneth "bestes" in Latyn tunge. And in the zodiak ben the 12 signes that han names of bestes, or ellis for whan the sonne entrith into eny of tho signes he takith the propirte of suche bestes, or ellis that for the sterres that ben ther fixed ben disposid in signes of bestes or shape like bestes, or elles whan the planetes ben under thilke signes thei causen us by her influence operaciouns and effectes like to the operaciouns of bestes. (*Astrolabe*, 1, 21, 49-62)

If Chaucer were a devotee of astrology one would expect something stronger than his offering the idea of celestial influence on people as one of three alternative explanations as to why the signs are named after animals. No preference is given to any of the alternatives: the "or ellis" formula introduces all three, and the terminal position of the theory of celestial influence could as easily diminish as augment its importance. Since even Oresme was quite willing to grant that the stars could influence complexions and inclinations of individuals, this statement seems more than non-committal; it seems to downgrade celestial influence. Chaucer also mentions the relationships of signs of the zodiac to parts of the body, but again only as part of a list and without judgment pro or con.

The second part of the *Treatise on the Astrolabe* consists of a series of "conclusions," most of which begin with a formula such as "To know the altitude of the sonne . . . ," or "Declaracioun of the ascensioun of signes," or "The conclusioun of equaciouns of houses after the Astrelabie." There are, however, two subdivisions that are called "special declarations"—both have to do with judicial astrology, that is with the application of astrological knowledge, and both are innovations beyond Chaucer's source. It is the first of these that we are concerned with. Chaucer has written on the problem of knowing "by nyght or by day the degre of eny signe that ascendith on the est orisonte, which that is clepid comounly the ascendent, or ellis horoscopum." Following his analysis of how to determine the precise degree of the sign ascending on the eastern horizon, Chaucer proceeds to a special statement about the ascendant which has to do with the definition and use of the ascendant by judicial astrologers:

A special declaracioun of the ascendent.
The ascendent sothly, as wel in alle nativites as in questions and

eleccions of tymes, is a thing which that these astrologiens gretly observen. Wherfore me semeth convenyent, syth that I speke of the ascendent, to make of it speciall declaracioun.

The ascendent sothly, to take it at the largest, is thilke degre that ascendith at eny of these forseide tymes upon the est orisounte. And therfore, yf that eny planete ascende at thatt same tyme in thilke forseide degre, than hath he no latitude fro the ecliptik lyne, but he is than in the degre of the ecliptik which that is the degre of his longitude. Men sayn that thilke planete is *in horoscopo*.

But sothly the hous of the ascendent, that is to seyn, the first hous or the est angle, is a thing more brod and large. . . . (*Astrolabe*, ii, 4, 1-8)

Here Chaucer gives us the astronomical definition of the ascendant, which is simply the degree of whatever sign is rising on the eastern horizon. Then he defines the astrological "house" of the ascendant, which is an area of thirty degrees. Finally he points out that for a planet to be "in the ascendant" in the astronomical definition it had to be in the single degree of longitude that was on the eastern horizon and in the latitude of the ecliptic, while a planet can be in the astrologers' "house" of the ascendant if it is anywhere within a thirty degree area of the zodiac.

The paragraph then proceeds to discuss the "lord of the ascendant," which is an astronomical term meaning the planet that has the most power over the sign of the zodiac in the ascendant:

Yit saien these astrologiens that the ascendent and eke the lord of the ascendent may be shapen for to be fortunat or infortunat, as thus:—A "fortunat ascendent" clepen they whan that no wicked planete, as Saturne or Mars or elles the Tayl of the Dragoun, is in the hous of the ascendent, ne that no wicked planete have noon aspect of enemyte upon the ascendent.

Chaucer notes, however, that the astrologers who sell their horoscopes can better sell good prospects than bad, so he continues directly with the hint that the astrologers "arrange" the facts to suit the customer:

But thei wol caste that thei have a fortunat planete in hir ascendent, and yit in his felicite; and than say thei that it is wel.

Having described what the astrologers called a fortunate ascendant, Chaucer observes that an unfortunate ascendant is the contrary, and then goes on to define what constitutes a fortunate lord of the ascendant:

> Further over thei seyn that the infortunyng of an ascendent is the contrarie of these forseide thinges. The lord of the ascendent, sey thei that he is fortunat whan he is in god place fro the ascendent, as in an angle, or in a succident where as he is in hys dignite and comfortid with frendly aspectes of planetes and wel resceyved; and eke that he may seen the ascendent; and that he be not retrograd, ne combust, ne joyned with no shrewe in the same signe; ne that he be not in his discencioun, ne joyned with no planete in his descencioun, ne have upon him noon aspect infortunat; and than sey thei that he is well.

Immediately following this comes Chaucer's explicit statement about astrology, which closes the special declaration:

> Natheles these ben observaunces of judicial matere and rytes of payens, in whiche my spirit hath no feith, ne knowing of her *horoscopum*. For they seyn that every signe is departid in thre evene parties by 10 degrees, and thilke porcioun they clepe a face. And although that a planete have a latitude fro the ecliptik, yit sey somme folk, so that the planete arise in that same signe with eny degre of the forseide face in which his longitude is reckned, that yit is the planete *in horoscopo*, be it in nativyte or in eleccion, etc.

We must now discover exactly what this last paragraph says and what it means. Perhaps the most important issue is to determine the antecedent of "these" in the first sentence. It seems unlikely that Chaucer would be referring only to the definition of the fortunate state of the lord of the ascendant, for while that is indeed "judicial matter" so is the fortunate or unfortunate state of the ascendant itself, which is discussed a few sentences previously in the same paragraph. Surely there is nothing any more or less objectionable in determining the fortunate or unfortunate state of the lord of the ascendant than that of the ascendant itself. A much more likely explanation is that Chaucer refers here to the entire discussion of the

astrological as opposed to astronomical ascendant. We should note that the denial is given its own paragraph and that it concludes the four paragraph special declaration of the astrological ascendant.

If that is what it says, what does it mean? Insofar as Chaucer's relationship to the practice of astrology is concerned, this passage means that he doesn't believe that lords of the ascendant or ascendants themselves are really fortunate or unfortunate. Furthermore, because he stated at the outset of this declaration that the ascendant is something "these astrologiens gretly observen," it means he has no faith in judicial astrology in general. Finally, because he specifically observes that the three areas in which astrologers use the ascendant are in elections of times, questions (the "interrogations" of Nicole Oresme), and nativities, we know from the very best kind of evidence that Chaucer did not believe in the validity of questions, elections, and nativities. In this he is aligned with Oresme, but he is more outspoken in his condemnation of nativities than is the noted opponent of astrology. Of course, it may well be that Chaucer believed, as so many men of his day did, that the stars at a person's birth inclined him in one direction or another; but, in the absence of evidence to the contrary, we should say that he did not believe that the stars caused irrevocable paths of destiny. Moreover, he says without any further qualification he holds no brief for nativities. In passing, it may also be remarked that he satirizes the casting of horoscopes. Thus, even if he did believe that the stars had some influence on complexions or inclinations (and he never says he does), he certainly had no confidence in the power of astrologers to determine what this influence might be.

The remaining sentences of the final paragraph are confusing to the modern reader, who may not be aware of what is being said. On a first reading the paragraph seems disjointed and out of value. Chaucer says that these things, presumably all these things, are pagan practices in which he has no faith. Then, by way of explaining why he has no confidence in them, he says that astrologers divide the signs in three parts of ten degrees called faces. "For they seyn that every signe is departid in thre evene parties by 10 degrees, and thilke porcioun they clepe a face." There seems to be a *non sequitur* here: why should Chaucer object to subdividing the signs of the zodiac? To do

so might be meaningless, but why offensive? The solution lies in the fact that we tend to stop reading after the sentence about the faces because the next and last sentence is about something we do not comprehend. Paraphrased, the sentence says, "although a planet is outside the ecliptic (a line running through the center of the zodiac), if it arises in the same degree as one of these arbitrary divisions called faces, which extend all the way across the breadth of the zodiac, some astrologers say that the planet is 'in the ascendant' or '*in horoscopo*.'" Chaucer phrases this in terms of celestial latitude and longitude, which is enough to make most of us forget why he objects. If, however, we backtrack to the early part of the special declaration of the ascendant, we find that there Chaucer pointed out that to an astronomer the ascendant was the exact degree, of the 360 degrees of the zodiac, that is arising at a given moment whereas to the astrologers the ascendant is an area 30 times as large. Secondly, he pointed out that to the astronomer a planet was in the ascendant only if it was in the exact degree of longitude that was rising and only if it was exactly on the ecliptic or path of the sun, which exactly bisects the sixteen degrees of latitude of the zodiac. The general tenor of the whole, then, is obvious: to have Mars, or Venus, or Saturn, or some other planet in the ascendant at the time of birth of any given person would be fairly unlikely. Since there are only seven planets and 360 degrees of longitude, and since a planet in one of the fifteen degrees of latitude outside of the ecliptic wouldn't count, the astrologers have come up with a system of a 30 degree ascendant (a longitudinal measurement) and a system of faces with sixteen degrees of latitude, so that many more people can have ascendants with planets "in" them and horoscopes will be more exciting. It is the last system that Chaucer introduces as a crowning blow to the pretentious machinations of the judicial astrologers.

Chaucer's own position, then, may definitely be charted as bearing more resemblance to that of Oresme, an opponent of astrology, than to that of the Wife of Bath, who is presumably a believer in the simplest sense. On the scale of fourteenth-century belief, Chaucer would rank high among the unbelievers, and it is indeed possible to argue that he accepted even less astrology than did Nicole Oresme. On the other hand, it would be very unsafe to argue that Chaucer

did not vouchsafe anything at all to astrology, or that his general disbelief was the only attitude among cultivated people in the age. As May McKisack has pointed out, Richard II was much interested in astrology in the declining years of his reign, and surely Chaucer was conscious that his own opinion was not universally accepted.[10] Artistically, of course, astrology was grist for the mill exactly as was alchemy, a pseudo-science that Chaucer held to be "clap-trap."[11]

There is, then, in the *Treatise on the Astrolabe* ample evidence of Chaucer's attitude, expressed without any intervening *persona* and addressed to his own son. In light of this it is remarkable that there has been much debate about Chaucer's attitude, but in fact there has been concern on the part of scholars to explain away this instance of Chaucer's poking fun at the casting of horoscopes. As a result, the typical scholarly opinion, epitomized in Professor Robinson's notes, is that Chaucer was not an "unbeliever." Indeed, Robinson's note to this statement in the *Astrolabe*, which is one of the few value judgments made by Chaucer on anything outside of a literary composition, says "on Chaucer's *own* attitude toward astrology, cf. *FranklT*, v, 1133, n." (italics mine). One wonders, if the attitude expressed in the *Treatise on the Astrolabe* is not Chaucer's, whose it is.

If we pursue the issue of Robinson's presentation of Chaucer's attitude toward astrology, we find that he refers us to three statements on the subject: two by J.S.P. Tatlock, and one by Canon Wedel, all of which temper Chaucer's condemnation of astrology in the *Treatise on the Astrolabe*. An analysis of these judgments shows that both

[10] May McKisack, *The Fourteenth Century: 1307-1399* (Oxford, 1959), p. 490. It has recently been suggested by Professor Pratt that Chaucer, through his dramatic use of astrology in the *Tales* and elsewhere, might have been suggesting himself as a possible court astrologer, in spite of his "pious disclaimer" in the *Treatise on the Astrolabe*. See *Selections from The Tales of Canterbury and Short Poems*, ed. Robert A. Pratt (Boston, 1966), p. xix. The contention argued here is that Chaucer utters more than just a "pious disclaimer" in the *Treatise*—he makes fun of the very heart of judicial astrology. Chaucer, who did not hesitate to lecture the king in "Lak of Stedfastnesse," would certainly not feel uncomfortable about holding an opinion different from the king's on astrology. Professor Speirs no doubt overlooked this poem when he argued that Chaucer would not presume that his poems ought to be attended to by the king himself. See John Speirs, *Medieval English Poetry: The Non-Chaucerian Tradition* (London, 1957), p. 267.

[11] Joseph E. Grennen, "The Canon's Yeoman's Alchemical 'Mass,'" *SP*, LXII (1965), 547.

Tatlock and Wedel believe that Chaucer's condemnation of judicial astrology cannot be assumed to be the last word on the subject because of other statements in his poetry, and both scholars believe that Chaucer's general and obvious interest in the relationship between astrological influence and human freedom was an outgrowth of his interest in the fourteenth-century debate about predestination.[12] The early and very influential study by Tatlock of Chaucer's attitude toward astrology divided the subject into three branches: general celestial influence on earthly affairs, belief that the future can be foretold by astrologers, and astrological magic. Tatlock believes Chaucer to have adhered to the last branch, because although the Franklin condemns astrological magic as "nat worth a flye," it nevertheless works in his tale and is not disreputable to his characters.

This is certainly not overwhelming argumentation. Professor Tatlock's judgments on Chaucer's beliefs in general celestial influences are also based on the assumption that Chaucer's characters speak for Chaucer, and he cites as an example the fact that Venus helped Troilus fare better in love because of her favorable position at his nativity. This, of course, leaves unanswered why Venus did nothing when Criseyde left Troilus and points up the weakness of this sort of argument. A similar problem is encountered with the position that Chaucer adhered to the second division, the ability to predict the future from the stars. To support this position Professor Tatlock is obliged to turn to the Man of Law's statement that the death of every man is written in the stars, but that man's wits are too dull to read it in full (*MLT*, 194-203). This requires the assumption that the Man of Law, who disparages Chaucer's poetic ability, nevertheless speaks for Chaucer on astrology, when the more logical approach would be to find in the Man of Law a figure of Chaucer's satire. As for the statement in the *Astrolabe*, Tatlock argues that Chaucer's condemnation occurs "only after a long and technical account for little Lewis' benefit of what astrologers say about the ascendant. . . ." This

---

[12] John S. P. Tatlock, *The Scene of the Franklin's Tale Visited*, Chaucer Society, Ser. 2, No. 51 (London and Oxford, 1914), pp. 17-37; and "Astrology and Magic in Chaucer's Franklin's Tale," *Anniversary Papers by Colleagues and Pupils of George Lyman Kittredge* (Boston and London, 1913), p. 350. Wedel, *Mediaeval Attitude*, pp. 142-53.

ignores the tenor of the whole passage, which is uncomplimentary.[13] Professor Tatlock's conclusion, although restrained, probably goes too far. He says, "The soundest conclusion as to Chaucer's feeling toward the whole subject of astrology and its arts is about this. He was greatly interested and in general believed there was a good deal in it, though his view probably varied from time to time; as to some of its applications in his own day he was sceptical and strongly disapproving."[14]

Canon Wedel's account of Chaucer's attitude, while not observing Tatlock's useful subdivisions, is quite similar in that it accepts the statements of Chaucer's characters as though they were Chaucer's. Although Canon Wedel is careful to point out that "Chaucer is first and foremost the literary artist [which] makes it unusually difficult to ascertain his own personal views on the subject of astrology," he feels that statements such as those by the Man of Law stand out because Chaucer "nowhere presents the other side of the case." As for the condemnation in the *Treatise on the Astrolabe*, Wedel says that "*if* Chaucer were to be held strictly to this statement, it would go far to nullify all the positive declarations regarding judicial astrology which can be found in any of his works" (italics mine). One wonders both why Chaucer should not be held strictly to this, and also what constitutes a "positive declaration" concerning astrology. In summation, Canon Wedel decides that the condemnation of astrology in the *Treatise on the Astrolabe* is a freak, perhaps put down "because he was writing to 'lyte Lowys my sone,'" but not ultimately convincing. Indeed, Canon Wedel goes somewhat beyond Professor Tatlock in

[13] Tatlock, *Scene*, p. 27. Professor Tatlock also argues that in the *Treatise on the Astrolabe* Chaucer "accepts" such ideas as the "influence of each sign on a particular part of the body," and "the (at least possible) general influence of the planets on man" (p. 23). The lack of an outright condemnation, however, does not imply acceptance. Like Professor Tatlock, Wedel believes that Chaucer's listing of the traditional characteristics of the signs of the zodiac and his stating the relationships of signs of the zodiac to parts of the body shows that Chaucer "espouses such notions" (*Mediaeval Attitude*, p. 151). Fig. 4 shows the influences of the zodiac on the body as presented in a Book of Hours. The religious context of the picture suggests that parts of astrology could be used without running counter to the church's opposition to determinism.

[14] Tatlock, *Scene*, p. 33.

involving Chaucer with astrology, and, wanting to forget about the condemnation in the *Treatise on the Astrolabe*, says: "Judging from the references to astrology apart from those in his *Treatise on the Astrolabe*, Chaucer subscribed to all the doctrines of the science as it was taught in his day. Judicial astrology, in so far at least as it undertook to define the individual's inclinations according to the configuration of the stars at birth, is nowhere condemned."[15]

3. THE DEBATE ABOUT PREDESTINATION

IF SERIOUS scholars feel compelled to temper Chaucer's denial of the whole of judicial astrology, there must be reasons. As has been suggested, the most prominent causative factors are a prevalent willingness to assume that Chaucer's characters speak for him and a reluctance to assume that Chaucer's denial of many facets of astrology might be taken as grounds for suspecting that Chaucer undercuts those of his characters who believe in astrology or astrological magic. There is a strong possibility that the complementary factor here, lying behind the reluctance to believe what Chaucer says, has powerfully and perhaps unnecessarily prejudiced scholars. Certain assumptions about the fourteenth-century debate on predestination have been influential forces in forming opinions about Chaucer's attitude toward astrology as well as about his attitude toward the more general but closely related problems of fate and free will. Of course there was a fourteenth-century controversy, but it has been recently shown to have been somewhat more complex than had been thought previously, and it must be emphasized that it was not simply a debate on whether or not there was predestination. Rather, the controversy was primarily about the relationship of merit and grace in salvation.

---

[15] Wedel, *Mediaeval Attitude*, pp. 144-52. Canon Wedel also observes that according to his Preface to the *Treatise on the Astrolabe*, Chaucer planned to discuss "tables of equaciouns of houses" and "tables of dignitees of planetes, and other notefull things. . . ." Both Tatlock and Wedel point out that this last means "other *useful* things," but that Chaucer thought that something was useful to know does not mean that he thought it to be of any intrinsic value. He thought it was useful to say a good deal about the astrologers' definitions and uses of the ascendant and of planets *in horoscopo*, but only in order to demonstrate that such things have no ultimate value.

Canon Wedel refers explicitly to the predestination debate as making up part of Chaucer's intellectual heritage and refers the reader to seminal remarks of Professor Carleton Brown, who had said, "As to the question of predestination, one recalls Chaucer's testimony to the zeal with which it was debated in his time."[16]

Chaucer's "testimony," which is often referred to, is in the *Nun's Priest's Tale*. The teller of the tale is commenting on the fact that Chauntecleer had been forewarned that the day was dangerous, but that he had chosen to listen to a woman's fallacious counsel:

> But what that God forwoot moot nedes bee,
> After the opinioun of certein clerkis.
> Witnesse on hym that any parfit clerk is,
> That in scole is greet altercacioun
> In this mateere, and greet disputisoun,
> And hath been of an hundred thousand men.
> But I ne kan nat bulte it to the bren
> As kan the hooly doctour Augustyn,
> Or Boece, or the Bisshop Bradwardyn,
> Wheither that Goddes worthy forwityng
> Streyneth me nedely for to doon a thyng,—
> "Nedely" clepe I symple necessitee;
> Or elles, if free choys be graunted me
> To do that same thyng, or do it noght,

---

[16] Wedel, *Mediaeval Attitude*, p. 124. Carleton F. Brown, "The Author of *The Pearl*, Considered in the Light of his Theological Opinions," *PMLA*, XIX (1904), 128. A typical outgrowth of Brown's observation is Professor Fansler's remark about the *Nun's Priest's Tale*, that "the humorous application of destiny and prescience to the fox's evil designs on Chanticler appears to be a satire on the belief of St. Augustine and Bradwardine in foreordination" (Dean Spruill Fansler, *Chaucer and the Roman de la Rose* [New York, 1914], p. 213). There is satire here, to be sure, but it is difficult to imagine either the Nun's Priest or Chaucer or any other mediaeval figure holding up St. Augustine as an object of derision. Nevill Coghill says that "whether or not our wills are free was a question never far from Chaucer's mind after he had read Boethius" (*The Poet Chaucer* [London, 1967], p. 51). Both scholars cited here have overstated the nature of the debate, which did not question whether or not our wills are free, but rather how free will can be explained. Professor Ackerman's judgment that for fourteenth-century thinkers "the freedom of man's will is illusory" also appears to misstate the conclusions of the controversy. See Robert W. Ackerman, *Backgrounds to Medieval English Literature* (New York, 1966), p. 119.

> Though God forwoot it er that was wroght;
> Or if his wityng streyneth never a deel
> But by necessitee condicioneel.

(NPT, 3234-50)

In spite of the obvious rhetorical exaggeration of the "hundred thousand men" this passage has been instrumental in fostering the impression that people stood around on street corners in the fourteenth century arguing that there was or was not free will. In fact, it is true, as the Nun's Priest notes, that some clerks contended that what God foreknows must needs be (*NPT*, 3234-35); but St. Augustine, Boethius, and others were capable of simultaneously defending God's foreknowledge—actually knowledge in an everlasting present—and man's free will. Thus, when the rest of the passage discusses the problem in terms of simple and conditional necessity, the borrowing of Boethius' language is no doubt intended to suggest Boethius' conclusions, which defended the freedom of the will. The Nun's Priest is, then, being ironic when he claims that he "kan nat bulte it to the bren" (*NPT*, 3240), for by his use of Boethian language he shows that he really knows the answers. All of this philosophical machination takes on more meaning when we place the tale in its proper framework—that is, following the *Monk's Tale*, which is a seemingly endless narration of Fortune's triumphs in the world. It is appropriately the Knight (whose story showed one character succeeding in the world) who interrupts the Monk, and the Nun's Priest follows with a tale involving Fortune, advance knowledge of a downward turn on Fortune's wheel, disregard of that knowledge, and yet ultimate success because of clever use of reason and will. This is a fine counter to the heavy-handed, destinal tone of the Monk's *De casibus* stories.[17]

---

[17] On the downgrading of Fortune in the *Nun's Priest's Tale*, although without specific analysis of the passage under discussion here, see Mortimer J. Donovan, "The *Moralite* of the Nun's Priest's Sermon," *JEGP*, LII (1953), 507-508. For an analysis of the Monk's inadequate treatment of destiny and providence see R. E. Kaske, "The Knight's Interruption of the *Monk's Tale*," *ELH*, XXIV (1957), 249-68. Professor Hatton sums up a series of very recent studies by concluding that "*The Nun's Priest's Tale* thus presents a Boethian answer to the problems raised by the Monk's misinterpretation of his tragedies." Thomas J. Hatton, "Chauntecleer and the Monk, Two False Knights," *PLL*, III (1967, supplement), 31.

For a great many years, however, critics have emphasized the Nun's Priest's assertion that there was disputation, while giving short shrift to his rejection of the Monk's emphasis on the power of Fortune. Chauntecleer's own emphasis on free will, epitomized in his blaming himself for having willfully been blind (*NPT*, 3431-32), has also been slighted in comments about determinism in the poem. Thus in 1947 Professor Bennett wrote:

> On one religious matter there was certainly "endless agitation." From the earliest times the problem of determinism and of man's free will had occupied theologians, and the question was very much alive in Chaucer's time, for, while he was a youth, Bishop Bradwardine in his *De Causa Dei* had stirred the troubled waters afresh. In the *Nun's Priest's Tale*, and in the revised version of *Troilus and Criseyde*, Chaucer shows his interest in the matter, although he characteristically shrugs his shoulders and declares that he must leave it to schoolmen "to bulte it to the bren." Here he was wise, for the finest minds had found it difficult to reconcile God's foreknowledge of events with man's free exercise of his will.[18]

Of course, it is not Chaucer but the Nun's Priest who shrugs his shoulders, and there is at least a possibility that his disclaimer of ability is more rhetorical than real, for the tone of the tale as a whole suggests that he held definite opinions favoring the freedom of the will. We should also note that Bishop Bradwardine may indeed have stirred the waters anew, but Bradwardine's mention by the Nun's Priest in connection with St. Augustine and Boethius might suggest that his opinions are the same as theirs; that those three stand together in their handling of the problem of fate and free will. Certainly the Nun's Priest's claim that a hundred thousand men have discussed the question should not be taken as an indication that a third of them sided with St. Augustine, a third with Boethius and a third with Bradwardine, for these three do not oppose one another. That the subject was debated there is no question, but the exact nature of the debate is sometimes overlooked.

Professor Morton W. Bloomfield has also spoken out emphatically about Chaucer's relationship to the problem of predestination, which

---

[18] H. S. Bennett, *Chaucer and the Fifteenth Century* (Oxford, 1947), p. 27.

he calls an issue that was "a preoccupation of his day." Bloomfield, however, has gone further than Bennett: instead of seeing in Chaucer a man who refrained from conclusions about free will and predestination, he has made him a determinist "like" Bradwardine. As Bloomfield sees it, Chaucer "stands with Bishop Bradwardine who, when Chaucer was still very young, thundered against the libertarians and the voluntarists."[19] Whether we put Chaucer with Bradwardine or against him, or leave Chaucer on the sidelines, will depend entirely on our assessment of Bradwardine's position on predestination and free will, but that is not an unvexed issue. We know that Bradwardine opposed astrology, because it seemed to him that it would undercut God's power. Partly because of this Gordon Leff has found in Bradwardine a man who "rejected not only all claims for the independent existence of free will, but denied any other form of determinism in the interest of God's," and has characterized Bradwardine's work as "distinguished by a lack of humanity; its traits are vigour and ruthlessness; its nature is proselytizing; its effects are to daze rather than to guide."[20]

It seems remarkable that a poet as abundantly humane as Chaucer would sympathize with ideas like this, but not everyone has been in agreement that Bradwardine was in fact inhumane and wholly deterministic. The problem for contemporary scholars is that there is something of a psychological fondness for free will in modern times, and when confronted with a mediaeval theologian who glorifies the

---

[19] Morton W. Bloomfield, "Distance and Predestination in *Troilus and Criseyde*," *PMLA*, LXXII (1957), 14-26; reprinted in *Chaucer Criticism*, ed. Richard J. Schoeck and Jerome Taylor (Notre Dame, 1961), II, 204-205. It is worthwhile noting that Professor Bloomfield thus places Chaucer at variance with his age. Bloomfield writes elsewhere that an emphasis on eminent free will is characteristically Scotistic, and that Scotism was "the dominant philosophy of fourteenth-century England" (*Piers Plowman as a Fourteenth-Century Apocalypse* [New Brunswick, n.d.], p. 122, n. 68). Another critic who has seen the *Troilus* as a tragedy of determinism is Professor Curry (*Mediaeval Sciences*, Chap. 10), who unhappily tries to link Boethius' Chain of Love (*Consolation*, Bk. IV, m. 6) with Albumasar (pp. 247-48), and who finds that Chaucer has created a world without free choice for dramatic effect in defiance of his personal beliefs (pp. 275-98). See the excellent rebuttal by Howard R. Patch, "Troilus on Determinism," *Speculum*, VI (1929), 225-43; reprinted in Schoeck and Taylor, *Chaucer Criticism*, II, 71-85.

[20] Gordon Leff, *Bradwardine and the Pelagians* (Cambridge, 1957), pp. 15, 118.

role played by God in man's acts, an adjustment in our thinking is required to realize that this is a device to raise up rather than debase God's creature. Professor Patch, in a study regrettably without influence, tried brilliantly although apparently in vain to redress the usual ideas about Bradwardine, but it is only very recently that a full-scale re-assessment of Bradwardine has appeared from Heiko Oberman.[21] At the heart of Oberman's compelling analysis is his insistence that Bradwardine, like St. Augustine before him, was commenting on predestination as part of a diatribe against Pelagianism or Neopelagianism, and in such theological debates the emphasis is laid on God's power in causing good actions rather than on man's strength to will the good freely. The issues at stake are too complex to be investigated in detail, but we may sketch them out briefly. The conclusion is that in the view of some historians Bishop Bradwardine "never denied free will; nor do his principles lead to such a denial. He saw more clearly than did his adversaries the precise relation between the First Cause of all reality and the free second causes of contingent events."[22] If this view is correct, then the hypothesis that Chaucer had the Nun's Priest group Bradwardine with St. Augustine and Boethius because of his similarity to them, not because of his differences from them, is considerably strengthened.

Thus, as the issue of attitudes toward astrology is encompassed by the larger issue of fate and free will, so are both questions related to the problem of grace, and that in turn must be seen as part of the realist-nominalist controversy. As it started out, the debate was between the Pelagians, who argued that man could take the initial step toward his own salvation without the assistance of grace, and St. Augustine, who felt that man was not able to do good or to merit salvation without help or grace from God.[23] For St. Augustine,

---

[21] Howard Rollin Patch, "Troilus on Predestination," *JEGP*, XVII (1918), 407-409. Heiko A. Oberman, *Archbishop Thomas Bradwardine, A Fourteenth Century Augustinian* (Utrecht, 1958). Citation from primary sources would perforce be prohibitively lengthy, as readers of Bradwardine are well aware, so only secondary sources are used here.

[22] Heiko A. Oberman and James A. Weisheipl, O.P., "The *Sermo Epinicius* Ascribed to Thomas Bradwardine (1346)," *Archives d'histoire doctrinale et littéraire du moyen âge*, XXV (1958), 306.

[23] Citation of all the relevant passages in Augustine and Pelagius is prohibited by lack of space. See, therefore, the following surveys: Eugène Portalié, S.J., *A*

good works follow grace and do not precede it; contrary to the Pelagians, man does not "merit" salvation, but God freely elects to give grace to some, whose wills are then free to reject sin. These people are predestined to eternal glory. Without grace, St. Augustine argued, Postlapsarian man is able only to sin, so in one sense the will is freed to make certain choices only by God's grace. St. Augustine felt that God "foreknows" that a man will or will not do a certain thing with his free (or "freed") will, but that God exists in an eternal present in such a way that his "foreknowledge" does not in any way abrogate the freedom of the will. Our free wills are secondary causes, God's will is a primary cause, and any resulting paradox is nevertheless true.[24]

Boethius defended the freedom of the will through the concepts of simple and conditional necessity, which are ideas intended to explain in more detail why God's foreknowledge does not preclude the freedom of the will, a question which St. Augustine had not fully answered. By the fourteenth century, however, the discussion of the question grew much more complicated due to the introduction of three-value logic on the one hand, and the realist-nominalist controversy on the other. William of Ockham's celebrated razor led him to dispose of universals—those commonalties such as "man," "dog," or "rose" that depend upon the mental perception of similarities—and other things as well. As part of his conviction that the abstract universals existed in name only (hence "nominalism") and were not "real," Ockham also denied the reality of grace as an intrinsic entity and thus decided, *contra* St. Augustine, that there was no reality to God's secondary causality in creatures, because freeing the will to cause a man to do good was dependent upon grace.[25] This led to a kind of Pelagian or semi-Pelagian attitude on the part of Ockham and some others, and it was to these others that Bradwardine ad-

---

Guide to the Thought of St. Augustine, trans. Ralph J. Bastian, S.J. (London, 1960), pp. 177-229; Paul Lehmann, "The Anti-Pelagian Writings," in *A Companion to the Study of St. Augustine*, ed. Roy W. Battenhouse (New York, 1955), pp. 203-34; *Basic Writings of St. Augustine*, ed. Whitney J. Oates (New York, 1948), I, xix-xxxiii.

[24] St. Augustine, *The City of God*, Bk. v, 9; *Basic Writings*, II, 66-67.

[25] Oberman and Weisheipl, "The *Sermo Epinicius*," p. 305.

dressed himself.[26] The introduction of three-value logic complicated the problem of free will because much of the "controversy" about predestination and free will is a controversy about the logic involved in discussing it, both in Oxford and Paris in the fourteenth century, and in Louvain somewhat later.[27] By the time of the full-blown arguments on the subject, one could argue whether a proposition concerning contingent futures, that is to say those future events that are neither necessary nor impossible, was a true proposition, a false proposition, or had a third value and was neither true nor false. Of course, the theological results of these logical debates were sometimes far from the original concerns, and one must shudder at the prospect of the theological deductions that could be arrived at when, as actually happened, it was debated whether Peter, after having been told by Christ that before the cock crowed he would deny his master thrice, had the power not to deny him as predicted.[28]

The fourteenth-century debate about predestination, then, can be seen as a debate about the relationship between justification and predestination, the reality of secondary causation, the validity of certain kinds of propositions, the nature of grace, and the relationship between time and eternity. Consequently, while the Neopelagians against whom Bradwardine argued, gave too much freedom to the will to suit him, Bradwardine's emphasis on God's primacy in causing the will to do things does not abrogate free will, anymore than it did for St. Augustine or for St. Thomas Aquinas. The latter, who is not as great an authority for the Middle Ages, but who is often more precise than his predecessor, said simply, "the providence of God produces effects through the operation of secondary causes. Therefore, that which flows from free choice is also of predestination."[29] Certainly we should not think that the Nun's Priest's ref-

[26] Konstanty Michalski, "Le problème de la volunté à Oxford et à Paris au XIVe siècle," Studia Philosophica, 2 (1937), in *Commentarii philosophicae Polonorum* (Lemberg, 1937), 292-93.

[27] Michalski, *Volunté*, pp. 286-95. Léon Baudry, *La querelle des futurs contingents* (Paris, 1950), p. 14. Oberman, *Archbishop Bradwardine*, pp. 108ff.

[28] Baudry, *La querelle*, p. 28. Contingency is here used in its philosophical sense. In addition to the references in note 27 above, see Léon Baudry, *Lexique philosophique de Guillaume D'Ockham* (Paris, 1958), s.v. "contingentia."

[29] St. Thomas Aquinas, *Summa Theologiae*, I, quaest. 23, art. 5. See also Oberman and Weisheipl, "The *Sermo Epinicius*," p. 306; and Patch, "Troilus on Predestination," p. 409.

erences to Augustine, Boethius, and Bradwardine indicated that no one in the fourteenth century knew where he stood on free will, for the reference to the "debate" is made in Boethian terminology of simple and conditional necessity; and as Baudry has pointed out, all the thinkers of the Middle Ages used his terms because they used his arguments as well.[30]

If Chaucer's reference to Bishop Bradwardine has played a part in making us think that Chaucer was in doubt about predestination and free will, and consequently about astrology, other considerations have led scholars to diminish Chaucer's denial of judicial astrology, the most important being the spirit of the age.

4. AUGUSTINIAN AND BOETHIAN IDEAS ABOUT FATE AND ASTROLOGY

THE APPROACH to Chaucer's attitude via *Weltanschauung* is the best possible way to put his personal remarks in their proper perspective. However, the same assumptions about mediaeval belief in predestination that can cause an erroneous emphasis on determinism in the later Middle Ages can also cause a dubious emphasis on the nature of the general mediaeval attitude toward astrology, for if we believe that determinism is part of the mediaeval theological framework, then any expression of astral influence seems to be a reinforcement of the essential world view. By way of illustration one can examine Canon Wedel's argument that the mediaeval attitude toward astrology moved from a condemnation, represented by St. Augustine, to a "revision" of the attitude in a "new compromise," expressed by Thomas Aquinas and Dante.[31] St. Thomas, along with others according to Wedel, saw in St. Augustine's admission that the stars could influence corporeal bodies the grounds for a further ramification. St. Thomas argues that while the intellect and the will are not corporeal and cannot be influenced directly, their intimate connection with the body makes it possible for them to be indirectly influenced by the celestial processes, although the will remains free to overrule the impulses of lower faculties. Canon Wedel believes that this constitutes an acceptance of astrology and that St. Thomas goes "just *as far as he dares* in freeing it from the restrictions with which it had

[30] Baudry, *La querelle*, p. 10.
[31] Wedel, *Mediaeval Attitude*, p. 23.

become *encumbered* in earlier Church doctrine." The very clear implication is that Wedel believes St. Thomas would have granted much more validity to astrology had he been bolder. There remains a "narrow portion of judicial astrology" that St. Thomas condemns, and this "narrow portion" consists of any certain prediction of a man's future actions and any prediction of fortuitous events. From this analysis of Aquinas' thought Canon Wedel concludes that "the long warfare of science with theology, carried on from the days of Tertullian and Augustine, had resulted in a distinct victory for science."[32]

Of course, we are once again faced with problems of definitions and emphasis. Are we to agree with Wedel that the obvious increase in the amount of astrological influence allowed by St. Thomas over St. Augustine represents a victory for astrology? Certainly it is not a victory for "science" as claimed. Should we, however, place the emphasis on the change in degree of astrological influence, or should we emphasize that which remains the same and say that the most notable feature of a comparison of the two views on astrology is that for a period of seven centuries church theologians stoutly maintained the freedom of the will? Certainly Thomas Aquinas differs from St. Augustine, but from what we have seen of the degree of astrological influence allowed by an opponent of the art such as Nicole Oresme, it would seem unwise to conclude that astrology is triumphant in the writings of St. Thomas, particularly in light of the fact that he denies the possibility of accurate predictions or predictions of fortuitous events. Another scholar, Pierre Duhem, surveyed a number of Aquinas' thirteenth-century contemporaries in theology and concluded that while different ones indeed allowed varying degrees of astral influence on terrestrial phenomena, ranging from the weather to the human body, not one accepted any stellar influence over anything also subject to the human will.[33]

Another study of the general mediaeval attitude toward astrology may be found in the writings of Professor Thorndike, who wisely declared that the position of Boethius, expressed in his *Consolation of Philosophy*, was "the usual one in the subsequent middle ages."[34] The influence of Boethius, a man rather slighted by the scholars we

[32] *Ibid.*, pp. 67-69 (italics mine).

[33] Pierre Duhem, *Le système du monde* (Paris, 1913-59), VI, 347.

[34] Lynn Thorndike, *A History of Magic and Experimental Science* (New York, 1923-58), I, 622.

have examined thus far, was extraordinary throughout the Middle Ages. Boccaccio availed himself of Boethius' definition of the nature of astral power, while Chaucer's decision to translate the *Consolation*, although not indicative of slavish adherence to every judgment therein, nevertheless makes Boethius of particular interest in our present endeavor. Thorndike's monumental study of magic and experimental science is justly appreciated by mediaevalists throughout the world, and in singling out a short paragraph for adverse criticism from such a massive work one runs the risk of appearing picayune. However, in large part because of his own high estimate of Boethius' influence on subsequent thought, Thorndike's assessment of Boethius' ideas needs re-examination. As Thorndike sees it:

> Boethius maintains the co-existence of the fatal series expressed in the stars, divine providence, and human free will, a thesis likely to reassure Christians inclined to astrology who had been somewhat disturbed by the fulminations of the fathers against the *genethliaci*, just as his constant rhapsodizing over the stars and heavens would lead them to regard the science of the stars as second only to divine worship.[35]

Once again we are faced with a problem depending upon small but extremely important differences in emphasis. It is true that Boethius maintains that free will, providence, and the "fatal series expressed in the stars" exist, and that all exist at the same time, but they by no means co-exist if by that term we understand some implication of equality other than temporal. One might almost think, from Professor Thorndike's phrasing, that the mediaeval Christian was given the option of ascribing phenomena to the exercise of free will, or to providence, or to stellar influence, but this was assuredly not the case. Thorndike bases his conclusions about Boethius' attitude upon certain statements set forth in Book IV, prose 6, of the *Consolation*, and we may profitably examine his treatment of the evidence:

> Fate may be exercised through spirits, angelic or daemonic, through the soul or through the aid of all nature or "by the celestial motion of the stars." It is with the last that Boethius seems most inclined to identify *fati series mobilis*. "That series moves sky and stars, harmonizes the elements one with another, and transforms

them from one to another. . . . It constrains human fortunes in an indissoluble chain of causes, which, since it starts from the decree of immovable Providence, must needs itself also be immutable."[36]

Such an equation is clearly impossible, for we cannot equate the stars themselves with the "series" that moves them, and Boethius himself not only does not make such an equation, but he takes some pains to point out that the stars are one of a number of secondary causes of terrestrial phenomena, all of which are subject to destiny, which is in turn subject to providence. There is, then, no "coexistence," but rather a hierarchy of movers. The basic distinction, easily perceived in Chaucer's translation, is between "purveaunce" ("providence") and "destyne" ("destiny") which translates "fati series mobilis." While "purveaunce disponith *alle* thinges," destiny is only the "disposicioun and ordenance clyvyng to *moevable* thinges." Thus the unfolding of temporal things, when seen from the perspective of God, is providence; but, as it happens, this unfolding is destiny. Boethius goes on to point out, however, that while both exist simultaneously, destiny is dependent upon providence: "And al be it so that thise thinges ben diverse, yit natheles hangeth that oon of that oother; forwhi the odre destynal procedith of the simplicite of purveaunce." God, then, in his eternal present of time, acts singularly and stably; destiny carries out the decree of providence in different ways and at different times. One of the six agents of the exercise of destiny mentioned by Boethius, is stellar power:

Thanne, whethir that destyne be exercised outhir by some devyne spiritz, servantz to the devyne purveaunce, or elles by som soule, or elles by alle nature servynge to God, or elles by the celestial

---

[36] *Ibid.*, I, 621. There is no doubt about Professor Thorndike's misreading here, as an examination of the Latin text will show. The "fati series mobilis" is less than providence but more than the stars or the elements. Thus, while its influences may be carried out by stars or angels or demons, it cannot be equated with any of these: "Igitur uti est ad intellectum ratiocinatio, ad id quod est id quod gignitur, ad aeternitatem tempus, ad punctum medium circulus, ita est *fati series mobilis* ad prouidentiae stabilem simplicitatem. *Ea series caelum ac sidera mouet . . .*" (*Anicii Manlii Severini Boethii philosophiae consolatio*, ed. Ludwig Bieler [Turnholt, 1957], p. 80; italics mine; future references to the Latin are to this edition). For a better assessment of Boethius' meaning here see Howard Rollin Patch, *The Tradition of Boethius* (New York, 1935), p. 42.

moevynges of sterres, or elles by vertu of aungelis, or elles by divers subtilite of develis, or elles by any of hem, or elles by hem alle; the destinal ordenaunce is ywoven and acomplissid. (Bk. iv, pr. 6)

The stars, then, can serve as agents of destiny, but they do not constitute destiny, nor have they any power of themselves. Professor Thorndike's equation of the stars with the "series" or "ordenaunce" that moves the stars is untenable, because this "series" is destiny, which is to be understood as providence in action. To believe in this is scarcely to believe in astrology, unless we broaden our definition of astrology overmuch.

Boethius wished to deny that there is such a thing as "fate" by showing that what we call fate is really the temporal operation of providence. On this point he is one with St. Augustine, who once said that human kingdoms are established by divine providence, "and if any one attributes their existence to fate, because he calls the will or the power of God itself by the name of fate, let him keep his opinion, but correct his language."[37] Boethius does, however, grant more power to the stars than does St. Augustine, and there is no question but that most people in the later Middle Ages, while defending the freedom of the will and downgrading celestial influence, would nevertheless admit more celestial influence than did St. Augustine, although somewhat less than is often imputed to them today. St. Augustine dismissed out of hand the idea that the stars might influence human behavior by themselves, but his denial of their instrumentality in carrying out the divine will was based on an objection done away with by Boethius. St. Augustine argued that the opinion that the stars are given power by God to act on their own in decreeing human behavior was wrong because this would refer human misdeeds to the glorious stars, and that those who would maintain that the stars carry out the divine commands are wrong because they would impute human misdeeds to God, whereas we should not even impute them to the stars.

Boethius was aware, no doubt, of the Augustinian objections to making the stars into providential agents, for immediately after the

[37] St. Augustine, *City of God*, v, 1; *Basic Writings*, ii, 54-55.

passage in which he says that the order of destiny moves heaven and the stars and constrains the fortunes and the deeds of men, he says that God's providence, effected by destiny, disposes all things to the good, and that people who do wicked things are seeking good, but have been misled:

> Natheles the propre maner of every thing, dressynge hem to gode, disponith hem alle; for ther nys no thing doon for cause of yvel, ne thilke thing that is doon by wikkid folk nys nat doon for yvel, the whiche schrewes, as I have schewed ful plentyvously, seken good, but wikkid errour mystorneth hem. (Bk. IV, pr. 6)

The objection which might be raised here is that if the order disposes all to the good and does not cause evil, how can providence constrain the deeds of men and yet men persist in vices? The answer of Boethius is very similar to that of St. Augustine: he maintains that there is free will and that there is predestination, but that man does not always exercise his reason, and consequently abrogates his freedom of choice (Bk. v, pr. 2). God's providence controls everything, but vice is man's doing, and those who find this an unacceptable paradox are themselves wicked:

> And yit ther folweth anothir inconvenient, of the whiche ther ne mai be thought no more felonous ne more wikke, and that is this: that, so as the ordre of thingis is iled and cometh of the pur-veaunce of God, ne that nothing is leveful to the conseiles of man-kynde (*as who seith that men han no power to don nothing ne wilne nothing*), thanne folweth it that oure vices ben referrid to the makere of alle good (*as who seith, thanne folweth it that God oughte han the blame of our vices, syn he constreyneth us by necessite to doon vices*). (Bk. v, pr. 3)

Boethius does admit more astral influence than St. Augustine, and it is perhaps because of his influence that so many humanists of the later Middle Ages accepted more celestial influence than they might have otherwise. However, they were not led to "regard the science of the stars as second only to divine worship" as Professor Thorndike would have it, unless we restrict that science to what might be called "philosophical astronomy" and divorce it from any study of celestial

influence. As Boethius said: "For it nis nat leveful to man to com-
prehenden by wit, ne unfolden by word, alle the subtil ordenaunces
and disposiciounis of the devyne entente" (Bk. IV, pr. 6). On the
other hand, while Boethius denied that the influence of the stars
could be known with propriety, he did think that the study of the
causes of things and of the motions of the heavens was a positive
good, and at the very beginning of the *Consolation* the first picture
we receive of a philosopher is that of the astronomer, "to whom the
hevene was opyn and knowen. . . . And, over this, he was wont to
seken the causes whennes the sounynge wyndes moeven . . . and what
spirit turneth the stable hevene . . ." (Bk. I, m. 2).

It is this concern for philosophy and not for astrology that is the
source of what Professor Thorndike calls Boethius' "constant rhapso-
dizing" about the stars, which Thorndike argued led mediaeval men
to regard the science of the stars as second only to divine worship.
This and other passages, however, are clearly about astronomy not
only as it differs from but even as it is opposed to astrology, for
we have seen that Boethius would not tolerate either any abrogation
of the freedom of the will or any interpretation or prediction of
whatever stellar influences there were. The beauty of the heavens is
not remarked upon by Boethius in order that the stars be worshipped,
but in order that God be worshipped, and the most famous of these
meters, the *O stelliferi conditor orbis* (Bk. I, m. 5), is a poem in praise
of God who made the heavens and commanded the stars to be
obedient to him:

> O thow makere of the wheel that bereth the sterres, which that
> art festnyd to thi perdurable chayer, and turnest the hevene with
> a ravysschynge sweigh, and constreynest the sterres to suffren thi
> lawe. . . .

If Professor Thorndike appears to be too quick to turn Boethius
into too much of a sympathizer with astrology, it is perhaps because
he, like Canon Wedel, sees attitudes toward astrology linked with
the larger issues of science and theology, and Thorndike is very much
on the side of "science" against the opponents of astrology. He calls
St. Augustine's arguments against astrology "narrow, partial, and
inadequate," and the conclusion of John of Salisbury's protestations

"lame." He says that many of Oresme's arguments are "trite," and says of Isidore of Seville's cavalier treatment of astrology that "Isidore might as well have taken the planets as signs in the astrological sense as have ascribed to them the absurd allegorical significance in passages of Scripture that he did."[38] Other Christian uses of things astrological are also derogated by Professor Thorndike. For example, when William of Conches says that the stars create the body but God the soul, Thorndike is led to reply that William committed a typical Christian "perversion" of the *Timaeus*.[39] This concern to emphasize astrology at the expense of whatever lies in its way leads Professor Thorndike to adopt a definition of the subject so wide as to be virtually without meaning for the discussion of mediaeval astrology, for he would argue that, since the author of a refutation of astrology believes that the stars can incline but not compel, the author has sanctioned the very subject he wrote against. He makes the same claim for another writer hostile to astrology who is nevertheless willing to assert that comets "signify" wars, pestilences and the like.[40] Unless we are willing to subdivide astrological beliefs more precisely than this we shall not proceed very far with an analysis of mediaeval attitudes toward the subject. It is unfortunate that as a historian of science Professor Thorndike has thought it advisable to bring so much of astrology into the scientific camp.[41]

[38] Thorndike, *Magic and Science*, for Isidore: I, 633; John of Salisbury: II, 166; Nicole Oresme: III, 412; St. Augustine: I, 517. Canon Wedel says, in a similar vein, "one is compelled to smile at the seriousness with which [St. Augustine] employed this mediocre argument [on twins]" (*Mediaeval Attitude*, p. 21). Professor Thorndike finds it difficult to be fair to an opponent of astrology like Nicole Oresme, for "we should like to have been able to present Nicolas Oresme simply as a critic of magic and astrology and as battling against superstition and the occult. But in his expeditions against what seemed to him error we sometimes find him on the side of theology in what looks very much like a warfare with science" (*Magic and Science*, III, 470).

[39] Thorndike, *Magic and Science*, II, 56.

[40] *Ibid.*, II, 592; I, 633.

[41] Professor Thorndike's over-enthusiasm for astrology as a science was criticized sharply by George Sarton in his review of the first two volumes of the *History of Magic and Experimental Science* (*Isis*, XXIII [1935], 472). For a more favorable review, which nevertheless deplored certain traits of argumentation, see Dana B. Durand, "*Magic and Experimental Science*: The Achievement of Lynn Thorndike," *Isis*, XXXIII (1941), 691-712. It is not without interest that Professor Thorndike felt obliged to disclaim in print any belief in the methods of astrology. See Lynn

5. FOURTEENTH-CENTURY VIEWS OF ASTROLOGY

No DOUBT the most profitable approach to placing in context Chaucer's attitude toward astrology is that adopted by Professor Tatlock, who suggests that Chaucer will be like most of the "best thinkers and writers of his own day. . . ." While Professor Tatlock is inclined to grant more assent to astrology to Chaucer's contemporaries than may perhaps be found in their views, his method is a good one.[42] The problem, of course, is in deciding what constitutes "belief," but because of our knowledge of the range of attitude of an opponent of astrology, like Oresme, we are in a better position today to judge to what extent a mediaeval man's statements committed him or did not commit him to the camp of the advocates. Thus, while some of the "best thinkers and writers" of Chaucer's day have positions vis-à-vis astrology that are not at all easy to analyze, there are other instances in which Tatlock's judgments seem to be based on the premise that the allowance of any weight whatsoever to astrology constituted at least partial belief or belief of a kind. However, we have seen that even the opponents of astrology, such as Oresme, and the opponents of judicial astrology, such as Boethius and Chaucer, would allow quite a lot of astrological influence on certain kinds of things without thinking of themselves as "believers." On the other hand, the professional astrologers often prefixed their writings with pious apologies, although as Professor Allen has pointed out for Renaissance thought, the astronomer might dabble in astrology, "but he knew when he crossed the line that limited the domains of the two areas."[43] That there were many believers and many who inclined toward more belief than they might publicly allow is not to be doubted, but some re-examination of key figures from a viewpoint that distinguishes more than one level of belief is in order.[44]

Thorndike, "The True Place of Astrology in the History of Science," *Isis*, XLVI (1955), 273-78.

[42] Tatlock, *Scene*, p. 23.

[43] Allen, *Star-crossed Renaissance*, p. 54.

[44] Professor Lemay has noted the somewhat contradictory history of the mediaeval attitude toward astrology: at each significant stage in the refutation of astrology there seems to have been a revival or an increase in its popularity. See Richard Lemay, *Abu Ma'Shar and Latin Aristotelianism in the Twelfth Century* (Beirut, 1962), p. xxxvii, n. 1.

The several figures Professor Tatlock adduces include Roger Bacon, who can perhaps serve as an illustration of a very distinct believer, and others like John Gower and John of Salisbury who are at the other end of the scale. Even here, however, it is necessary to inquire after Tatlock's use of evidence, for he emphasizes the fact that both the latter allowed some astrology rather than that both denied much. Gower, for example, is first found to be a stout emphasizer of man's freedom from astral determinism, but is subsequently modified by Tatlock's citation of his statement that "all things . . . including . . . fortune and temperament are governed by the planets."[45] Now it is true enough that Gower puts this opinion down in black-and-white, but his presentation of the view is only in order to refute it, which he does directly:

> And thus seith the naturien
> Which is an Astronomien.
> Bot the divin seith otherwise,
> That if men weren goode and wise
> And pleasant unto the godhede,
> Thei scholden noght the sterres drede;
> For o man, if him wel befalle,
> Is more worth than ben thei alle
> Towardes him that weldeth al.
> Bot yit the lawe original,
> Which he hath set in the natures,
> Mot worchen in the creatures,
> That therof mai be non obstacle,
> But if it stonde upon miracle
> Thurgh preiere of som holy man.
> (*Confessio Amantis*, vii, 649-63)

From this it is plain enough that Gower was concerned to discount and not to promulgate the claims of astrology, and the whole passage on astrology and astronomy is prefaced by a form of the popular Latin tag, *"Vir mediante deo sapiens dominabitur astris,"* "the wise man governs the stars through the aid of God."[46]

[45] Tatlock, *Scene*, p. 25.
[46] Canon Wedel has correctly assessed Gower as having "a general hostility to the occult arts," although his bias is apparent when he applauds Gower's "emanci-

In a similar fashion Tatlock's assessment of John of Salisbury's position appears to be debatable, for he argues that John would agree with Gower about the stars' influence on fortune and temperament (which we have seen Gower did not believe), and further that John's goal was "to minimize, but not to deny, the influence of the stars." Of course, even the opponents of astrology did not entirely deny the power of the stars, and while Tatlock's conclusion is that John of Salisbury granted quite a lot, Canon Wedel has unceremoniously lumped him in with the Church Fathers as an outspoken opponent, on the grounds that the tenor of his statements in general is so clearly anti-astrological.[47]

---

pated" attitude toward magic. Wedel curiously believes that whatever Gower's general attitude toward occult arts, he shows an "enthusiastic interest in astrology" (*Mediaeval Attitude*, pp. 142; 121-22).

[47] Tatlock, *Scene*, pp. 25-26; p. 26, n. 1. Wedel, *Mediaeval Attitude*, p. 39. It is very doubtful that John of Salisbury believed that the stars governed fortune and temperament as Tatlock claims. While John grants that nothing on earth happens without a cause, and that the sun can augment or decrease the humours in people as well as warmth in the weather, this is the standard belief of both opponents and proponents of astrology, as we have seen. "Nichil etenim est eul fit, cuius ortum legitima causa et ratio non praecedant; et, ut alius ait, nichil fit in terra sine causa. . . . Asserunt quoque communiter solem caloris auctorem esse, humorumque augmentum et defectum, quoniam id sensus probat, motui lunari accomodant; et in hunc modum plurima" (*Ioannis Saresberiensis episcopi carnotensis policratici*, ed. Clement C. J. Webb [Oxford, 1909], Bk. II, chaps. 1 and 19; I, 66 and 108). Such power as the stars may have exists for John of Salisbury, as it does for one of John's favorite authors, Boethius, in the fact that the stars sometimes act as agents of God's providence: "Multipharie siquidem multisque modis suam Deus instruit creaturam, et nunc elementorum uocibus nunc sensibilium aut insensibilium rerum indiciis, prout electis nouerit expedire, quae uentura sunt manifestat. Futuras itaque tempestates aut serenitates signa quaedam antecedentia praeloquuntur, ut homo, qui ad laborem natus est, ex his possit exercitia sua temperare" (I, 68). "Qui enim sideribus legem dedit, qui curricula temporum uoluntatis suae freno moderatur, qui rerum momenta temporibus suis accommodat, quando uult et quo modo uult, nouum stupente natura aut rarum potest producere effectum ex causis concurrentibus, quae aliter parere consueuerant. Quis enim consiliarius eius fuit, aut dicet ei, Cur ita facis? Vtique Dominus est; quod beneplacitum est in oculis suis faciet" (I, 134). Professor Tatlock's statement that John of Salisbury was concerned "to minimize, but not to deny, the influence of the stars" (*Scene*, p. 26, n. 1), is, strictly speaking, true, but the tone and the content of the minimization put John of Salisbury squarely in the camp of the opponents of the mass of astrology. Canon Wedel's judgment is much more to the point in this instance, for he observes that John of Salisbury found in astrology "little more than a dangerous philosophical doctrine" (*Mediaeval Attitude*, p. 40).

The same kinds of problems in the use of evidence are to be found when we approach other writers, for they can be considered as proponents or opponents depending on our weighting of their remarks. Professor Tatlock has argued, for example, that Chaucer's literary acquaintance Deschamps wrote two *ballades* in which it is said that the stars would irresistibly control men were it not for free will. The problem is whether we are to assume from this that Deschamps inclined toward strong belief in the power of the stars, or that he was trying to emphasize the power and freedom of the will. Deschamps actually wrote a diatribe against divination of various kinds, the *Demoustracions contre sortilèges*, which transcribes part of Nicole Oresme's *Livre de divinacions*. In spite of this, both Tatlock and Wedel emphasize whatever astrological allowances he makes, and the latter quotes approvingly an editor who suggested that Deschamps wrote his attack on astrology while in the throes of religious fervor.[48] With Petrarch, another literary acquaintance of Chaucer's, there is an almost identical situation. Professor Tatlock would have it that Petrarch "admits" that the stars can control the weather, but in view of the fact that this "admission" occurs in Petrarch's famous letter to Boccaccio in which he brilliantly and hilariously attacks the follies of the astrologers, it is surely to be downgraded in importance, and indeed, as we have seen, statements of this sort are the rule among the frankest enemies of the greater part of astrology.[49]

Boccaccio, to whom Petrarch wrote his letter ridiculing astrology, is styled by Canon Wedel as a "firm believer in stellar influence," yet to believe in stellar influence and to believe in judicial astrology are not always the same thing.[50] Thus, when Boccaccio says that Mars and Venus in a horoscope fashion people who become lovers, we should not leap to the conclusion that he embraced the whole of astrology any more than we should suspect that he accepted the whole or even a part of pagan mythology simply because he talks about the pagan gods as having ancestors and descendants. Indeed

---

[48] Wedel, *Mediaeval Attitude*, pp. 139-40; 139, n. 3. For Deschamps' use of Nicole Oresme see Coopland, *Oresme*, pp. 8-9. For the *Demoustracions contre sortilèges* see *Oeuvres Complètes des Eustache Deschamps, SATF* (Paris, 1891), VII, 192-99.

[49] Tatlock, *Scene*, p. 29. Petrarch, *Lettere Senile*, ed. and trans. Giuseppe Fracasetti (Florence, 1870), Bk. III, 1; vol. I, 133-59.

[50] Wedel, *Mediaeval Attitude*, p. 88.

Boccaccio is rather careful to qualify just what he thinks about astrology: he says that Mars and Venus do not cause passion to come about, but rather that these planets can produce people who have the bodily disposition toward producing passion themselves.[51] Or, we might say, these planets produce people like the Wife of Bath who choose to follow their inclinations. Moreover, it should be pointed out that Boccaccio is indebted for his position on astrology to Boethius, and in fact silently cites Boethius when he says that the planets operate as ministers of God just as angels and devils do. Any such allegiance to Boethius should do much to counter such elements of allegiance to astrology as we may find elsewhere in Boccaccio.[52] There is no doubt that Boccaccio would grant a larger sphere of influence to astrology than would some of the opponents of the art, but that would scarcely suffice to bring him into the other camp. However far Boccaccio might progress toward belief in astrology, and he probably would progress further than Chaucer, his decision to speak of astral influences as secondary causes in the

[51] ". . . et sic ex Marte et Venere non generatur passio, sed . . . homines apti ad passionem suscipiendam secundum corpoream dispositionem producuntur; quibus non existentibus, passio non generaretur" (Giovanni Boccaccio, *Genealogie deorum gentilium libri*, ed. V. Romano [Bari, 1951], II, 453).

[52] "Nec tamen negamus Deo ministros esse, alios iustitie ut Demones, alios gratie ut Angelos, alios opportunitatum et victus, ut supercelestia corpora" (*Genealogie deorum*, II, 537). Cf. Boethius, *Philosophiae consolatio*, Bk. IV, pr. 6; p. 80: "Siue igitur famulantibus quibusdam prouidentiae diuinis spiritibus fatum exercetur seu anima seu tota inseruiente natura seu caelestibus siderum motibus seu angelica uirtute seu daemonum uaria sollertia seu aliquibus horum seu omnibus fatalis series texitur, illud certe manifestum est immobilem simplicemque gerendarum formam rerum esse prouidentiam, fatum uero eorum quae diuina simplicitas gerenda disposuit mobilem nexum atque ordinem temporalem." Professor Osgood observes of the mythological element here that to conceive of it "not as mere make-believe, but as describing, however dimly, the operations of the Celestial Hierarchy, gives [mythology] dignity, reality, and a certain perennial truth" (*Boccaccio on Poetry*, trans. Charles G. Osgood, Library of Liberal Arts [New York, 1956], p. xxi). Had Professor Osgood perceived the Boethian origin of the statement, however, he might have decided that Boccaccio, like Boethius, was more concerned to downgrade than to dignify gods, demons, and planets, by making them secondary rather than first causes. It is also of interest that Boccaccio uses the Boethian passage cited here in his commentary on Dante, wherein he also defends free will and denies the ability of human reason to predict the future from the stars: Giovanni Boccaccio, *Il Comento sopra La Commedia di Dante Alighieri*, ed. A. Penna (Florence, 1831), I, 71-72; II, 158.

Boethian sense means that however much they influenced the world they did not abrogate the freedom of the will, which was also seen as a secondary cause. This Boethian attitude figures very prominently in evaluating mediaeval belief because it opened an avenue for subsequent authors to find a place for celestial influence that at once granted its reality and denied both its impingement on free will and its exact predictability.

Another figure whose attitude toward celestial influence may be said to be Boethian is Dante, whose admiration for Boethius is well-known from his remarks in the *Convivio* (Bk. II, Chap. 13). Because of this strain of Boethianism one can reassess the evidence for Dante's attitude with a greater ability to distinguish nuance, for while it is one thing to say that so much and no more nor less was believed, it is quite another to make a judgment of the whole. Canon Wedel, for example, has contrasted Dante's condemnation of astrologers in the *Inferno* with what he takes to be Dante's admiration for heavenly powers in the *Paradiso*. He says, "For Dante, the influence of the stars upon human life was indeed an awe-inspiring fact. The heavens are the instruments of God. It is to them that the First Mover has delegated the power to mould the destinies of the world. . . ."[53] There is no question here about the evidence—Canon Wedel is undeniably accurate in his summations—but his interpretation is perhaps open to question. We may reasonably ask if the force of the evidence is to show that Dante believed that the stars had an awe-inspiring influence on human life, or that God had an awe-inspiring influence on human life. Whatever the influence, Marco Lombardo's defense of free will in *Purgatorio* XVI, as Canon Wedel points out, admits that the heavens initiate impulses ("Lo cielo i vostri movimenti inizia"), but Marco insists that man is free to choose whether or not he will follow those impulses. Since even an opponent of astrology like Oresme was not wholly opposed to conceding some degree of stellar influence on human inclinations, this really puts Dante as much with the opponents as with the proponents of the art. For Dante, the ultimate powers of the stars lie beyond them in God, and whether he is arguing that Fortune, like the heavens, is both a guide for those

---

[53] Wedel, *Mediaeval Attitude*, p. 80. He cites a number of *loci* in Dante, among them *De monarchia* II, 2; *Paradiso* VIII, 91ff.; *Purgatorio* XVI, 67-84.

below, and guided from above, or whether he is arguing that the origin of worldly dissatisfaction is in man's departing from the providential order, he is being very Boethian.[54] Similarly, when Cacciaguida says that contingent futures are unknowable to humans and known to God, although deriving no necessity from God's knowledge, he is merely stating in the philosophical language of the fourteenth century Boethius' distinction between absolute and conditional necessity.[55]

The emphasis here on Boethius and Oresme as touchstones for later writers has been necessitated to redress the balance effected by earlier scholars who mistakenly felt that mediaeval men either vacillated in their views, or, in admitting some fraction of astrology, were hinting that they would accept the whole openly if it were not for the fear of reprisal. Neither of these alternatives adequately expresses the situation, and the study of the history of attitudes toward astrology is indeed a good deal more complex and subtle than has usually been thought. The definitive history of the subject is yet to be written, and when it is done it will comprise many, many volumes. As a consequence the techniques employed here have scarcely been exhaustive, but, through an examination of the way in which some standard works on the subject manipulate evidence according to certain preconceived suppositions, it is hoped that the previous over-simplification of the problem has revealed itself.

---

[54] For Fortune see *Inferno* VII, 73-79: "Colui, lo cui saper tutto trascende / Fece li cieli, e diè lor chi conduce, / Sì ch'ogni parte ad ogni parte splende, / Distribüendo igualmente la luce. / Similemente a li splendor mondani / Ordinò general *ministra e duce*, / Che permutasse a tempo li ben vani . . ." (italics mine). The second proposition is more complicated. Canon Wedel has argued that Dante says that "were it not for the influences of the stars, children would be exactly like their parents" (*Mediaeval Attitude*, p. 80, with reference to *Paradiso* VIII, 91ff.). In the strict sense this is true, but Wedel fails to point out that it is providence that guides the stars in forming inclinations, and people are free to follow these inclinations or not, which is sometimes the cause of human dissatisfaction. "Lo ben che tutto il regno che tu scandi / Volge e contenta, fa esser virtute / Sua provedenza in questi corpi grandi" (*Paradiso* VIII, 97-99). See also Boccaccio's commentary, III, 209. All Dante citations are from *Il Convivio*, ed. G. Busnelli and G. Vandelli (Florence, 1964), 2 vols.; or *La Divina Commedia*, ed. C. J. Grandgent (Boston, 1933).

[55] " 'La contingenza, che fuor del quaderno / De la vostra matera non si stende, / Tutta è dipinta nel cospetto etterno; / Necessità però quindi non prende, / Se non come dal viso in che si specchia, / Nave che per corrente giù discende' " (*Paradiso* XVII, 37-42). See also note 28 above.

6. ARTISTIC EXPRESSIONS OF PROVIDENCE,
ASTROLOGY, AND FREE WILL

THE REDUCTIVE view of astrology, which divides people into be-
lievers and unbelievers, is at its most inadequate when dealing with
astrology in an artistic or poetic framework. The place of astrology
with regard to providence and free will is difficult enough to fix when
dealing with a prose essay or letter, but in artistic contexts there is
even greater room for error because we are forced to look further
afield for the complete picture or the proper perspective. An excellent
example of this problem is afforded by the horoscope of the fifteenth-
century humanist Agostino Chigi, which he ordered to be represented
artistically on the vault of his Farnesina Palace (Fig. 1). By itself
this vault seems to indicate that Chigi was a devotee of astrology and
possibly very deterministic in his outlook, but if we look at the vault
of the chapel of Santa Maria del Popolo (Fig. 2), where he is buried,
we find the planets arranged in a circle with an angel over each, while
God is shown above at the center, with his arms raised up in a gesture
of command. This obviously Boethian motif, in which the stars are
instruments of the divine will, puts the horoscope of the Farnesina
Palace into a very different perspective.[56] A similarly deceptive in-
stance of the artistic employment of astrology is afforded by the rep-
resentation of the night sky of Florence as it was on July 9, 1422
(Fig. 3). Once again the artistic representation considered *in vacuo*
suggests a very high level of astrological belief, but in fact this par-
ticular image comes from the cupola of the Old Sacristy of San Loren-
zo in Florence, and it is a representation of the heavens as they stood
on the date of the consecration of the main altar.[57]

Of course, the complex interrelationships between destiny and

[56] Jean Seznec, *The Survival of the Pagan Gods*, trans. Barbara F. Sessions (New
York: Harper Torchbooks, 1961), pp. 79-82. See also C. S. Lewis, *The Discarded
Image* (Cambridge, 1964), p. 87. For a somewhat different, but nevertheless
Christian, interpretation of the cupola, which sees the planets descended from the
Timaeus with God's gesture one of reception of souls, see John Shearman, "The
Chigi Chapel in S. Maria del Popolo," *JWCI*, XXIV (1961), 129-60. For an ex-
cellent survey of the mediaeval narrative tradition in which fatalism is contrasted
with providence, see T. McAlindon, "Magic, Fate, and Providence in Medieval
Narrative, and *Sir Gawain and the Green Knight*," *RES*, n.s. LXII (1965), 121-39.
[57] Seznec, *Survival of the Pagan Gods*, p. 119.

providence, fate and free will, are vastly more subtle in literary than in artistic contexts. Therefore it is even more important to exercise caution and to look for possible Boethian perspectives when dealing with poetry than when dealing with art, whether we confront Ariel in *The Tempest* saying "I and my fellows / Are ministers of Fate," or whether we note that the *Parson's Tale*, with its emphasis on personal responsibility, is introduced with a reference to the zodiac. There are two instances in Chaucer's poetry that especially invite this kind of cautious consideration, because they have so often served as springboards for arguing that Chaucer believed to a great extent in celestial influences. The passages in question are in the *Knight's Tale* and in the *Troilus and Criseyde*.

In the *Knight's Tale* the role of stellar influence or fate has been elevated to a position of some eminence by Professor Curry, who argued that Chaucer abandoned the mythology he found in his source and substituted "as a motivating force that formative and impelling influence of stars in which his age believed."[58] The problem here, however, is that if the stars are in fact both formative and impelling, if indeed, as Curry says, the story is spread against the backdrop of "the destinal power of the stars," then the motivation of the story and its backdrop have been poorly chosen, for human action of any kind is ultimately meaningless if it is accomplished in a wholly deterministic universe.[59] Perhaps a more useful definition of the role of the stars in the *Knight's Tale* would note that the stoicism of Arcite

---

[58] Curry, *Mediaeval Sciences*, p. 119. Curry does not deal with the subject as lucidly as he might, but it must be remembered in his defense that the basic situation verges on the paradoxical—that is, the stars have influence but providence controls them and yet leaves the will free, so the stars only incline and do not compel except in those instances when they are carrying out the decrees of providence, at which time they can compel without abrogating the freedom of the will or causing man to sin. In addition to calling the stars the "motivating force" of the *Knight's Tale* Curry terms the tale itself an "occult story of conflicting planetary influences" (p. xxiii), and says that behind the human narrative Chaucer has spread the "destinal power of the stars" (p. xxiii). On the other hand, Curry also says that "Chaucer will not permit these things to be left ultimately to the cold, unsympathetic direction of the stars; life would be unbearable if it were subject to these natural or mechanical processes alone" (p. 154). Similarly, ". . . the *Knight's Tale* is in no sense presented to illustrate the influence of Saturn and Mars in the affairs of the two heroes" (p. 153).

[59] Contrast Bronson who argues that astrological allusion is present "to give

and Palamon, which is engendered by their belief in astral determinism, is not to be found in Theseus, the hero of the story; differs from the belief of the Knight, who narrates it; and need not be imputed to Chaucer, who wrote it.

Palamon is sure that he must be in prison because of the influence of Saturn (*KnT*, 1328), and Arcite not only agrees, but shows himself a stoic, too:

> Fortune hath yeven us this adversitee.
> Som wikke aspect or disposicioun
> Of Saturne, by som constellacioun,
> Hath yeven us this, although we hadde it sworn;
> So stood the hevene whan that we were born.
> *We moste endure it*; this is the short and playn.
>
> (*KnT*, 1086-91)

The one explicit statement by the narrator, the Knight, about the relationship of destiny and human freedom is somewhat different. At first glance it appears that the Knight endorses a kind of astral determinism, for he says that destiny can perform a thing that might not happen again for a thousand years, but a closer inspection reveals that on the one hand destiny is only the agent of God's providence, and on the other its designs are accomplished through the promptings of human appetites or inclinations.

> The destinee, *ministre general*,
> That executeth in the world over al
> The *purveiaunce* that God hath seyn biforn,
> So strong it is that, though the world had sworn
> The contrarie of a thyng by ye or nay,
> Yet somtyme it shal fallen on a day
> That falleth nat eft withinne a thousand yeer.
> For certeinly, *oure appetites* heer,
> Be it of werre, or pees, or hate, or love,
> *Al is this reuled by the sighte above.*
>
> (*KnT*, 1663-72)

---

greater dignity and a sense of cosmic perspective to [the characters'] conduct" (Bertrand H. Bronson, *In Search of Chaucer* [Toronto, 1960], p. 15).

This, of course, is not granting very much to the stars by mediaeval standards, since the usual corollary is that man's will remains free to reject his impulses.

The Knight's emphasis on providence, on the stars as ministers of the divine will, and on celestial influence on appetites is there to give us a picture of "determinism" that is to be contrasted to that painted by Arcite. These distinctions between the Knight and Palamon and Arcite, and between Theseus and Palamon and Arcite, are essential to make, for without them we can fall into a casual reading of the several statements on destiny that insufficiently distinguishes between them. Theseus' concern to make virtue of necessity (*KnT*, 3042) refers to the necessity of mortality, not fortune, and the lack of stoic utterances on his part suggests that his position is closer to what we would expect of the orthodox Christian Knight than it is to what we discover in the young lovers' willingness to "endure" fate. This further suggests that the distinction being underscored in the poem is between Theseus' wisdom and the young lovers' lack of it rather than the distinction between the pagan characters of the poem and the Christian Knight who narrates it.[60]

The other very famous Chaucerian pronouncement about fate and the heavens has also been taken as an admission of determinism because of the failure of critics to recognize or properly make use of the Boethian emphasis and its function in the poetry. The passage is the apostrophe to Fortune in the third book of the *Troilus and Criseyde*, which is one of the elements of that work which led Professor Curry to say that "destiny in this poem is perhaps more hugely spread than has been hitherto conceived. . . ."[61] When we take a close look at this particular passage, however, we find that it is couched in the familiar

---

[60] Theseus, who stands in relationship to Palamon and Arcite approximately as does the Knight to the Squire, says he was once a fool in love, but now knows better. "A man moot ben a fool, or yong or oold,— / I woot it by myself ful yore agon, / For in my tyme a servant was I oon" (*KnT*, 1812-14). Professor Huppé has incisively argued that the *Knight's Tale* is told for the benefit of the Squire— "to lead him from courtly folly back to an ideal of Christian chivalry" (Bernard F. Huppé, *A Reading of the Canterbury Tales* [State University of New York, 1964], p. 54).

[61] Curry, *Mediaeval Sciences*, p. 241. See Howard R. Patch's articles on "Troilus on Determinism," and "Troilus on Predestination," cited above in notes 19 and 21 for a more closely argued view of the problems.

Boethian language that conceives of Fortune and the stars as executors of the providential order:

> But O Fortune, *executrice* of wyrdes,
> O influences of thise hevenes hye!
> Soth is, that *under God* ye ben oure hierdes,
> Though to us bestes ben the causes wrie.
>
> (*T&C*, III, 617-20)

Even more to the point than the Boethian concept of the stars as ministers of the divine will, however, is the way in which the heavens and/or Fortune conspire to implement God's plan. The situation in the third book of the *Troilus* is that Pandarus is conspiring to bring together Troilus and Criseyde at his house through the pretext that Criseyde should dine with him while Troilus is said to be out of town. This is easy enough to get Criseyde to agree to, but the more difficult problem is for Pandarus to get Criseyde to stay the night, and it is here that "Fortune" acting "under God" forces Criseyde to remain:

> This mene I now, for she gan homward hye,
> But execut was al bisyde hire leve
> The goddes wil; for which she moste bleve.
>
> (*T&C*, III, 621-23)

We should expect here, if we're taking all of this seriously, that some great planetary conjunction would ineluctably force Criseyde to be rooted to the spot so that she would be powerless to leave. We do in fact get a great planetary conjunction—indeed a conjunction of Saturn and Jupiter, which is the rarest and most awe-inspiring of the conjunctions—but instead of withering Criseyde's will on the spot, this phenomenal conjunction causes it to rain, and Criseyde decides not to go home in the rain!

> The bente moone with hire hornes pale,
> Saturne, and Jove, in Cancro joyned were,
> That swych a reyn from heven gan avale,
> That every maner womman that was there
> Hadde of that smoky reyn a verray feere.
>
> (*T&C*, III, 624-28)

Rather than one of Chaucer's more awe-inspiring passages or destinally darkened places, this is one of his funniest touches. The conjuring up of one of the "great conjunctions" for such a paltry business reminds us of the true perspective we should have both with regard to Pandarus' shallow scheming and with regard to the uncataclysmic, private love affair. The whole, exaggerated phenomenon was hinted at when Chaucer invoked Calliope, the Muse of Epic, for the very mundane seduction of Book III.[62]

For Chaucer, then, a very solemn comment on destiny as providential agent could be turned promptly to humorous effect, and, while Chaucer was no doubt serious when he translated the *Consolation of Philosophy* and when, in the *Treatise on the Astrolabe*, he denied any belief in judicial astrology, he was at one with his age in finding much of the machinations of astrology to be very funny. Professor Tatlock shrewdly observes that Chaucer certainly disapproved of magicians and astrologers, so many of whom, it should be added, abused what little art there was in astrology; while Canon Wedel adduces Petrarch as an early example of the sort of person who looked ahead to the day "when astrology would be universally laughed to scorn."[63] It is somewhat difficult for us in this day of

---

[62] Some years ago Professors Root and Russell argued that the *Troilus* could be dated by determining just when in Chaucer's lifetime such a conjunction took place (R. K. Root and Henry N. Russell, "A Planetary Date for Chaucer's Troilus," *PMLA*, XXXIX [1924], 48-63). A more promising line of approach is that taken by Professor O'Connor, who argues that the "great" or "superior" conjunctions were associated in general with great catastrophes such as Noah's Flood and the fall of kingdoms (John J. O'Connor, "The Astronomical Dating of Chaucer's *Troilus*," *JEGP*, LV [1956], 556-62). Nicole Oresme remarks that the great conjunctions regularly mark major events in history. Chaucer's use of this particular conjunction of Saturn and Jupiter to bring about the unexceptional event of the love affair between Troilus and Criseyde may have been ironic in that this conjunction usually foretold great catastrophes, or significant in pointing toward the tragedy that would befall Troy as a partial result of the tragedy that befalls Troilus. Yet another possibility is that the love affair is to be contrasted both in character and fame with the happy event of the birth of Christ, which was associated with the conjunction of Saturn and Jupiter by Bradwardine. See Eugenio Garin, *Studi nel Platonismo Medievale* (Florence, 1958), p. 60, n. 1.

[63] Tatlock, *Scene*, pp. 33-34. Wedel, *Mediaeval Attitude*, p. 86. The habit of satirizing astrologers was very widespread. One of the more amusing instances may be found in Benvenuto da Imola's commentary on *Inferno* XX, the canto of the Diviners: "Unde bene Petrus de Abano paduanus, vir singularis excellentiae, veniens ad mortem, dixit amicis, magistris, et scholaribus et medicis circumstantibus, quod dederat operam praecipuam diebus suis tribus scientiis nobilibus; quarum una

high regard for the experimental method to realize that in the four-teenth century people could make fun of astrology even when it was not being abused but was simply being methodical and "scientific" in arguing its claims. Consequently it is startling to encounter a sober writer like Robert Holkot making a joke about astrology in his *Commentary on the Book of Wisdom*. Holkot inquires whether or not it is legitimate to try to foreknow the future by the observation of signs. On the *pro* side he argues that it is because many ancient writers "proved" it true through experimentation, but then he adds that on the other hand experimentation itself is less than perfect, for many have "proven" that the meeting of two religious with each other was a sign that they had been frustrated in hunting![64]

When Chaucer uses astrological imagery, then, we must be on our guard to distinguish just what kind of imagery it is, who employs it, and for what purpose. When we read in Boethius that the philosopher is the man who observes the courses of the heavens and seeks the causes of the motions of the heavens (Bk. 1, m. 2), we discover the portrait of the good astronomer in idealized terms that Chaucer's audience probably knew well. It is because the true astronomer was so highly regarded that the astrologer, and especially the opportunistic astrologer, was so severely condemned. When Chaucer introduces into the *Miller's Tale* the portrait of the astrologer who was walking along looking at the stars and who consequently fell into a marl pit, there is not only laughter at the follies of astrology per se, but there is also some sadness about those who corrupt philosophy.[65] Chaucer's other uses of astrology and astrologers, however, deserve chapters to themselves.

---

fecerat eum subtilem, et haec erat philosophia; secunda fecerat eum divitem, scilicet medicina; tertio vero mendacem, scilicet astrologia" (*Comentum super Dantis Comoediam*, ed. J. P. Lacaita [Florence, 1888], II, 68).

[64] "Utrum obseruatio signorum ad praecognoscendum euentus futuros sit licita: vel superstitiosa Videtur primo quod sit licita: quia licitum est illo vtique antiqui per multa experimenta probauerunt esse verum sed multi probauerunt quod occursus religiosorum est signum frustrationis artis venatorie" (Robert Holkot, *Ropertus Holkot super libros sapientie* [Haguenau, 1494], sig. D₂ʳ). Holkot goes on to cite St. Augustine's objections to divination.

[65] The story has changed a good deal from its origin in the *Theaetetus*, where Socrates acknowledges the jest but praises the philosopher's lack of practical knowledge and sees in his falling into wells a sign of high-mindedness.

CHAPTER II

The Conventions and Possibilities of Astrology

I. CHURCH DECORATION AND ASTROLOGY

IF WE GRANT that Chaucer was quite high among the skeptics on the mediaeval scale of belief in astrology, we must look upon his employment of numerous astrological images as more poetic than biographical, "scientific," or "destinal." To do so is to take on a rather formidable task. It is formidable because it requires that every astrological image be examined in its immediate context in order to determine Chaucer's particular usage in different poetic matrices. Once it is assumed that Chaucer uses astrological imagery for something more than clandestine hints at his personal belief on the subject, there are a great many different artistic possibilities available, just as there are for his use of mythological imagery, alchemical motifs, and the conventional dream vision. It should be emphasized, moreover, that while astrological images were widely used in a variety of artistic media and modes, Chaucer characteristically draws upon extant conventions only to vary their themes, to use them in new contexts, or to appropriate them with such skill of execution that they become fresh and poetically vital rather than artistically desiccated. In a very general way it is possible to say that his models for the employment of astrological imagery are primarily Dante and Boccaccio. Yet, as we shall see presently, his close borrowings from Boccaccio are nevertheless arranged in such a way that it is clear that only sometimes does he share Boccaccio's goals; at others he emphatically does not.[1] By the same token one of the most famous astrological images in Dante turns up in Chaucer's *Squire's Tale* in what seems to be a humorously incongruous position.

It is not pertinent here to examine the personal belief of either Dante or Boccaccio in any more detail than has been done already, but we may note that Chaucer's decision to use astrological imagery in

---

[1] Kittredge long ago posited Dante and Boccaccio as the obvious sources for Chaucer's common device of defining the time in terms of astrology. See George Lyman Kittredge, "Chaucer's Lollius," *Harvard Studies in Classical Philology*, XXVIII (1917), 118-20.

his poetry, if indeed prompted in part by his readings in Dante and Boccaccio, would not have been affected much one way or another by the degree of belief of either of the two Italians. In Chaucer we inevitably find that his "sources" have been subsumed to his own designs. Insofar as astrology is concerned, Chaucer did not break any new ground in using astrological material artistically without putting credence in the material per se. We have already seen that the age old Boethian pattern, in which the planets are both given power over earth and yet made servants of the providential order, was a powerful artistic stimulus in the Middle Ages, and lasted into the Renaissance. Professor Thorndike to the contrary notwithstanding, Chaucer did not find in Boethius a "constant rhapsodizing" that would encourage him to think of astrology as "second only to divine worship." He did find in Boethius a famous philosopher whose deliberations on the serious matters of fate and free will were adorned with metric apostrophes to the heavens couched in solar and lunar images, but to Boethius and Chaucer these matters probably seemed more "astronomical" and "philosophical" than "astrological." Indeed, many of the Chaucerian images that are commonly discussed as "astrological" because they involve the planets or the zodiac or some combination thereof have in fact very little to do with astrology. Thus for many instances of Chaucer's astrological imagery, we may say that astrology serves as the mode of the image, but its function is not at all astrological. This can even apply, with some qualification, to Chaucer's enthusiastic poetic use of horoscopes (which have no place whatsoever in "astronomy") while he disclaims actual belief.

Chaucer's artistic use of materials that were in certain ways intrinsically repugnant was characteristically mediaeval. As everyone who has confronted the sculptured signs of the zodiac in the Labors of the Months on mediaeval cathedrals knows, astrological images were comfortably used by a church that steadfastly opposed the deterministic element of astrology.[2] In some ways this is not too astonishing a phenomenon, for the stars and planets, whether or not connected with the signs of the zodiac and the deterministic element which they implied, were obvious sources for artistic motifs indi-

---

[2] Émile Mâle, *The Gothic Image*, trans. Dora Nussey (New York: Harper Torchbooks, 1958), pp. 64-75.

cating the relationship between earth and heaven, both as mere spatial links and as links in a chain of providential influence. Because the essential religious concern of the men of the Middle Ages was the relationship of this world and heaven, and because so much verbal and pictorial art is related in one way or another to religious concerns, astrological or astronomical motifs are commonplace in areas that are not at all astrologically oriented.

For St. Bonaventure the heavenly bodies did not need to be put into either a providential or an astrological chain of determination in order to be employed in a figure of thought; they served to illustrate the link between heaven and earth by their philosophical "nature." One sees, he argues, that some things are earthly and therefore mutable and corruptible, others are celestial, hence mutable but incorruptible, and it follows that some things are supercelestial and consequently both immutable and incorruptible. After this image of the stars and planets as a *tertium quid* Bonaventure explains the utility of the figure: "From these visible things, therefore, one mounts to considering the power and wisdom and goodness of God as being, living, and understanding; purely spiritual and incorruptible and immutable."[3] Here, as in Boethius, images of the planets are used only as a means and not as an end in themselves.

The cycles of the signs of the zodiac and the Labors of the Months should be understood, then, as means of expressing man's relationship to eternity, rather than as a manifestation of paganism, whether conscious or latent. As Émile Mâle has observed, the cycle of the Labors reminded the mediaeval man of the penalty of the Fall, but as that same scholar also observed, the relationship of these cycles to Christ or the Virgin (and one might add to the symbolic zodiac) reminded the worker that he did not labor without hope.[4] The impact of this concept on the art of the Middle Ages can

---

[3] St. Bonaventure, *The Mind's Road to God*, trans. George Boas, Library of Liberal Arts (New York, 1953), p. 12.

[4] Mâle, *Gothic Image*, pp. 64-66. Mâle notes that an eighteenth-century scholar thought that the signs of the zodiac on the façade of Notre Dame at Paris indicated the survival of Mithraism into the 13th century! The origin of the Labors of the Months has received a good deal of discussion, but the current opinion is that there is no significant break in content between late antiquity and the early Middle Ages. Doro Levi has observed that pictorial calendars of this sort have always been

be seen in the Labors of the Months and the signs of the zodiac found both on churches—as at Amiens—and in lay devotional manuals of the yearly calendars as in the very simple Queen Mary Psalter and the breathtakingly elaborate *Très riches heures* of Jean de France (Figs. 5-8).

The ramifications of the use of the cycles of the Labors and the zodiac in church architecture may be better understood through reference to Professor Katzenellenbogen's analysis of the Royal Portal at Chartres.[5] In the three tympana of the Royal Portal Christ is shown in the same frontal pose, situated exactly in the center, and has the same gesture of blessing. By this device the artist managed to unify the three basic scenes of Christ's Incarnation, his Ascension, and his Second Coming. The Incarnation tympanum, on the right, has as its secondary theme the seven liberal arts, which are represented in the archivolts, each accompanied by an author representative of the particular art. It is in the left or Ascension tympanum, however, that we find the secondary theme to be the signs of the zodiac and the Labors of the Months (Fig. 9). The relationship of the signs of the zodiac and the Labors of the Months to the Ascension is also found at Vézelay in the archivolts of the Ascension tympanum (Fig. 10), and at Autun in connection with the Last Judgment. Thus the function of the zodiac on the exterior of all of these cathedrals would seem to be to link heaven and earth in order to show Christ "as lord of heaven and earth, and of time with its various activities." There is more, however. As Professor Katzenellenbogen observes, the left

---

artistic interpretations of *"Menologia rustica* which contains human, civil, and religious activities" (Doro Levi, "The Allegories of the Months in Classical Art," *Art Bulletin*, XXIII [1941], 288). An introduction to the Labors that dwells more on the Middle Ages is James Carson Webster's *The Labors of the Months* (Princeton, 1938). For the relationships between the mediaeval Labors and the classical seasons and *horae*, see George M. A. Hanfmann, *The Season Sarcophagus in Dumbarton Oaks* (Cambridge, Mass., 1951), I, 262-80. Hanfmann's emphasis on the mediaeval "sentimental" response to nature is not beyond question.

[5] Adolf Katzenellenbogen, *The Sculptural Programs of Chartres Cathedral*, reprinted by the Norton Library (New York, 1964), pp. 7-26. Katzenellenbogen observes that while in mediaeval art a zodiacal sign is usually related to the month in which the sun enters the sign (thus, Aries to March and Taurus to April), at Chartres the signs are linked with the months in which the sun remains in the sign (thus, Pisces to March, and Aries to April) (p. 114, n. 88).

and right tympana of the Royal Portal at Chartres are related in that intellectual work is represented by the seven liberal arts, and manual labor by the Labors of the Months. Thus the labors of penance for the Fall are balanced by the labors of the intellect, which have Christ himself as their goal. The words of Daniel 2:21 are very much to the point: "Et ipse mutat tempora et aetates . . . dat sapientiam sapientibus, et scientiam intelligentibus disciplinam."[6]

Whereas the zodiac is balanced with the liberal arts at Chartres, the seven planets are connected with the seven liberal arts in the Florentine Cappella degli Spagnuoli (Fig. 11). In an artistic appropriation of astrological material outside the realm of pictorial art, Dante set forth an elaborate relationship between the spheres of the planets and the liberal arts in the *Convivio*. The relationship is based upon three resemblances: both the heavens and the arts revolve around something that they do not move, in that no art demonstrates its own subject but presupposes it; both illuminate things, in that the heavens illuminate visible things and the arts illuminate intelligible things; both infuse perfection into things that are duly disposed.[7] That this fantastic argument was no doubt considered an admirable ornament by its author is some indication of the distance between our own century and the fourteenth in the matter of the artistic or literary use of cosmology.

The coupling of the spheres of the planets and the liberal arts that occurred in Dante's *Convivio* was paralleled in a less strict format in some mediaeval floor mosaics, specifically those at St. Remi in Rheims, where the rivers of paradise, the elements, the seasons, the months, the zodiac, the liberal arts, the cardinal points of the com-

[6] The signs of the zodiac also occur on archivolts of the right bay of the porch on the north transept façade at Chartres, where they are thematically linked with the tympanum illustrating the sufferings of Job. As Katzenellenbogen says, this is neither a thoughtless repetition of the imagery of the Royal Portal nor a meaningless embellishment, but is a direct outgrowth of Job 38:33: "Numquid nostri ordinem caeli, Et pones rationem eius in terra?" See Katzenellenbogen, *Sculptural Programs*, pp. 74-75.

[7] Dante, *Il Convivio*, II, xiii; vol. I, 188-212. It should be noted that the numbering of the Chapters is different in the English translation, there being an additional chapter after chapter three. The editors note that correspondence between the seven planets and the liberal arts may derive from Trivet's commentary on Boethius' *Consolation of Philosophy*. Various other correspondences were also known.

pass, and the cardinal virtues were depicted.[8] It may be remarked
that the planets were also used for decoration in secular art: the bed-
room of the Countess of Blois, the daughter of William the Con-
queror, featured images of the heavens and the earth on the ceiling
and floor, while statues of philosophy and the liberal arts carry the
baldachin over the bed, perhaps indicating the knowledge required
to understand the motions of the heavens pictured above and the
meaning of the mythological scenes on tapestries on the walls.[9] The
relationship of the zodiac to the virtues and vices was not at all
uncommon in the Middle Ages, and there is an elaborate scheme in-
volving the zodiac with both the virtues and the vices on the west
portal of St. Gilles at Argenton-Château. As Professor Katzenellen-
bogen has observed, the function of the zodiac in this complicated
figure is to link human life with the last judgment in such a way
that the faithful will be reminded to shun the vices and emulate the
virtues in view of the coming judgment day.[10] Another relationship
of things astrological to virtues may be found in the writings of the
Englishman, Alexander Neckam, who aligns the seven planets with
the seven gifts of the Holy Spirit as itemized in Isaiah 11:1-3—
sapientia, intellectus, consilium, fortitudo, scientia, pietas, and *timor
dei.*[11]

Another vein of astrological convention that did not necessarily

[8] Adolf Katzenellenbogen, *Allegories of the Virtues and Vices in Mediaeval Art*,
reprinted by the Norton Library (New York, 1964), p. 52, n. 1. See also Katzenel-
lenbogen, *Sculptural Programs*, pp. 15 and 110, n. 45, for a reference to Saint-Irénée.

[9] See Seznec, *Survival of the Pagan Gods*, p. 127, n. 15; and Katzenellenbogen,
Sculptural Programs, pp. 15-16.

[10] Katzenellenbogen, *Allegories*, pp. 17-18, and Fig. 18. The zodiacal figures are
very indistinct, and consequently no reproduction is offered here. For a detailed
picture of the archivolts—indistinct though they may be—see Paul Deschamps,
French Sculpture of the Romanesque Period (New York, n.d.), Fig. 74a.

[11] Alexander Neckam, *De naturis rerum*, ed. Thomas Wright (London, 1863),
Bk. I, ch. 7; pp. 41-44. Also see Seznec, *Survival of the Pagan Gods*, p. 49. Neckam
goes out of his way to deny belief in astral determinism while using the theory of
astrological influences to explain the gifts of the Holy Spirit: "Absit autem ut ipsos
aliquam inevitabilis necessitatis legem in inferiora sortiri censeamus. . . . Voluntas
enim divina certissima est rerum causa et primitiva. . . . Sciendum etiam est quod,
licet superiora corpora effectus quosdam compleant in inferioribus, liberum tamen
arbitrium animae non impellunt in ullam necessitatem hoc vel illud exequendi"
(pp. 39-40).

reflect any belief in astrology was the concern to parallel the Muses with the planets. Martianus Capella, who is referred to by Chaucer in the *Merchant's Tale*, was the most influential early writer to follow the Pythagoreans in aligning the planets and the Muses; he added the earth and the sphere of the fixed stars to the seven planets in order to match them up evenly with the nine Muses.[12] Obviously the existence of seven planets and twelve signs of the zodiac goes a long way toward explaining the popularity of astrological symbolism in the Middle Ages, when numerological mysticism was remarkably popular. Mâle observes that the contemplative man of the Middle Ages could find in the four seasons and twelve months of the year a figure of Christ, of whom the four evangelists and twelve apostles are members.[13] Thus it comes as no great surprise to discover that the twelve apostles themselves were linked with the signs of the zodiac in the frescoes of the Salone at Padua, and that there is a fascinating although much neglected passage in Dante's *Convivio* in which he subtly changes his emphasis on the precession of the equinoxes in order to have the best of both worlds with his allegorical or figurative interpretations. The importance of this passage for the study of Chaucer is indeed great, for whether or not Chaucer had read it, we are vouchsafed an insight into the attitude toward astronomy of another mediaeval writer. That Dante unhesitatingly quibbled with the sense of his astronomy for the sake of his allegory is interesting food for thought.

2. DANTE'S METAPHORICAL COSMOLOGY

AT THE heart of the problem in the *Convivio* is the proper explanation of the phenomenon known as the precession of the equinoxes. This rather complicated phenomenon is perhaps best understood if we

[12] Martianus Capella, *De nuptiis Philologiae et Mercurii*, ed. Fransiscus Eyssenhardt (Leipzig, 1866), Bk. I, 28; p. 12. This work was not only known to Chaucer but was sufficiently popular throughout the Middle Ages to attract a number of commentators, among them Dunchad, John the Scot, Remigius of Auxerre, and Alexander Neckam. There were numerous Renaissance editions of Martianus, and even the commentary by Remigius is extant in over 70 MSS. See the Introduction to *Remigii Autissiodorensis commentum in Martianum Capellam*, ed. Cora E. Lutz (Leyden, 1962-65), I, 40-41. See also Seznec, *Survival of the Pagan Gods*, pp. 49-50.

[13] Mâle, *Gothic Image*, p. 66.

refer to two kinds of movement: a gradual change in the date of the vernal equinox (calendrical precession), and a small precessional motion of the sphere of the fixed stars. In the most complete and most complicated treatment of the subject, which may be encountered in the thirteenth-century Alfonsine Tables, a Crystalline Sphere was posited to account for the phenomenon of calendrical precession. This was necessary because the sun's annual course around the heavens (the sidereal year) is approximately 365¼ days, which the Alfonsine astronomers chose to regard as a constant, but its course through the zodiac (the tropical year) from entrance into the vernal equinox and back again, is slightly less than that—actually by about 20 minutes a year. Over the centuries, however, this sort of thing mounts up, and it comes to about 3 days in every 400 years. The Crystalline Sphere was supposed as a sphere in which the sun made one revolution in precisely 365¼ days, and which was consequently thought to move around the zodiac at the rate of about 1° per century. Today, of course, we compensate for this difference by omitting Leap Year at the beginning of the century every three out of four times.

Because the longitude of celestial bodies is measured along the ecliptic or path of the sun through the zodiac, the sun's tardiness in its entrance of the signs of the zodiac will have an effect on the relationship of the vernal equinox to the constellations behind it. Since the sun enters the first degree of Aries in some twenty minutes of time less than a sidereal year, it completes a cycle of the zodiac in some 50 seconds of space less than it completes its sidereal year. This would mean that if the sun entered Aries against a certain backdrop of stars, one year later the sun would enter the same sign very slightly to the west of its previous backdrop. This difference is virtually indistinguishable in a year's time, but over the centuries it has resulted in the displacement of the signs of the zodiac from the constellations of the zodiac so that today the sun enters the sign Aries while its backdrop constellation is Pisces. To account for this precessional motion of the sphere of the fixed stars or constellations, they were given a small motion of their own. It was thought by some that this sphere oscillated back and forth, and so its motion was called "Trepidation." Thus it may be seen that the oft-en-

countered statement that "the Crystalline Sphere accounts for precession" tells only half the story.[14]

Happily for our present purposes Dante does not refer in his *Convivio* or elsewhere to this rather involved theory of precession, but relies rather on the much older theories which tried to account for the precession of the equinoxes with a motion of the eighth sphere —that of the fixed stars.[15] The primary distinction, in Dante's view,

[14] The precession of the equinoxes according to late mediaeval theory is best explained in *The Equatorie of the Planetis*, ed. Derek Price (Cambridge, 1955), pp. 104-107. See also M. A. Orr (Mrs. John Evershed), *Dante and the Early Astronomers* (London, 1956), pp. 92-100, and 290-97; Edward Moore, *Studies in Dante* (Oxford, 1903), III, 6-18; J. L. E. Dreyer, *A History of the Planetary Systems from Thales to Kepler* (n.p., 1953), pp. 202-206 and 277-79. For a useful and very detailed history of the theories of precession and trepidation see Pierre Duhem, *Le système du monde* (Paris, 1913-59), II, 180-266. There are certain problems connected with the work of Thâbit ibn Qurra and az-Zarqâlî. For more recent treatments of the two see *The Astronomical Works of Thabit B. Qurra*, ed. Francis J. Carmody (Berkeley and Los Angeles, 1960), pp. 15-22 and 84-101; and José Maria Millás Vallicrosa, *Estudios Sobre Azarquiel* (Madrid and Granada, 1943-50).

[15] It is not entirely clear why Dante does not refer to the theory of the Crystalline Sphere, since he was undoubtedly familiar with the writings of Brunetto Latini the Florentine, who had been sent in 1260 to Alfonso X of Castile, the king under whose guidance the Alfonsine Tables were drawn up. Brunetto was memorialized as Dante's teacher in *Inferno*, XV, 28-124. However, Dante uses the word Crystalline only as a synonym for the Primum Mobile, which, he says, it was called by many (Dante, *Convivio*, II, iii; vol. I, 113-14). Certainly this term was used in Dante's time as a synonym for the Primum Mobile, e.g. by Iacapóne da Todi and Cecco d'Ascoli. (See the *Grande Dizionario della lingua Italiana*, s.v. "cristallino," 4. No entry of the other meaning of crystalline is found prior to the 16th century.) It may be that Italy was slow in adopting the concept of the Crystalline Sphere. Sacrobosco's widely used *De sphaera* has no mention of it, and the commentaries on that work by Cecco d'Ascoli and Michael Scot ignore it. (Scot is mentioned in *Inferno* XX, 115-118. Cecco, who lectured on Sacrobosco at Bologna until 1324, mentions Dante in his *Acerba*.) Moreover, the *Tractatus spere materialis* of Andalò di Negro, Boccaccio's teacher, does not mention the Crystalline Sphere. On the other hand, John Peckham, Archbishop of Canterbury from 1279-92, wrote a *De sphaera* in which he clearly distinguishes a Crystalline Sphere from the Primum Mobile: "Quidam tamen in hiis periti litteris ponunt unum intermedium celum inter cristallinum et empyreum collocatum, motum motu simplicissimo, ut infra declarabor. Secundum hos primos igitur sunt undecim orbes celestes . . ." (Lynn Thorndike, *The Sphere of Sacrobosco and its Commentators* [Chicago, 1949], p. 448; for the other remarks thus far see pp. 24, 35, 77, 283, 359, and 448; as well as Orr, *Dante and the Early Astronomers*, pp. 156-57). In spite of Peckham's work in England, Chaucer refers to only nine spheres in the *Parlement of Foules* (ll. 59-61), and he

is between the eighth sphere of the fixed stars, which moves in order to account for both kinds of precession, and the motion of the Primum Mobile, which turns all the heavens in their daily course from east to west. Thus, writing in *Convivio* II, iii, he argues that Aristotle thought there were only eight heavens, the last being that of the fixed stars, but that Ptolemy, perceiving there was a motion of precession and wanting to have a First Mover of absolute simplicity, laid down the existence of a ninth sphere, the Primum Mobile, outside of the fixed stars, which would make a revolution from east to west in just a fraction less than 24 hours. (Actually, Ptolemy thought there were only eight spheres, but Dante is probably using a commentary.) In this way one could avoid having the sphere of the fixed stars simultaneously revolve in different directions around different poles. Indeed, the positing of a Crystalline Sphere such as has been discussed grew out of the same concern for simplicity of motion, and this intermediate sphere is required when calendrical and equinoctial precession are distinguished. To these nine spheres of the pagan astronomers Dante adds a tenth, the unmoved and unmoving celestial Empyrean, for which justification he appeals to Catholic rather than astronomical or philosophical authority.

---

refers to the Toledan Tables in the *Franklin's Tale*, but does not mention the slightly later Alfonsine Tables, which introduced the theory of the Crystalline.

At one juncture Dante says that he has counted the Crystalline as the Primum Mobile ("Lo Cielo cristallino, che per Primo Mobile dinanzi e contato" [*Convivio*, II, xiv; vol. I, 223]), which might suggest that he knew of the existence of another sphere named the Crystalline, but this is mere supposition. There is, interestingly, a clear statement of the idea of a Crystalline Sphere, although without mention of it by name, in Albertus Magnus' *De coelo*, which was the source for some of Dante's ideas on the spheres: ". . . ante orbem stellarum oportet esse duos orbes. . . . quia diximus in coelo stellarum fixarum deprehensos esse tres motus; et ideo oportet quod ante ipsum sit coelum duorum motuum tantum. . . . natura non venit de extremo in extremum nisi per medium. . . . ergo erunt decem sphaerae, quarum prima habet motum diurnum, et secunda vocatur circulus signorum non stellatorum . . . " (cited by Busnelli and Vandelli without remarks on its significance for this aspect of the *Convivio*, I, 247). Even if Dante had been aware of the theory of the Crystalline Sphere as separate from the Primum Mobile, the idea that there were nine moving heavens and one unmoving, Empyrean heaven so appealed to his sense of harmony and his feeling for mystical numerology that it is doubtful that he would have included a separate Crystalline in a work like the *Convivio*, which, after all, is a work in which a number of ideas are made to serve a central theme.

At a later juncture in the *Convivio*, however, Dante quibbles with the existence of a Primum Mobile to account for diurnal motion. In *Convivio* II, xiv, Dante has finished relating the spheres of the planets to the seven liberal arts, and is faced with the no doubt delightful metaphorical possibilities of the remaining spheres. His first choice is to relate the eighth sphere of the fixed stars to physics and metaphysics, because of its two motions: its daily motion signifies the corruptible things of nature, which physics treats of, and its extremely slow motion of precession signifies incorruptible things, which are the proper subject of metaphysics. Now here is the quibble: Dante does not actually contradict himself and say that the eighth sphere of fixed stars causes the diurnal motion, but only that it has one.[16] However, all the planets have this motion, so it is not a particular quality of the eighth sphere unless it originates there, and Dante skirts around this problem without coming to grips with it. Dante attributed to each of the seven planets two unique properties that related the respective planet to a liberal art; he also used two properties for the eighth sphere, although these were related to two branches of study and one of them was not at all peculiar to the eighth sphere. Following this passage Dante immediately goes on to ascribe the origin of diurnal motion to the ninth sphere or Primum Mobile, which he compares to moral philosophy on the grounds that it regulates the motions of the planets beneath it so that they receive the virtue of their parts from above. Of course, this does not align well with Dante's emphasis on the diurnal motion of the eighth sphere as one of its own "properties"; it is also further evidence that he is as much concerned with philosophy as he is with cosmology. Dante is never a slavish imitator: he uses the materials that are at hand and is not afraid to vary his emphasis or to disagree with his sources in order to implement his own philosophical and artistic goals. It may be remarked that in this sequence about the spheres he disagrees with Aristotle in favor of Ptolemy, then, on the authority of the Catholic church, disagrees with Ptolemy in order to add a sphere, and later disagrees with Aristotle in relating the diurnal movement (which Aristotle had seen as the

---

[16] Professor Moore (*Studies in Dante*, III, 15-16) thought that Dante was cosmologically inconsistent, but Busnelli and Vandelli follow Nardi in emphasizing Dante's care to avoid an actual contradiction (I, 220).

symbol of permanence and eternity) to the corruptible things of the world. Moreover, he finishes his chapter by tacitly arguing with St. Thomas' description of philosophy as the handmaiden of theology, preferring to see philosophy and theology as queens, paramours, and handmaidens together, and yet to see theology as a perfect "dove."[17]

3. ASTROLOGY AND MYTHOLOGY

No DOUBT the source for at least some of the manifold artistic uses of astrology may be traced to the lack of any distinction between a planet and a planetary "god" in the Middle Ages—a situation that does not indicate a "confusion," but rather a disinclination to distinguish—which made it possible for the church to appropriate astrology and astrological images for its own designs as part of the heritage of pagan antiquity that it ubiquitously put to work in the vineyards of the Lord. Thus when we encounter a fourteenth-century portrayal of Jupiter as a monk on the campanile in Florence (Fig. 12), it is a person that is portrayed, but the association of Jupiter with monks comes from an astrological relationship of the planet Jupiter with the western or Christian countries, and from an exhortation to those who would invoke his aid to dress like Christians and particularly like monks.[18] This association of gods and planets is extremely old, and arose because the planets were discovered sometime after early societies had created their pantheons. Franz Cumont has pointed out that it is impossible to have any very sophisticated system of astrology until there is a well-developed calendar with which to compute the motions of the planets, and Cumont would put the existence of such a calendar at the rather late date of 747 B.C. This would mean that the planets would naturally be associated as forces with the already

---

[17] On the disagreement with Aristotle on corruptibility, see Duhem, *Système du monde*, IV, 226. For philosophy and theology see Étienne Gilson, *Dante the Philosopher*, trans. David Moore (New York, 1949), pp. 114-20. Dante's ascription to Ptolemy of the necessity for simple motion in the eighth sphere is actually Neoplatonic, not Ptolemaic. In the later Middle Ages it was suggested that the whole Ptolemaic system be modified in order to bring it into accord with Neoplatonic philosophy. See Bruno Nardi, "Dante e Alpetragio," *Giornale Dantesco*, XXIX (1926), 41-53; and al-Bitrûjî, *De motibus celorum*, ed. Francis J. Carmody (Berkeley and Los Angeles, 1952), pp. 11-37.

[18] Seznec, *Survival of the Pagan Gods*, pp. 161-63. Of course, this is the origin of the association, not the meaning of the figure on the campanile.

existing gods of the Babylonians, and the same thing happened later with the Greeks and Romans. Thus every planet took on two natures: one traditional and pre-existent, linked with an extant god, and the other essentially adventitious, based on observation of the planet's color, motion, and presumed nature.[19] If we jump many centuries to Greek and Roman times, it is possible to trace the development by which a planet would at one juncture be called the "star of Zeus" or the "star of Aphrodite" and not long afterwards be referred to simply as "Zeus" or "Aphrodite," and later still as "Jupiter" or "Venus."[20] This complete identification of gods and planets was furthered by the literary device of "catasterism," in which the story of a god or goddess is terminated by translation to the heavens and memorialization in a constellation—the device being best known in Ovid's *Metamorphoses*.[21] By the time of Cicero this complete interchangeability of gods and planets had become the usual attitude of the pagan world.[22]

If planets and pagan gods could be identified one with another, then the various arguments for the use of things pagan could be extended without much trouble to cover planets, and, by a series of easy extensions, the zodiac, stellar influence in general, and so forth. These arguments for the use of things pagan have become much better known in recent years, but not much emphasis has been put on the fact that parts of astrology managed to include themselves under the aegis of potentially useful errors. Not only was there the tradition of the interchangeability of gods and planets available to the artist casting round for means of expression, but also there was among some of the Fathers a revival of Euhemerism that made it possible to think of the planet/gods as ways of talking about human characteristics brought to perfection in a single, historical figure. St. Augustine referred to the theories of Euhemerus (who, as early as the third century B.C., advanced the idea that the "gods" were merely famous

[19] Franz Cumont, *Astrology and Religion Among the Greeks and Romans* (New York, 1912), pp. 8, 25, and 45-46.
[20] Franz Boll and Carl Bezold, *Sternglaube und Sterndeutung*, rev. Gundel (Leipzig and Berlin, 1931), p. 49.
[21] See Cumont, *Astrology and Religion*, p. 117.
[22] Seznec, *Survival of the Pagan Gods*, p. 37.

heroes) in order to attack the pagan gods, but in some ways this very revival helped give them a new life in art.[23]

St. Jerome's "captive maiden" from Deuteronomy was one of the early examples of the use of things pagan. Classical writings were, like the beautiful captive, to be shorn of their distracting beauty (the hair and the fingernails of the maiden were to be cut) and then after a decent interval appropriately employed (the maiden was to be kept for a time and then married).[24] Similar figures are the classical declaration "aurum in stercore quaero," which had been adapted by Cassiodorus, among others, and the very famous argument about Egyptian gold that St. Augustine used to characterize those things of value among the pagans that the good Christian might carry away, just as the Israelites carried away the gold and silver of their Egyptian captors.[25] In general this whole process of adaptation of classical myth may be called allegorization, and studies indicate that it was closely modelled on Biblical exegesis.[26] This metaphorical interpretation of pagan myth is better known than the corresponding allegorization of astrology, but because of the correspondences between the two, some figurative use of astrology should be expected in mediaeval art. However, few scholars have seen as well as Ceslaus Spicq that allegory is a principal characteristic of astronomy and astrology themselves, as well as of art, architecture, and Biblical exegesis.[27] When we encounter astrology in a work of mediaeval art, then, we should expect that the astrology itself will as often as not be subsumed under the artistic goal at hand: while sometimes astrology will function as astrology, sometimes it will function in art quite figuratively,

[23] *Ibid.*, pp. 11-17.

[24] Henri de Lubac, S.J., *Exégèse médiévale*, Part 1 (Paris, 1959), I, 290-93. Father de Lubac observes that in fact Origen had used the same idea.

[25] *Ibid.*, I, 274-77, and 294. See also D. W. Robertson, Jr., *A Preface to Chaucer* (Princeton, 1962), pp. 337-56, which is an excellent survey of the tradition and of its relation to mediaeval humanism, and see the same author's translation of St. Augustine's *On Christian Doctrine*, pp. xiii-xiv.

[26] Jean Pépin, *Mythe et allégorie* (Paris, 1958), pp. 44ff.; and see Robertson, *Preface*, pp. 286ff.

[27] Ceslaus Spicq, *Esquisse d'une histoire de l'exégèse latine au moyen âge* (Paris, 1944), p. 28, n. 1. The doctrine of "plenitude" is the probable cause of the mediaeval concern to apply allegory to an understanding of the universe. See Arthur O. Lovejoy, *The Great Chain of Being* (New York: Harper Torchbooks, 1960), pp. 99-143.

as in the parallels we have seen between the planets, the signs of the zodiac, and a whole catalogue of virtues, arts, vices, apostles, and the like. Indeed, at times an astrological image will be so forced in an artistic context that it is difficult to conceive of it as astrology at all, as when we encounter Jupiter as a monk, or parallels between Aries the Ram and Christ the Lamb.[28]

Whether we speak of astrology or astronomy, we must remember that we are speaking of raw material ready to be used in various ways in different artistic matrices, and we must be prepared to turn to a variety of sources and resources if we are to attempt to explicate Chaucer's poetic use of astrology. Thus when Boccaccio is writing as a mythographer in his *Genealogy of the Pagan Gods* he is writing as one explicating things both pagan and mythic. Yet he does not confine himself in his discussions of sources to the works of other writers on pagan gods, such as Ovid, but cites as his authorities Paul of Perugia on pagan mythology, Paul the Geometrician on arithmetic and astrology, Dante on poetry, myth, and theology, and Andalò di Negro on astrology.[29] In short, a mythographer like Boccaccio felt obliged to know astrology, arithmetic, and theology, as well as mythology. It follows, then, that if we are to interpret astrology we shall at least have to be ready to resort to mythology and theology, and perhaps even arithmetic.

The most significant result of the linking of astrology and astrological images with the gods of pagan mythology is that they will often take on more rather than less meaning. In the continual moralizations of the mediaeval classics from Servius, Lactantius Placidus, and Fulgentius right on into the Renaissance, men assumed that a fable meant something and that this meaning was discoverable.[30] This is well enough known today not to require further discussion, but the curious interplay of astrology with mythography is less well known.

---

[28] Seznec, *Survival of the Pagan Gods*, p. 50, nn. 59 and 60; and H. Flanders Dunbar, *Symbolism in Mediaeval Thought* (New York, 1961), pp. 120; 161, n. 176; and 407.

[29] Boccaccio, *Genealogie deorum*, II, 760-62.

[30] The tradition of moralization has been discussed by many of the scholars already cited here, notably Robertson, Pépin, and Seznec. See also Erwin Panofsky, *Studies in Iconology*, reprinted by Harper Torchbooks (New York and Evanston, 1962), pp. 18-31.

We have already noted that Boccaccio cites an astrologer, Andalò di Negro, as one of his authorities; it is also worth noting that Boccaccio unhesitatingly draws him into one of his analyses and contrasts Andalò's opinion with that of Albericus the mythographer. Thus, in discussing the nature of Hermaphrodite, Boccaccio first submits the opinion of Albericus that Hermaphrodite was born of the union of Mercury and Venus, following a seduction accomplished through Mercury's eloquence, and should have been wholly male but was made partly feminine because of the abundance of tender language that had accompanied the conception. Boccaccio then presents and indicates his preference for Andalò's astrological analysis of Mercury, which says it is a "masculine" planet when with other "masculine" planets, and "feminine" when with "feminine" planets. Consequently Boccaccio ascribes the dual sexuality of the non-astrological Hermaphrodite to the vagaries of a planet.[31] By the same token the astrologers themselves drew upon other traditions, so that Mercury's association with eloquence, which we have just observed and which no doubt originated with Martianus Capella's *Marriage of Mercury and Philology*, finds its way into the astrological manuals as one of the characteristics influenced by Mercury at a person's birth. To eloquence is added wisdom, doubtless also due to the influence of Martianus' opus.[32]

Similarly we may observe that the planetary goddess, Venus, had a wealth of associations in the later Middle Ages precisely because she was both a planet and a goddess, as well as a person and the personification of a quality. Thus in the discussion of the adultery of Mars and Venus in the *Ovide moralisé*, a discussion that will be referred to again in the analysis of the *Complaint of Mars*, we find that the author first discusses the story of Mars and Venus as an allusion to

[31] "Hermofroditum ex Mercurio et Venere genitum vult Albericus lascivientem preter oportunitatem esse sermonem, qui, cum virilis esse debeat, nimia verborum mollicie videtur effeminatus. Ego vero Hermofroditum habere utrumque sexum ad naturam Mercurii refero, quem venerabilis Andalo aiebat, eo quod cum masculinis planetis masculus esset, cum feminis autem femina . . ." (Boccaccio, *Genealogie deorum*, I, 140-41).

[32] "Si uero dominus ascendentis Mercurius fuerit in bono loco, liber ab infortunijs, largitur nato eloquentiam, sapientiam, suauitatem, pulchritudinem, scripturae peritiam, scientiam, & excellentiam solertiamque in inueniendo ac componendo" Albohali Alchait, *De judiciis natiuitatem* . . . (Nuremberg, 1546), sig. C_3^{r-v}. Cf. Albumasar, *Introductorium in astronomiam* . . . (Venice, 1506), sig. H_1^v.

the natures of the two planets and their influences on one another. He then gives us a Euhemeristic interpretation in which Venus is merely the *nom de guerre* of a woman who deceived her blacksmith husband with a very "chevalereuz" young warrior. Following this there is an apostrophe against adultery, after which there is an allegory in which Venus figures as the personification of "luxure."[33] There is no particular preference expressed for one or another of the explanations given in the poem; all are given equal footing. Clearly then, an artistic reference to Venus might imply the planet, the goddess, the personification of Love, or it might center on one but have overtones of the others. Just as Martianus Capella suggested to the astrologers some influences that Mercury might have here below, so the myth of the adultery of Venus and Mars, which is at least as old as Homer, suggested that when both of these planets were involved in a nativity the "native" would be inclined toward fornication and adultery.[34] There is, however, a further corollary of some importance: the astrologers make value judgments about this particular sort of venereal influence, continually referring to sin, turpitude, corruption, debauchery, wickedness, and law-breaking. In other words, to say that something is astrological is often to link it with something mythological, which in turn would often be "moralized." Even a study of astrological images solely in astrological manuals gives us a "moralization" of sorts, in that there existed among the astrologers (or among their translators) a set of normative moral values, whatever opinion they might have had about the degree of astral determinism extant in the world.

Any planet or god, of course, can mean different things in different contexts and can be construed variously depending upon which particular myth is cited and whether the deity in question is cited as a god or as a planet, and so forth. The problem for the literary student is that poets do not always make it clear which set of attributes we are to think of when a planet or a god is presented. This

---

[33] *Ovide moralisé*, ed. C. de Boer, in *Verhandlingen der Koninklijke Akademie van Wetenschappen te Amsterdam*, Afdeeling Letterkunde, XV, XXI, XXX, XXXVII, XLIII (1915-1938), Bk. IV, ll. 1488-1755: vol. XXI, 44-49.

[34] Many examples are cited in Chapter III, but actually occurrences of this are so numerous as to defy meaningful documentation.

usually does not mean that a specific response is not intended, but rather that the figure in question is to be understood in its immediate poetic context and that the correct mythical or astrological associations are to be summoned up by the reader, not listed didactically by the poet. An excellent example of this is afforded in Boccaccio's *Teseida*, where we are once again concerned with the goddess Venus. In the text proper Boccaccio gives us some hints as to which Venus we are dealing with, but he is certainly not tautological. Palemone goes to Venus' temple and invokes her as the wife of Vulcan, who makes the mountain of Cytheron happy, and asks that he be granted Emily by the love that Venus bore for Adonis.[35] That Venus is linked with Vulcan might make us suspicious, but she is merely the wife here, not the deceiver, and the reference to Venus and Adonis, while mightily condemned by generations of mythographers, is here cited in a completely neutral tone. In the *Chiose* to the poem, however, Boccaccio offers a full analysis of Venus, *in bono* and *in malo*, and tells us that only the latter is the one we are concerned with in the *Teseida*. Mars, Boccaccio tells us, signifies the irascible passions and Venus the concupiscent, but of the latter there are two kinds: the legitimate desire for sexual relations in order to have children within the bonds of matrimony and lascivious desire, commonly represented by the Goddess of Love. Moreover, he goes on, it is possible to deduce from an inspection of the text that the former and not the latter Venus is intended.[36]

It would seem, then, that we should maintain a very flexible posture toward astrological imagery, for its interpretation may depend upon sifting through various sets of associations, but, come what may, we can test our ideas by going back and inspecting the poem and deciding that our interpretations of the astrological images do or do

[35] " 'O bella dea, del buon Vulcano sposa, / per cui s'allegra il monte Citerone, / deh, i'ti priego che mi sii pietosa / per quello amor che portasti ad Adone' " (Giovanni Boccaccio, *Teseida*, ed. Aurelio Roncaglia [Bari, 1941], Bk. VII, 43: p. 191).

[36] "Ad evidenzia della quale cosa è da sapere che come di sopra, dicendo Marte consistere nello appetito irascibile, cosí Venere nel concupiscibile. La quale Venere è doppia, perciò che l'una si può e dee intendere per ciascuno onesto e licito disiderio, sí come è disiderare d'avere moglie per avere figliuoli, e simili a questo; e di questa Venere non si parla qui. La seconda Venere e quella per la quale ogni lascivia e disiderata, e che volgarmente e chiamata dea d'amore; e di questa disegna qui l'autore il tempio e l'altre cose circustanti ad esso, come nel testo appare" (*Teseida*, Chiose, p. 417).

not make sense in their poetic contexts. Moreover, along with a certain generosity of latitude for the interpretation of astrological imagery, we also ought to allow considerable latitude in our definition of what constitutes an astrological image. There was, as we have seen, a large area of overlap in the mediaeval definitions of astrology and astronomy, even though distinctions between the two were often drawn, and for the study of astrological imagery in Chaucer more would be lost than gained if we tried to distinguish between the two. For example, the discovery of the sun in Taurus at the opening of *The Canterbury Tales* is certainly not anything we would associate with judicial astrology or divination, and yet the idea of defining the time of year with reference to the sun's entrance into a sign of the zodiac could only be referred to a mediaeval and not a modern definition of astronomy. Other complications might also arise, such as the question of where to pigeonhole the planetary hours in which the protagonists pray to the god or goddess of their choice in the *Knight's Tale*.

If astrological imagery is broadened to include much that might today be subsumed under the rubric of astronomy, cosmology, or myth, it immediately becomes apparent that Chaucer uses a great deal of astrological imagery in his poetry. It should, however, be observed that, with the exception of the *Complaint of Mars*, Chaucer uses astrology incidentally; aside from the exception just mentioned, astrology is never the subject or the mode of his poetry. Thus, although Chaucer is not an astrologer and clearly ranks high among the unbelievers in astrology, we may fairly say that at one juncture he did write an astrological poem.[37]

4. ASTROLOGY AND MYTHOLOGY IN THE *KNIGHT'S TALE* AND *TROILUS AND CRISEYDE*

In this brief and necessarily eclectic survey some idea of the scope and complexity of the artistic possibilities of astrology, all based on

---

[37] The term "astrological poem" is accurate when applied to the "Mars," but it potentially confuses means and ends, so its use in this study has been deliberately avoided as much as possible. The study of Professor Soldati employs the term "astrological poetry" to describe the writings of men who had quite varying attitudes toward the practice of the science, and illustrates the limitations of describing poetry only with reference to its form and mode. See Benedetto Soldati, *La Poesia Astrologica nel Quattrocento* (Florence, 1906), pp. 84, 171, and 230ff.

conventional uses of particular elements of astrology, has been emphasized. There are, of course, numerous occasions when an astrological image will not have obscure ramifications, when it will stand only for itself, when it will mean what it says. In the *Knight's Tale*, for example, Chaucer uses a good deal of astrological imagery in conjunction with mythological imagery, but it needs very little explication. We have already noted that Arcite ascribes the necessity of his and Palamon's imprisonment to the condition of the heavens at their birth, particularly to "som wikke aspect or disposicioun / Of Saturne, by some constellacioun" (*KnT*, 1087-88). The astrology here, such as it is, is straightforward enough: the association of Saturn with imprisonment is made by Saturn himself in the same poem, when he lists "the prison in the derke cote" (*KnT*, 2457) among the phenomena under his control. Shortly after Arcite's speech on Saturn, Palamon also ascribes his imprisonment to Saturn, adding, however, a reference to the non-astrological figure of Juno as a kind of co-conspirator: "But I moot been in prisoun thurgh Saturne, / And eek thurgh Juno, jalous and eek wood" (*KnT*, 1328-29). Although the astrology here is clear enough, its poetic use cannot be understood without reference to the poetic context. If we note only that both ascribe imprisonment to Saturn, we see that they are styled by Chaucer as deterministic characters; but when we reflect that Arcite said they were both in prison because of Saturn and that Palamon ascribes his own imprisonment to Saturn even after Arcite has been released, then we may fairly judge that Chaucer is not only saying that both are deterministic but also that to be deterministic and pessimistic in the face of evidence to the contrary is to be short-sighted.

The planetary gods of the *Knight's Tale* are portrayed most dramatically in the descriptions of the temples of Venus, Mars, and Diana, and in the self-description of his powers by Saturn. Here astrology, astronomy, and mythology are nicely mixed and are conveyed with extremely forceful terms that draw upon iconographic traditions, mythographic writings, astrological conventions, and even upon such disparate subjects as French poetry and the pseudo-science of geomancy. The deities in the temples are portrayed as gods, not planets, so that we discover Venus "naked, fletynge in the large see" (1956), and Mars in his cart, "Armed, and looked grym as he were wood"

(2042). On the other hand, all three deities are portrayed along with the "children of the planet," that is, with the types of character, occupation, and future that were supposedly created by the influence of the respective planets at a person's birth. For an illustration of the unpleasant things in store for the children of Saturn, the ultimately influential deity in the *Knight's Tale*, see Figs. 13a and b. This astrological influence is made poetically most obvious in the description of Mars, which says: "Ther were also, *of Martes divisioun*, / The barbour, and the bocher, and the smyth" (*KnT*, 2024-25). Saturn, on the other hand, speaks like a god, but describes himself as a planet when he promises Venus to give Emily to Palamon and even volunteers a statement of his astrological peculiarities:

> My cours, that hath so wyde for to turne,
> Hath moore power than woot any man.
>
> . . . .
>
> I do vengeance and pleyn correccioun,
> Whil I dwelle in the signe of the leoun.
>
> (*KnT*, 2454-62)

Whether this last is some obscure historical allegory or whether it is simply an astrological fact is not entirely clear, but in all events the astrology is essentially self-interpreting in that Chaucer gives us both the situation and its meaning.[38]

[38] Professor Parr has argued that vengeance and correction are not to be found as peculiar to Saturn in astrological manuals, and that the planet is not often said to be more malignant in Leo than in other signs. Because Saturn was in Leo from July 1, 1387, to August 15, 1389, Parr argues that "vengeance" refers to the Duke of Gloucester's persecution of the young Richard II and his friends, after Richard had been forced to submit to a regency the previous year. "Pleyn correccioun" would consequently signify Richard's successful demand that the Privy Council dissolve the regency, which was made in May of 1389. See Johnstone Parr, "The Date and Revision of Chaucer's *Knight's Tale*," *PMLA*, LX (1945), 307-14. On the whole this is an attractive interpretation for those who are predisposed to accept historical allegories, but it may be objected that such an allusion would be obtrusive and inartistic in a list of traditional Saturnine influences. Professor Weese has made two further objections to Parr's position: (1) both "vengeance" and "pleyn correccioun" are activities that may be legitimately associated with Saturn, and (2) Chaucer would not describe Gloucester's usurpation as "vengeance." See Walter E. Weese "'Vengeance and Pleyn Correccioun,'" *MLN*, LXIII (1948), 331-33. The first point is well taken, and it may well be that some astrological document will

Although the several gods and goddesses of the *Knight's Tale* are described in such a way that we know what they mean, not much attention has been paid to the meaning of the meaning: the poetic function of the planetary deities. To put it another way, it is one thing to say that here Venus represents Love, Mars represents War, and so forth, but it is quite another to look at what kind of love and what kind of battle. If we ask this question, we are led at once to two provocative insights. The first is that all four deities involved with Palamon, Arcite, and Emily are associated with distinct unpleasantness. The second is that three of these deities are also associated with Theseus, but with a different emphasis.

In the temple of Venus we find depicted lovers, as we might expect, but there is neither sweetness nor light in either the lovers' actions or the series of portraits of famous servants of the goddess:

> Wroght on the wal, ful pitous to biholde,
> The broken slepes, and the sikes colde,
> The sacred teeris, and the waymentynge,
> The firy strokes of the desirynge
> That loves servantz in this lyf enduren;
>
> . . . .
>
> Lo, alle thise folk so caught were in hir las,
> Til they for wo ful ofte seyde "allas!"
>
> (*KnT*, 1919-52)

This is the Venus that Palamon will pray to, and if we remember the double Venus of Boccaccio we have some idea of what is intended here. Conversely, Theseus, although he does not mention Venus by name, does say that he was a servant of the God of Love at one time, and elsewhere Venus is styled as the Goddess of Love, mother of Cupid

---

eventually turn up these precise terms. In this regard it is worth noting that Professor Parr himself found an astrological source for the "cherles rebellyng" associated with Saturn, which many had thought to be not astrological but rather a covert reference to the Peasants' Revolt (Johnstone Parr, "Chaucer's *Cherles Rebellyng*," *MLN*, LXIX [1953], 393-94). The second of Weese's objections is somewhat less forceful in that Parr did not equate "vengeance" with the usurpation of power in 1387, but rather with the persecution of Richard beginning in 1386. With this noted, however, there is still doubt that Gloucester's acts could properly be termed "vengeance" on the king for his youthful indiscretions.

(*KnT*, 1904 and 1963). Theseus mocks the strife of Palamon and Arcite, presumably indicating that he now thinks Venus' game not worth the candle:

> Se how they blede! be they noght wel arrayed?
> Thus hath hir lord, the god of love, ypayed
> Hir wages and hir fees for hir servyse!
> And yet they wenen for to been ful wyse
> That serven love. . . .
>
> . . . .
>
> A man moot ben a fool, or yong or oold,—
> I woot it by myself ful yore agon,
> For in my tyme a servant was I oon.
> (*KnT*, 1801-14)

Parallel to the two attitudes toward Venus that are displayed are two perspectives on Mars. The temple of Mars is in itself a rather uninviting place, being comparable to the "grisly place / That highte the grete temple of Mars in Trace" (*KnT*, 1971-72), and it is lighted only by what little northern light comes through the door, "For wyndowe on the wal ne was ther noon, / Thurgh which men myghten any light discerne" (*KnT*, 1988-89). All this, however, is nothing in comparison to the various "martial" figures that are then listed in a series that is more notable for morbidity than for heroism. Following the personifications of Felony, Ire, and Dread, we see the pickpurse and the famous smiler with his knife, followed by pictures of burning stables, treasonable murder, suicide, the nail driven into a sleeper's temple, the tyrant with his prey, the hunter strangled by briars, and the sow devouring a child in its cradle. Finally, there is an ugly prolepsis for Arcite, "who shal be slayn or elles deed for love" (*KnT*, 2038). These personifications are, of course, "conventional" but form only a part of the conventional associations of Mars. Chaucer chooses his details to give the tone he wants. The Mars of "open werre" is mentioned only once in this catalogue, and the Mars that Neckam linked with "consilium" is absent. Conversely, when Theseus listens to the plea of the women in the temple of "Clemence" and with "herte pitous" swears to avenge their wrong, it is Mars who "So shyneth in his white baner large, / That alle the feeldes glyteren

up and doun" (*KnT*, 976-77). Needless to say, although this is the "same" Mars, the emphasis is a good deal different, and to some extent it is justifiable to speak of a "double" Mars after the example of Boccaccio's double Venus.

Theseus is also associated at one juncture with Emily's patron deity, albeit fleetingly, and in the linkage with him Diana is clearly nothing more or less than the familiar goddess of hunting—the favorite sport of Chaucer's day:

> For in his huntyng hath he swich delit
> That it is al his joye and appetit
> To been hymself the grete hertes bane,
> For after Mars he serveth now Dyane.
> (*KnT*, 1679-82)

Indeed, it would seem difficult to present an unattractive portrait of the goddess of virginity and hunting, but Chaucer does exactly that in his description of her temple. There she is accompanied by portraits of Callisto, turned into a bear by Diana's anger; Daphne, turned into a tree; Actaeon, slain by his hounds in Diana's "vengeaunce"; and Atalanta and Meleager, to whom Diana "wroghte hym care and wo" (*KnT*, 2072). Under Diana's feet is a moon that is waxing and will soon wane—a traditional symbol of inconstancy—and she is casting her eyes down into those realms "Ther Pluto hath his derke regioun" (*KnT*, 2082). Pluto is styled elsewhere by Chaucer as the king of hell (*T&C*, III, 592), and Diana's downcast eyes would consequently appear to be a sign of something other than, say, modesty. The last image adduced for the description refers to Diana's role as goddess of childbirth, and while this might be presented positively, Chaucer prefers to concentrate on the picture of the woman who calls on the goddess for help "pitously" because her child "so longe was unborn" (*KnT*, 2084).

Saturn, of course, is more often malevolent than any other planet, but it may be noted that he is not always so; Chaucer couples him with Mars in the *House of Fame* and there presents the seven "wise and worthy" men of the "secte saturnyn" who are under his influence (*HF*, 1438). In the *Knight's Tale*, however, there is no such tempering of the customary picture of Saturn who now outdoes even

Mars in his necrological affinities, having virtually no other influences. Saturn is not associated at all with Theseus, and we may properly inquire to what degree we are to applaud the events involving Palamon, Arcite, and Emily, when they voluntarily associate with such unpleasant deities, and when the deities are in turn manipulated by the disquieting figure of Saturn.

One way of approaching the astrological imagery and the general involvement with the pagan gods that is found in the tale is to abandon any idea of astral determinism for self-determination on the basis of character. It is certainly clear enough that although Arcite prays to Mars, and Palamon to Venus, both are interested in battle only insofar as it is a possible prelude to the enjoyment of Emily. That lady's service of Diana, in turn, seems to be less the result of a desire for the positive virtues of chastity or legitimate child-bearing than it is the product of self-indulgence, for she says she is

> A mayde, and love huntynge and venerye,
> And for to walken in the wodes wilde,
> And noght to ben a wyf and be with childe.
> > (*KnT*, 2308-10)

Further confirmation of Emily's character may be found in her devotion to Fortune, which matches her devotion to Diana. For, although she asks Diana to send her the one who most desires her if she must indeed marry, she first warms to Arcite when it seems that he has won, then loves Palamon "tenderly" (*KnT*, 3103) when she is married off to him. Surely her devotion to chastity is being satirized when Chaucer remarks upon her favorable attitude toward Arcite:

> And she agayn hym caste a freendlich ye
> (For wommen, as to speken in comune,
> Thei folwen alle the favour of Fortune).
> > (*KnT*, 2680-82)

We may argue, then, that when people indulge in the self-serving chastity here associated with Diana or the lust symbolized by Venus and its resultant fury against friend, there is a certain determination of

75

the future that does not depend upon planetary intervention, but rather upon logical probabilities.[39] The actions of Palamon and Arcite lead to the death of one friend at the hands of another over a girl who, in Theseus' words, "woot namoore of al this hoote fare, / By God, than woot a cokkow or an hare!" (*KnT*, 1809-10). The marriage that occurs after this is indeed *post hoc*, but not *propter hoc*: it is the result of Theseus' attempt to make virtue of necessity.

Death as the result of the service of Venus, is not found only in the *Knight's Tale* but may be encountered in the *Troilus* as well. Troilus is actually provided with a horoscope of sorts by Chaucer, although the fact has not attracted much critical attention, and typically it is a simplified affair. Like the horoscopes of the Wife of Bath, Hypermnestra, and Constance, all of which will be discussed later, this horoscope is abbreviated in order to gain in artistic utility, even at the cost of a loss in astrological verisimilitude. This fact in itself suggests that Chaucer uses astrology in his artistic creations because he is interested in different and striking ways of saying things about his literary characters and is not much interested in the astrology of horoscopes *per se*. In Book II Chaucer discusses the fact that at the time of Criseyde's first sight of Troilus, after she has learned that he loves her, Venus was in the seventh house of heaven—in Libra, which is one of her houses—and did not have any planets in bad aspect to her.[40] To this information, which clearly is intended to suggest the propitiousness of the moment for the start of a love affair, Chaucer adds the remark that Venus was also in a good position in the heavens at Troilus' birth—something that would not run counter to the present favorable indications:

[39] In this connection compare Professor Robertson's incisive remarks about Arcite: "as a devotee of Mars (Wrath), he meets his death through the action of an infernal fury (a wrathful passion) sent by Pluto (Satan) at the instigation of Saturn (Time, who consumes his 'children'), who was, in turn, prompted by Venus (Concupiscence). That is, concupiscence frustrated leads to wrath which in time causes self-destruction" (Robertson, *Preface*, p. 110).

[40] Robinson follows Skeat in thinking that this refers to the seventh "house" in the division made for horoscopes and elections. However, because Chaucer says "her" seventh house, it seems more likely that he had in mind the houses of the planets in the signs of the zodiac, the seventh of which is one of Venus' houses. Because the seventh divisional house is the house of love or marriage, the poetic meaning would be about the same in either case.

And also blisful Venus, wel arrayed,
Sat in hire seventhe hous of hevene tho,
Disposed wel, and with aspectes payed,
To helpe sely Troilus of his woo.
And, soth to seyne, she nas not al a foo
To Troilus in his nativitee.

(T&C, ɪɪ, 680-85)

Of course, for a real horoscope we would want to know the positions of all the planets, both the signs they were in and the divisional houses, but this one is not intended to do more than indicate that Troilus is one of the "children" of Venus.[41] The depiction of Troilus as possessing venereal influences is of a piece with his name, for in some respects Troilus is a personification of Troy itself; as the commentary by Bernard Silvestris indicates, the city of Troy is like a body brought low by lechery.[42] Without resorting to the commentators, however, it is possible to see that Paris' choice of Venus over Juno or Pallas is now echoed in the make-up of Troilus.

Chaucer follows his source closely at the end of the *Troilus* in having Troilus die as the ultimate (although indirect) result of this kind of love: "Swich fyn hath, lo, this Troilus for *love!* (Cotal fine ebbe il mal concetto amore) (*T&C*, v, 1828). But Chaucer soon departs from Boccaccio's *Filostrato* in order to relate Troilus' death not only to love in general, but also to the pagan deities that have represented various aspects of character throughout the poem. Once again we would do well to recall the Mars who is associated with those who die for love. Another of these deities is, of course, the Venus whose favorable position in Troilus' nativity might have prompted him toward love, but it should be noted that any folly in love would have to be credited to Troilus, not Venus. Thus, at the end of the *Troilus*, Chaucer links the pagan deities with "wretched worldly

---

[41] Later on in the poem Troilus, hesitating outside Criseyde's bedroom, prays to Venus and asks that if she had any astrological impediments at his birth that she would ask her "father" to overcome them now (ɪɪɪ, 715-21). The fact that Troilus first hesitates and later faints in attempting what turns out to be an easy conquest suggests that the only impediments are his and not Venus'.

[42] *Commentum Bernardi Silvestris super sex libris eneidos Virgilii*, ed. W. Riedel (Greifswald, 1924), pp. 15-16, and 102-103. On Troy and Troilus see D. W. Robertson, Jr., "Chaucerian Tragedy," *ELH*, xix (1952), 14, n. 11.

appetites," and it would seem that the end result of the astrology in this poem is to show us that worldly appetites should be controlled and not indulged:

> Lo here, of payens corsed olde rites,
> Lo here, what alle hire goddes may availle;
> Lo here, *thise wrecched worldes appetites*;
> Lo here, the fyn and guerdoun for travaille
> Of Jove, Appollo, of Mars, of swich rascaille.
>
> (*T&C*, v, 1849-53)

5. ASTROLOGY AS A RHETORICAL DEVICE

No DISCUSSION of the conventions and possibilities for the use of astrology in art in general and in Chaucer in particular would be complete without some treatment of its commonest form: the astronomical periphrasis, sometimes called *chronographia*. This rhetorical device, in which the time of day, or time of year, is indicated by a circumlocution involving some reference to the motions of the heavens, is one of the oldest of all such phenomena. As Ernst Curtius has pointed out, the astronomical periphrasis was common enough in classical antiquity that Quintilian could claim the necessity of an acquaintance with astronomy for an understanding of the poets; that this importance continued unabated is evidenced by Gervase of Melkley's thirteenth-century treatise on poetics which urges its use for every conceivable treatment of time: "Perfecto versificatori non hymet, non estuet, non noctescat, non diescat sine astronomia."[43] In Chaucer the device is evident in the opening lines of the General Prologue, which refer to the sun's having run its half-course in Aries, and in the closing imagery of the Parson's Prologue, which refers to Libra's rising and the sun's setting. In addition to employing the astronomical periphrasis in the framework of the *Tales*, Chaucer also uses the device roughly a dozen times within the tales themselves, once in the *Legend of Good Women*, and about eight times in *Troilus and Criseyde*. Elsewhere in the late Middle Ages the device

---

[43] Ernst Robert Curtius, *European Literature and the Latin Middle Ages*, trans. Willard R. Trask (New York and Evanston: Harper Torchbooks, 1963), pp. 275-76. Curtius traces periphrasis from antiquity down to Shakespeare and Goethe, but draws only on Dante and not on Chaucer for mediaeval examples.

is also common, particularly in the Italian literature that influenced Chaucer so much. Boccaccio uses a number of astronomical periphrases in the *Teseida,* and Curtius lists some twenty-three instances in the *Divine Comedy.*

As with most of Chaucer's uses of astrology, the problem is not so much with explicating the technical aspects of these periphrases, which are usually straightforward enough, but with determining just what Chaucer's poetic purposes are in employing them.[44] Unfortunately, this determination is made more complicated by the incomplete knowledge we have at present about Chaucer's precise knowledge of rhetoric and his attitude toward what may be lumped together as "rhetorical effects." The problem, reduced to its essentials, is that although Manly argued in 1926 that Chaucer knew and consciously followed the teachings of the mediaeval rhetoricians, his opinion has been questioned.[45] This, of course, could, but probably does not, call into question the validity of the very large body of Chaucer criticism based on the premise that Chaucer did know the rhetoricians.[46] The reason it does not is that much of the "rhetoric" in Chaucer that critics have discussed has to do with various literary devices which,

[44] This is not to imply that the device is always straightforward. The technical problems posed by *chronographia* can sometimes lead to disagreement over literal interpretation, and it should be remembered that not everyone is in accord over the position of the sun at the opening of *The Canterbury Tales.*

[45] John Matthews Manly, "Chaucer and the Rhetoricians," reprinted in Schoeck and Taylor, *Chaucer Criticism,* I, 268-90. James J. Murphy, "A New Look at Chaucer and the Rhetoricians," *RES,* n.s. xv (1964), 1-20. Murphy argues that what seems to be one of the major pieces of evidence for Chaucer's knowledge of the rhetoricians, his reference to Geoffrey of Vinsauf in *NPT,* 3347-50, is in fact modelled on something in Nicholas Trivet, and is consequently evidence against rather than for Chaucer's acquaintance with Vinsauf. However, Murphy's contention that Chaucer did not know Vinsauf's work directly has not been universally accepted, some scholars arguing that Chaucer shows his knowledge of Vinsauf in places other than *NPT.*

[46] Some idea of the extent of the body of criticism may be gathered from Murphy's calculation in 1964 that more than 40 studies along these lines were extant. There is a useful bibliography of primary and secondary works involving Chaucer and rhetoric in the one book-length treatment of the subject: Robert O. Payne, *The Key of Remembrance: A Study of Chaucer's Poetics* (New Haven and London, 1963). Payne does not discuss the astronomical periphrasis in Chaucer, presumably because his interests are mainly in what he calls "over-all structural patterns" (p. 115).

by the later Middle Ages, were grouped together under the heading *colores rhetorici*. These "colors" may be found not only in the manuals of the rhetoricians, but also in grammatical handbooks, manuals of prose-writing, and in handbooks of rhythmical language for use in hymns and letters. What is particularly important in this is that while Professor Murphy has argued against the existence of an active rhetorical tradition in England in the fourteenth century, he has noted that grammars such as the *Graecismus* by Évrard of Béthune and the *Barbarismus* (the third book of Donatus' *Ars maior*) were among the most popular books in libraries and schools. Thus, whether or not Geoffrey of Vinsauf's *Poetria nova* and Matthew of Vendôme's *Ars versificatoria* were known widely in fourteenth-century England—indeed whether or not there was any "rhetorical" tradition at all—it is quite possible to discuss the figures or colors of rhetoric and their various employments with reference to a "grammatical" tradition that undeniably existed.[47] Although two of the traditional three parts of rhetoric—*inventio, dispositio*, and *elocutio*—may not have been known to Chaucer, the grammars more than took care of the problems of embellishment and ornamentation of the *materia* of poetry, which fell under the last of the divisions.[48] Consequently, whatever the situation was with regard to Chaucer's

[47] Murphy, "New Look," pp. 4-5. Alexandre de Villedieu's *Doctrinale* was another widely used grammar. See L. J. Paetow, *The Arts Course at Medieval Universities with Special Reference to Grammar and Rhetoric, University of Illinois Studies*, III (1910), 38. For further information on grammar and rhetoric see Charles Sears Baldwin, *Medieval Rhetoric and Poetic* (New York, 1928); and R. H. Robins, *Ancient and Mediaeval Grammatical Theory in Europe* (London, 1951).

[48] The distinction between a grammarian and a rhetorician is important, and more work is needed on the subject. Murphy, for example, styles both Geoffrey of Vinsauf and Matthew of Vendôme as grammarians rather than rhetoricians (p. 17). Thus, even if Chaucer knew Vinsauf, one would have to speak of a "grammatical" influence on Chaucer. However, Professor Kelly, in a more detailed analysis, has shown that Vinsauf's concern for *inventio* and *dispositio* as well as for *elocutio* makes him a rhetorician, while Vendôme may properly be called a grammarian. See Douglas Kelly, "The Scope of the Treatment of Composition in the Twelfth- and Thirteenth-Century Arts of Poetry," *Speculum*, XLI (1966), 261-78. Dante follows the customary distinction between a rhetorician (concerned with arrangement) and a grammarian (concerned with syntax) in *Convivio* II, xi. The distinctions have been turned around in Professor Gilbert's translation: Allan H. Gilbert, *Dante and his Comedy* (New York, 1963), p. 39.

knowledge of the structural matters touched on by the rhetoricians, he knew a good deal about the colors of rhetoric and could expect his audience to know enough about them to appreciate both their use and their misuse.

This last is important, for while the line between admirable rhetorical ornament and ludicrously inflated style is thin, the line is nevertheless usually discernible, and it particularly invites our scrutiny because, of all the rhetorical devices of *amplificatio*, the astronomical periphrasis is the one that most readily invites abuse. Indeed, there is a tradition of parodic use of the figure that is almost as old as the device itself.[49] Upon reflection this is not really so surprising, for as Curtius has stated, the classicist will decorate his discourse with approved *ornatus*, but in some epochs the *ornatus* will be piled on meaninglessly or indiscriminately, and we have Mannerism as a result.[50] Now of all the rhetorical ornaments that are listed by both the grammarians and the rhetoricians, perhaps the most dangerous is periphrasis, a subspecies of which is the astronomical periphrasis or *chronographia* under discussion here. For in spite of the great emphasis placed on the *amplificatio* of material in the mediaeval rhetoricians, and in spite of the fact that devices like periphrasis and *repetitio* were among the colors of rhetoric, various kinds of unskillful repetition and redundancy were widely condemned.

Aristotle had warned against far-fetched and inappropriate metaphors in his *Art of Rhetoric* and had observed that the comic poets used metaphors for their effects too. Moreover, there is a general warning against impropriety in Horace's *Ars poetica* that is broadly paraphrased by Chaucer himself in the *Troilus*, although Chaucer's direct source was probably the *Policraticus* by John of Salisbury.[51]

[49] Otto Weinreich, *Phöbus, Aurora, Kalender und Uhr. Schriften und Vorträge der Wurttenbergischen Gesellschaft der Wissenschaften*, IV (1937), 1-37. Curtius, *European Literature*, pp. 276ff., uses the abuse and parody of the astronomical periphrasis to introduce his discussion of "Mannerism." Professor Enkvist sees no degeneration of descriptions of the time of year into "rhetorical formulae" until we encounter Chaucer's successors, but he does not discuss all the occurrences in Chaucer. Nils Erik Enkvist, *The Seasons of the Year*. Societas scientiarum Feinnica, *Commentationes Humanarum Litterarum*, No. 22 (Helsinki, 1957), p. 113.

[50] Curtius, *European Literature*, p. 274.

[51] Aristotle, *Art of Rhetoric*, trans. John Henry Freese, Loeb Classical Library (London and New York, 1926), III, ii and iii: pp. 359 and 365. Horace, *Satires*,

For a more detailed statement on the dangers of periphrasis, however, we must go to Quintilian, who observed that *macrologia*, or more words than necessary, is a fault, but *"periphrasis*, which is akin to this blemish, is regarded as a virtue." Quintilian proceeds with the observation that *pleonasm*, another kind of redundancy, can be bad or good depending upon the manner in which it is used, and he later returns to the subject of periphrasis to note that when it ceases to be decorative it degenerates into the fault called *perissologia*.[52] Thus Quintilian named three of the four species of excess that were later condemned in the manuals of the grammarians.

It is worth remembering that along with lists of the various rhetorical devices one should use, the grammarians regularly paid attention to various kinds of errors one should avoid, and along with errors of grammar, they listed deviations of taste. These must have been widely studied, for the third book of Donatus' *Ars maior*, concerning barbarisms, solecisms, and *ceteris vitiis*, circulated separately as the *Barbarismus*. It is here that we find the best definitions of *pleonasmos, perissologia, macrologia,* and *tautologia*.[53] The same terms are used in the very popular *Doctrinale* of Alexandre de Ville-dieu, although listed with the barbarisms and solecisms. They appear again in the *Graecismus* by Évrard of Béthune, who, while condemn-

---

Epistles and Ars Poetica, trans. H. Rushton Fairclough, Loeb Classical Library (London and New York, 1932), p. 451. No suggestion that Chaucer knew either of these works at first hand is intended here, but it is worth noting that both existed in mediaeval English libraries. See Ernest A. Savage, *Old English Libraries* (London, 1911), Appendix B. In passing it may be noted that there is little on the specific subject of the dangers of certain kinds of rhetorical figures in either Cicero's *De inventione* or *De oratore*, or in the pseudo-Ciceronian *Ad Herennium*.

[52] Quintilian, *Institutio oratoria*, trans. H. E. Butler, Loeb Classical Library (London and New York, 1921-22), VIII, iii and vi; vol. III, 241 and 337. As with Aristotle, Horace, and the rhetorical works of Cicero, no first hand knowledge of Quintilian can be claimed for Chaucer, but the *Institutio* was extant in England. See Savage, *Libraries*, Appendix B.

[53] "Pleonasmos est adiectio verbi supervacui ad plenam significationem, ut 'sic ore locuta est' pro 'sic locuta est.' Perissologia est supervacua verborum adiectio sine ulla vi rerum, ut 'ibant qua poterant, qua non poterant non ibant.' Macrologia est longa sententia res non necessarias conprehendens, ut 'legati non inpetrata pace retro, unde venerant, domum reversi sunt.' Tautologia est eiusdem dictionis repetitio vitiosa, ut 'egomet ipse'" (Donatus, *Ars grammatica*, ed. Henrich Keil in *Grammatici latini* [Leipzig, 1864], IV, 395).

ing these faults of supererogation, could simultaneously praise the color he calls *repetitio*.[54] This is not really self-contradictory, however, for while empty repetition is a fault to be avoided, this sort of repetition for intensification is an excellent device, as his example clearly shows:

> *Tu mihi lex, mihi rex, mihi lux, mihi dux, mihi iudex,*
> *Te colo, te cupio, te diligo, te peto, Christe.*[55]

Thus, even while avoiding the "cult of Vinsauf" that Professor Murphy has warned against, it is possible to show that any educated person would know something of the tradition of periphrasis and would also be aware of the possibilities of various errors of redundancy, whether or not he found them directly linked with the virtue of periphrasis. When we further consider that Chaucer was an extremely sensitive literary artist, we may assume that he knew what he was doing when he used an astronomical periphrasis and that he would be conscious of the risk one necessarily runs when using this sort of device. But Chaucer is not a static artist who has one set of principles that regulate his whole artistic career, as even the standard division into French, Italian, and English periods of influence suggests. More specifically, it may be argued that Chaucer was at one time far more enamoured of the astronomical periphrasis than he was at another, later period and that by the time of the writing of *The Canterbury Tales* he was able to use the device for both elegance and parody in the same poem. The problem concerns both matters of taste and matters of genre.

To begin with, it is easy enough to show that Chaucer enthusiastically used the astronomical periphrasis when he wrote the *Troilus*: indeed, so enthusiastically that every single usage is an innovation beyond his source, the *Filostrato*, some being paraphrased from the *Teseida* and others created for the occasion.[56] Later, however, when Chaucer drew upon the *Teseida* directly for his *Knight's Tale*, instead

---

[54] Alexandre de Villedieu, *Doctrinale*, ed. Dietrich Reichlung in *Monumenta germaniae paedagogica* (Berlin, 1893), XII, 157-58. Évrard of Béthune, *Eberhardi Bethuniensis graecismus*, ed. I. Wrobel (Wroclaw, 1887), Ch. II, ll. 16ff.

[55] *Graecismus*, Ch. III, ll. 4-5.

[56] Kittredge, "Chaucer's Lollius," p. 118. It is assumed here that the *Troilus* precedes the *Tales*, although the matter is not entirely settled.

of adding to the eight astronomical periphrases that he found there, he reduced the number to just one. Moreover, although the astronomical periphrasis is used very prominently by Chaucer in the framework of the *Tales*, at the beginning and at the end, there are not very many occurrences within the tales themselves; after the one instance in the *Knight's Tale*, all the remaining usages are to be found in just three tales: the *Squire's Tale*, the *Merchant's Tale*, and the *Franklin's Tale*.[57] Moreover, these three tales occur in a sequence, with the *Squire's Tale* in the middle, and the device is used almost as often in the *Squire's Tale* as in the other two combined. All of this suggests that Chaucer was being conservative in using the astronomical periphrasis *in propria persona* when he wrote the *Tales* and that we ought to be very alert to whatever is going on in the *Squire's Tale*, because it manifests a characteristic literary device that Chaucer uses at one time and in one place and not at another time and in another place.

This discrepancy, of course, is partly due to Chaucer's conscious effort to write a tragedy in *Troilus*, and for that genre the astronomical periphrasis, which had its origin in epic poetry, is more suitable than it is for a romance like the *Squire's Tale*, where the effects built up tend to crumble of their own weight. This, however, brings up the very difficult problem of tone, for some judgments must be made about when Chaucer is serious and when he is not in his use of the device. Kittredge, borrowing an admirable phrase from Scott, called the astronomical periphrasis a typical feature of the "big bow-wow style," and felt that when Chaucer used it at one juncture in the *Franklin's Tale* and at another in the *Troilus*, he was not being naive but rather was consciously and humorously indulging in fancy style.[58] It would seem, nevertheless, that although the two passages are much alike, one is not funny and the other is. The difference is not because of their rhetorical grounding, but rather because of the kind of poem in which they are used and the sort of person who uses them. The

---

[57] The computation of the time of day by reference to the sun's altitude, found in the Headlink to the *Man of Law's Tale* and in the *Nun's Priest's Tale*, is not considered here since it is different in tone. The two examples of the phenomenon are treated briefly at the beginning of Chapter VII.

[58] Kittredge, "Chaucer's Lollius," p. 119. Robinson also thinks the passage is humorous.

point to be made is that looked at objectively almost any periphrasis is funny, and yet some are intended to be funny and some are not. When Wordsworth commented on the opening line of Johnson's "Vanity of Human Wishes" that it might well be paraphrased as "Let *Observation* with extensive *observation observe* . . . ," one doubts that Dr. Johnson would have appreciated the *reductio*. There are, however, some occasions in which the essential extravagance of periphrasis is made the point of its use, as in the magnificent parody of the device in the playlet in *Hamlet*:

> Full thirty times hath Phoebus' cart gone round
> Neptune's salt wash and Tellus' orbed ground,
> And thirty dozen moons with borrow'd sheen
> About the world have times twelve thirties been.[59]

The lines in *Troilus* that may or may not be intentionally humorous are certainly not nearly as broad as the Shakespearean parody:

> The dayes honour, and the hevenes yë,
> The nyghtes foo—al this clepe I the sonne—
> Gan westren faste, and downward for to wrye,
> As he that hadde his dayes cours yronne.
>
> (*T&C*, ii, 904-907)

On the whole this is not a very extravagant example of the astronomical periphrasis, surely not more so than many others in the same poem, so it is only the vaguely self-conscious "al this clepe I the sonne" that could be thought to give the passage a humorous cast. On the other hand, if the passage is intentionally humorous, the humor is intrusive, for the passage is set in the middle of a series of events that could in no way be construed as funny. Criseyde has been debating with herself the desirability of a love affair; she listens to Antigone's song in praise of love; the sun sinks; she goes to bed; after listening to the nightingale sing of love, she falls asleep and has an ambiguous dream about an eagle who exchanges his heart with hers. Indeed, if one thinks of the eagle dream as unsettling, if not worse, it may well be that the epithets given to the sun by Chaucer

---

[59] Pointed out by Curtius, *European Literature*, p. 276.

(the night's foe and the day's honor) make some sense in context, since there is a contrast set up between the happy daytime songs of Antigone and the nightingale and the nocturnal actions of the eagle, who "Under hire brest his longe clawes sette, / And out hire herte he rente" (*T&C*, II, 927-28). The context makes it doubtful that this periphrasis was intended to be funny.

This periphrasis, like all of those in the *Troilus*, comes not from the mouth of a character but from the narrator and, in its major features, forms part of a series of periphrases in the poem. For, unlike the use Chaucer makes of the device elsewhere, he seems to have a definite purpose here, and without over-analyzing the details of the several images we may say that the themes underscored by this astronomical periphrasis are earthly mutability and the universality of the power of love. To some extent it must be admitted that any astronomical periphrasis will involve mutability, simply by definition, but it seems that Chaucer was particularly concerned to emphasize it here. If we examine the periphrases of the time of year, for example, we find that they depict spring, summer, then three winters with three springs:

> Whan Phebus doth his bryghte bemes sprede,
> Right in the white Bole, it so bitidde,
> As I shal synge, on Mayes day the thrydde. . . .
>
> > (*T&C*, II, 54-56)

> Byfel that, whan that Phebus shynyng is
> Upon the brest of Hercules lyoun. . . .
>
> > (*T&C*, IV, 31-32)

> The gold-ytressed Phebus heighe on-lofte
> Thries hadde alle with his bemes clene
> The snowes molte, and Zepherus as ofte
> Ibrought ayeyn the tendre leves grene. . . .
>
> > (*T&C*, V, 8-11)

The three passages stand at the openings of Books II, III, and V, and, like the zodiacs in the devotional manuals and on the cathedrals, they remind us of the endless change on earth. Moreover, Chaucer's arrangement of the images is such that one is reminded that summer

follows spring and both are succeeded by winter, that this is a harsh world and we must not be deceived by appearances, especially when the flowers of spring tempt us to forget the withering blasts of winter. Moreover, it may well be that Chaucer wanted to be specific about the particular aspect of this world that is most subject to this kind of mutability—namely love. The poem itself is undeniably about a love affair that begins slowly, flares into the heat of passion, and is then figuratively "cooled" when Criseyde forsakes Troilus: all this is echoed in these images. First, the time of year is stated in terms of the sun in Taurus, the house of Venus and the sign always associated with love.[60] Next, the time of year is stated in terms of the sun in Leo—which it entered on July 12 in the Middle Ages—either to indicate the heat of passion already seen in Book III or, more likely, to call attention to the change from love to wrath, also in the sense of heat, since Book IV is begun with an invocation of the furies and Mars. The final image takes us through winter to spring again, but now there is massive irony in the reference to spring, for Troilus in this final book loses his loved one. Much of the imagery used in these periphrases gains meaning at the end of the poem, for there Chaucer departs from his basic source to have Troilus rise up through the spheres, whose revolution has thus far symbolized mutability, and look back in understanding so that harmony now appears from the apparently erratic motions of the stars:

> His lighte goost ful blisfully is went
> Up to the holughnesse of the eighthe spere,
> In convers letyng everich element;
> And ther he saugh, with ful avysement,
> The erratik sterres, herkenyng armonye
> With sownes ful of hevenyssh melodie.[61]

[60] It may be that by including a reference to May 3, the date of the Invention of Holy Cross, on which St. Helena overthrew the temple of Venus and raised up the true cross, Chaucer is being proleptic about the sorrowful outcome of this spring-begun love affair. Not everyone, however, is in precise agreement about the significance of May 3. See D. W. Robertson, Jr., "Chaucerian Tragedy," *ELH*, XIX (1952), 19; John P. McCall, "Chaucer's May 3," *MLN*, LXXVI (1961), 201-205; George R. Adams and Bernard S. Levy, "Good and Bad Fridays and May 3 in Chaucer," *ELN*, IV (1966), 245-48.

[61] *T&C*, V, 1808-13. For a survey of opinions on Troilus' exact position and the possible meaning thereof, see Chapter IV:3.

This ascent through the spheres is a basic metaphor for the ascent to wisdom and may be discovered as such in Boethius' *Consolation*, Bk. IV, m. I. That the nature of this wisdom has to do with the evanescence of love and the mutability of this world we may be sure:

> Swich fyn hath, lo, this Troilus for love!
>
> . . . .
>
> Swych fyn hath false worldes brotelnesse!
>
> . . . .
>
> . . . thynketh al nys but a faire
> This world, that passeth soone as floures faire.
>
> (*T&C*, v, 1828-41)

It may be that Chaucer got the germ of his idea to use the changing seasons symbolically from Boccaccio's *Chiose* to the *Teseida*, for Boccaccio had marked the season's change from spring to fall and interpreted it roughly along the lines of "as ye sow, so shall ye reap." He is careful not to be over-obvious in relating the astronomical periphrasis to the events of the poem, but he observes that autumn takes from the world the beauty that spring had given it, and the application of this to the *Teseida* is left to the reader.[62]

The astronomical periphrases for the time of day in the *Troilus* are quite similar in function to those for the time of year in that the variation of evening, morning, morning, evening, and morning again echoes the basic theme of inconstancy that is everywhere throughout the poem. Indeed, it is possible that Chaucer's dwelling on the change from day to night and from night to day is in itself significant: in this poem the diurnal astronomical periphrasis is reserved for sunrise and sundown. It may also be that these images of daily as opposed to yearly time are in part to remind us of the universality of the problems encountered by Troilus, emphasizing that mutability in love, like the mutability of time itself, is daily re-enacted. Whether or not we can go that far in our reading, there is little doubt that

---

[62] "Ariete è uno de'XII segni del sole e Libra è uno altro. Sta in Ariete il sole da mezo marzo infino a mezo aprile, e in questo tempo tutto il mondo si rifà bello di frondi, di fiori e d'erbe. In Libra sta da mezo settembre infino a mezo ottobre: in questo tempo non solamente si seccano tutte le frondi, ma caggiono tutte degli alberi, sí che Libra toglie al mondo quella bellezza che Ariete gli aveva data" (Boccaccio, *Teseida*, Chiose, p. 386).

Chaucer intended to relate these several images of change in the time of day to love, for four out of the five instances are complicated by reference to more than just the sun.

The first of the periphrases of the time of day is the one already discussed in regard to its possible humor, and it is the simple image, involving only the sun. The next, in Book III, is a much more complicated affair, and is a dawn not sundown image:

> But whan the cok, comune astrologer,
> Gan on his brest to bete and after crowe,
> And Lucyfer, the dayes messager,
> Gan for to rise, and out hire bemes throwe,
> And estward roos, to hym that koude it knowe,
> *Fortuna Major*, that anoon Criseyde,
> With herte soor, to Troilus thus seyde. . . .
>
> (*T&C*, III, 1415-21)

Here the dawn is signalled not by the rise of the sun but by the rise of Lucifer—that is, Venus, the morning star—accompanied by the geomantic figure of *Fortuna Major*. Whatever the exact significance of this figure in geomancy, and whatever precise meaning it has in Dante, where it also occurs, the general impact is clear enough: Venus is linked with good fortune, but ironically so at dawn, when the lovers must part.[63]

The remaining three periphrases of the time of day are all in Book v, which is the book in which Criseyde's infidelity occurs. It is not surprising in view of this that the first of the images involves both the sun and the moon, the moon being the age-old symbol of inconstancy:

> On hevene yet the sterres weren seene,
> Although ful pale ywoxen was the moone;
> And whiten gan the orisonte shene

---

[63] See Robinson's notes and note 70 below for a summary of opinions on *Fortuna Major*. Professor Kaske's argument that the aube which follows this periphrasis is a comic device reinforces the ironic interpretation of the periphrasis proposed here. See R. E. Kaske, "The Aube in Chaucer's *Troilus*," in Schoeck and Taylor, *Chaucer Criticism*, II, 167-79.

Al estward, as it wont is for to doone;
And Phebus with his rosy carte soone
Gan after that to dresse hym up to fare.
(T&C, v, 274-79)

The second image also seems to make a silent comment on the action
of Book v, for it involves the moon, Signifer (the zodiac), and
Venus in addition to the sun, and presumably links love, inconstancy,
the change of time of day, and the cycle of the seasons:

The brighte Venus folwede and ay taughte
The wey ther brode Phebus down alighte;
And Cynthea hire char-hors overraughte
To whirle out of the Leoun, if she myghte;
And Signifer his candels sheweth brighte.[64]

As far as their relation to the action is concerned, certainly the two
passages are appropriate. The sunrise with its reference to the
mutable moon begins the day on which Troilus tells Pandarus that

[64] *T&C*, v, 1016-20. The imagery of Cynthia the moon leaving the sign Leo
is a continuation of an earlier theme. In Book IV Criseyde swears by the notoriously
inconstant moon that she will be constant: "certes, herte swete, / Er Phebus suster,
Lucina the sheene, / The Leoun passe out of this Ariete, / I wol ben here . . ."
(*T&C*, IV, 1590-93). It is then specified that for the moon to accomplish this
journey will take ten days, or a little more than one third of its mean period of 28
days. Troilus subsequently apostrophises the moon and says it was at quarter when
Criseyde left, and when it comes quarter again she will return. In view of the fact
that Criseyde leaves Troilus for Diomede, Chaucer's emphasis on the "horned"
quarter moon is doubtless ironic:

"Ywis, whan thow art *horned* newe,
I shal be glad, if al the world be trewe!

I saugh thyn *hornes* olde ek by the morwe,
Whan hennes rood my righte lady dere,
That cause is of my torment and my sorwe;
For which, O brighte Latona the clere,
For love of God, ren faste aboute thy spere!
For whan thyne *hornes* newe gynnen sprynge,
Than shal she come that may my blisse brynge."
(T&C, v, 650-58)

Then comes the passage cited in the text, indicating that the moon has moved from
Aries to Leo and is now ready to "whirl" out of Leo. In other words, the ten days
are up.

he believes he "mot nedes dye" because of his "maladie" (*T&C*, v, 316 and 318), thus reminding us of the ultimate mutation of life into death. On the other hand, the sunset image with Venus and the moon introduces the moment of Criseyde's inconstant change of heart, for with the evening she retires, considers her situation and Diomede's great estate,

> . . . and thus bygan to brede
> The cause whi, the sothe for to telle,
> That she took fully purpos for to dwelle.
> (*T&C*, v, 1027-29)

The last of the astronomical periphrases of the time of day is another dawn scene, and like the preceding ones it marks in splendid imagery the dawn of an unhappy day, for this is the day on which Troilus will wait all day long at the city gates for Criseyde, who does not come:

> The laurer-crowned Phebus, with his heete,
> Gan, in his course ay upward as he wente,
> To warmen of the est see the wawes weete,
> And Nysus doughter song with fressh entente.
> (*T&C*, v, 1107-10)

Here it is the mythological "Nisus' daughter" or Scylla, rather than the astrological moon or Venus who is brought in to emphasize the meaning of the periphrasis, but again the imagery of the device echoes the action of the poem. Nisus' daughter is one who suffered from unrequited love and so properly introduces the day when Troilus will be denied by his loved one. It is not necessary to go far afield for the meaning here, for Nisus' daughter figures in the *Legend of Good Women*:

> . . . Nysus doughter stod upon the wal,
> And of the sege saw the maner al.
> So happed it that, at a scarmishyng,
> She caste hire herte upon Mynos the kyng,
> For his beaute and for his chyvalrye,
> So sore that she wende for to dye.

And, shortly of this proces for to pace,
She made Mynos wynnen thilke place,
So that the cite was al at his wille,
To saven whom hym leste, or elles spille.
But wikkedly he quitte hire kyndenesse,
And let hire drenche in sorwe and distresse.

(LGW, 1908-19)

In Chaucer's hands, then, the astronomical periphrasis is more than mere "puffing": it can be used in the same way other imagistic devices are used to sum up and put into perspective the action of the poem. Chaucer, however, makes much less use of the device after he writes the *Troilus,* and certainly does not attempt the kind of elaborate interplay of images that he used there. His two most significant uses of the periphrasis, at the beginning and end of *The Canterbury Tales,* have sections to themselves in this study. In the General Prologue the astronomical periphrasis is less important for the imagery used than for the time indicated (although the imagery of Taurus is meaningful, as it was in the *Troilus*), and in the Parson's Prologue both the imagery used and the time of day indicated require lengthy expositions. In the *Knight's Tale,* as already noted, Chaucer actually leaves out a large number of astronomical periphrases that were in his source, the *Teseida,* and the one he does use, marking the morning on which Arcite happens upon Palamon in the woods, seems to have little connection with the action unless one would want to see some purpose in having the sun shine on the leaves of a forest just before the heroes meet there:

The bisy larke, messager of day,
Salueth in hir song the morwe gray,
And firy Phebus riseth up so bright
That al the orient laugheth of the light,
And with his stremes dryeth in the greves
The silver dropes hangynge on the leves.

(KnT, 1491-96)

When Chaucer subsequently uses astronomical periphrases frequently in the *Tales,* they are indeed linked, but as much by humor as by subtlety of imagery. There are, however, some imagistic links

too. First of all it should be noted that the three tales which include some eight astronomical periphrases are sequential tales whether we number by the Ellesmere order or adopt the Bradshaw shift. Furthermore, there are some points to be noted which suggest that Chaucer might ultimately have linked up these tales more than they are in the manuscripts. In the first place, all three tales—the Merchant's, the Squire's, and the Franklin's—have to do with eloquence as a kind of sub-theme, and thus Chaucer's abundant employment of very eloquent astronomical periphrasis provides an echo to the sense. It must be cautioned, however, that "eloquence" in these tales is not exactly of the kind that was known from Martianus Capella and the wedding of Mercury and Philology. Here we are concerned with the self-saving "eloquence" that Proserpina gives to May in the *Merchant's Tale* so that she may deceive her husband, and with the self-consciously vain attempts at "rhetoric" of the Squire and the Franklin in their tales.[65]

The second possible indication that Chaucer intended to link up the tales even more is the Franklin's astronomical periphrasis of the time of year which is a clear imitation of the Merchant's periphrasis of the same thing, the major difference being that one introduces the sun at the summer solstice and the other, the sun at the winter solstice. The Franklin clearly echoes the Merchant's plot and setting in using a squire in love with his mistress and an elaborate garden. If the periphrasis is also intended to be an imitation of the Merchant by the Franklin, it would be a device of characterization parallel to the Franklin's concern to imitate the Squire's "gentility" and rhetorical "colors." In this case, we would see him imitating the Merchant's rhetorical devices as he imitates the Squire's, and this would provide an amusing comment on the Franklin's expostulation against wealth,

[65] This analysis of rhetoric and humor in the *Squire's Tale* and the *Franklin's Tale* is greatly indebted to the excellent essays of Messrs. Haller and McCall, and to the writings of Professors Pearsall, Berger, and Huppé. Robert S. Haller, "Chaucer's *Squire's Tale* and the Uses of Rhetoric," *MP*, LXII (1965), 285-95; John P. McCall, "The Squire in Wonderland," *The Chaucer Review*, I (1966), 103-109; D. A. Pearsall, "The Squire as Story Teller," *UTQ*, XXXIV (1964), 82-92; Harry Berger, Jr., "The F-Fragment of the *Canterbury Tales*," *The Chaucer Review*, I (1966), 88-102 and 135-56; Bernard F. Huppé, *A Reading of the Canterbury Tales* (State University of New York, 1964), pp. 163-74.

the major concern of the Merchant: "Fy on possessioun, / But if a man be vertuous withal" (Franklin's Headlink, 686-87). An inspection of the two passages will show how similar they are in form, although opposite in detail:

> Bright was the day, and blew the firmament;
> Phebus hath of gold his stremes doun ysent,
> To gladen every flour with his warmnesse.
> He was that tyme in Geminis, as I gesse,
> But litel fro his declynacion
> Of Cancer, Jovis exaltacion. (*MerchT*, 2219-24)

This is a fairly straightforward description of the impending summer solstice. The sun is in Gemini but is about to move into Cancer, the sign in which it attains its maximum angle of declination. In short, this is a description of midsummer's eve. The golden sun and the blue skies are picked up for inversion by the Franklin, along with the very overt reference to the change from the summer solstice to the winter one:

> And this was, as thise bookes me remembre,
> The colde, frosty seson of Decembre.
>   Phebus wax old, and hewed lyk laton,
> That in his hoote declynacion
> Shoon as the burned gold with stremes brighte;
> But now in Capricorn adoun he lighte,
> Where as he shoon ful pale, I dar wel seyn.
> The bittre frostes, with the sleet and reyn,
> Destroyed hath the grene in every yerd.
> Janus sit by the fyr, with double berd,
> And drynketh of his bugle horn the wyn;
> Biforn hym stant brawen of the tusked swyn,
> And "Nowel" crieth every lusty man.
>   (*FranklT*, 1243-55)

This is periphrasis with a vengeance, and what the Merchant managed to say in six lines the Franklin redundantly marches through in thirteen. It is almost as though Chaucer had the Merchant use an astronomical periphrasis for the summer solstice the

better to set off the overly elaborate and very long periphrasis by the Franklin. The Franklin not only tells us the time straight out (December), but also defines the date astronomically with reference to the sun in Capricorn; he not only tells us what the sun is like in Capricorn (once old and twice pale), but also what it was formerly like at the summer declination (like burnished gold). The Merchant employed a reference to the weather in his periphrasis; the Franklin employs two, first defining December as cold and frosty, then noting that the bitter frosts along with sleet and rain have destroyed the green in every yard. To this he adds a little description of January, taken from a calendar illumination of Janus sitting by the fire, and finishes the whole with a hearty cry of "Noel." But the worst feature of the periphrasis is that it is temporally indistinct, for whereas the Merchant's periphrasis defined the time of year within a few days, this passage refers to the sun's entrance into Capricorn (December 12), to the month of December by name, to the month of January by implication, and to Christmas (December 25) or perhaps to the whole Christmas feasting period, which lasted into January, with the cry of Noel.

Even at that, one should be very cautious in deciding that this is meant to be a parody of the astronomical periphrasis. After all, Chaucer occasionally used a seven line periphrasis in the *Troilus*, the astronomical periphrasis at the opening of the General Prologue is both lengthy and possibly confusing, and Chaucer employs the sun's motion, the month of the year, and the weather in that same opening periphrasis. What may tip the balance in favor of seeing this periphrasis as parodic is that while Chaucer's use of the device in the *Troilus* and in the General Prologue is in a neutral narrational guise, the Franklin has been introduced to us in the Prologue of his tale as one who is self-conscious about rhetoric. He claims no knowledge of rhetoric at great length but uses some rhetorical devices to do so, and his characteristic handling of one of the rhetorical colors, namely paronomasia or word-play, is in egregious punning:

> But, sires, by cause I am a burel man,
> At my bigynnyng first I yow biseche,
> Have me excused of my rude speche.

95

I lerned nevere rethorik, certeyn;
Thyng that I speke, it moot be bare and pleyn.
I sleep nevere on the Mount of Pernaso,
Ne lerned Marcus Tullius Scithero.
Colours ne knowe I none, withouten drede,
But swiche colours as growen in the mede,
Or elles swiche as men dye or peynte.
Colours of rethoryk been to me queynte;
My spirit feeleth noght of swich mateere.
                              (*Frankl Prol*, 716-27)

In view of this, the astronomical periphrasis that the Franklin uses
for the time of year should be seen as a conscious, or rather self-
conscious, use of a rhetorical device. When considered in that light
its possible defects seem to be real, and we should credit them to the
Franklin and not to Chaucer. By the same token, the Franklin's sub-
sequent periphrasis for the time of day is more succinct than his
periphrasis for the time of year, but it is even more self-conscious:

But sodeynly bigonne revel newe
Til that the brighte sonne loste his hewe;
For th'orisonte hath reft the sonne his lyght,—
This is as muche to seye as it was nyght!
                              (*FranklT*, 1015-18)

Scholars from the time of Kittredge on have compared this
passage with Chaucer's periphrasis in the *Troilus* when the narrator
says "al this clepe I the sonne," but the two passages function quite
differently. There is no real reason for the narrator in the *Troilus*
to apologize for his dilatory speech at that particular juncture in the
work, but for the Franklin to be self-conscious about his use of rhe-
torical colors is an amusing characteristic that was strongly emphasized
in the Prologue of his tale. Thus, although the periphrasis for the
time of day is not all that elaborate, the very use of a periphrasis
embarrasses the Franklin and so he blurts out a "burel" equivalent
directly after the ornate device.[66]

---

[66] It must be emphasized that the shortened summation of a flowery statement is
not in itself funny, but can be so in certain circumstances, such as when the speaker
is a hopeful *rhetor*. Fulgentius, for example, in the *Mitologiarum*, has eleven lines

While the Franklin's astronomical periphrasis of the time of year seems to be patterned after the description of the summer solstice in the *Merchant's Tale*, his general concern for rhetorical color is probably the result of an attempt to imitate the Squire. In his fumbling praise of the young man, the Franklin pays particular attention to the eloquence of his speech:

> "In feith, Squier, thow hast thee wel yquit
> And gentilly. I preise wel thy wit,"
> Quod the Frankeleyn, "considerynge thy yowthe,
> So feelyngly thou spekest, sire, I allow the!
> As to my doom, ther is noon that is heere
> Of *eloquence* that shal be thy peere,
> If that thou lyve; God yeve thee good chaunce,
> And in vertu sende thee continuaunce!
> For of thy *speche* I have greet deyntee."
> *(Frankl Headlink,* 673-81)

Just what it is in the Squire's speech that constitutes eloquence we are not told, but certainly the Franklin's introductory remarks about the colors of rhetoric suggest that it is the Squire's eloquence which he admires. If so, his admiration is unduly excited, for both Professors Haller and McCall have demonstrated that the essence of the *Squire's Tale* is his inability to manage rhetorical devices and to have command of the story line. It follows that the Squire's astronomical periphrases should be demonstrably weak, and so they are.[67]

The first of these is by far the most astrologically oriented of all the astronomical periphrases in Chaucer. Chaucer himself referred to the sign Libra as the "moon's exaltation" in the Parson's Prologue,

---

of verse about the evening, after which he says, "et, ut in uerba paucissima conferam, nox erat." See Eleanor Prescott Hammond, "Chaucer and Lydgate Notes," *MLN,* XXVII (1912), 91-92.

[67] In speaking of the various astronomical periphrases in the *Squire's Tale,* Haller notes that "there is a thin line between useful ornament and circumlocution" (p. 288), and McCall has observed a certain lack of coherence in one periphrasis in that the sun is described as being clear and jolly even though it is in a choleric, hot sign (p. 108). Both critics point out that the elegant astronomical periphrasis of the time of day inserted when Cambyuskan departs from the dinner table is very intrusive.

but nowhere in his own narrations does he give the wealth of astrological refinement of detail that we find here:

> The laste Idus of March, after the yeer.
> Phebus the sonne ful joly was and cleer;
> For he was neigh his exaltacioun
> In Martes face, and in his mansioun
> In Aries, the colerik hoote signe.
> Ful lusty was the weder and benigne,
> For which the foweles, agayn the sonne sheene,
> What for the sesoun and the yonge grene,
> Ful loude songen hire affecciouns.
> Hem semed han geten hem protecciouns
> Agayn the swerd of wynter, keene and coold.
>
> *(SqT, 47-57)*

If the Franklin went overboard in the matter of periphrasis, here there is a similar excess in astrology. We are told that the sun was in Aries; that Aries is a hot, choleric sign; that the sun was not only in Aries, but was indeed approaching the specific degree within the confines of the sign in which it has its astrological exaltation. What is more, that this particular degree happens to fall in one of the ten degree divisions of the signs known as faces, and the particular face happens to be one assigned to the planet Mars. This has to be parody.

Critics have pointed out the inability of the Squire to live up to his father the Knight whether in battle or in tale-telling; but while the Squire's general difficulties in managing his material seem to contrast him to the Knight, this particular astronomical periphrasis with its references to the sun in Aries, the singing "foweles," and the month of March unmistakably reminds us of Chaucer's own opening of the *Tales*. It seems possible that Chaucer created a primary figure of self-parody in the pilgrim figure named Chaucer, who cannot remember any stories, etc., and a secondary figure of self-parody in the Squire, who is, as Haller has noted, the only poet among the pilgrims. Certainly Chaucer's audience would know that Chaucer himself had been a squire, and it seems difficult to believe that the Squire's first astronomical periphrasis was not constructed to be

similar enough to Chaucer's own use of the device as narrator to be compared. Chaucer here humorously exaggerates his own writing, pretending that all squires cannot control rhetoric. Some remarks on the details of difference are thus in order.

> Whan that Aprill with his shoures soote
> The droghte of March hath perced to the roote,
> And bathed every veyne in swich licour
> Of which vertu engendred is the flour;
> Whan Zephirus eek with his sweete breeth
> Inspired hath in every holt and heeth
> The tendre croppes, and the yonge sonne
> Hath in the Ram his halve cours yronne,
> And smale foweles maken melodye,
> That slepen al the nyght with open ye
> (So priketh hem nature in hir corages);
> Thanne longen folk to goon on pilgrimages.
>
> (*Gen Prol*, 1-12)

The basic difference in the periphrasis that Chaucer uses is in its application. Chaucer uses his periphrasis to introduce the time of year when people want to go on pilgrimages, albeit many for the wrong reasons, while the Squire's periphrasis introduces a birthday party. Chaucer here uses the simple words "sun" and "Ram," while the Squire chooses the more aureate "Phebus" and "Aries." Chaucer's periphrasis is remarkably unified, speaking of the rebirth of plants through water and wind in the springtime and the accompanying concern for procreation in birds and hopefully for spiritual re-creation in man, but the Squire wanders in his maze of astrological detail and only comes out again to contradict his earlier statement that the weather was benign by saying that the birds were singing because they felt it afforded them some protection against the sword of winter.[68]

The Squire's second astronomical periphrasis is not patterned after anything as obvious as the opening of *The Canterbury Tales*, but it is as bizarre as the first. Its employment for the time the hero leaves the dinner table is particularly curious because it is uneventful in the

---

[68] The dates involved are different too, by about a month. For the significance of the date of the General Prologue see Chapter IV:1.

first place, and unconventional in the second. The hour is just past midday, and Chaucer elsewhere uses the periphrasis for time of day only to indicate dawn or dusk:

> Phebus hath laft the angle meridional,
> And yet ascendynge was the beest roial,
> The gentil Leon, with his Aldiran,
> Whan that this Tartre kyng, this Cambyuskan,
> Roos fro his bord, ther as he sat ful hye.
> Toforn hym gooth the loude mynstralcye,
> Til he cam to his chambre of parementz,
> Ther as they sownen diverse instrumentz,
> That it is lyk an hevene for to heere.
> Now dauncen lusty Venus children deere,
> For in the Fyssh hir lady sat ful hye,
> And looketh on hem with a freendly ye.
>
> (*SqT*, 263-74)

As some of the images Chaucer used in the *Troilus* were complicated by the addition of another planet, so is this one, but with a planet Chaucer often adduced himself in order to symbolize love in the *Troilus*. What is different here is that the Squire has placed Venus in Pisces (where she is powerful) thus perverting one of the most beautiful and important astrological images in mediaeval poetry, the opening of Dante's *Purgatorio*.[69]

> Lo bel pianeta che d' amar conforta
> Faceva tutto rider l' oriente,
> Velando i Pesci ch' erano in sua scorta.
>
> (*Purgatorio* I, 19-21)

In the *Purgatorio* as in the *Squire's Tale* Venus symbolizes love, but love of a very different quality. Dante uses the image for the dawn when he emerges from Hell and invokes the sacred Muses to help him with his poetry as he prepares to cross the lake to the mountain

---

[69] In his notes Robinson says that *Purgatorio* I, 19-21, is less likely as a source for this passage than it is for *T&C*, III, 1257, or *KnT*, 1494, for which he thinks it is a definite source. However, in the *Troilus* passage there is no mention of Pisces, and in the passage from the *Knight's Tale* there is no reference to either Pisces or Venus.

of Purgation. The Squire, on the other hand, invokes Venus in Pisces at midday, when the hero arises from the dinner table and proceeds to a music room. He invokes no sacred Muse.[70]

The third of the Squire's periphrases is so convoluted that it scarcely appears to be one unless it is read carefully. The Squire starts out by praising a lady's beauty, and ends with a description of the time of day:

> Up riseth fresshe Canacee hireselve,
> As rody and bright as dooth the yonge sonne,
> That in the Ram is foure degrees up ronne—
> Noon hyer was he whan she redy was—
>
> (*SqT*, 384-87)

To praise a lady in terms of the time of year is not beyond the bounds of customary rhetoric in Chaucer, indeed the Knight compares Emily to the month of May, but comparisons of young ladies with March are certainly uncommon, if they exist at all. Moreover, note the specification of time: not just the sun in the Ram, but the sun four degrees into the Ram, bringing us to the fifteenth day of March, the very Ides on which Cambyuskan celebrates his birthday. Thus the passage says that the lady was as bright as March fifteenth, which is today. This is not very impressive rhetoric, and the closing line is actually ludicrous. Robinson's notes argue that the sun is four degrees above the horizon in its daily course when Canacee arises, and she gets dressed before it rises any more; but surely the sense is that the young sun in the fourth degree of the Ram is like the young sun that has run its half-course in the Ram in the General Prologue. That is, in both cases we are concerned with the sun's annual motion, not its daily motion. Thus, since the sun goes round the zodiac at the rate of about one degree a day, the sense of the passage is that Canacee rose up looking like the ruddy, bright March sun and managed to get herself ready the same day! This is in fact no compliment, but is damning with faint praise.

[70] In *T&C*, III, 1415-21, Chaucer borrowed the image of *Fortuna Major* from *Purgatorio* XIX, 4-6, and used it in connection with Venus. There, however, no violence is done to the sense, for Chaucer takes an image from Dante's canto of the Slothful and uses it to introduce the lovers in bed and Troilus' long speech protesting the coming day and the necessity "to hennes go."

The last of the astronomical periphrases is mercifully cut short, like the tale itself:

Appollo whirleth up his chaar so hye,
Til that the god Mercurius hous, the slye—
(*SqT*, 671-72)

As Professor Haller has justly observed, a tale with no beginning and no middle can scarcely have an end, and this tale is "complete" if not finished at any point.[71] It is fitting, certainly, that the tale is cut off in the middle of one of the astrological embellishments the Squire loves so well and uses so badly, and this one promised worse things yet, for now we have Apollo instead of Phebus, whirling his chariot instead of entering a sign or leaving an angle. Chaucer used Phebus for the sun as a regular matter in the *Troilus*, but he never used Apollo in an astronomical periphrasis.

There is a lot of humor in Chaucer's parody of the astronomical periphrasis in the *Squire's Tale*, and surely some of the game is in poking fun at his own poetic enthusiasms. This is what he does in the *Thopas*, which is all activity and no action, all *solaas* and no *sentence*. Here he takes up a device that he himself used very skillfully in the *Troilus* but chose to de-emphasize in his redaction of the *Teseida* into the *Knight's Tale*, possibly because he saw that the dangers of its excesses outweighed its value as a traditional adornment.

---

[71] Haller, "Uses of Rhetoric," p. 293.

CHAPTER III

The *Complaint of Mars*

I. HISTORICAL ALLEGORY

IF CHAUCER's *Complaint of Mars* has not attracted the least amount of criticism of any of the poet's works, it must surely rank very near the bottom of the list, and the lack of scholarly interest in the poem is probably the result of its vexatious astrological detail on the one hand, and its seeming lack of unity on the other. It must be confessed that the poem proceeds with a good many changes of direction; starting out with a Valentine's Day invocation, it continues with a long astrological discourse and concludes with a "complaint" proper that involves philosophical questioning of the purpose of love and classical allusions to the Brooch of Thebes. Even so, it is remarkable that the full scale approaches to the poem may be numbered at only three— the works of J. M. Manly, Gardiner Stillwell, and George Williams—one of which was done in the last century. Of these there is one that needs special treatment because of its difference from the others and because of its difference from customary criticisms of Chaucer. This is the chapter on the *Complaint of Mars* in George Williams' *A New View of Chaucer*, a book devoted to reading various Chaucerian poems as though each were a *roman à clef*. In the case of the *Complaint*, however, more than any other Chaucerian poem, the use of historical allegory may be defended on the grounds that the figures in the poem were identified as prominent fourteenth-century people by an early commentator.[1]

The copyist Shirley introduced into his copy of the poem in the Trinity College Manuscript a unique comment identifying the personages involved: "þus eondeþe here þis complaint whiche some men

---

[1] George Williams, *A New View of Chaucer* (Durham, 1965). The chapter is a revision of the author's article in *JEGP*, LVII (1958), 167-73. The other major pieces of criticism are J. M. Manly, "On the Date and Interpretation of Chaucer's *Complaint of Mars*," *Harvard Studies and Notes in Philology and Literature*, V (1896), 107-26; Gardiner Stillwell, "Convention and Individuality in Chaucer's *Complaint of Mars*," *PQ*, XXXV (1956), 69-89. An essay that follows Stillwell very closely is Wolfgang Clemen, *Chaucer's Early Poetry*, trans. C. A. M. Sym (London, 1963), pp. 188-97.

sayne was made . by my lady of york doughter to þe kyng of Spaygne and my lord of huntyngdon . some tyme duc of Excestre. . . ."[32] In this curious statement Shirley said that the poem concerns "my lady of York, daughter to the King of Spain," who is probably Isabella, Duchess of York and wife to Edmund, Duke of York. Note that Shirley errs in saying that she is the King of Spain's, that is, John of Gaunt's daughter; rather, she is his sister-in-law. The other personage mentioned, "my lord Huntingdon," is one John Holland, Lord Huntingdon. While there is no historical evidence to link John Holland with Isabella, John of Gaunt's sister-in-law, there is evidence that he was involved in a scandal with Gaunt's daughter Elizabeth. Holland apparently seduced her while she was engaged to another man, and she broke the engagement and married Holland.[3] All this, in turn, must be regarded in light of the fact that Shirley also said that the entire poem was written at the instigation of John of Gaunt: "Loo yee louers gladeþe and comforteþe you . of þallyaunce etrayted bytwene þe hardy and furyous Mars . þe god of armes and Venus þe double goddesse of loue made by Geffrey Chaucier . at þe comandement of þe renommed and excellent prynce my lord þe duc John of Lancastre."[4]

If Shirley is correct in saying that the poem was written at the request of John of Gaunt—and it must be granted that he is correct in saying that the next poem, the *Complaint of Venus*, was translated from the French of Oton de Graunson—it remains to be decided why the Duke wanted a poem about a liaison between Isabella and John Holland. Professor Brusendorff suggested that the poem is a reproach, and that Gaunt wanted to have Chaucer jeer at the man who had deprived his daughter of her honor; but this assumes that the Duke, having saved appearances with the hasty marriage of his daughter to John Holland, wished to destroy them with a poetic re-enactment of another embarrassing affair involving Holland and his sister-in-law, which would surely put his own daughter in a much worse

---

[2] Cited by Aage Brusendorff, *The Chaucer Tradition* (London and Copenhagen, 1925), p. 263.

[3] Brusendorff, *Chaucer Tradition*, p. 267. See also Sydney Armitage-Smith, *John of Gaunt* (Westminster, 1904), pp. 310 and 459.

[4] Cited by Brusendorff, *Chaucer Tradition*, p. 263.

light than it would his new son-in-law.[5] Professor Cowling argued that Shirley was only partly right and that it must have been the affair with Elizabeth, rather than Isabella, which was memorialized in the poem. He also points out that Chaucer would not dare publicly cast aspersions on the honor of the Duke and Duchess of York, for in those days debts of honor were satisfied by blood.[6] One would think, however, that casting aspersions on the honor of John of Gaunt's daughter might as easily expose Chaucer to Lancaster's wrath as the alternative might to York's, and Cowling ignores the implications of Shirley's statement that the poem was ordered by John of Gaunt. Gaunt's reaction to Holland's seduction of his daughter was first to marry him to her and then to appoint him Constable of the Spanish Expedition, which is not consonant with his presumed ordering of a poem like the *Complaint*, even if instead of finding it "jeering" as Brusendorff does, we should call it "apologetic, and yet dignified and poetic," as Cowling does.

Professor Williams observes that there is no evidence that Gaunt was enraged by his daughter's change in fiancés, that there is no reason why Chaucer should write an "apology" for the lovers, and that there is no likelihood that he would present Gaunt as unsympathetically as he presents Phoebus in the poem.[7] Professor Williams' own interpretation, however, is not based upon impregnable grounds. He argues that the poem is about the affair between John of Gaunt and Katharine Swynford (Chaucer's sister-in-law), and that Phoebus represents common gossip. His argument for these identifications abandons Shirley and depends instead on the perception that the poem is shot through with non-astronomical language describing the "conjunction" of Mars and Venus, such as "unto bed thei go," in a "chambre," while Venus flees to a "tour," and hides in a "smokyng cave." The specific identifications of Mars/Gaunt and Venus/Kath-

---

[5] Brusendorff is very emphatic in endorsing the historical allegory, saying "I do not see how it can be reasonably challenged any more" (p. 268). However, apart from Shirley's attestation much of his evidence for the existence of historical allegory is very weak. For example, he argues that the mediaeval attire of Mars and Venus in the illumination of the poem in the Fairfax MS points to a contemporary significance, but as will be argued below, the two are conventionally portrayed.

[6] George Cowling, *Chaucer* (London, 1927), pp. 61-62.

[7] Williams, *New View*, pp. 56-57.

arine Swynford depend upon Chaucer's use of the line "with seint John to borwe" in this poem and his similar reference to John of Gaunt as "Seint Johan" in the *Book of the Duchess*. Moreover, Williams argues, Mars is called "the thridde hevenes lord" in the poem, and Gaunt was the third son of the king, the third male heir in line for the throne after Prince Lionel's death, the third most celebrated military figure in the kingdom, and so forth. Professor Williams also calls attention to the fact that Mars is not easily counted as the ruler of the third heaven, since he is in the fifth sphere if we count from the moon outwards, and in the fourth if we count inward from the Primum Mobile.

Some objections to this may be stated. In the first place, Mars *is* the third heaven's ruler if we give both the daily and precessional motions to the eighth sphere of the fixed stars and number the next inmost (the sphere of Saturn) as the first beyond it, a system used in a work Chaucer knew, Macrobius' *Commentary on the Dream of Scipio*. Moreover, the many puns in the *Book of the Duchess* about long castle and Lancaster, rich hill and Richmond, St. John and John of Gaunt are clustered so as to be noticeable and are included in a poem clearly concerning the Lancaster family. The *Complaint of Mars*, on the other hand, has no other overt connections with the Duke of Lancaster. In addition to this, it may be observed that the phrase "with St. John to borwe" is a commonplace, used elsewhere by Chaucer (*SqT*, 596). Finally, it may be remarked that while Chaucer's language is sometimes non-astronomical, the chambers, towers, caves, and so on that he speaks of are all good synonyms for technical terms and accurately describe technical phenomena of astrology.

An even greater exception to this particular approach, however, is that, like Cowling's argument for the identification of Mars and Venus with Holland and Elizabeth, it must necessarily conclude that the poem is an "apology" for an extra-marital liaison, and yet the poem very clearly shows its "hero," Mars, being forced to leave Venus and spending fully half the poem bewailing his "peyne," "distresse," "harm," and "distruccioun." Thus it is hard to see in the *Complaint* an apology for adultery, since it seems rather to say that transient liaisons are unfortunate in their very transitoriness. Further-

more, since half of the poem is given over to Mars' fulminations after his separation from his lady by powers over which he had no control, it is difficult to relate the events of the poem to the history of John of Gaunt, who kept Katharine Swynford for thirty years and finally married her, or to John Holland, who married Elizabeth shortly after the seduction. The same problem prohibits any serious consideration of Shirley's historical ascriptions, for Shirley may have copied the poem, but he most certainly did not read it with any care, since his genial advice to lovers to be cheerful because of the alliance of Mars and Venus runs exactly counter to Mars' own injunctions to "Compleyneth eke, ye lovers, al in-fere." Moreover, Shirley errs in thinking that the Duchess of York is John of Gaunt's daughter—an error that does not inspire confidence in his historical knowledge.

Certainly the issue of the poem's tone should be squarely faced before any historical allegory is determined, and yet the majority of critics seem to have put the cart before the horse and have determined the attitude toward illicit love at least in part from their ideas about possible historical interpretations. Indeed, Brusendorff's contention that the poem's tone is "jeering" constitutes a barely represented minority view, for not only do Cowling and Williams see the poem as apologizing for illicit love, but Professor Root called it a poem "to the greater glory of illicit love," while Wells' *Manual* has termed it a poem "in glorification of illicit love."[8] Professor Stillwell has partially redressed the balance by saying that the poem exhibits "sympathetic, but nonetheless very pointed irony and humor." Even at that the complaining of Mars is perhaps not sufficiently explained, for if Chaucer is indeed "sympathetic" to imitators of Mars and Venus, it would be hard to find the evidence for his sympathy in this poem.[9] The fact of the matter is that Chaucer's attitude, as well as that of his audience, toward the story of Mars and Venus

[8] Robert Kilburn Root, *The Poetry of Chaucer* (New York, 1950), p. 63; John Edwin Wells, *A Manual of the Writings in Middle English: 1050-1400* (New Haven and London, 1916), p. 635.

[9] Stillwell, "Convention and Individuality," p. 69. Professor Stillwell correctly sees that Chaucer, with this tale of woe, tells the lovers the opposite of what they might hope to be told on St. Valentine's Day, but Stillwell takes this to be humorous rather than cautionary (p. 72).

was rather well fixed in the direction of condemnation, and the "good" interpretation of Mars and Venus that became common in the Renaissance was only used outside of any reference to planetary conjunction or mythological adultery in the Middle Ages and so cannot fit the situation in the *Complaint of Mars*. Thus the generally unfavorable tone of the poem resulting from Mars' long complaint makes most of the historical allegories dubious and suggests that we should look for a general theme rather than a specific ascription. Professor Manly's demonstration that the astrological situation as described did not occur in Chaucer's lifetime is also an encouragement to expect in the poem a conventional attitude toward a standard theme with astrological details that will echo the customary attitude toward the events rather than serve as memorials of a recent astronomical or historical phenomenon.[10]

2. VERSIONS OF THE MARS AND VENUS STORY

THE STORY of Mars and Venus in western literary history is a comedy in its earliest versions. Moreover, it is a comedy about the embarrassment of two lovers caught in the act of adultery by a wronged husband. One of the very earliest versions of the story is in the eighth book of Homer's *Odyssey*, where a minstrel sings the story for the entertainment of the guests in the palace of Alcinous. In this version Mars and Venus at first commit adultery secretly, but then are discovered by Apollo, who tells Vulcan of his wife's unfaithfulness. Vulcan forges fetters that he sets as a snare around the bed, and after pretending to leave, he catches the lovers *in flagrante delictu*. Vulcan calls out to the other gods to come and see a matter that is both

---

[10] Manly, "Date and Interpretation," 107-11. Professor Koch, using the astronomical computations of Turein, had thought that the poem could be referred to the conjunction of Mars and Venus on April 14, 1379, but Skeat observed that the demands of the poem are that the conjunction be broken up on the 12th, and Koch's conjunction did not even begin until the 14th. Manly further observed that the conjunction adduced by Koch does not fulfill the other conditions of the poem either: that the conjunction be in Taurus; that it have neither planet retrograde; that a few days after leaving Mars, Venus shall have reached the second degree of Gemini. Manly also calculated that no conjunction in Chaucer's lifetime fitted *all* the conditions. See John Koch, "Das Datum von Chaucer's 'Mars und Venus,'" *Anglia*, IX (1886), 582-84; and *The Complete Works of Geoffrey Chaucer*, ed. Walter W. Skeat (Oxford, 1896), I, 66.

"laughable" and yet "monstrous," and the gods are indeed amused by the discomfiture of the principals, but along with their "unquenchable laughter" they draw a moral about the event: "ill deeds thrive not. . . ."[11]

Homer had no direct influence upon Chaucer, of course, but this very early version of the story was a model for the form it took in Plutarch and Ovid, the latter of which is the probable source for Chaucer's version. Passing over Plutarch, who is next chronologically, let us look at the two versions of the story in Ovid. In the fourth book of the *Metamorphoses* Mars and Venus are discovered in their adultery by the sun and are entrapped by Vulcan. Exactly as in Homer, Vulcan then invites in the other gods to see the disgrace of the pair, and the gods laugh at them; one, however, pays tribute to the power of Venus by saying that he would not mind being so disgraced. In the *Art of Love*, Ovid again relates the story, and again it is essentially comic, but here the discomfiture of the adulterers receives more emphasis. Not only do they afford a spectacle for the other gods, but Venus cries, and both are unsuccessful in their attempts to cover their faces and their "lewd parts." Again one of the gods offers to change places with Mars.[12]

Although Chaucer would have found an incidental suggestion of the power of Venus in both versions of the story in Ovid, he would certainly have seen it as essentially a funny story about embarrassment brought about by misbehavior. Thus, if he meant to change it into an apology or glorification of this misbehavior, he would have had to signal his intentions more obviously than he did. Rather, the complaining of Mars at such length seems ample indication that Chaucer is not apologizing for the situation, but is following the Ovidian form in which misbehavior leads to discomfiture and unhappiness. There is, however, the suggestion of a sub-theme in one of Ovid's versions that demands more scrutiny, for Chaucer uses it in addition to the main theme.

[11] Homer, *The Odyssey*, trans. A. T. Murray, Loeb Classical Library (London and New York, 1931), I, 281-83.

[12] Ovid, *Metamorphoses*, trans. Frank Justus Miller, Loeb Classical Library (London and New York, 1916), I, 191. Ovid, *The Art of Love*, trans. J. H. Mozley, Loeb Classical Library (London and Cambridge, Mass., 1962), pp. 105-107. Robinson and Skeat refer only to the version in the *Metamorphoses* as the source.

This sub-theme is the tempering effect that Venus has on Mars. Obviously this can receive various interpretations ranging from tacit condemnation to something quite at variance with the Homeric and Ovidian story in which Mars and Venus are symbols of the disgrace of adultery discovered. In Ovid's *Art of Love*, Venus makes Mars change from a terrible captain to a lover, but Ovid elsewhere compares the soldier and the lover to the detriment of the latter. In Plutarch's *Moralia*, however, this aspect of the relationship of Mars and Venus is separated from the adultery *per se*, and Plutarch argues that Concord or Harmony is the issue from the union of Mars and Venus, that is, of Love and War.[13] It should be remarked that when Plutarch speaks in this vein he carefully avoids reference to the discovery of Mars and Venus by the sun, for that account of the union necessarily leads to a different analysis of its meaning. Indeed, Plutarch himself makes such an analysis in his essay on "How the Young Man Should Study Poetry," while discussing Homer's version of the story. He not only claims that Homer intended there to be a moral interpretation of the story, but also denies that a currently circulating "astrological" interpretation has any validity—this interpretation being that the conjunction of Mars and Venus portends births conceived in adultery, which cannot be kept secret![14] Of course, no direct influence on Chaucer can be claimed for either of these works of Plutarch, but the extent of the tradition in which Venus is the pacifier of Mars, ultimately bringing Harmony, must be examined.

Professor Panofsky has argued that this treatment of the two planetary deities was at least alluded to in mediaeval mythography, specifically in two of the Vatican Mythographers, and was known to the western Middle Ages from Statius' *Thebaid*.[15] However, a close

[13] Plutarch, *Isis and Osiris* (*Moralia*, 370), trans. Frank Cole Babbitt, Loeb Classical Library (Cambridge, Mass., and London, 1936), V, 117. For a discussion of Ovid's amusing handling of the *miles amoris* figure, see Robertson, *Preface*, pp. 408-10.

[14] Plutarch, "How the Young Man Should Study Poetry," *Moralia*, 10-20, trans. Frank Cole Babbitt, Loeb Classical Library (London and New York, 1927), pp. 101-102.

[15] Panofsky, *Studies in Iconology*, 162-64. Panofsky also remarks that there is a passage on Venus' ability to neutralize the destructive powers of Mars in Lucretius, *De rerum natura*. However, this work is not listed earlier than 1520 by

inspection of the evidence suggests that while the idea that Venus could temper the fury of Mars was well-known in the Middle Ages, the more positive idea that the union of the two produced Harmony seems to be discoverable only in the Renaissance. In the two Vatican Mythographers, for example, it is said that Hermiona was conceived at the adultery of Mars and Venus, but there is no attempt to link her with Harmony, nor do the stories that follow demonstrate any sort of concord, but rather the opposite. They are concerned with the Brooch of Thebes, given by Vulcan to Hermiona, which brought misfortune to all who wore it. Thus the second Vatican Mythographer writes, "Nupsit Cadmus Hermionae, quae nata erat ex adulterio Martis et Veneris; sed malo omine."[16] By the same token, Statius' story of Venus' pacifying Mars, which Chaucer surely knew, shows her only partially successful, for she halts Mars momentarily, but cannot stop him altogether. Moreover, Statius' Venus refers to the misfortunes of her daughter brought about as a punishment for the adultery.[17] By the time of the Renaissance, it must be granted, the situation is very, very different, and Professor Wind, drawing upon the writings of Pico della Mirandola about the tempering of Mars by Venus, is able to demonstrate that certain iconographic representations of Mars and Venus by Botticelli, Piero di Cosimo, and Paolo Veronese are in fact depictions of the theme of *discordia concors*.[18] Professor Panofsky, moreover, has demonstrated that Titian's

---

Savage, and was discovered in the Middle Ages in 1518. See Savage, *Old English Libraries*, p. 260.

[16] *Scriptores rerum mythicarum*, ed. G. H. Bode (Cellis, 1834), p. 101.

[17] Statius, *Thebaid*, trans. J. H. Mozley, Loeb Classical Library (London and New York, 1928), III, 260-323; pp. 469-75. See also B. A. Wise, *The Influence of Statius upon Chaucer* (Baltimore, 1911), pp. 42-44.

[18] Edgar Wind, *Pagan Mysteries in the Renaissance* (London, 1958), pp. 81-88. Wind also includes a representation of Mars and Venus from the Palazzo Schifanoia in Ferrara that will be discussed below, as an example of the adulterous Mars and Venus. Except when direct Neoplatonic influence on the artist can be demonstrated, as is the case with Botticelli, it is dangerous to interpret renaissance paintings as Neoplatonic allegories. On Botticelli's "Mars and Venus," one of the classic examples of Neoplatonic influence, see E. H. Gombrich, "Botticelli's Mythologies: A Study in the Neoplatonic Symbolism of his Circle," *JWCI*, VIII (1945), 45-60; and Nesca A. Robb, *Neoplatonism of the Italian Renaissance* (London, 1935), pp. 218-19.

"Allegory of the Marquis d'Avalos" is a type of Venus and Mars painting, probably a wedding portrait, and that the two gods figured in other quite decorous pictures, one demonstrably a wedding picture, by such artists as Paris Bordone and Rubens.[19]

The idea that Venus tempered Mars was by no means unknown in the Middle Ages, but until the advent of Italian Neoplatonism, it was not stressed as an important philosophical doctrine; rather, it was seen as an interesting astrological phenomenon. Perhaps no better illustration of this could be afforded than a look at Chaucer's own uses of the idea. In the story of Hypermnestra in the *Legend of Good Women*, for example, he notes that at Hypermnestra's birth the planet Mars is in one of the signs in which Venus has great power; consequently his "malice" is taken from him, and the native is born with no warlike or even self-preservational capabilities:

> The rede Mars was that tyme of the yeere
> So feble that his malyce is hym raft;
> Repressed hath Venus his crewel craft,
> That, what with Venus and other oppressioun
> Of houses, Mars his venim is adoun,
> That Ypermystra dar nat handle a knyf
> In malyce, thogh she shulde lese hire lyf.
> (*LGW*, 2589-95)

It should be noted that there is no mention of a conjunction of Venus and Mars, nor of any "discovery" by the sun, nor is the repression of Mars necessarily an entirely good thing, since Hypermnestra disobeys her father's orders to kill her husband, and consequently dies in prison.

A more positive statement, majestic in tone, of the effect Venus has on Mars may be found in the Prologue to Book III of the *Troilus*. Here Chaucer is clearly concerned with a multiple Venus, whose might is felt "In hevene and helle, in erthe and salte see" (*T&C*, III, 8), and whose inspiration of Jove is not condemned but seen as the cause of his love for humankind—"and amorous him made/ On mortal thyng . . ." (*T&C*, III, 17-18). Thus Venus here represents many kinds of love, and her relationship to Mars is not depicted as

[19] Panofsky, *Studies in Iconology*, pp. 160-63.

adulterous, but is ideally similar to her power to hold "regne and hous in unitee" (*T&C*, III, 29), which is modelled on the harmonious love of Boethius III, m. 8.

> Ye fierse Mars apaisen of his ire,
> And as yow list, ye maken hertes digne;
> Algates hem that ye wol sette a-fyre,
> They dreden shame, and vices they resygne.
>   (*T&C*, III, 22-25)

Whether or not Venus makes Troilus' heart "digne" through pacification of Mars is another matter. It may be remarked on the contrary that one of the characteristics of Chaucerian servants of Venus is a tendency toward warlike endeavors rather than the opposite, and we may note in this regard that rather than being peaceful the Squire fights "In hope to stonden in his lady grace" (*Gen Prol*, 88), while Troilus himself fights not to preserve besieged Troy, "But only, lo, for this conclusioun:/ To liken hire the bet for his renoun" (*T&C*, I, 480-81).

Whatever the implications of the cosmic Venus' effects on Mars for the characters in the *Troilus*, the significance of her appeasement of Mars' ire in the *Complaint of Mars* is clearly in accord with the generally comic tone of the adultery and discovery story and is emphatically not an instance of *discordia concors*. Chaucer gives us a lengthy description of the rules Venus lays down for Mars when she is "won" by him, but it will be noted that all the rules are in Venus' favor, so that Mars' presumed virtues, such as a lack of jealousy, represent license for Venus rather than virtue on the part of Mars. Thus, while he agrees to "perpetuall obeisaunce," in spite of Venus' many other lovers, she binds herself to love him only as long as he does not "trespass" against love. Furthermore, in the course of the poem she breaks her lesser vow by leaving the still-faithful Mars to go off with Mercury, who receives her as his "frend."

> Whilom the thridde hevenes lord above,
> As wel by hevenysh revolucioun
> As by desert, hath wonne Venus his love,
> And she hath take him *in subjeccioun*,

And *as a maistresse taught him* his lessoun,
Commaundynge him that nevere, in her *servise*,
He nere so bold no lover to dispise.

For she *forbad him* jelosye at al,
And cruelte, and bost, and tyrannye;
She made him at her lust so humble and tal,
That when her deyned to cast on hym her ye,
He tok in pacience to lyve or dye.
And thus she *brydeleth him* in her manere,
With nothing but with scourging of her chere.

Who regneth now in blysse but Venus,
That hath thys worthy knyght *in governaunce?*
Who syngeth now but Mars, that serveth thus
The faire Venus, causer of plesaunce?
He bynt him to perpetuall obeisaunce,
And she bynt her to loven him for evere,
But so be that his trespas hyt desevere.[20]

Shades of the Wife of Bath![21] Venus here makes Mars less warlike, but there is certainly no ennoblement in the process. Rather, Mars binds himself to a one-sided agreement that he keeps, while Venus pledges only to be true if he is true and doesn't keep her promise. This is clearly modelled on Ovidian satire of the *miles amoris* and is not a praise of harmony.

The story of Venus and Mars as we have it in the *Complaint of Mars,* then, is modelled after a humorous Ovidian story, and the sub-theme of Mars' change from warrior to lover, effected by Venus, is put to comic, not philosophical, use. Before proceeding to a close reading of the poem, however, there is more to be said about the raw materials for the basic story as Chaucer found them. While Ovid is the source for the *Complaint of Mars,* it is noteworthy that the

[20] *Complaint of Mars,* 29-49. Gombrich missed Chaucer's irony here, and thought the tone was consonant with Neoplatonic symbolism ("Botticelli's Mythologies," p. 48).

[21] For the significance of proper and improper bridles, see Boethius, Bk. I, m. 7, and Bk. II, m. 8. It is the bridle of mastery that the Wife of Bath triumphantly wrests from Jankyn (*WB Prol,* 813). See further Robertson, *Preface,* pp. 22-23 and his Fig. 6.

story was moralized by the mythographers. Moreover, while Chaucer took the basic elements of his poem from Ovid, he cast them in a significant astrological form that is not classical.

3. ASTROLOGICAL SIGNIFICANCE OF
THE CONJUNCTION

THERE ARE two basic points about the astrological situation in the *Complaint of Mars* to be taken into consideration: the first is that it concerns a conjunction of the planets Mars and Venus, and the second is that the conjunction takes place in the sign Taurus, the "house" of Venus, in which Mars has his *casus* or fall. Thus, just from a consideration of the literary sources of the *Complaint* we would assume that Chaucer was concerned with an astrological representation of the adultery of Mars and Venus through the phenomenon of conjunction, and that in choosing to have it occur in a sign wherein Venus is powerful and Mars weak, he wished to satirize those love relationships in which men subject themselves to women. Certainly the most important occurrence of Taurus elsewhere in Chaucer's poetry is in the little horoscope of the Wife of Bath, which also involves Mars in Taurus, and we may assume that the Wife of Bath's desire to have "maistrie" in marriage does not run counter to her horoscope. Venus in the *Complaint of Mars* is similarly dominant and, granting that in the *Tales* Chaucer is undercutting the relationships between the crude, bourgeois Wife and her several husbands, he is undercutting and not apologizing for the relationship between the "courtly" Mars and Venus in this poem. Aristocratic carnality was as readily condemned as the bourgeois variety in the Middle Ages, and we should remember that Dante's famous line about love that quickly repairs to the gentle heart is used in a description of eternally damned adulterers.

The astrological situation described in the *Complaint* does not constitute a horoscope by any stretch of the imagination, but we may gain some understanding of the mediaeval attitude toward the astrological interrelationships of Mars and Venus through a study of astrological manuals, and these devote most of their attention to various relationships of the two in horoscopes. It is, however, the general tone that we are interested in, and the tone is very clear. As already seen in the

citation from Plutarch, there was a tendency among the astrologers from the very earliest times to conceive of any association of Mars and Venus in a horoscope as a sign that the native would be inclined toward adultery, fornication, or sexual depravity, whether the two planets were in conjunction or merely in aspect with regard to one another, whether one was in one of the houses of the other or just in one of the subdivisions of a sign—a decan or term—that was arbitrarily linked with the other. Thus, although Chaucer could observe that Venus was capable of quelling Mars' "venim" so that Hypermnestra would be unmartial, there is another, even stronger tradition that saw in the association of Venus and Mars an augury of lustfulness. Indeed, the astrologers so often refer to this in so many different guises that the whole subject defies full documentation, but a sampling is instructive.

As early as Ptolemy, who wrote a four part work on astrology variously called the *Tetrabiblos* and *Quadripartitum* in addition to his purely astronomical works, we find that Venus is important in influencing people in matters of love and that when she is in conjunction or other association with Mars she inspires an excess of lust:

> In the genitures of women one must examine Venus. For if Venus is in aspect with Jupiter or likewise with Mercury, she makes them temperate and pure in love. If Saturn is not present, but she is associated with Mercury, she makes them easily aroused and full of desire, but generally cautious, hesitant, and avoiding turpitude. But if Venus is together with Mars only, or is in some aspect to him, she makes them lustful and depraved and more heedless.[22]

It should be noted that not all planetary associations of Venus cause an excess of lust, but only those with Mars, while some associations, such as that with Jupiter, produce women who are pure in love. Chaucer apparently had something like this in mind when he said of Hypermnestra in the *Legend of Good Women* that although she had great beauty from Venus, Jupiter was so compounded with Venus that Hypermnestra thought that the greatest felicity was to keep her good name in wifehood (*LGW*, 2584-88). On the other hand, the

----

[22] Ptolemy, *Tetrabiblos*, trans. F. E. Robbins, Loeb Classical Library (Cambridge, Mass., and London, 1940), p. 407.

Wife of Bath's horoscope is not specific about the relationships be-
tween Venus and any other planets, but the Wife claims that Venus
gave her lust, and "likerousnesse," and she is no doubt correct,
astrologically speaking.

Another way of approaching the significance of the astrology in
the *Complaint of Mars* is to examine what the astrologers say about
horoscopes in which Mars is in a good position in one of his own
houses, when associated with Venus, as well as those where he is in
a bad position in one of Venus' houses such as Libra or Taurus
wherein Mars has his *casus*. The contrast points out again that Mars
is not always an evil harbinger, but only when he is in a "contrary"
position—as he is in the *Complaint*.

> Allied with Venus, in honourable positions, Mars makes his
> subjects pleasing, cheerful, . . . given to misconduct in matters of
> love, but still successful, circumspect, and sensible. . . . In contrary
> positions he makes them leering, lascivious, profligate . . . adulter-
> ers . . . corrupters of women and maidens . . . profligate, fond of
> adornment, bold, disposed to base practices, and shameless.[23]

The boldness, fondness of adornment, and shamelessness certainly
remind one of the Wife of Bath, but it is the general suggestion that
Mars and Venus together cause "misconduct in matters of love" at
best, and adultery at worst, that is most important for an analysis of
the *Complaint*.

The Roman astrologer Firmicus Maternus, who writes from a well
delineated moral stance, says that Mars and Venus in conjunction
cause adultery and that this does violence to the laws of matrimony.
The tone of the whole is instructive:

> Si Mars et Venus in eodem signo pariter constituti aequabili
> societatis potestate iungantur, ista Martis Venerisque coniunctio
> stupratores adulterosque perficiet, ut pravo cupiditatis ardore pos-
> sessi, et indomitae libidinis stimulis incitati, captiosis pollicitationibus
> stupri perpetrandi causa alieni matrimonii iura sectentur.[24]

[23] *Ibid.*, pp. 353-55.

[24] Julius Firmicus Maternus, *Matheseos libri VIII*, ed. W. Kroll and F. Shutsch
(Leipzig, 1897-1913), II, 124. Cf. II, 248, where it is said that adulterers will be
born when Mars and Venus are found together in the horoscope or when Mars

This diatribe by Firmicus Maternus, when considered along with Ptolemy's use of "depraved" to describe the effects of Venus and Mars in the genitures of women, clearly shows that well before the advent of Arabian astrology there was a native western astrological tradition which not only interpreted Mars and Venus in a horoscope as prognosticating a life of lechery and adultery, but which also frankly condemned the effects.

The Arabic astrologers continued to associate various sorts of involvements of Mars and Venus with adultery, fornication, and lechery. Messehalla, for example, wrote that the person born with Mars in one of the terms (a five-fold division of a sign) ascribed to Venus would be involved unfortunately with women, and like the earlier writers on astrology Messehalla does not glorify or apologize for what he clearly calls sin:

> Si fuerit [Mars] in termino Veneris, malam uitam habebit ex euentu mulierum, & accipiet uxorem ex euentu peccati, & capient eum in concubitu peccati uel fornicationis, & accipiet fornicarias, & habebit eas, & transibunt multi dies, & opera eius non erunt bona . . . & fide sua non permanet. . . .[25]

Other Arabic astrologers are similar. Albohali speaks of the power of Venus to cause a singular list of sexual sins. For him she signifies an influence toward "foeditatem, calliditatemque ac mulierositatem, prostitutam pudicitiam & uerecundiam ac turpitudinem luxuriae." In Albumasar's famous work on the great conjunctions we read that the conjunction of Mars and Venus "significat multam fornicationem et adulterium et malum in mulieribus. . . ."[26]

The encyclopedists among the Arabic astrologers summed up what their forerunners had said, recapitulated it, and often added some remarks of their own. Typical of these writers is Albohazen Haly,

---

is within any of the boundaries of Venus, or vice versa, or when Venus is under the rays of Mars.

[25] Messehalla, *In reuolutionibus annorum mundi* . . . , in Omnibus #12 as described in Carmody's bibliography (Nuremberg, 1549), sig. K₃ʳ⁻ᵛ. See also K₄ʳ⁻ᵛ.

[26] Albohali Alchait, *De iudiciis natiuitatem* (Nuremberg, 1546), sig. C₃ʳ; cf. K₁ᵛ. Albumasar, *De magnis coniunctionibus* (Augsburg, 1489), sig. E₃ᵛ.

who in his massive work describes Mars in good aspect to Venus in a nativity and finds that even then the native will lie with women "against the law," which is not only sinful, but apparently cannot alleviate the unhappiness the native will be subject to:

Sed si planeta [Mars] habuerit conuenientiam cum Venere, & fuerit in bono statu sicut praediximus, procreant natum conueni-entem cum hominibus, mobilem, bonae credulitatis, deceptorem amicorum suorum: hic enim uitam diligit uitiosam, quietem amat simplicem, pulchrae formae, amat psallere & saltare, amore cor-ripitur, conuiuator est, iacet cum mulieribus contra legem & in quo est peccatum, nihilominus felix est.[27]

An interesting comment on the variety of possible relationships between Venus and Mars in a nativity and their essentially similar effect on the native is to be found in the writings of Albubatur. Here we find conjunction, quadratic aspect, opposition, and each in the house of the other all discussed as inclining the native toward fornica-tion, with the further distinction that under certain astrological situations involving Venus, the native will be inclined towards un-natural sex acts:

Quando Venus in domo Martis fuerit, et Mars in domo Veneris, natus erit manifestus fornicator, et sine uerecundia. Quando Venus cum Marte iuncta fuerit, aut in quadrato uel oppositio aspectu, natus malas ac turpes fornicationes committet. Si Mars et Venus in signo masculino fuerint, natus erit fornicator. Si Venus effoeminata fuerit, natus erit multum effoeminatus, et fornicationes ultra nat-uram diliget.[28]

Guido Bonatti, whose writings on astrology earned him a place in Dante's *Inferno* next to Michael Scot, is another whose analysis of Mars and Venus mentions unnatural acts. After this comment he cites Albohali to the effect that Mars in Taurus signifies the birth of a fornicator:

[27] Albohazen Haly, *De iudiciis astrorum* (Basle, 1551), sig. P_1^v; cf. Kk_5^r ("Qvando Venus iungitur cum Marte significat multas fornicationes & mala, et multas fornicationes in mulieribus . . .") and A_6^v.

[28] Albubatur, *De natiuitatibus* (Nuremberg, 1540), sig. G_2^v.

Quod si fuerit mars in tauro vel libra: fueritque natiuitatis signator signabit natum luxuriosum fornicatorem sodomitam et in omnibus venereis abusibus sceleratum futurum deceptorem.... Et dixit abolay quod si fuerit in tauro signat natum proditorem falsum malignum minatorem atque fornicatorem futurum.[29]

We may say with some assurance, in light of this evidence, that in the Middle Ages the conjoining of Mars and Venus in classical legend was echoed in the accounts of the astrologers, who associated various kinds of lecherous behavior with various relationships of the two planets. Thus, Chaucer would know that in writing a poem about Venus and Mars and executing part of it in astrological terms he would be doubly concerned with adultery and fornication. From its classical background his audience would expect the story to be funny; from its astrological nature, to be unfortunate.[30]

4. THE MYTH AND THE MYTHOGRAPHERS

ANOTHER aspect of the story of Venus and Mars that deserves consideration prior to an attempt to analyze Chaucer's treatment of the theme is the tradition of mythological interpretation of the Ovidian story. As Seznec has pointed out, mediaeval commentaries on Ovid and other classical writers were essentially moral expositions, and they were in very widespread use by the fourteenth century.[31] Of

[29] Guido Bonatti, *Liber introductorius ad iudicia stellarum* (Augsburg, 1491), sig. CC₅ᵛ.

[30] There are a number of other comments in the astrologers that link various relationships of Mars and Venus with adultery and fornication, sometimes with and sometimes without a condemnation. For further comment, see the following: John of Seville, *Johannes Hispalensis isagoge epitome totius astrologie* (Nuremberg, 1548), sig. N₄ᵛ; Ptolemy, *Centiloquium*, in *Astronomici scriptores* (Basle, 1551), sig. G₃ᵛ; Abraham ibn Ezra, *De natiuitatibus* (Marburg, 1537), sig. F₂ᵛ; Abraham ibn Ezra, *The Beginning of Wisdom*, ed. and trans. Raphael Levy and Fransisco Cantera, *Johns Hopkins Studies in Romance Literatures and Languages*, extra vol., XIV (1939), 43; Pico della Mirandola, *Disputationes adversus astrologiam divinatricem*, ed. Eugenio Garin (Florence, 1946-52), I, 480; Albumasar, *Introductorium in astronomiam* (Venice, 1506), sigs. D₂ʳ, H₁ʳ⁻ᵛ, and G₆ᵛ.

[31] Seznec, *Survival of the Pagan Gods*, pp. 84-121. Seznec gives a valuable outline of the more important mediaeval works. There is a convenient summary of Ovidian commentaries in Irving Lavin, "Cephalus and Procris: Transformation of an Ovidian Myth," *JWCI*, XVII (1954), 262, n. 1. See also Erwin Panofsky, *Renaissance and Renascences in Western Art* (Copenhagen, 1960), p. 78, n. 2.

course, as Robertson has cautioned, the commentaries do not provide us with material that can be applied mechanically in the interpretation of a poem, but they are useful in indicating conventional areas of meaning that are in turn helpful guides.[32] With regard to the story of Mars and Venus we are fortunate that it was commonly treated in the commentaries and that the expositors were quite consistent in their interpretation of it. Professor Robert P. Miller has studied both the mediaeval and the Renaissance interpretations of the myth as preface for the study of Shakespeare's "Venus and Adonis," and his remarks on the nature and continuity of the tradition are informative:

> For the renaissance, as for the medieval, reader, a fable *meant* something; and in this case the mythographers, without substantial discrepancy from Fulgentius (c. 500) to George Sandys (1640), find the relation of Venus and Mars to illustrate a highly conventional "moral": the impossibility of concealing a *virtus conrupta libidine* (*i.e.*, the corruption of an inner *virtus*, symbolized by the "warrior" Mars, by an inordinate desire, or lust).[33]

The mythographers examined by Miller in his admirable study are Fulgentius, Giovanni del Virgilio, Arnulf of Orleans, Pierre Bersuire, Boccaccio, Natalis Comes, and Abraham Fraunce. Although this is more than a merely representative selection, it is nevertheless possible to adduce even more mythographic material. All of the so-called Vatican Mythographers relate the story of the adultery of Mars and Venus, and two of them substantially agree with the interpretation already noted in Fulgentius. There is also a commentary on the meaning of the Ovidian story in the *Ovide moralisé*, which has been suggested by Professor Stillwell as the closest analogue to the *Complaint* and which Chaucer certainly knew.[34] Finally, although Pro-

---

[32] Robertson, *Preface*, p. 359.

[33] Robert P. Miller, "The Myth of Mars's Hot Minion in *Venus and Adonis*," *ELH*, XXVI (1959), 472; also see p. 471. It is noteworthy that through the long history of moral interpretation the laughter of the gods is not forgotten. As late as the end of the 16th century Spenser could say that the exposure of Mars and Venus caused laughter: "That all the Gods with common mockerie / Might laugh at them and scorne their shameful sin" ("Muiopotmos," ll. 372-73).

[34] Stillwell, "Convention and Individuality," p. 75. Stillwell is perhaps too conservative in calling the *Ovide moralisé* an analogue rather than a source. On

fessor Miller cites Boccaccio's moral comment on the myth of Mars and Venus, the same author also has a long astrological exposition of the conjunction of Mars and Venus, which is treated here rather than in the section on astrology because Boccaccio writes primarily as a mythographer in his *Genealogy of the Pagan Gods*.

That the import of the adultery of Mars and Venus is that *virtus* can be corrupted by libido is attested by both the second and the third Vatican Mythographers, who also variously interpret Vulcan's chains as the bonds of fervor and the habit of seduction:

Venus cum Marte rem habuit, quam Sol manifestans, Vulcano prodidit. Nam virtus, corrupta libidine, sole teste apparet, et turpiter catenata fervoris constrictione tenetur.

. . . .

Dicitur etiam cum Venere Mars furtim concubuisse, quod Sol videns Vulcano prodidit. Ille adamanteis catenis eos coeuntes ligans, diis omnibus turpiter ostendit jacentes. . . . Mars igitur complexu Veneris pollutus, id est, virtus libidinis illecebris corrupta, sole teste apparet, id est, tandem veritatis indicio rea esse cognoscitur. Quae quidem virtus prava consuetudine illecta vinclis constrictioribus ostenditur catenata.[85]

One important detail here is that the sun, which represented merely a sort of common gossip in Ovid, is styled by the third Vatican Mythographer as the "sign of truth" by which this kind of activity must at last be judged. By the time of the Renaissance this interpretation had gone so far as to identify the sun with God's justice, and even in the Middle Ages it is clear that the sun was interpreted by the commentators as a variant on the popular conception of the *"sol iustitiae,"* a figure ultimately dependent upon Malachi 4:2. This interpretation may help to explain a puzzling feature in the one manuscript illumination of the poem, as we shall see.

Chaucer's use of the *Ovide* as a source for parts of the *Legend of Good Women* see John Livingston Lowes, "Chaucer and the *Ovide Moralisé*," *PMLA*, XXXIII (1918), 302-25; and Sanford Brown Meech, "Chaucer and the *Ovide Moralisé*— A Further Study," *PMLA*, XLVI (1931), 182-204.

[85] *Scriptores rerum mythicarum*, pp. 85 and 231-32.

The exact significance of the relationships between the *Ovide moralisé* and Chaucer's *Complaint of Mars* is not easy to specify, in part because we cannot be sure that the *Ovide* always constituted a direct source for Chaucer, and in part because there are some major differences between the two works. Oftentimes the *Ovide* is a difficult work to bring into relationship with other mythographic writings because it has many new interpretations. In the case of the story of Mars and Venus the anonymous author of the *Ovide* is in the mainstream of the mythographic tradition that condemns the affair as disgraceful adultery; he does not, however, give any indication that Mars represents *virtus* corrupted, but symbolizes rather "li siens avoultierres," that is, adulterous people. The allegorization as a whole, however, does not differ substantially from other interpretations in tone:

> —Or vous dirai l'alegorie
> Que ceste fable signifie.
> Venus avoit par amistié
> Le dieu de bataille acointié.
> Venus, c'est a dire luxure,
> Feme de Vulcan, c'est ardure
> Qui les cuers fet ardoir et frire,
> Fist celeement avoultire.
> Mars estoit li siens avoultierres.
> Mars vault autant con "destruisierres."
> Grief mort et grief destruction
> Vienent par fornication.
> Par luxure et par avoultire
> Sont li pluiseur mis a martire
> Et desnué de bones mours.
> Aucun dient que c'est amours,
> Mes je di qu'amours n'est ce mie,
> Ains est pechiez et vilonie,
> Que nulz predom ne doit amer,
> Et qui le veult amours clamer:
> D'amours vient malz, paine et poverte,
> Ire, angoisse et mors et grief perte.[36]

[36] *Ovide moralisé*, Bk. IV, ll. 1630-51.

The allegorization continues with a very lengthy diatribe against this kind of love and concludes with an interpretation of the sun as the "diex de sapience" who discovers the lovers—quite similar to the interpretations we have seen of the sun as the sign of truth. The whole exposition is terminated with the comment that Vulcan's binding the lovers represents "mauvese ardure" which subjects the adulterers to "honte et a laidure, / A mort et a perdicion, / A dampnable derision."[37]

In addition to the allegorization of the fable, the author of the *Ovide* also retells the basic story, retells it in an astrological *rifacimento*, and retells it as a Euhemeristic allegory about historical people of the past. Of these retellings it is the astrological version that is more pertinent to the present purpose, but it is somewhat different from Chaucer's. There is a conjunction of the two planets, as in Chaucer, but there the resemblance ends. In the *Ovide* the conjunction is described with rather more astrological detail, in that it is insisted that the conjunction occur when Venus is at apogee and Mars at perigee and that no other planet come between them; but there is no indication of the sign of the zodiac in which the conjunction occurs, whereas Chaucer clearly states that the conjunction occurs in Taurus. Another major difference is that the author of the *Ovide moralisé*, in addition to having the sun discover the lovers, also permits the unastrological figure of Vulcan to enter the picture as outrageous ardor, which grows in the conjunction of the planets, while Chaucer makes use of the astrologically unexceptionable sun only. Finally, while Chaucer gives a humorous exaggeration to the astrological idea that Venus tempers the malevolent qualities of the planet Mars, the author of the *Ovide* instead has Mars deprive Venus of her customary "debonaireté" and make her "male et enrevre." Although the passage is lengthy it is of sufficient importance to be cited in full:

> —Or vous vueil espondre ces fables.
> Mars est une planete errables,
> Plains de colerique nature,
> C'est de secheresce et d'ardure;

[37] *Ibid.*, IV, 1753-56.

The Complaint of Mars

Pour ce faint la fable, sans faille,
Qu'il soit mestre diex de bataille,
Qu'il est nuisans et damageus,
Si predomine aus corageus,
Aus mellis et aus irascibles.
Venus et planete paisibles,
Moiste, chaulz, de bone atemprance,
Plains de grace et de bienvueillance.
Li sanguin, qui sont moiste et chaut,
Pour l'umour puant, pour le chaut,
Desirrent l'oeuvre de luxure,
Si sont amoureus par nature
Et debonaire et gracieus.
Pour ce qui li luxurieus
Sont samblable a Venus de mours
L'apele on deesse d'amours.
Quant Mars fet son cours par le ciel
Ou plus bas point de son cerciel
Et Venus ou plus hault dou sien,
Si qu'il n'a entr'aux nulle rien
Qui les departe ne dessevre,
Venus devient male et enrevre,
Et pert pour la prochaineté
De Mars sa debonaireté
Et l'umour qu'el soloit avoir.
Tout ce puet l'en apercevoir
Par le soleil, qui les descuevre.
Vulcans les prist en presente oeuvre:
Vulcans c'est l'outrageuse ardure
Qui double et croist par la jointure
De ces deus estoiles ensamble,
Qui a Venus soustrait et emble
S'amour et sa bone atemprance
Et sa grace et sa bienvueillance,
Si qu'ele avoutire et forsligne,
Quant elle est en la droite lingne
Souz Mars, sans autre entremoien.[38]

[38] *Ibid.*, IV, 1488-1528.

The question that must now be asked is what exact influence may we discern? We know that Chaucer made use of the *Ovide moralisé* elsewhere in his writings, but if it is a source here, what can we say of the nature of Chaucer's use of it? For Professor Stillwell, who first called attention to the importance of the *Ovide* for the *Complaint of Mars*, the influence on the whole is not very extensive. "All in all, the *Ovide* gave Chaucer relatively little for *Mars*—not much more, if anything, than the idea for the combination mythology-astrology-generalization. The chief value of the analogue is that in its plain moralizing it provides a contrast to Chaucer."[39] However, one may note that the combination of astrology and mythology is also to be found in Boccaccio's treatment of the Mars and Venus story in his *Genealogy of the Pagan Gods*. More to the point is Stillwell's argument that the overt moralizing of the French poet is not to be found in Chaucer. Here, though, some caution must be exercised lest we think that there is no moralizing at all in Chaucer's poem. The casting of the story as a "Complaint" and the devotion of almost half of the poem to Mars' expostulations of his distress are clear indications that Chaucer wanted to show the moral of the story rather than tell it. Thus, although the two poets are most dissimilar in their handling of the moralization, and although Chaucer's *Complaint* is not solely modelled on the conventional interpretation of the myth in terms of *virtus* corrupted by libido (there being no great emphasis on prior *virtus* in Chaucer's Mars), nevertheless Chaucer closely follows the French poet's conclusion that love of this kind brings about "malz, paine et poverte, / Ire, angoisse et mors et grief perte."

Another interpretation of the myth that is harmonious in tone but slightly different in its interpretation of the details is that of Boccaccio. Actually, Boccaccio both interprets the myth of Mars and Venus and quotes the astrologers as to the significance of Venus and Mars in a nativity, quite expectably saying approximately the same thing in both cases. His exposition of the classical story may at first strike us as quite different in tone from those allegorizations that emphasized the corrupting power of libido, for Boccaccio styles the affair as typical of love in marriage, rather than as adultery. He goes on to observe, however, that in this particular case the wedded lovers let

[39] Stillwell, "Convention and Individuality," pp. 76-77.

the fires of love press on to a greater flame, and that although this is natural, it is reprehensible. The whole passage is easily understood if we remember that for Chaucer's Parson sexual congress in marriage for its own sake, when people "take no reward in hire assemblynge but oonly to hire flesshly delit," is technically categorized as a sub-species of adultery. Boccaccio's interpretation, then, grows quite naturally out of a mediaeval attitude toward the adultery of Mars and Venus:

> Si autem acutius velimus sensum huius fictionis excutere, arbitror intelligi posse pro Venere concupiscibilis appetitus, Vulcano ignis deo, id est, calori naturali, matrimonio, id est indissolubili vinculo alligatus; hic more ignis dum in maius incendium nititur, Martem tanquam ferventissimum amare dicitur, et ab eo tanquam sibi simile amatur, et in idem desiderium iunguntur lascivientes, quod a Sole, id est a sapiente viro dum cernitur redarguitur, et excedens iusto calori accusatur. Verum dum incontrarium, fervor inordinate concupiscientie fertur, fit ut occultis vinculis, id est cogitationibus atque delectationibus lascivis artius alligetur insipiens, a quibus effeminatus solvi non possit, et iam palam factis obscenis commixtionibus a sapientibus rideatur.[40]

In styling the sun as "sapience" Boccaccio is at one with the author of the *Ovide moralisé*, but the idea that the adultery of Mars and Venus represents immoderate marital delight seems to be Boccaccio's own. The tone of the passage is, however, typical, and Boccaccio elsewhere adduces an astrological digression on Mars and Venus which confirms the impression that he did not mean to minimize or to undercut traditional interpretations of the myth. It is clear that Chaucer did not get anything of the plot of the *Complaint of Mars* from Boccaccio's explication of the myth of Mars and Venus; but, on the other hand, if Chaucer had read Boccaccio's account, he would not have found anything therein that ran counter to the general tenor of the mythographic interpretations.

Not many pages after his mythographic exposition of Mars and Venus, Boccaccio offers a sort of astrological interpretation—a phenomenon quite frequent in his *Genealogy*. In this he simply quotes

[40] Boccaccio, *Genealogie deorum*, II, 448-49.

from the astrologers the very same sort of thing we have already seen: namely, the theory that Mars in Taurus in a nativity signifies the birth of a lascivious person, and that when Mars and Venus both participate in a horoscope, with no regard to the sign, the native will be captious, luxurious, and a fornicator:

Volunt namque astrologi, ut meus asserebat venerabilis Andalo, quod, quando contingat Martem in nativitate alicuius in domo Veneris, in Tauro scilicet vel in Libra reperiri, et significatorem nativitatis esse, pretendere hunc, qui tunc nascitur, futurum luxuriosum, fornicatorem, et venereorum omnium abusivum, et scelestum circa talia hominen. Et ob id a phylosopho quodam, cui nomen fuit Aly, in Commento quadripartiti, dictum est, quod quandocunque in nativitate alicuius Venus una cum Marte participat, habet nascenti concedere dispositionem phylocaptionibus, fornicationibus atque luxuriis aptam.[41]

In the classical story, in the astrological manuals, and in the writings of the mythographers, the story of Mars and Venus is never associated with any sort of true love, never glorified or apologized for but always seen as luxury, fornication, immoderate delight, or simple adultery, and is regularly condemned. In view of the evidence, it is inconceivable that Chaucer could have transformed the story into something positive without running the risk of being very much misunderstood, and the tone of the poem suggests that he made no such attempt. Professor Stillwell has argued that, unlike the author of

---

[41] *Ibid.*, II, 452. There is also an astrological exposition in the excerpts made by Ghisalberti from Bersuire's *Metamorphoses Ouidiana moraliter* . . . : "Vel si vis dic quod aliqui dicunt sensum licteralem phisice. Aiunt quandoque quod Mars et Venus qui sunt duo planete, coniunguntur. Sed quia sol efficitur tunc fervencior, propter Martem, ideo dicitur revelare coniunctionem. Vulcanus autem deus ignis ad hoc currere dicitur quia ardor igneus in aere duplicatur. Venus etiam dicitur tunc adultera s. quando natura sua begnivola per Martis violenciam est mutata." It should be noted that here Venus is affected by Mars, and not otherwise. The commentary continues with an interpretation that is at once more familiar in tone while new in detail: "Istud potest applicari contra ecclesiasticos luxuriosos, quia pro certo sepe fit quod sol i. aliquis doctor vel ecclesiasticus prelatus alicuius mulieris malo amore vexatur, et ibi taliter occupatur, quod illuminare doctrinis et exemplis bonis suis mundum dedignatur . . ." (F. Ghisalberti, " 'L'Ovidius Moralizatus' di Pierre Bersuire," *Studj Romanzi*, XXXIII [1933], 115-16).

the *Ovide moralisé*, "Chaucer does not take love to be a damnable
sin, mere 'luxury' and fornication," but it might be better to say that
Chaucer is not treating of any sort of good "love" at all, and the
relationship he was re-creating was so well known and so commonly
interpreted that he chose to let the characters' actions speak for them-
selves.[42] Of course literary conventions do change, as do astrological
and mythographic traditions, but they do not often do a sudden
about-face, and when they are reversed there are invariably some
signals of the artist's intention.

In Chaucer's England one attitude toward the myth of Mars and
Venus was predominant prior to Chaucer's poem, and there are no
clear-cut indications that Chaucer is striking out in new directions.
To all the evidence thus far cited there can be added yet another
indication that Chaucer and his audience were conditioned to see in
the story of Mars and Venus something derisive. In the one English
literary treatment of the myth (although written in Latin), Walter
Map makes use of the story in his very amusing and very popular
"Dissuasio Valerii ad Ruffinum ne uxorem ducat," which is a work
that Chaucer knew and made use of in the *Wife of Bath's Tale*. Map
is not really against marriage, of course, but rather against lechery,
and the whole work is of a figurative turn, as is indicated by his sum-
mary statement, "I do not wish thee to be the bridegroom of Venus,
but of Pallas." In the "Dissuasio" the story of Venus and Mars is
one of a series showing how the pursuit of women leads to self-
denigration. Map remarks that Jupiter permitted himself to bellow
like a bull for Europa, and that Phoebus came to lack his own light
because of his love for Leucothoe. Then follows the story of Mars
and Venus:

> Then there was Mars, who attained the name of 'God of Battles'
> through the well-known number of victories, in which his ready
> valour stood him greatly in stead. Although he knew no fear for
> himself, he was bound with Venus by Vulcan in chains, invisible, to
> be sure, but tangible—this too amid the mocking applause and the
> derision of the heavenly court. My friend, meditate at least upon
> the chains which thou dost not see and yet already in part feel, and

[42] Stillwell, "Convention and Individuality," p. 75.

snatch thyself away while they are still breakable, lest that lame
and loathsome smith whom 'no god ever honoured at his board
nor goddess with her bed' shall chain thee in his fashion to his
Venus and shall make thee like unto himself, lame and loathsome,
or, what I fear more, shall render thee club-footed; in such wise
that thou canst not have the saving grace of a cloven hoof, but,
bound to Venus, thou wilt become the distress and laughing-stock
of onlookers, while the blind applaud thee and those with sight
threaten.[43]

5. ICONOGRAPHIC TREATMENTS OF
MARS AND VENUS

IF WE GRANT that there was every reason for Chaucer and his audi-
ence to be predisposed to condemn the story of Mars and Venus,
and if we grant that there is little in Chaucer's poem to show a theme
of approbation running counter to the usual attitude, then the prob-
lem remaining is whether or not the audience in fact responded to
the story as their predispositions inclined them. Of course no solid
answer can be given, but there is a hint at least that the reaction to
Chaucer's poem was very much conditioned by the mythographic
interpretations of the story of Mars and Venus. Such little evidence
as there is depends upon an interpretation of the illumination of the
Complaint of Mars in the Fairfax MS (Fig. 14). The manuscript is
dated 1450, so it was done well after the poet's lifetime, but the
mediaeval conventions of mythography and iconography persisted
well into the Renaissance. We have already noted that mythographers
were busy throughout the Middle Ages writing moral interpretations
of the myths. In addition to this it should be noted that the mythog-
raphers often described the appearances and the accompanying para-
phernalia of the gods, so that artists who wished to represent them
could go to the manuals for "rules" of portrayal as well as for an
interpretation of the various actions of the deities in question. A

---

[43] Walter Map, *De nugis curialium*, trans. Frederick Tupper and Marbury
Bladen Ogle (London, 1924), pp. 187-88. For another literary analogue see Peter
Abélard: "But shame gradually disappeared and made us more shameless and it
became less as acts became easier. What the poet tells us of Mars and Venus caught
in the act happened also to us" (J. T. Muckle, *The Story of Abélard's Adversities*
[Toronto, 1954], p. 27).

further complication is that in some (but not all) of the mythographers, the details of portraiture are not merely stated but are also moralized, so that the iconographic representations of the pagan gods become subject to mythographic, moral analysis on the same basis as mediaeval redactions of the myths themselves.

Not all scholars, however, have been persuaded that these moral interpretations are valuable for the study of later mediaeval art, and Professor Seznec has sternly denigrated them. Speaking of Petrarch's *Africa*, for example, which recreates the pictorial details of the pagan gods as described in the third Vatican Mythographer but omits the allegorizations found there, Seznec writes, "Thus Petrarch preserves only those details which have the value of images; as a humanist and man of taste, he disregards what was meant to improve or instruct."[44] That it was necessary in the fourteenth century to disregard that which was meant to improve or instruct in order to qualify as a man of taste, let alone a humanist, is a curious judgment indeed. It would be a shame to deny, say, Boccaccio the title of humanist because in his *Genealogy* he chose to reiterate much of the moral teaching that accompanied the iconography of the pagan gods. Seznec also argues that the excision of moral commentary in an anonymous work of about 1400 called the *Libellus de deorum imaginibus* is an avoidance of "the mythological substance encumbered with the mediaeval glosses," and its virtue is that it "offers us a clear text, determinedly profane and purely iconographical." Yet, another art historian, Panofsky, who has taken a larger view of the general tendency toward this sort of moralization in the latter part of the Middle Ages, has argued that the *Libellus* omits the moralizations merely for the sake of brevity.[45] Moreover, recent scholarship has proven that Chaucer's word-pictures of the gods do not depend upon the unmoralized *Libellus*, as was once thought, but come from Pierre Bersuire's moralized Ovid.[46]

[44] Seznec, *Survival of the Pagan Gods*, p. 174.

[45] *Ibid.*, p. 176; Panofsky, *Studies in Iconology*, p. 23.

[46] Professor Wilkins has argued that two details in Chaucer's descriptions of Venus in the *Knight's Tale* and in the *House of Fame* were definite indications that Chaucer used the unmoralized *Libellus* rather than Bersuire's *Metamorphosis Ovidiana moraliter*. The details are Venus' holding an object in her right hand and her roses being both white and red. However, Professor Steadman has noted that in neither

In spite of the existence of works like the *Africa* and the *Libellus* that do not include the conventional moralizations of the iconographic descriptions of the pagan gods, there is no doubt that more mythographic treaties included rather than omitted them, and they are of considerable interest in an analysis of the illumination of the Fairfax MS. There we see a tri-partite division of the illumination into panels, with Mars on the left, Venus on the right, and (very curiously) Jupiter rather than the sun above. Jupiter is not mentioned in the *Complaint*, nor does he figure in any of the classical stories nor in any known mediaeval redactions, so his inclusion here may be simply a mislabeling, or it may be that he has been substituted for the sun for reasons that will be discussed presently. Mars in the illumination is somewhat different from the Mars that Chaucer described in the *Knight's Tale*.

> The statue of Mars upon a carte stood
> Armed, and looked grym as he were wood;
> And over his heed ther shynen two figures
> Of sterres, that been cleped in scriptures,
> That oon Puella, that oother Rubeus—
> This god of armes was arrayed thus.
> A wolf ther stood biforn hym at his feet
> With eyen rede, and of a man he eet;
> With soutil pencel depeynted was this storie
> In redoutynge of Mars and of his glorie.
>
> (*KnT*, 2041-50)

---

of the Chaucerian descriptions does she hold a conch shell, but the "citole" of the *Knight's Tale* is probably descended from Bersuire's explication of the *conca marina*. Professor Quinn has further noted that the Paris edition of Bersuire indeed specifies the right hand for the object being held, in contrast to the edition Professor Wilkins used, which did not specify which hand held the conch. Panofsky has remarked that the Chaucerian descriptions are at variance with both the *Libellus* and Bersuire in that they describe Mars as standing rather than sitting in his cart. Panofsky has also urged that some allowance be made for poetic inventiveness. On the whole it would seem that the moralized Bersuire is the more likely source for Chaucer's descriptions than the unmoralized *Libellus*. See Ernest H. Wilkins, "Descriptions of the Pagan Divinities from Petrarch to Chaucer," *Speculum*, XXXII (1957), 511-22; John M. Steadman, "Venus' *Citole* in Chaucer's *Knight's Tale* and Berchorius," *Speculum*, XXXIV (1959), 620-24; Betty Nye Quinn, "Venus, Chaucer, and Peter Bersuire," *Speculum*, XXXVIII (1963), 479-82; Panofsky, *Renaissance and Renascences*, p. 78, n. 2.

Lacking in the Fairfax illumination are the grim expression, the figures from geomancy, the cart, and the man being eaten by the wolf. On the other hand, there is a wolf and Mars is armed. Mars does not have the conventional whip but the sword he carries here exists elsewhere in iconographical representations, and his mediaeval armor is expectable enough. The two figures kneeling behind him are difficult to explain. They certainly do not seem to be the shrieking furies that Petrarch mentions, nor can they represent the killing of Remus by Romulus, which the *Libellus* describes and illustrates.[47] It may be that the artist has taken them from the poem itself, which says that lovers ought to complain about Mars' state. The most interesting detail, and one very difficult to explain, is the fact that Mars has one leg armed and the other bare from toe to tunic.

Of these several iconographic attributes only the wolf receives attention from the mythographers. In one sense the wolf is an obvious symbol of violence—he eats a sheep in the *Libellus* and a man in Chaucer's *Knight's Tale*—but according to the third Vatican Mythographer the wolf is said to be associated with Romulus and Remus, the sons of Mars, because of the lechery of the Romans:

> Romulum et Remum ejus fingi filios constat, quia viri fuerunt bellicosi. Nam quod lupa dicuntur alti, fabulosum figmentum est ad celandam avorum Romani generis turpitudinem. Nec incongrue excogitatum est. Nam et meretrices ab obscoenitatis et odoris ac rapacitatis similitudine *lupas* vocamus; unde et *lupanaria* dicimus. Constat hoc animal etiam esse in tutela Martis.[48]

It is also possible that Mars' bare leg is also a sign of lechery. While the evidence is not at all conclusive, it is nevertheless possible to speculate that the artist knew of some convention in which lecherous gentlemen are so depicted. In Titian's two versions of the "Rape of Lucretia," Tarquin has one knee covered and one bare, while in

[47] For a series of pictures of Mars see Seznec, *Survival of the Pagan Gods*, Figs. 74-77. For a collation of iconographic descriptions of Mars see Hans Liebeschutz, *Fulgentius metaforalis* (Leipzig and Berlin, 1926), p. 64. Liebeschutz also includes the anonymous *Libellus de deorum imaginibus* and its illuminations, pp. 117-28.

[48] *Scriptores rerum mythicarum*, p. 235. Boccaccio sees the wolf only as a symbol of rapacity: "Lupus vero ob id illi dicatus est, quia rapax et ingluviosum sit animal, ad insatiabilem voracitatem sequentium castra monstrandam" (*Genealogie deorum*, II, 449).

Michelangelo's figures of David and Bathsheba on the ceiling of the Sistine chapel, David is also depicted with one knee bared. The idea must be advanced very tenuously, of course, but certainly the artist who did the illumination was very conscious of iconographic conventions, and it was presumably no accident that he drew Mars as as he did.[49]

With the figure of Venus we are on much surer ground. She bears a strong resemblance to the Venus described in the *Knight's Tale*:

> The statue of Venus, glorious for to se,
> Was naked, fletynge in the large see,
> And fro the navele doun al covered was
> With wawes grene, and brighte as any glas.
> A citole in hir right hand hadde she,
> And on hir heed, ful semely for to se,
> A rose gerland, fressh and wel smellynge;
> Above hir heed hir dowves flikerynge.
> Biforn hire stood hir sone Cupido;
> Upon his shuldres wynges hadde he two,
> And blynd he was, as it is often seene;
> A bowe he bar and arwes brighte and kene.
>
> (*KnT*, 1955-66)

In addition to the conventional attributes, the artist has included a picture of Vulcan working at his forge, and although Vulcan is not mentioned in Chaucer's poem, the association of Mars and Venus certainly brings him to mind; one writer on mythology, Bernard Silvestris, tells us that when we encounter Venus with Vulcan she should be understood as symbolizing the voluptuousness of the flesh.[50] While neither Vulcan nor the three graces are mentioned in the description of Venus in the *Knight's Tale* or in the *Complaint of Mars*, both may be found in the unmoralized description of Venus in the

---

[49] I am indebted to Professor D. W. Robertson, Jr., for this suggestion. For illustrations see Hans Tietze, *Titian: The Paintings and Drawings* (New York, 1950), Figs. 275 and 276; Charles de Tolnay, *The Sistine Ceiling* (Princeton, 1945), Figs. 167 and 168.

[50] "Ubi ergo invenies Venerem uxorem Vulcani matrem Ioci et Cupidinis, intellige voluptatem carnis, quia naturali calori iuncta est et iocum et cohitum parit" (Bernard Silvestris, *Super sex Eneidos*, p. 10).

Libellus de deorum imaginibus. The graces may also be encountered moralized *in bono* in the third Vatican Mythographer, and *in malo* in Bersuire, while the remaining paraphernalia is moralized by both the third Vatican Mythographer and Boccaccio. The moralizations are very close, and Boccaccio follows the earlier writer without much change. Although moralizations of the peripheral figures are easily found—Cupid, for example, is moralized by both Boccaccio and the third Vatican Mythographer—the moralization of Venus herself and her attributes sums up the situation rather well. In the third Vatican mythographer her appearance, the sea, her doves, roses, and conch shell are all moralized:

Nuda pingitur seu quod crimen libidinis minime celetur, seu quod nudis conveniat, seu quod libido consilium cujuslibet nudet et celari non sinat. Rosae ei adscribuntur. Rosae enim rubent et pungunt; itemque libido ruborem ingerit e pudoris opprobrio, pungitque peccati aculeo. Sicut enim rosa delectat quidem, sed celeri motu temporis tollitur; ita et libido. Columbae ei consecrantur, quod illae aves (ut frequens innuit foetura) maxime in coitu fervidae creduntur. Pingunt eam in mari natantem, quia libido rebus naufragia inferre non dubitetur. Unde Porphyrius in epigrammate: *Nudus, egens, Veneris naufragus in pelago.* Concha etiam marina portari pingitur, quia hoc animal aperto simul toto corpore in coitu misceatur.[51]

[51] *Scriptores rerum mythicarum*, pp. 228-29. Cf. Boccaccio, *Genealogie deorum*, I, 151-52: "Nuda autem ideo pingitur ut ad quid semper parata sit ostendatur. Seu quia nudos qui illam imitantur persepe faciat. Aut quia luxurie crimen et si in longum perseveret occultum, tandem, dum minus arbitrantur obsceni, procedit in publicum, omni palliatione remota, vel potius quia absque nuditate committi non possit. Natantem autem ideo Venerem pingunt, ut infelicium amantium amaritudinibus immixtam vitam procellis agitatam variisque et eorum naufragia crebra demonstrent, unde et Porphyrius in epygrammate dicit: Nudus, egens, Veneris naufragus in pelago. . . . Illi rosas in tutelam datas aiunt, eo quod rubeant atque pungant, quod quidem libidinis proprium esse videtur. Nam turpitudine sceleris erubescimus et conscentia peccati vexamur aculeo, et sicut per tempusculum rosa delectat, parvoque lapsu temporis marcet, sic et libido parve brevisque delectationis et longe penitentie causa est, cum in brevi decidat quod delectat, et quod officit vexet in longum. Marinam concam manibus gestat, ut per eam Veneris ostendatur illecebra toto enim adaperto corpore, refert Juba, conca miscetur in coitum."

Both Venus and Mars, then, are depicted with attributes that may indicate libidinous tendencies—Mars possibly so, and Venus very definitely so. In a consideration of the picture as a whole this makes good sense, for the two deities are waving to one another, much as Mercury "salueth" Venus in the poem (146), and above Venus' head Cupid is aiming his arrow at Mars. Even without recourse to the iconographic interpretations, the picture is obviously a representation of Mars and Venus, the characters in the poem, greeting one another. What the iconographic interpretations do is remind us that the two pagan gods have the most dishonorable intentions toward one another.

The figure of Jupiter overhead is puzzling, since he does not appear in the poem or in any known version of the story. His hand, however, extended outward and down, seems to be in a gesture of rebuke. That Jupiter as king of the pagan gods should be the one to rebuke those who were upsetting the domestic life of Olympus is a natural enough interpretation, and the extension to the Christian world is also straightforward. Jupiter was very frequently likened to the Christian God, for obvious reasons, and was frequently used as a symbol for God or Christ as in Dante's *Purgatorio* VI, 118. By the same token, the sun was likened to God by Dante and by many other writers, so it is difficult to understand why the illustrator chose to substitute Jupiter for the sun, which was already present in the poem as the discoverer of the lovers. It may be that the fiery figure behind Jupiter represents the sun, but this still does not explain the presence of Jupiter. Certainly there would be nothing untoward in showing Jupiter or the sun as God rebuking the adulterous pair, for as Chaucer's Parson is at some pains to spell out, lechery more than other sins is particularly offensive to God, and he has often punished it:

God woot, this synne is ful displesaunt thyng to God; for he seyde hymself, "Do no lecherie." And therfor he putte grete peynes agayns this synne in the olde lawe. . . . Forther over, by the synne of lecherie God dreynte al the world at the diluge. And after that he brente fyve citees with thonder-leyt, and sank hem into helle.

(*ParsT*, 837-39)

Another way of approaching the interpretation of the illumination of the *Complaint of Mars* is through a comparison of it with other renditions of the same theme. Several of these exist from a period contemporary with or shortly after the mid-fifteenth century illumination in the Fairfax MS, and we may also examine the eighteenth-century version by Boucher. This rendition (Fig. 15) is included here because of its complete dissimilarity from the earlier versions. Here, for the benefit of some critics of Chaucer, we in fact find a glorification of illicit love, with the discovery and not the adultery seeming to carry the burden of reproof. Where Jupiter rebuked the lovers from above in the Fairfax illumination, now several *putti* gracefully pull back the silken veil.

As we have already noted, Professor Wind has demonstrated that Botticelli's "Mars and Venus" (Fig. 16) is in fact a representation of the theme of *discordia concors*, and it is worth noting some of the differences between this painting and the Fairfax illumination. In Botticelli the clothing of the figures is reversed and Mars is nearly nude, while his armor is stripped from him and has become the plaything of some *putti*. Venus is dressed, and her clothing is very similar to that which she wears in Botticelli's "Primavera," wherein Professor Gombrich has argued she represents *Humanitas*.[52] Mars' stupor is, of course, to be contrasted to Venus' wakefulness, and both, in turn, may be contrasted with the greeting of the two gods in the Fairfax illumination. Botticelli's painting also shows a swarm of wasps in the conch shell held by one of the *putti*, who vainly tries to wake Mars, which Gombrich has suggested is a punning reference to the Vespucci family, by whom the painting may have been commissioned. All in all, the great difference in theme between these pictures, which are not far apart temporally, is echoed in the treatment of the subject matter.

The "Mars and Venus" of Piero di Cosimo (Fig. 17) dates from the closing years of the fifteenth century, not long after the Botticelli version, and indeed it has been argued that it was commissioned as a pendant to it.[53] While Professor Wind has merely lumped it in with

[52] Gombrich, "Botticelli's Mythologies," pp. 18-19.
[53] R. Langton Douglas, *Piero di Cosimo* (Chicago, 1946), pp. 54-59.

the Botticelli version of the theme, Professor Panofsky has noted that Piero has changed the starkly allegorical treatment to a pastoral one, and there are other interesting differences as well.[54] The most noticeable difference is that Venus is accompanied by a child and a rabbit; this symbol and fruit of *Venus genetrix* combine to suggest that the picture is meant to symbolize wedded love. Venus' traditional doves also put in an appearance here, but they are transformed from the earlier doves that fluttered around Venus' head into a pair of billing and, presumably, cooing turtle doves, located between the two lovers.

A far more difficult picture to analyze than either of these is the representation of Mars and Venus in the Taurus panel of the fresco cycle at the Palazzo Schifanoia in Ferrara (Fig. 18a). Professor Wind has arbitrarily called this another illustration of *discordia concors*, while Seznec says the fresco shows the "conversion of an antique fable into a romance of chivalry."[55] There are, however, elements in the painting which suggest that it is nearer in meaning to the Fairfax illumination than to the works of Botticelli and Piero di Cosimo, even though its date and provenience are somewhere in between: it is Italian but not Florentine, and dates from about 1470. Perhaps the major difference is that while Venus is dressed, as she is in the two Neoplatonic paintings just discussed, Mars is not nude, nor is he asleep, nor is his armor lying unused. Rather Mars is dressed in his armor, and instead of lying peacefully opposite Venus, he is chained to her shell-chair. Thus, while the fresco shows Mars and Venus above the astrological sign Taurus, wherein Venus is powerful and Mars weak, the theme seems to be less *discordia concors* than Venus' placing the "bridle" on a man. Mars is not pacified, but humiliated. Moreover, while there is no precedent for a chain binding Mars to Venus in Ficino's allegorization of the myth, the mythographers, drawing on the wicked chain of delight in Boethius (Bk. III, m. 10), made much of the chains of fervor and evil habits that bound the lecherous. Moreover, Walter Map urged Ruffinus to "meditate

[54] Panofsky, *Studies in Iconology*, p. 63, n. 77.

[55] Seznec, *Survival of the Pagan Gods*, p. 206. For an analysis of the entire fresco cycle see Aby Warburg, "Italienische Kunst und Internationale Astrologie im Palazzo Schifanoia zu Ferrara," *Gesammelte Schriften* (Leipzig, 1932), II, 459-81. Identification of details here follows Paolo d'Ancona, *The Schifanoia Months at Ferrara* (Milan, 1954), pp. 35-37.

at least upon the chains which thou dost not see and yet already in part feel."

Venus is perhaps depicted in a shell (the detail is not clear) rather than holding one as in the Fairfax illumination, but this is not to be judged one way or another, for Botticelli adapted the shell to his "Birth of Venus," another Neoplatonic allegory. On the other hand, she definitely retains some of the other imagery that Botticelli and Piero deleted: she is crowned with roses (both white and red as specified in the *Libellus*); there are doves over her head; Cupid is painted on her girdle; the graces are present in the picture. The swans drawing the boat are an addition to the story and were thought by Warburg to be related to the swan of Lohengrin in *Parsifal*. A more likely derivation, however, is from one of the commentaries on Jove's disguise as a swan in the rape of Leda. Boccaccio, for example, said that the swan was a great singer, and song was one of the "hooks" of Venus.[56] More provocative still is the apple she holds in one hand—the ultimate symbol of *virtus conrupta libidine*—and the flower she holds in the other—perhaps symbolizing the *flos faeni* of 1 Peter 1:24. When we study the "children" of the planet on either side of the swan-boat we see that we are, in fact, dealing with lechery rather than *discordia concors*, or what Seznec chose to call "chivalry." On the right hand side, for example, a young man is rather indelicately approaching a young girl, using a technique favored by Nicholas in the *Miller's Tale*, and now known to be a conventional iconographic motif for lechery.[57] (Fig. 18b)

As in Piero di Cosimo's version of the subject, there are rabbits in this picture, but, unlike Piero's rabbits, these are not associated with children. These rabbits seem rather to be linked with the activities of the lecherous young man on the right hand side of the picture; indeed, rabbits were commonly associated with lechery in the later Middle Ages. As Professor Abraham has demonstrated, the Latin *cunnus* became Old French *con* and then with an "endearing diminutive" *conin*, while Latin *cuniculus* became first *conil* and then *conin*. Many literary puns inevitably followed, and the motif of the rabbit hunt became a popular iconographic theme. Abraham refers to

[56] Boccaccio, *Genealogie deorum*, II, 547.
[57] See Robertson, *Preface*, p. 193, and his Figs. 5, 18, and 59.

several instances of paintings on valves of the first half of the four-teenth century that show hounds chasing rabbits while gentlemen engage in chin-chucking ladies.[58] Rabbits were also sometimes asso-ciated with the Virgin because it was thought that they could give birth parthenogenetically (modern biology bears this out), and they were sometimes associated with the sixth sign of the zodiac through a confusion between Libra and the French *lièvre* ("hare") or Spanish *liebra*.[59] However, the meaning of an iconographic motif is best judged by the context in which it appears, and here the rabbits cer-tainly must echo the love-making that goes on throughout the up-per band of the fresco.

The rabbits and the lecherous gesture are in accord with the lutes held by the young ladies surrounding the couple on the right. These lutes are first cousins to the *citole* held by Venus in Chaucer's *Knight's Tale* (1959), which Mr. Steadman has seen as descended from the moralization of Venus' *conca marina* in Bersuire's *Metamorphosis Ouidiana moraliter.* . . .[60] Bersuire had thought the conch was pri-marily a musical instrument, and consequently related it to the *cithara* of the *meretrix* in Isaiah 23:16. Steadman believes that Chau-cer's attribution of a *citole* to Venus is prompted by this exposition. Although Steadman is probably right about this, it is worth noting that *citole* in Middle English means dulcimer or zither, while Bersuire's *cithara* means lute.[61] The instruments held by the ladies in the Schifanoia fresco are clearly lutes with their characteristic crooked necks, and because of their association with other venereal activities in the picture, they may very well be descended from the *cithara* of Isaiah, via some mythographer—in all probability Bersuire.

[58] Claude K. Abraham, "Myth and Symbol: The Rabbit in Medieval France," *SP*, LX (1963), 589-97. See also Robertson, *Preface*, p. 113 and n. 107; as well as his Figs. 23-28, 35, 61, 64, and 110.

[59] Seznec, *Survival of the Pagan Gods*, p. 182; Wind, *Pagan Mysteries*, p. 127; Abraham, "Myth and Symbol," p. 596.

[60] Steadman, "Venus' Citole," p. 620.

[61] *Middle English Dictionary*, ed. Hans Kurath, et al. (Ann Arbor, 1956-), s.v. "citole." Panofsky translates *citole* as "little lyre" (*Renaissance and Renascences*, p. 78, n. 2). Though Chaucer may have transformed the kind of instrument in-volved here, there is no doubt that Bersuire's *cithara* is a more proximate source than the unmoralized *conca marina* of the *Libellus*.

In sum, the judgment of Wind and Seznec about the Schifanoia fresco of Taurus is probably wide of the mark, and it should be emphasized that while the renditions of Mars and Venus by Botticelli, Piero di Cosimo, and Veronese can be traced to certain Neoplatonic allegories for their inspiration, the Schifanoia frescoes have not been so related. Indeed, elsewhere in the same fresco series, on the fresco for Libra, the upper band shows what has been identified as the "Triumph of Lust," while elsewhere in the same panel Mars and Venus are discovered in bed. It would perhaps be unlikely that two completely different interpretations of the Mars and Venus story would occur in the same cycle.[62]

6. THE PROEM TO THE *COMPLAINT*

ALL THIS IS but *prologomena* to the poem itself, but useful in establishing the probable tone of the poem insofar as Chaucer would have received it from his sources, and insofar as his audience would have been prepared to respond to it. In short, although the astrological power of Venus to temper Mars was well known in the Middle Ages, it was not made a positive virtue very often, and never figured in interpretations of the story of the adultery of Mars and Venus except, as in the *Complaint of Mars*, when exaggerated for humorous effect. Thus we can expect the *Complaint of Mars* to be a poem showing the penalties of the wrong kind of loving, and so it is. Professor Stillwell has said that if the lovers addressed at the outset follow the advice given them in the Proem they are "heading straight for woe," but this is only partially right, for the "woe" involved comes about only if one imitates Mars and Venus, while the lovers addressed in the Proem are given more latitude than that.[63]

The *Complaint of Mars* is a Valentine's Day poem. In order to understand what this implies it is necessary to observe that in Chaucer's other Valentine poem, the *Parlement of Foules*, the condition of lecherous folk who are condemned to "whirl around the earth, always in pain" leads us to the theme of the poem: the futility of earthly love. As Professors Robertson and Huppé say, this theme is suggested in the opening of the poem and is in full concord with

[62] D'Ancona, *The Schifanoia Frescoes*, p. 78.
[63] Stillwell, "Convention and Individuality," p. 72.

the mediaeval concept of St. Valentine, who was seen as one who illustrated in his personal life the marriage of the soul to Christ.[64] Chaucer introduces the whole subject in a rather devious way, having some dozen lines of Proem before revealing that he has been recounting the words of a bird that sang on St. Valentine's Day: "Seynt Valentyne, a foul thus herde I synge / Upon thy day, er sonne gan up-sprynge (13-14)."

What the little bird sang is ambiguous until we realize that we are involved with a Valentine poem. In retrospect, the ideas are clear enough. The bird tells lovers (birds) to rejoice, but warns those who "lye in any drede" to flee lest the rising sun discover them:

> Gladeth, ye foules, of the morowe gray!
> Lo! Venus, rysen among yon rowes rede!
> And floures fressh, honoureth ye this day;
> For when the sunne uprist, then wol ye sprede.
> But ye lovers, that lye in any drede,
> Fleeth, lest wikked tonges yow espye!
> Lo! yond the sunne, the candel of jelosye! (1-7)

That there are two kinds of love involved here is at once obvious, but at first glance we seem to be dealing with lovers like the birds who have nothing to fear and lovers who are in danger of discovery by gossips. A casual reading might thus incline us to think that Chaucer is implying that the only "drede" there is in love is the dread of discovery by neighborhood gossips, but "wikked tonges" are not to be interpreted as a Chaucerian condemnation of spoilsports. Rather, these types are literary descendants of Wikked Tonge in the *Romance of the Rose*, who is a good character, not a bad one— being, with Daunger and Shame, a guardian of the rosebush at the request of Chastity. Wicked Tongue, then, is the proper enemy of lechery and is "wicked" only to the lecherous. The lovers who lie

[64] Bernard F. Huppé and D. W. Robertson, Jr., *Fruyt and Chaf* (Princeton, 1963), pp. 101-108 and 123. In the *Legend of Good Women* the small birds defy the fowler and praise St. Valentine, and immediately the God of Love appears with Alceste, who taught "of fyn lovynge, / And namely of wifhod the lyvynge" (*LGW*, [G] 534-35). Thus St. Valentine is regularly linked with wedded love, good love, etc. For a detailed interpretation of the function of St. Valentine in the *Legend*, see B. G. Koonce, "Satan the Fowler," *Medieval Studies*, XXI (1959), 176-84.

in dread are not only in danger of discovery, but are in danger because of improper love. This explains why the sun is called the "candel of jelosye" in line 7, and is later referred to as "jelous Phebus" (140). There is nothing in either Chaucer's story or its antecedents to suggest that the sun has anything to be jealous about, or is in fact jealous; but there is a parallel with the jealous god of the Bible, who is jealous in that he does not wish other "gods" to be preferred before him. Fornication is just such a form of "idolatry," and Chaucer's Parson observes that Holy Matrimony is one of the remedies of lechery. Of course, virginity and continence are to be chosen even above marriage. The first stanza of the Proem, then, advises the lecherous that they should abandon one kind of love for another, marriage or spiritual love—one that does not need to hide from the sun. Venus, of course, stands as symbol for all these loves. It should also be noted that it is the sun's daily course that threatens the lovers in the Proem, while in the main part of the poem it is the sun's annual motion through the zodiac that routs the lovers. Thus, the opening imagery gives us a kind of daily re-enactment of the action of the main part of the poem, broadening its significance and giving it a more emphatic universality: any lesser love should be changed for a better on any day of the year.

The next stanza urges these lovers who are in dread to leave their loves but not to sorrow overmuch, for their sorrows will cease. Then follows the seemingly illogical statement that a glad night is worth a sad morning after:

> Wyth teres blewe, and with a wounded herte,
> Taketh your leve; and with seint John to borowe,
> Apeseth sumwhat of your sorowes smerte.
> Tyme cometh eft that cese shal your sorowe:
> The glade nyght ys worth an hevy morowe! (8-12)

If the glad night is really worth the price of a sad departure the next morning, then why should the speaker-bird tell the lovers who are "in dread" that they should not mourn because they will be happier *soon?* If the glad night is really worth the sad morning, they should be happy *now.* A better reading is to see the phrase "ys worth" as meaning "has become," as it does elsewhere in Chaucer's

poetry.[65] The message with that reading becomes "the glad night has become a sad morning, but do not despair, things will improve after you leave your love." This interpretation accords well with the speaker-bird's oath by St. John "for a surety," for Chaucer's Parson employs St. John in an admonishment against adultery, and his name was commonly invoked in vows of celibacy![66] The message to the lovers, then, is that they should abandon this kind of love for one more favored by St. John, and that if they do their sorrows will cease. This, in turn, is a commonplace in mediaeval thought, and it is not necessary to go any further than the *Romance of the Rose* to find Reason telling the Lover exactly the same thing: if you want to be happy, flee this kind of love:

> For I ne preise that lovyng
> Wherthurgh men, at the laste eendyng,
> Shall calle hem wrecchis full of woo,
> Love greveth hem and shendith soo.
> But if thou wolt wel Love eschewe,
> For to escape out of his mewe,
> And make al hool thi sorwe to slake,
> No bettir counsel maist thou take
> Than thynke to fleen wel, iwis;
> May nought helpe elles, for wite thou this,
> If thou fle it, it shal flee thee;
> Folowe it, and folowen shal it thee.
> (*RofR*, 4773-84)

In the next stanza the speaker-bird leaves off addressing only the lovers that lie in dread, and speaks to everyone, telling them to awake; to choose their mates (not sweethearts), if they have not already done so; and if they have chosen (if they are married in the world or figuratively married to God), to make good use of St. Valentine's Day for renewing their vows of love:

[65] Cf. "And in this world no lyves creature / Withouten love is worth, or may endure" (*T&C*, III, 13-14).

[66] *Parson's Tale*, 841. J. Burrow, *A Reading of Sir Gawain and the Green Knight* (London, 1965), p. 101, n. 35.

> Yet sang this foul—I rede yow al awake,
> And ye that han not chosen in humble wyse,
> Without repentynge cheseth yow your make;
> And ye that han ful chosen as I devise,
> Yet at the leste renoveleth your servyse;
> Confermeth hyt perpetuely to dure,
> And paciently taketh your aventure. (15-21)

The coupling of an injunction to awaken with an exhortation to choose one's mate or to renew one's vows of love is quite possibly modelled on a passage in St. Paul that begins by urging people to awake, proceeds with an exhortation to put off the works of darkness and put on the armor of light, and finishes with an injunction to put on Christ and make no provision for the concupiscence of the flesh. The passage is forceful enough to be recognizable on its own merits, but it is worth noting that the last sentence is the key passage in the conversion of St. Augustine, as described in his *Confessions*:

> Et hoc scientes tempus: quia hora est iam nos de somno surgere. Nunc enim propior est nostra salus, quam cum credidimus. Nox praecessit, dies autem appropinquavit. Abiiciamus ergo opera tenebrarum, et induamur arma lucis. Sicut in die honeste ambulemus: non in comessationibus, et ebrietatibus, non in cubilibus, et impudicitiis, non in contentione et aemulatione: sed induimini Dominum Iesum Christum, et carnis curam ne feceritis in desideriis. (Romans 13: 11-14)

If, in fact, Chaucer hoped to rouse echoes of this passage in the minds of his audience, then the import of this stanza of the *Complaint* would be that everyone should awake to the approaching day of judgment (this "day" is associated with the "sol iustitiae" in the *Glossa ordinaria*), that those who are awaking from a "night" of sin should put off sin and choose a new "mate," while those who have already chosen a spouse or made a spiritual decision (or both) should renew those vows.[67] This leads directly into the last stanza of the Proem, in which Chaucer takes off his mask of speaker-bird and says

[67] *Glossa ordinaria*, PL, 114, col. 414.

145

that he will "in my briddes wise" sing the "sentence" of the story of Mars and Venus. The "sentence" is plain enough: Mars binds himself to Venus and suffers both her loss and the sun's punishment ("So feble wax he for *hete* and for his *wo.* . . ."), while Venus suffers through entering an astrological "cave" that is like "helle" and then goes off in fickle fashion with Mercury. Clearly the "sentence" here is the same as that adduced by Walter Map in his dissuasion of Ruffinus: do not marry Venus; marry Pallas. All in all, this is both appropriate advice for St. Valentine's Day and just about what the audience would expect from a redaction of the Mars and Venus story.

7. THE ASTROLOGICAL SECTION OF THE POEM

PERHAPS the most difficult feature of the actual astrological reworking of the Mars and Venus myth is the business about Venus' bridling Mars, but this has already been discussed above and its exaggerated humor pointed out. In this middle section of the poem there are, however, some more astrological difficulties to be ironed out, and there are a few non-astrological passages that call for explication. The astrological situation in general is not too complicated. Mars and Venus have been in some aspect with regard to each other—we do not know whether in triune, quartile or sextile—and subsequently they will join in conjunction in the next "palace" of Venus, which we later discover is Taurus, rather than Libra, because the date is in April:

> Thus be they knyt, and regnen as in hevene
> Be lokyng moost; til hyt fil, on a tyde,
> That by her bothe assent was set a stevene,
> That Mars shal entre, as fast as he may glyde,
> Into hir nexte paleys, and ther abyde,
> Walkynge hys cours, til she had him atake,
> And he preide her to haste her for his sake. (50-56)

The planet Mars, then, is to be thought of as "ahead" of Venus in their course through the zodiac; also, both planets are moving directly and are not in retrograde. Chaucer next notes that Venus travels about twice as fast as Mars in their mean annual motion, which is a fact and has to be taken into consideration by a poet trying

to work out a plan for having the two planets be first apart, then in conjunction, and then apart again with no immediate prospects for Mars to catch up with Venus. "Wherfore she sped her as faste in her weye / Almost in oo day as he dyde in tweye" (69-70). The next astrological phenomenon is the conjunction itself, which is described by Chaucer in purely non-astrological terms, with the succinct remark, "Ther is no more, but unto bed thei go" (73). This is not as astonishing a metaphor for a conjunction as one might think, for the common verb used to describe conjunction in the astrological manuals is *copulare*.

Chaucer now digresses to a more elaborate description of the place of the conjunction. Although we eventually find out that it has to be Taurus, we do not know in what subdivision within the sign the conjunction takes place. At the same time that Chaucer describes this "chambre" within the "paleys" he tells us that the sun in its annual course through the zodiac has entered the "paleys" of Taurus too:

> Sojourned hath this Mars, of which I rede,
> In chambre amyd the paleys prively
> A certeyn tyme, til him fel a drede,
> Throgh Phebus, that was comen hastely
> Within the paleys yates sturdely,
> With torche in honde, of which the stremes bryghte
> On Venus chambre knokkeden ful lyghte.
>
> The chambre, ther as ley this fresshe quene,
> Depeynted was with white boles grete. (78-86)

Manly has made the only serious attempt to determine the identity and the location of this "chambre" and his arguments deserve to be quoted in full:

> I cannot find that chamber was ever an established technical name for any of the subdivisions of the sign as house. . . . If we examine all the subdivisions of Taurus, as given by Johannes Hispalensis, chapter ii, we shall find that Venus has a term, consisting of degrees 1-8, a decanate, consisting of degrees 1-10, a novene, $13\frac{1}{3}°$ — $16\frac{2}{3}°$, and three dodecatemoria, 1-$2\frac{1}{2}°$, $17\frac{1}{2}$-$20°$, and 25-$27\frac{1}{2}°$. That the second dodecatemorion is indicated here, is perhaps little

better than a guess. Some confirmation of the guess I once thought might be derived from the fact that upon the chamber of Venus the rays of the Sun are said to strike lightly as he enters the palace gate. According to Wilson and Heydon, a planet is under the Sun's beams when within seventeen degrees of that luminary. . . . That this chamber, whatever it may be, should be decorated with paintings of bulls, is not strange; but, inasmuch as the colors of Taurus are red and citron, it may seem strange that the bulls should be white. White, however, is one of the colors signified by Venus.[68]

Manly's idea that the chamber must be located somewhere near the middle of the sign because of the sun's distance from it is probably correct, but the suggestion that it is the second dodecatemorion is perhaps open to question because of the infrequent reference to these subdivisions by the astrologers. A way out of this difficulty may be found if we do not insist that the chamber be thought of as belonging to Venus, which Manly never questions. It is true that Chaucer once refers to it as "Venus chambre," but he may merely have meant that it was the chamber that Venus was in at the moment and not that it was astrologically associated with her, and Chaucer's other two references to the chamber do not specify that it is Venus'. If we look for a terminus or decan near the center of the sign Taurus that is somehow identifiable, we might try to link it with Jupiter rather than Venus on the grounds of the white bulls on the chamber walls. Manly noted that these were not really to be expected in a chamber of Venus, but the white bull was regularly associated with Jupiter in his guise as abductor of Europa, and this incident was the origin of the sign Taurus.[69] Chaucer elsewhere uses the white bull to refer to Taurus itself (*T&C*, ii, 53-56), but there is nothing to prevent him from using it here to characterize a subdivision of Taurus associated with Jupiter. Moreover, such a subdivision can be found in at least some astrological manuals.

[68] Manly, "Date and Interpretation," pp. 117-18.

[69] "Agenor, rex Lydiae, qui et in Tyro et Sidone regnavit, filiam habuit mirificae formae, nomine Europam, quam Juppiter in specie candidi tauri rapuit. Unde postea in signum honoris taurus translatus est in caelum, et ex eo factum signum quod dicitur Taurus" (*Scriptores rerum mythicarum*, p. 253).

While the details of the subdivisions called "termini" do not always agree, Albumasar's very popular *Introductorium* mentions a terminus of Jupiter in the center of Taurus, extending from the sixteenth to the twenty-fourth degree. In Figure 19 we see a terminus of Jupiter in a manuscript of Firmicus Maternus, extending from approximately the twelfth to the twenty-second degree.[70] (To find the terminus in the illustration, first find Taurus at 8:00 o'clock, then look at the subdivisions in the outer ring.) Chaucer probably wanted the conjunction to occur somewhere near the center of the sign, and thus called attention to the subdivision of Jupiter located there, not in order to emphasize the importance of Jupiter or the astrological significance of this particular terminus, but simply because his other concerns demanded this location. Chaucer was concerned to show Mars being left behind Venus in their courses through the zodiac and to show the sun overtaking him. In that way could Chaucer say ". . . ys *double* thy penaunce" (109). Double in that Mars is deprived of Venus and is "burned" by the sun: "So feble he wex, for hete and for his wo, / That nygh he swelte . . ." (127-28). In order for all this to work out, the mean motions of the planets must be taken into account. The sun moves through the zodiac at the rate of one degree per day, and Venus travels at about the same speed, while Mars moves only half as fast. Thus if Mars and Venus are to be alone in Taurus before the sun arrives there, and if Venus must travel to the next sign while the sun gets ever closer to Mars who remains in the sign of Taurus, a central location for the conjunction is neatest. Although it would be possible to arrange the conjunction elsewhere within the sign and still have Venus reach Gemini while Mars was close to the sun, it would mean abandoning the nice conceit that the sun reaches the "palace" while the lovers are within.

The remaining astrological cruxes involve the destination of Venus and its meaning for the poem. After leaving Mars, Venus is said to proceed to Cyllenius' (i.e., Mercury's) "tower," and once she is there, she is said to flee into a "cave" that stands two degrees within the "gates" of the sign.

[70] Albumasar, *Introductorium*, sig. d₉ᵛ.

Now fleeth Venus unto Cilenios tour,
With voide cours, for fere of Phebus lyght.
Alas! and ther ne hath she no socour,
For she ne found ne saugh no maner wyght;
And eke as ther she hath but litil myght;
Wherfor, herselven for to hyde and save,
Within the gate she fledde into a cave.

Derk was this cave, and smokyng as the helle;
Not but two pas within the yate hit stod.

(113-121)

Since the next sign after Taurus, Gemini, is Mercury's house or "palace," (the word Chaucer uses to describe Taurus when he calls it Venus' palace), the phrase "Cilenios tour" might be just a synonym for "Mercury's palace," but several scholars have felt that a tower is really a part of a palace, and is thus a more likely name for one of the subdivisions of the signs.[71] A study of iconographic representations of the signs of the zodiac shows that in fact either interpretation is possible, but the equation of tower with palace is more likely. Figure 20 shows the decans of Scorpio as a series of peaked attic dormers on an astrological "house," and it is possible that some such representation as this prompted Chaucer to refer to the first terminus (not decan) of Gemini, which belongs to Mercury, as his tower. Some very definite towers, however, may be found in Figure 21, where Saturn, Jupiter, Mars, and the Sun are shown in crenelated towers representing their astrological palaces, each palace having two towers representing the two signs of the zodiac, except for the sun which has only one. The vexing phrase, then, means no more than that Venus fled to Mercury's palace, i.e., Gemini.

It should be emphasized that once in Gemini Venus is not well off. Chaucer notes that she has no "socour" there, and she remains frightened and tries to hide herself in a "cave." Skeat long ago noted that this is a translation of the astrological term *puteus* and that one is to be found in the second degree of Gemini.[72] Although Venus' aim is to improve her situation, the *puteus* she enters is dark and smokes

[71] Robinson's note to line 113 has a summary of opinions.
[72] Skeat, *Works*, I, 499.

like hell, so presumably she, like Mars, is suffering after the love affair. In fact, it may be argued that Chaucer is here meting out appropriate justice to his characters by having the astrologically described affair now receive astrologically described punishment. Mars is clearly in a very bad way in his closeness to the sun, being technically in the state called "combust," and we remember that Troilus hoped that in his nativity Venus had not been "combust" or "let," both unfavorable positions. Now Venus enters a sign that is not fortunate for her, and within it she enters a *puteus*, which the illuminations of the astrological manuals inform us was a kind of devil's cauldron or hellmouth. Figure 22 shows us a *puteus* surrounded by grotesque, inimical figures, and possessing a tusked, wicked-looking mouth. One figure on the lower right holds a bellows, indicating that the *puteus* is a place of astrological heat. At the bottom of Figure 23 we see a *puteus* as a kind of cauldron, again attended by hostile grotesques, and both of these representations may be compared with a more or less typical hellmouth from the *Hours of Catherine of Cleves* in Figure 24. All in all, a most unpleasant place for a planet to be.

This poem, however, is to be a complaint of Mars rather than a complaint of Venus, and Chaucer does not leave Venus in her place of punishment for too long, but shows her breaking her vow to love Mars forever by taking up with the lord of the zodiacal house she is in, Mercury.

> But, as God wolde, hyt happed for to be,
> That, while that Venus weping made her mone,
> Cilenius, rydinge in his chevache,
> Fro Venus valaunse myghte his paleys se,
> And Venus he salueth and doth chere,
> And her receyveth as his frend ful dere. (142-47)

We may assume, then, that another conjunction is in the offing, and the mythological background is no more savory for this one than it was for that of Mars and Venus. The adultery of Mercury and Venus gave birth to Hermaphrodite in classical mythology, and to the mediaeval glossators this suggested that Mercury or eloquence, whom Sophia did not want to marry, was not sufficiently concerned with

wisdom and was too much concerned with exterior ornament.[73] In other words, just as Venus' seduction of Mars represented *virtus conrupta libidine*, so the affair with Mercury was emblematic of the sacrifice of wisdom to "lasciviousness of word." In effect both principals are punished for their actions, but to underscore the evanescence of this kind of love Chaucer shows Venus "saved" by Mercury.

This middle section of the poem has some noteworthy passages in addition to the astrological cruxes just discussed. The first of these follows the initial statement about Mars' subjection by Venus and shows to what extent Mars' rational powers have been compromised by his passion for Venus. He observes that the zodiacal sign in which the assignation is scheduled to take place is unfortunate for him, indeed possibly fatal, but the beauty of Venus makes him contemptuous of death:

> Then seyde he thus: "Myn hertes lady swete,
> Ye knowe wel my myschef in that place;
> For sikerly, til that I with yow mete,
> My lyf stant ther in aventure and grace;
> But when I se the beaute of your face,
> Ther ys no drede of deth may do me smerte,
> For al your lust is ese to myn herte." (57-63)

Mars here sounds much like the hero of a mediaeval romance expressing lofty sentiments, but it is possible that the contempt of death is meant to undercut Mars. Chaucer uses the exact same phrasing in *The Canterbury Tales* to describe the emotions of another *miles amoris*, Chauntecleer, whose infatuation with the beauty of his lady's face is elaborated with a hilarious apostrophe to her red eyes and is concluded with the famous mistranslation of *mulier est hominis confusio*. As Mars has knowledge of his danger in Taurus but disregards it because of the beauty of his lady's face, so Chauntecleer successfully

---

[73] "Juxta deliramentum fabularum [Mercurius] adhuc adolescentulus cum Venere fertur concubuisse, et Hermaphroditum, a suo et Veneris nomine nomen habentem, genuisse. . . . Hermaphroditus autem significat quandam sermonis lascivitatem, quia plerumque, neglecta veritatis ratione, superfluus sermonis ornatus requiritur. Hinc est, quod Sophiam legimus Mercurio nubere noluisse. Licet enim sermo magnum sit rationalis creaturae ornamentum, sapientia tamen superfluum verborum ornatum respuit . . ." (*Scriptores rerum mythicarum*, p. 214).

refutes Pertelote's analysis of his dream but immediately dismisses
the forthcoming "adversitee" from his mind because of Pertelote's
beauty. Both characters are portrayed first using their reason and
then abusing it because of feminine attractiveness.

> Now let us speke of myrthe, and stynte al this.
> Madame Pertelote, so have I blis,
> Of o thyng God hath sent me large grace;
> For whan I se the beautee of youre face,
> Ye been so scarlet reed aboute youre yen,
> It maketh al my drede for to dyen;
> For al so siker as *In principio,*
> *Mulier est hominis confusio,*—
> Madame, the sentence of this Latyn is,
> 'Womman is mannes joye and al his blis.'
> (*NPT,* 3157-66)

Another passage that deserves further explication is the description
of the conjunction of Mars and Venus in non-astrological terms:

> This worthi Mars, that is of knyghthod welle,
> The flour of feyrnesse lappeth in his armes,
> And Venus kysseth Mars, the god of armes. (75-77)

By itself this description would seem to be nothing more than a
momentary straying outside the bounds of the basic astrological meta-
phor—the kind of thing that Chaucer does elsewhere in the poem
when he says that Mars' armor makes it difficult for him to walk
over land. However, when considered along with the fact that Mars
and Venus are elsewhere said to begin their relationship by being in
astrological aspect ("Be lokyng moost"), the lines describing the
embrace may be seen as part of a traditional way of describing the
progression of lechery, which graduates from looking to touching,
from touching to talking, thence to kissing, and at last to the deed it-
self. Chaucer's Parson gives a representative exposition of these phe-
nomena, conceiving of them as the five fingers of lechery that grip a
man by the reins (Mars has been bridled by Venus) and throw him
into hell:

The firste fynger is the fool lookynge of the fool womman and of the fool man. . . . The seconde fynger is the vileyns touchynge in wikkede manere. . . . The thridde is foule wordes, that fareth lyk fyr. . . . The fourthe fynger is the kissynge; and trewely he were a greet fool that wolde kisse the mouth of a brennynge oven or of a fourneys. . . . The fifthe fynger of the develes hand is the stynkynge dede of Leccherie.[74] (*ParsT*, 853-62)

The only part of the process left out in the *Complaint* is the "foule wordes," but they may be present too, since "foule wordes" have the goal of lechery and are not necessarily offensive to the ear. In the *Ayenbite of Inwit* each of the five steps is said to be "foul." Thus Mars' and Venus' exchange of vows and their appointment of a place of assignation might correspond to the "foule wordes." While it is not possible to be certain of an echo of the five steps of lechery in the poem, especially since the exact order is not maintained, certainly there is a good chance that Chaucer had this in mind, and it would be harmonious with his other devices in the poem.

8. THE COMPLAINT OF THE *COMPLAINT*

THE ACTUAL complaint that Mars makes takes up almost half of the poem and is a characteristically Chaucerian exercise in extended irony. Here, precisely as with Palamon and Arcite in the *Knight's Tale* and with Troilus in the *Troilus and Criseyde*, Chaucer shows us characters who have to some degree begun to behave irrationally because of love; he then has them "explain" or question their dilemma with some quasi-philosophical choplogic, usually depending upon Boethian arguments that are followed with some care all the way to a sudden, erroneous conclusion.[75] In this sort of literary maneuver, tone is all important, and yet the proper perception of the tone of an extended irony depends upon a careful reading of other parts of the poem as well as some agreement about generally accepted ideas

[74] The breakdown of lechery into five steps is ultimately from Gregory. For another mediaeval example see Dan Michel's *Ayenbite of Inwit*, ed. Richard Morris, *EETS*, o.s. No. 23 (London, 1866), p. 46. It has been noted that this progression is probably alluded to in the *Parlement of Foules*, ll. 225-28. See Huppé and Robertson, *Fruyt and Chaf*, p. 118 and n. 25.

[75] See Robertson, *Preface*, pp. 270 and 493 for the analyses of the *Knight's Tale* and the *Troilus*.

in the fourteenth century. In other words, those who believe that
Chaucer could not make up his mind how he felt about Boethius will
not be convinced about his use of Boethian (or any other) ideas for
ironic purposes, but those who believe that he felt Boethian ideas to
be normative will see in them a ready source of humor.

Chaucer leads into Mars' actual complaining with a pleasingly am-
biguous injunction that every man should have joy in his mate, the
tacit corollary being that if your "mate" is Venus you will not have
any more joy than Mars does.

> And what his compleynt was, remembreth me;
> And therfore, in this lusty morwenynge,
> As I best can, I wol hit seyn and synge,
> And after that I wol my leve take;
> And God yeve every wyght joy of his make!
> (150-54)

Mars then begins to speak, and in a little Proem to his complaint he
notes that his wit is "troubled," thus adumbrating the folly of the
conclusions he will later reach:

> Wherfore the ground and cause of al my peyne,
> So as my troubled wit may hit atteyne,
> I wol reherse. . . . (160-62)

One might think, in view of the fact that Mars entered into his
association with Venus knowing that he was going to be in danger
in the sign Taurus ("Ye knowe wel my myschef in that place"), that
the "ground" and "cause" of his "peyne" would be his own stupidity,
but this is not the case. Rather, Mars' troubled wit hits upon the
idea that the blame for his present misfortunes should not be placed
on himself nor on Venus, but rather upon the creator of Venus—
God:

> So fareth hyt by lovers and by me;
> For thogh my lady have so gret beaute
> That I was mad til I had gete her grace,
> She was not cause of myn adversite,
> But he that wroghte her, also mot I the,

That putte such a beaute in her face,
That made me coveyten and purchace
Myn oune deth; him wite I that I dye,
And myn unwit, that ever I clamb so hye.

(263-71)

The line of illogic Mars follows here is no doubt gratifying to him
for removing the burden of blame from its obvious sources, but
in the Middle Ages the concept of crediting "he that wroghte her"
(who is throughout this section of the poem identified as God) with
being the source of our vices was not approved of as a way out of
self-censure. Indeed, an important part of the discussion of providence
and free will in Boethius notes that there must be free will in order
to account for man's choice of vice, for there is no sin more odious
than blaming man's vices on the source of all good:

> And yit ther folweth anothir inconvenient, of the whiche ther ne
> mai be thought no more felonous ne more wikke, and that is this:
> that, so as the ordre of thingis is iled and cometh of the purveaunce
> of God, ne that nothing is leveful to the conseiles of mankynde
> (*as who seith that men han no power to don nothing ne wilne
> nothing*), thanne folweth it that oure vices ben referrid to the
> makere of alle good (*as who seith, thanne folweth it that God
> oughte han the blame of our vices, syn he constreyneth us by neces-
> site to doon vices*). (Bk. v, pr. 3)

This, then, is the ultimate penalty for submitting *virtus* to Venus
rather than to Pallas. Mars is so thoroughly enmeshed in his own
self-interest that he cannot even see the source of his problem.
Like Troilus, who cursed the gods, his birth, himself, his fate, nature,
and every creature except his lady (*T&C*, v, 207-10), Mars ignores
Venus' fickleness and his own rash decision and curses God. By such
an action he not only fails to improve the situation, but rather makes
it worse. The source of this mental blindness is the original decision
to perform a dubious and dangerous action, to conjoin with Venus
in a dangerous place, and that decision was based, in part, upon a
failure to discriminate between one Venus and another. This insuf-
ficient distinction is brought out in the third tern of the complaint
proper, in which Mars asks why God made love and why love doesn't

last. Like Arcite, who asks what the world is and what men want to
have, Mars has asked two questions that are somewhat incompatible.
Thus, just as the mediaeval answer to the first of Arcite's questions
implies that the second is ill-conceived (since the world is a place
where you cannot "have" anything permanently), so Mars' first
question about love is not in harmony with his second about the
transitoriness of love (because the kind of love God ordains in man
is not the evanescent variety characterized by lust). Note too that
Mars amusingly accuses God of forcing people to love in spite of
themselves—another device to remove his own burden of responsi-
bility:

> To what fyn made the God that sit so hye,
> Benethen him, love other companye,
> And streyneth folk to love, malgre her hed?
> And then her joy, for oght I can espye,
> Ne lasteth not the twynkelyng of an ye,
> And somme han never joy til they be ded.
> What meneth this? What is this mystihed?
> Wherto constreyneth he his folk so faste
> Thing to desyre, but hit shulde laste?
>
> (218-26)

Of course, God does implant the desire or love of something in his
creatures: Boethius called it "the covetise of verray good," and it is a
desire for something that does indeed last.

Mars continues in this vein by arguing that God is inimical to lovers
and that he is like a fisherman who baits his hook with something
attractive (woman's beauty) but wounds with the hook. In this argu-
ment Mars does violence to the mediaeval concept of God as a
benevolent fisherman, baiting his hook with Christ to catch Satan,
and shows once more that he does not understand about the uses of
beauty in general and of female beauty in particular.[76] The distinction
between those things that were to be used and those things that were
to be enjoyed was clearly set forth by St. Augustine, and in the four-
teenth century even a person of very modest education would have

---

[76] For Christ on God's hook, see Mâle, *Gothic Image*, Fig. 184.

been unlikely to argue that God created beauty in order to make man miserable.[77]

Mars is, all in all, somewhat less than a formidable disputant about these questions, and in general it is safe to say that the complaint proper of the poem is simply a demonstration of the subjection of reason to passion as it was astrologically acted out earlier in the poem. The final demonstration of this is in Mars' references to the Brooch of Thebes, which he tries to use as a vehicle for the argument that the creator of an object and not the object itself is responsible for the resultant misfortunes. Here, however, he has the grace to allow that the person who covets the fair object is at least in part to blame:

> The broche of Thebes was of such a kynde,
> So ful of rubies and of stones of Ynde,
> That every wight, that sette on hit an ye,
> He wende anon to worthe out of his mynde;
> So sore the beaute wolde his herte bynde,
> Til he hit had, him thoghte he moste dye;
> And whan that hit was his, then shulde he drye
> Such woo for drede, ay while that he hit hadde,
> That wel nygh for the fere he shulde madde.
> And whan hit was fro his possessioun,
> Then had he double wo and passioun
> For he so feir a tresor had forgo;
> But yet this broche, as in conclusioun,
> Was not the cause of his confusioun;
> But he that wroghte hit enfortuned hit so
> That every wight that had hit shulde have wo;
> And therfore in the worcher was the vice,
> And in the covetour that was so nyce.
>
> (245-62)

This has a kind of logic to it in the abstract, but we may assume that Chaucer would expect his audience to know what the Brooch of Thebes was and in what way it was unlucky. Chaucer got the story of the Brooch from the second book of Statius' *Thebaid*, and the basic

[77] For a discussion of the problem of the use and abuse of beauty in mediaeval aesthetics, see Robertson, *Preface*, pp. 65-113.

point to be noted is that the Brooch (a necklace according to Statius) was made by Vulcan, the wronged husband, in order to punish the adultery of Mars and Venus by bringing misfortune on the daughter of the union, Harmonia. This takes something of the force out of Mars' argument that the creators of beauty are to be blamed for the ill-starred results of the desire for that beauty. Moreover, the Brooch was noted for its bad effects on certain women; it is introduced into Statius' narrative when Argia wears it while approaching the temple of "unmarried Pallas" and is frightened away by a trumpet blast. Another possessor of the jewel, Semele, died when her lover Jove revealed himself as the wielder of lightning, and Eriphyle persuaded her husband to go to war, where he met his death, in order to gain the jewel. In general, then, the Brooch of Thebes symbolizes the punishment of adultery, the dangers of unchastity, and even danger to selfish wives, for Eriphyle's actions ultimately brought about her death.[78] In the later Middle Ages the story of Harmonia, her necklace, and her unhappy marriage to Cadmus was glossed by Boccaccio as the result of a marriage based upon "flagrant libido."[79]

Mars fails to convince us that the Brooch of Thebes is a good analogy for arguing, in the next stanza, that God is to be blamed for creating Venus; indeed, the only thing he does convince us of is his inability to reason properly. Chaucer then brings the poem to a close by having Mars forego his several arguments, as though aware of their weakness, and appeal to knights, ladies, and lovers "al in-fere," on the basis of homelier grounds.

> But to yow, hardy knyghtes of renoun,
> Syn that ye be of my devisioun,
> Al be I not worthy to so gret a name,
> Yet, seyn these clerkes, I am your patroun;
> Therfore ye oghte have som compassioun
> Of my disese. . . .

. . . .

[78] Statius, *Thebaid*, I, 413-17; II, 244-305. Professor Thomas P. Roche, in an unpublished study, examines a number of mediaeval commentaries on the legend and concludes that the Brooch symbolizes the subjection of man to woman. The pertinence of this to the *Complaint of Mars* is obvious.

[79] Boccaccio, *Genealogie deorum*, II, 478.

> And ye, my ladyes, that ben true and stable,
> Be wey of kynde, ye oughten to be able
> To have pite of folk that be in peyne.   (272-83)

Of course, compassion and pity are very much in order here—not, as Mars thinks, for his woe, but rather for his unreasonableness. With this last delicate touch of irony Chaucer brings the poem to a close, adding only an admonition to all lovers to "complain" for Venus. What began as a Valentine's Day poem thus finishes as a Valentine's Day poem. Chaucer has been concerned with proper and improper love throughout, and this is an ideal topic for the genre of the Valentine poem. What is remarkable is not the subject, but the dazzling execution of it.

CHAPTER IV

Three Astrological Cruxes

I. THE APRIL DATE IN THE
GENERAL PROLOGUE

WE HAVE ALREADY examined the several ways in which Chaucer uses the astronomical periphrasis of time in *The Canterbury Tales* and the *Troilus*, but the two periphrases that open and close the *Tales* deserve further scrutiny, for it seems that Chaucer is reaching for significance beyond either eloquence or rhetoric in both cases.

The first problem with the periphrasis in the General Prologue is to determine what time of year it points to; the second is to determine what that means, after which some speculation as to the significance of the opening date for the *Tales* as a whole is in order. The passage itself is one of Chaucer's more extended periphrases, and both the literal and metaphorical interpretations of it depend upon a careful reading of the text. Thus, even though the opening lines of the Prologue are among the most often quoted in all English poetry, let us look at them again:

> Whan that Aprill with his shoures soote
> The droghte of March hath perced to the roote,
> And bathed every veyne in swich licour
> Of which vertu engendred is the flour;
> Whan Zephirus eek with his sweete breeth
> Inspired hath in every holt and heeth
> The tendre croppes, and the yonge sonne
> Hath in the Ram his halve cours yronne,
> And smale foweles maken melodye,
> That slepen al the nyght with open ye
> (So priketh hem nature in hir corages);
> Thanne longen folk to goon on pilgrimages. (1-12)

Chaucer is here being quite roundabout, even for a periphrasis. Our first impression is that the sun has run a half-course in the Ram, and the time must consequently be half a month after the sun's entrance into the Ram (Aries) on March 12, which would bring the date to

about March 27. However, the first line of the poem suggests that April has already succeeded March, and the reference to the time of year in the Headlink to the *Man of Law's Tale* clearly establishes the date then as April 18. Because the *Man of Law's Tale* has traditionally been considered among the tales of the second day, the majority of scholars from Skeat to Robinson have assumed that in order to reconcile the half-course in the Ram with a date past mid-April we must understand that the sun has run through both the first and the second half-courses in the Ram, and that the half-course referred to is the second.[1] This would mean that the time would be somewhat after the sun's entrance into the next sign, Taurus, which occurred on April 12, and would harmonize rather well with the subsequent reference to April 18. Although the necessary reading seems forced, it is worth noting that the periphrasis of the time of year in the *Nun's Priest's Tale* is handled in a similar fashion: our natural response to the first part of the passage is proven wrong when we come to a clearer statement of the time at the end of the passage.[2]

Even so, our rather complicated reading of the line about the

---

[1] Of course, not all scholars have agreed. Several Chaucerians have assumed, usually without discussion, that the pilgrimage begins in late March or early April. Tatlock, however, discusses the matter vigorously; he maintains that too much emphasis on harmonization of dates in an unfinished work like the *Tales* is a dubious practice and that consequently Skeat's complex reading of the opening lines is not justifiable. See John S. P. Tatlock, "Boccaccio and the Plan of Chaucer's *Canterbury Tales*," *Anglia*, XXXVII (1913), 88, n. 3.

[2] Whan that the month in which the world bigan,
That highte March, whan God first maked man,
Was compleet, and passed were also,
Syn March bigan, thritty dayes and two

. . . .

Caste up his eyen to the brighte sonne,
That in the signe of Taurus hadde yronne
Twenty degrees and oon, and somwhat moore.

(*NPT*, 3187-95)

One major difference between the two passages is that in the *Nun's Priest's Tale* the astrological material is very clear. However, Chaucer's statement that March was complete and that 32 days had passed since March began would make us think that the date was April 2, did we not subsequently encounter the statement that the sun had proceeded 21 degrees in Taurus, which unequivocally means that the date is May 3. We must therefore suppose the statement about March to mean that 32 days had passed since March began and ended.

sun's half-course through the Ram would benefit from some further confirmation, such as might be afforded by a precedent for the date. Happily such a precedent exists, for the Bible recounts a mid-April pilgrimage—the pilgrimage of Noah in his journey on the ark, which began on April 17 as recounted in Genesis 7:11:

> Anno sexcentesimo vitae Noe, mense secundo, septimo decimo die mensis, rupti sunt omnes fontes abyssi magnae, et cataractae caeli apertae sunt.

In spite of the many ways of numbering the months in the Middle Ages, we may be reasonably confident that to Chaucer a reference to the seventeenth day of the second month would imply the seventeenth of April, for in his poetry he twice suggests that the first month is March:[3]

> Whan that the month in which the world bigan,
> That highte March, whan God first maked man. . . .
> (*NPT*, 3187-88)

> The laste Idus of March, after the yeer. (*SqT*, 47)

The computation in which March is the first month of the year is derived from the ordinance concerning the Hebrew month Nisan in Exodus 12:2: "Mensis iste, vobis principium mensium: primus erit in mensibus anni." The problem, however, is in determining the proper relationship between the Hebrew month Nisan, based on a lunar calendar, and the mediaeval, Christian months of a solar calendar. Opinion was varied in the Middle Ages, but in the fourteenth century the famous exegete Nicholas de Lyra wrote decisively about the problem in a commentary on Exodus 12:2, and argued for a correspondence to March rather than April:

> . . . tamen est sciendum quod hoc est regulaliter [*sic*] verum quod primus mensis hebreorum semper incipit a principio lunationis

---

[3] Poole's standard work on the beginning of the year argues that in England the year officially began with Lady Day (March 25), but Chaucer's statement that the Ides of March came "after the year" is a clear indication that he was using a system that could begin the year earlier in March than the 25th. See Reginald L. Poole, "The Beginning of the Year in the Middle Ages," *Proceedings of the British Academy*, x (1921-23), 125.

propinquioris equinoctio vernali: siue principium dicte lunationis sit ante equinoctium siue post siue ibidem. dictum autem equinoctium est propinquius principio martii quam fini: quare est .xii. die martii secundum veritatem: lumen aliter signetur in kalendariis nostris: Ex quo partem verum quod dictum est sic quod primus mensis hebreorum magis correspondet martio quam aprili.[4]

The coincidence of the departure of the Canterbury pilgrims with the date of the departure of Noah's ark furnishes us with a precise and not unlikely rationale for Chaucer's choice of a specific month and day for the beginning of his poem, and this possible analogue would in turn strengthen Skeat's readings of the astrological passages. It is even more important, however, that if indeed Chaucer had this Biblical analogue in mind, then an understanding of it can enhance our knowledge of Chaucer's meaning in the Prologue and perhaps even in the entire *Canterbury Tales*. The prominent position of the passage describing the time of the year invites us to consider its

---

[4] *Biblie iampridem renouate . . . vna cum glosa ordinaria: et litterale moralique expositione Nicolai de Lyra . . .* (Basle, 1502), I, sig. x₆ʳ, col. 2. For Nicholas' exegesis on the date of Noah's flood, which he says is in April, see sig. h₃ʳ, col. 2. Nicholas' explanation of the system of months referred to in the Bible and their relation to the months of the fourteenth century was important, since it corrected the earlier idea of Rabanus Maurus, which was quoted in the *Glossa ordinaria* and printed along with Nicholas' commentary in the edition used here. The earlier argument was that the first month—Nisan, the month of the Passover—usually corresponded to April (see the *Glossa ordinaria*, PL, 113, cols. 110 and 218). The interpretation of Nicholas, however, was anticipated as a possibility as early as the thirteenth century by Hugh of St. Cher, who glossed Exodus 12:2 thus: "Mensis iste. Hic est Aprilis, idest, lunatio Aprilis, quae in Martio saepe inchoat imo semper, nisi embolismus impediat. . . . Sed nota, quod in *Glossa* Nisan quandoque vocatur Aprilis, quandoque Martius; et hoc ideo, quia Martius noster et Aprilis Judaeorum in parte simul concurrunt" (*Hugonis Cardinalis opera omnia in universum vetus, et Novum testamentum tomi octo . . .* [Venice, 1732], I, sig. L₈ʳ, col. 2). The difference is more in the degree of insistence than in the approach; Hugh wants both possibilities, while Nicholas insists on March. Calculations might show that the changing relationship of the lunar and solar year across the centuries makes it possible for both exegetes to be correct in their statements. We have seen that Rabanus Maurus related Nisan to April, while an exegete as early as Ambrose wrote that Nisan corresponded to March (*PL*, 14, col. 410). Whatever the astronomical truth may be, it is interesting to note that Chaucer was abreast of the Biblical scholarship of his day. I am grateful to Professor R. E. Kaske for direction of my attention to the pertinent passage in Hugh of St. Cher.

value for the events that follow, but while the Biblical analogue is a possible explanation for the choice of the date, it is not the only possible explanation. Does its precision and appropriateness make it a better explanation than others, such as the conventionality of spring openings and the realistic appropriateness of the time of year? Let us consider.

Rosemond Tuve has pointed out the doubtfulness of Chaucer's having had any specific source in mind for his spring description,[5] but the remarkable similarity of a passage in Guido delle Collonne's *Historia Destructionis Troiae* to Chaucer's opening lines has prompted several scholars to see in it a possible source:

> It was the season when the sun, hastening under the turning circle of the zodiac, had now entered its course under the sign of the Ram, in which the equinox is celebrated, when the days of the beginning of spring are equal in length to the nights; then when the season begins to soothe eager mortals in its clear air; then when as the snows melt, gently blowing zephyrs wrinkle up the waters. . . .[6]

In spite of the obvious similarity in wording and tone to Chaucer's Prologue, there is an important difference in the astrological material. Guido says that the sun *had now entered* (*iam intrauerat*) the sign of Aries, the Ram, which in Chaucer's time extended from March 12 to April 12; but the emphasis on the entrance into the

---

[5] Rosemond Tuve, "Spring in Chaucer and Before Him," *MLN*, LII (1937), 9-16. Essentially similar conclusions are reached by Enkvist and Schaar. The latter notes that Chaucer allows the abstract element of his description to predominate over the graphic. See Enkvist, *The Seasons of the Year*, pp. 110-112; and Claes Schaar, *The Golden Mirror* (Lund, 1955), p. 413.

[6] "Tempus erat quod sol maturans sub obliquo zodiaci circulo cursum suum sub signo iam intrauerat arietis, in quo noctium spatio equato diebus celebratur equinoctium primi ueris, tunc cum incipit tempus blandiri mortalibus in aeris serenitate intentis, tunc cum dissolutis niuibus molliter flantes zephiri crispant aquas . . ." (Guido de Columnis, *Historia Destructionis Troiae*, ed. Nathaniel Edward Griffin [Cambridge, Mass., 1936], pp. 34-35). The translation is from Muriel Bowden, *A Commentary on the General Prologue to the Canterbury Tales* (New York, 1948), p. 20. It is worth noting that Guido refers to the wetness of April; "Tunc quasi medium mensis Aprilis effluxerat" (*loc. cit.*). The line occurs outside the "tunc cum" formula, however, and is therefore merely a metaphor which does not affect the astrological dating.

sign, as well as on the equinox, clearly points to a date closer to the middle of March than to the middle of April.[7] The close similarity of the two passages in so many respects makes Chaucer's difference in the date of a full month all the more noticeable; it emphasizes that his choice of the time of year is not necessarily governed by convention or by a particular source, but by his own demands and specific purposes.

Chaucer drew upon sources, to be sure, but he was quick to change conventional material for his own poetic ends and would arrange the events of a poem to suit his purposes. It is easy to say that mediaeval poems begin in the spring because it is a convention, but this is begging the question. It is as easy to discuss Chaucer's pilgrims as though they were real people and to say they went on pilgrimages in the spring because of the beautiful weather (ideal for romance). But although April is a nice time of year for a trip, who wants to go riding in all that rain? The fact of the matter is that there is no historical evidence to show that a majority of pilgrims went on their journeys in the spring; indeed, the major pilgrimages to Canterbury were undertaken in December and July.[8] In short, we are not deal-

---

[7] Miss Bowden emphasizes the similarities between Chaucer's passage and Guido's (e.g., both mention the Ram), but it is difficult to pass over the very large discrepancy in time. See Bowden, *Commentary*, p. 20 and n. 6.

[8] For the festivals in December and July, see Bowden, *Commentary*, p. 34. Miss Bowden also points out that Chaucer's pilgrimage was not at the time of one of these great festivals. Sidney Heath says that spring was the favorite time of year for English pilgrimages to domestic shrines, but he does so without documentation (*Pilgrim Life in the Middle Ages* [Boston and New York, 1912], p. 46). J. J. Jusserand gives great emphasis to the problem of muddy roads in mediaeval England, which could be so bad for travel that on at least one occasion the opening of Parliament was held up because so few members had arrived on time (*English Wayfaring Life in the Middle Ages* [New York, 1925], pp. 86-87). One would think, in view of this, that the showers of April would be less appealing for travel than the drought of March or a morrow of May. The only two pilgrimages to Canterbury at a specific time of year that Jusserand describes are the famous one of Henry II on July 12, 1174, and that of Manuel II, Paleologus, Emperor of Constantinople, who arrived at Canterbury in December, 1400 (Jusserand, *op.cit.*, pp. 352-55). No denial of the obvious suitability of spring as a time to travel is intended here. Rather, the fact that a pilgrimage to Canterbury is not necessarily taken in April serves as a warning not to believe that Chaucer is either slavish in following traditions or capricious in changing them. Care must always be exercised when trying to distinguish between what is based upon a poet's observation and what is the re-

ing with realism as historicity in this passage, although it is quite
likely that at least someone went to Canterbury on April 17 every
year. Rather, what Chaucer does here is to add to a very meaningful
literary tradition of spring-openings both in his arrangement of
detail and sequence, and in his specification of a symbolically signifi-
cant date. This does not detract from what we are accustomed to call
realism, but rather adds to it another dimension of reality—one that
Chaucer, like Dante, thought important for the opening of a poem.[9]

Having established a parallel between the departure of the Canter-
bury pilgrims and the departure of Noah, it behooves us to consider
the meaning of the symbolism here. Yet, just as Chaucer's periphrasis
of the time of year must be considered in terms of other such literary
devices, so the symbolism of the parallel departures deserves to be
considered in the wider context of the symbolism of spring. In the
Middle Ages spring in the solar calendar was the time of rebirth in
nature and the time for planting of crops, while in the ecclesiastical
calendar, spring is the time of both the beginning and the end of
Christ's life on earth—the Annunciation and the Passion and Resur-

---

sult of the manipulation of traditional material. Here the emphasis has been placed
on Chaucer's variations on a convention in order to gain figurative meaning. Con-
versely, an element of the General Prologue that has long been thought to be a
rhetorical convention and not observational—the drought of March—has recently
been accounted for empirically. See James A. Hart, " 'The Droghte of March': A
Common Misunderstanding," *TSLL*, IV (1962-63), 525-29.

[9] As J. V. Cunningham has noted with regard to this passage, realism depends
upon artifice (*Tradition and Poetic Structure* [Denver, 1960], p. 75). Professor
Spitzer downgrades historical realism in this passage to emphasize the idea of world
harmony presented therein, which he further argues is appropriate because the pil-
grimage itself is inspired by love (Leo Spitzer, *Classical and Christian Ideas of
World Harmony* [Baltimore, 1963], p. 179). Professor Peck has referred to the
"generally accepted assumption that the pilgrims begin a four-day pilgrimage to
Canterbury on the Wednesday before Easter. . . ." While it is not clear just how
widely this assumption is in fact accepted, such an idea would account for the
choice of date primarily to coincide with the middle of Holy Week in a particular
year. This does not, however, necessarily rule out the associations with Noah and
the Flood, which Chaucer might have intended as a sort of lagniappe, or which
he might have had in mind when choosing a specific year. In either case the se-
lection of the date of departure would be primarily determined by symbolic con-
cerns and would accord adventitiously with actual pilgrimages, which apparently
occurred throughout the year. See Russell A. Peck, "Number Symbolism in the
Prologue to Chaucer's *Parson's Tale*," *ES*, XLVIII (1967), 209, n. 13.

rection. The latter, heralding man's rebirth after death because of Christ's death and rebirth, was traditionally associated with the sacrament of baptism, which represents man's rebirth in life in a purified state, ready to begin his pilgrimage to his spiritual home. Because baptism is a kind of beginning, it in turn was associated with spring, the beginning of the year and the time of rebirth in nature.[10]

In Biblical commentaries Chaucer could have found material pertinent to both the solar and ecclesiastical calendars. Nicholas de Lyra's explanation of the date of Noah's flood is literal, but one also encounters spiritual and moral explanations in the commentaries. If Chaucer chose the analogue of the flood to determine the date for the departure of his pilgrims, then the principle of analogy itself would suggest that the coincident dates would constitute an intermediate link in Chaucer's suggested imagery, not the final goal.

In the Middle Ages the flood was understood to have occurred at a specific time and place, but it was also interpreted mystically as a symbol of baptism, the idea being that just as Noah was saved by the water of the flood and the wood of the ark, so the individual Christian is saved by the water of baptism and the wood of the cross.[11] With this in mind, the "when . . . when . . . then" formula of the Prologue takes on another dimension; not only is Chaucer saying "when April and warm weather come along, then it is a good time to travel," but also the analogies of the date, flood, pilgrimage, and baptism imply the message that "when one is baptized, then one starts on the pilgrimage of life." Judging from the varying degrees of virtue of the characters in the *Tales*, one might add, "for better or worse." The image of the pilgrimage of the individual on the

---

[10] On the two calendars see Chapter II. In poetry the rhetorical paralleling of the rebirth in nature and the Resurrection has been found in Troubadour poetry and in Christian Latin poetry by D. Scheludko, who speaks of the "Verbindung der Auferstehung Christi mit dem Frühlingserwachen." Mr. Scheludko has argued for a less sentimental view of nature in mediaeval poetry than has hitherto been evidenced: ". . . des Parallelismus, der nicht emotionaler, sondern rational-rhetorischer Natur ist" ("Zur Geschichte des Natureinganges bei den Trobadors," *ZFSL*, LX [1935], 261-62).

[11] See the *Glossa ordinaria*, *PL*, 113, col. 107. There are fuller treatments of this commonplace elsewhere in the exegetical tradition, for example, in Peter Damian (*PL*, 145, col. 847); Rabanus Maurus (*PL*, 107, col. 515); and Bede (*PL*, 91, col. 91).

voyage of life is a commonplace in Anglo-Saxon and mediaeval poetry, and Chaucer has Theseus' father, wise, old Egeus, "that knew this worldes transmutacioun," say, "This world nys but a thurghfare ful of wo, / And we been pilgrymes, passynge to and fro" (*KnT*, 2847-48). This is not to argue that the Canterbury pilgrims are to be seen as a procession of innocents toward a heavenly reward. The flood is a two-sided symbol that is ideal for Chaucer's purposes: it was sent to punish sin, and yet the event itself shows the way to salvation, through the ark for Noah and through baptism and the other sacraments for the individual Christian. The image of the flood is the perfect banner under which Chaucer can unite such disparate philosophies as those of "hende Nicholas" and the Parson—the one reminding us of man's fallen nature and its possible consequences, and the other directing our vision toward the Augustinian ideal of using the world rather than enjoying it.

The final traditional element in Chaucer's spring-opening is the astrological imagery itself, and again it would be unwise to focus upon the literary use of things astrological to the exclusion of a consideration of any of the other arts. There is no need to inquire into the astrological lore about Aries or Taurus, since the zodiac was widely used in a non-astrological way that is clearly more in line with Chaucer's intentions. As we have seen, the zodiac was commonly used in church architecture as a calendar of the year and was often accompanied by a series of illustrations of the Labors of the Months. Thus, the mediaeval man, condemned to labor because of Adam's sin, kept pace with the turning circle of the zodiac and was constantly reminded of the cycle of the Christian year and of the fact that he did not labor without hope. Chaucer's use of the zodiac would call his audience's attention to the meaning of the time of year just by the very nature of the device. In the Prologue, Chaucer drew not only upon a literary tradition of spring-openings, but also upon a more basic treasury of seasonal associations in mediaeval art—associations with various dates of importance in the ecclesiastical calendar. As we have seen, a very general reference to spring could possibly remind a mediaeval audience of the sacrament of baptism, but Chaucer is careful to make his point clear. The first line of the Prologue, with its reference to the "sweet showers of April" might

have served to remind Chaucer's audience of another rain in April, but he labors the point somewhat to give the suggestion time to clarify itself. By directing the audience's attention to the time of year first in terms of the months and then in terms of the zodiac, Chaucer gradually focusses upon a short period of time—thus excluding other dates of ecclesiastical importance in the spring—and he simultaneously underlines his meaning with references to the rain and to the pilgrimage. In the first few lines of the Prologue, Chaucer makes specific a framework for his poem that would have been much less meaningful from the general connotations of spring or even of April.[12]

Both the best substantiation for the assertion that Chaucer intended his readers to think of the flood and the best illustration of the import of this intention for the *Tales* as a whole is the appropriateness of the *Miller's Tale* for this scheme. Coming as it does on the first day of the pilgrimage there is irony in having the Miller tell a story of a false "Nowelis flood" on the very day of the true one. Moreover, by studying an individual tale we may gain a vantage point from which to consider the import of the analogue of the flood for the entire set of Canterbury tales.

Professor John J. O'Connor has pointed out an aspect of irony in Chaucer's having John the carpenter succumb to the astrological predictions of Nicholas, because Noah himself was reputed to be an astrologer. With the information of the identity of dates, it is pos-

---

[12] Once again it should be emphasized that while the parallel of the flood is the primary cause of Chaucer's choice of date, he manipulates his periphrasis so as to extract the maximum meaning from all elements of it. Chaucer did not have to describe the date the way he did, so we must assume that the details were chosen, and, if chosen, chosen for symbolic as well as literal or rhetorical effectiveness. For example, Professor Hoffman has observed that while the birds impel, the Saint beckons (Arthur W. Hoffman, "Chaucer's Prologue to Pilgrimage: The Two Voices," *ELH*, XXI [1954], 2). Professor Robertson, well aware that dates do not have to be defined astrologically, suggests that the sun in Taurus was conjured up because Taurus is the house of Venus, who variously motivates the pilgrims with love of God or the world (*Preface*, p. 373). Professor Huppé notes that a fourteenth-century encyclopedist likens the sun's passage through the first three signs of the zodiac to Christ's "passage" through the three parts of penitence: contrition, confession, and satisfaction (*Reading of the Canterbury Tales*, p. 19). These observations seem heightened rather than set aside by the parallel dates of the departure and the flood.

sible to see further humor in the tale.[13] Because the flood is a symbol of both punishment and reward, Chaucer is able to have Nicholas, in order to reap his own reward, offer John the chance to be "saved." Chaucer then carries the whole affair one step further and metes out poetic justice to each character according to his crime. The need for water is great; in its absence, Absolon is forced to scrub his mouth with "sond, with straw, with clooth, with chippes" (*MillT*, 3748). Nicholas screams for water as a local anaesthetic, and, for want of it, John the carpenter breaks his arm in his fall from the roof. From Nicholas' first invocation of the deluge as a means of salvation for John, we move to the position in which the lack of water is a form of punishment. The association of the flood with the sacrament of baptism—a ceremony of purification—is certainly in Chaucer's mind here, for each character needs a portion of cleansing. On the other hand, an actual deluge is not needed, for the absence of water can punish as effectively as the presence of it. Chaucer's Parson is the best glossator here, for he says very clearly that the flood was sent to punish lechery (*ParsT*, 839), thus when Nicholas invokes it to encourage lechery, its absence is not only fitting but effective.

From the prominent position of the image of the flood in the *Miller's Tale* the critic is invited to survey the point-counterpoint of humor based on the two sides of God's justice, reward and punishment, not only in this tale but in all the *Tales*. Chaucer's interest in the subject of God's justice is amply attested to by his translation of Boethius and by the *Parson's Tale*, which stands in the *Tales* at the opposite pole from the suggestion of Noah's pilgrimage, and which is concerned with the pilgrimage of the Christian through life:

Stondeth upon the weyes, and seeth and axeth of olde pathes (that is to seyn, of olde sentences) which is the goode wey, / and walketh

[13] John J. O'Connor, "The Astrological Background of the *Miller's Tale*," *Speculum*, XXXI (1956), 125. Professor Stokoe further observes that the astrological-mythological machinery that is at the service of providence in the *Knight's Tale* is maliciously distorted by the Miller. See William C. Stokoe, "Structure and Intention in the First Fragment of *The Canterbury Tales*," *UTQ*, XXI (1952), 124. A consideration of the date of the tale and the poetic justice encountered by the principals suggests, however, that while the astrological emphasis has changed from elegant descriptions of classical deities to false astrologers, providence remains much the same.

in that wey, and ye shal fynde refresshynge for youre soules, etc. /
... Of whiche weyes, ther is a ful noble wey and a ful covenable,
which may nat fayle to man ne to womman that thurgh synne
hath mysgoon fro the righte wey of Jerusalem celestial; / and
this wey is cleped Penitence. . . . (*ParsT*, 77-81)

Noah escapes punishment through God's grace (Genesis 6:8) and
the Parson concludes Chaucer's group of tales with a sermon on how
that grace may be achieved. Noah and the Parson are used by Chau-
cer to define what a pilgrimage should be, while the *Tales* themselves
illustrate the range of human achievement and failing.[14]

Dante too stood "upon the weyes" at the opening of his journey
to God, and although Chaucer's pilgrimage may be located geograph-
ically and temporally, while Dante's is a journey of the mind, Chau-
cer's ideal destination is also a spiritual home. Both poems have a
degree of orientation to the world at their outset, but both are ulti-
mately directed to a destination beyond it. Both poems may be con-
sidered as spiritual roadmaps, even though their technique is very
different, for their goal is not to show us the Heavenly City, but
rather to instruct us how we may find it for ourselves. As Chaucer's
Parson puts it:

> And Jhesu, for his grace, wit me sende
> To *shewe yow the wey*, in this viage,
> Of thilke parfit glorious pilgrymage
> That highte Jerusalem celestial.
> (*Pars Prol*, 48-51)

The only place in which the spiritual pilgrimage to God may be
accomplished is in "this viage"—the voyage of our life—and by
synecdoche the journey of Chaucer's pilgrims is both.

2. THE WIFE OF BATH'S HOROSCOPE

THE HOROSCOPE of the Wife of Bath is as abbreviated as any to be
found in Chaucer, but has received detailed critical attention, doubt-

---

[14] Essentially similar conclusions about the importance of the pilgrimage, but
from somewhat different premises, have been reached by Ralph Baldwin, "The
Unity of the *Canterbury Tales*," *Anglistica*, V (1955), in the section on the Par-
son's Prologue.

less because of the intriguing character to whom it belongs. The horoscope itself is simple enough, and like most of Chaucer's literary horoscopes it is much too simplified to suggest that it is a "real" horoscope. Its emphasis on Venus and Mars is a forceful reminder of the associations of adultery surrounding any astrological linking of those planets as was pointed out in Chapter III. In short, it is inescapable that the horoscope will somehow be a symbol for lechery or adultery or both, and the Wife interprets it just this way, saying that she followed her "constellation" and did not refrain from lechery. As we have seen in Chapter I, this suggests that some value judgment should be made about the Wife: no one had to follow the inclination set forth by the stars, but she seems not to take note of this, in spite of her citations of Ptolemy and her generally high level of awareness of astrology.

> For certes, I am al Venerien
> In feelynge, and myn herte is Marcien.
> Venus me yaf my lust, my likerousnesse,
> And Mars yaf me my sturdy hardynesse;
> Myn ascendent was Taur, and Mars therinne.
> Allas! allas! that evere love was synne!
> I folwed ay myn inclinacioun
> By vertu of my constellacioun;
> That made me I koude noght withdrawe
> My chambre of Venus from a good felawe.
> Yet have I Martes mark upon my face,
> And also in another privee place.
> For God so wys be my savacioun,
> I ne loved nevere by no discrecioun,
> But evere folwede myn appetit,
> Al were he short, or long, or blak, or whit;
> I took no kep, so that he liked me.
>   (*WB Prol*, 609-25)

The Wife's enthusiastic account of her horoscope and her subsequent interpretation of its influence on her judgment in love ("I ne loved nevere by no discrecioun") combine to build up a picture of the most astrologically concerned person among the Canterbury pil-

grims. Other pilgrims tell about astrologers—for example, the Miller tells of Nicholas, and the Franklin of the Orleans clerk—and give horoscopes or other astrological data about the characters in their tales—such as the Man of Law about Custance—but only the Wife of Bath twice quotes Ptolemy, tells us her own horoscope, and treats us to a hilarious astrological explanation of why clerks don't praise women. This is thoroughly consistent with the rest of her character. The Wife's concern to invert the traditional hierarchy of Christian marriage, her factitious interpretations of the Bible, and her complacent reliance on her own "experience" all combine to paint the picture of one whose ego has caused a certain mental blindness making truth completely subjective. This, in turn, is not far removed from the traditional picture of the divinatory astrologer, whose attempts to see into the future were judged to be false prophecy, and whose concern for the "truth" of the heavens often blinded him to more immediate realities—like the astrologer of John the carpenter's fable in the *Miller's Tale*. Thus the Wife's astrological concern in itself tells us something about her character, so does her horoscope and her interpretation of her horoscope.

Of actual astrological detail we have very little in the Wife's horoscope, but it is enough. We know only that the ascendant sign was Taurus and that Mars was in Taurus, but this information alone is significant, without examining any of the other planets and their locations. Venus also figures somehow in the horoscope, but we cannot be sure just how since we have no indication of her location; all that is said is that she gives the Wife her lust and lecherousness.[15]

---

[15] Professor Curry has argued that Venus was in conjunction with Mars in Taurus because the Wife says she has the "prente of Seinte Venus seel," and Venus must be in the ascendant to leave a mark. Thus, if she is in the ascendant she must be in conjunction with Mars (*Mediaeval Sciences*, p. 329, n. 3). However, Chaucer does not say that both planets are in the ascending sign Taurus, and the imprint Venus leaves may not be a mark on the body—thus determining that Venus was in the ascendant—but may merely be a figurative reference to the Wife's gap-toothed appearance. Even if both planets are to be discovered in the ascendant, they are not necessarily in conjunction, as Curry supposes. In a way it is unfortunate that Chaucer did not clearly indicate that Venus was in conjunction with Mars in the Wife's horoscope, for one of the meanings of the conjunction in nativities of women is the inclination to dominate their husbands. See *Alchabitius cum commento* . . . (Venice, 1512), sig. b₂ᵛ.

Mars' influence on the Wife probably amounts to about the same thing, according to the astrologers, but this is not really inconsistent with the Wife's claim that he gave her her "sturdy hardynesse." As we have already seen, the possible relationships of Mars and Venus could be considered separately and together simultaneously by the astrologers, and the various combinations and permutations did not necessarily cancel one another out. Thus, although in the horoscope of Hypermnestra in the *Legend of Good Women* Mars is said to lose his "venom" because of the oppression of Venus and other "houses," his appearance in Taurus, an unfortunate house for him, in the Wife's Prologue does not necessarily mean that all his war-like influence is taken from him. On the other hand, his appearance in Taurus is significant in and by itself, and the significance was noticed by the scribe of the Ellesmere MS, who inserted an explanatory gloss:

Mansor Amphorisoun 14 Cumque in ascendente fuerint infortune turpem notam in facie pacietur In natiuitatibus mulierum cum fuerit ascendens aliqua de domibus Veneris Marte existente in eis vel e contrario erit mulier inpudica Idem erit si habuerit capricornum in ascendente He[c] Hermes in libro fiducie Amphoriso 25.[16]

The essential message of this rather abrupt gloss is that, according to the *Aphorisms* of Almansor, when Mars is in either of the houses of Venus in the nativities of women, they will be unchaste, and the documentation for this may be found in the *Aphorisms* of Hermes Trismegistus. As a check on this one may note that indeed the anonymous glossator was correct, and Hermes says exactly the same thing:

In natiuitatibus mulierum, cum fuerit ascendens aliqua de domibus Veneris, Marte existente in eis, uel de domibus Martis, Venere existente in eis, erit mulier impudica: idem erit, si in ascendente Capricornum habuerit.[17]

[16] John M. Manly and Edith Rickert, *The Text of the Canterbury Tales* (Chicago, 1940), III, 499. It is of interest that Robinson notes the existence of this gloss, but neither reproduces it nor tells what it says.

[17] Hermes Trismegistus, *Centiloquium*, in the 1551 *Omnibus* volume as described by Carmody, sig. H₁ᵛ.

Not surprisingly this interpretation of the significance of Mars in Taurus in a nativity was sufficiently widespread so that it came to the attention of Boccaccio's astrological mentor Andalò, who informed Boccaccio that people born when Mars was in Taurus or Libra, Venus' other house, would be venereal in all things.[18] The famous Guido Bonatti said that Mars in Taurus or Libra in a nativity portended the birth of one who would be a sinful deceiver in every venereal abuse, and for support he cited Albohali, who had written that those born when Mars was in Taurus would not only be fornicators, but also traitors.[19] This same Albohali elsewhere gives a slightly more general treatment of Mars as the lord of the ascendant, in both good and bad positions: he says that in a bad position (such as he would be in Taurus) Mars portends the births of devious people, while when Venus is with or in aspect to Mars in such a location a female born at the time will be a garrulous, mendacious virago![20] This is hitting close to home in a description of the Wife of Bath, but it should be remembered that Chaucer does not make it clear that Venus is in any aspect to Mars or in conjunction with him.

The significance of Mars in Taurus, then, is easily documented with reference to the astrologers and to the passages cited here that are specifically concerned with one of the houses of Venus. Many

[18] "Perciocchè secondochè gli astrologi voglione, e così affermava il mie venerabile precettore V. Andale, quando avviene che nella natività d'alcuno, Marte si trovi esser nella casa di Venere in Tauro o in Libra, e trovisi essere significatore della natività di quel cotale che allora nasce, ha a dimostrare, questo cotale che allora nasce devere essere in ogni cosa venereo" (Giovanni Boccaccio, *Il Commento sopra La Commedia di Dante Alighieri*, ed. A. Penna [Florence, 1831], II, 55).

[19] Guido Bonatti, *Liber introductorius*, sig. EE₆ᵛ: "Quod si fuerit mars in tauro vel libra: fueritque natiuitatis signator signabit natum luxuriosum fornicatorem sodomitam et in omnibus venereis abusibus sceleratum futurum deceptorem. . . . Et dixit abolay quod si fuerit in tauro signat natum proditorem falsum malignum minatorem atque fornicatorem futurum." Cf. Albohali Alchait, *De iudiciis natiuitatem*, sig. O₁ᵛ-O₂ʳ: "Eodem in domo Veneris existente, erit natus luxuriosus, fornicator, perpetrans scelus cum uxoribus consanguineorum suorum, uel cum suis consanguineis, uel desponsabit mulierem, cum qua antea moechatus est, & patietur detrimentum a mulieribus." Also, Messehalla, *In reuolutionibus*, sig. H₂ʳ.

[20] "Eodem [Mars] uero impedito a malis in loco malo, significatur timiditas ac uilitas animi, mala suspitio, & multitudo inuolutionis in operibus ac dictis. . . . Et si fuerit [Venus] cum Marte, aut ei applicans, significat garrulitatem uerborum, mendacium ac falsitatem, deceptionem, Si masculus fuerit, mulierosus erit, Si foemina, uirago" (Albohali Alchait, *De iudiciis natiuitatem*, sig. C₃ʳ⁻ᵛ).

more could be added if we were to study the writings of the astrologers on Mars in bad positions generally or just *in horoscopo*.[21] Similarly, if we were to search the astrologers for references to the influence of Venus and Mars together in a horoscope the number of citations could be multiplied greatly, but the meaning of Mars in Taurus would not be significantly modified, and the precision of Chaucer's imagery would be needlessly set aside. In view of the clear meaning of Mars in Taurus and the Wife's plain statement that she followed her "constellation," which made her unable to keep her "chamber of Venus" from a "good felawe," it is noteworthy that the major investigator of the Wife of Bath's horoscope, Professor Curry, has analyzed the whole thing very differently and has come up with quite different conclusions about the significance of the horoscope. The basic difference is that while the present interpretation emphasizes the importance of Mars in Taurus without further ramifications, Professor Curry has tried to account for both Mars and Venus in his analysis. Even though it is not clear where Venus is located in the horoscope, he assumes that she is the dominant planet but that her generally benign influence has been subverted by Mars' malevolent impulses. The assumption that Venus is the dominant planet in the horoscope is based upon the fact that the Wife uses the phrase "My dame taughte me that soutiltee" (*WB Prol*, 576), which Curry argues is a reference to Venus. Robinson, however, has observed that this reading is "hardly to be accepted."[22] Surely it is a bold reading, since Venus is not mentioned at all in the passage about "my dame." Because Curry's interpretation of the astrology depends so much on Venus' domination, it is unfortunate that there is no evidence that she is in fact the dominant planet.[23] Moreover, by trying to account for influences of both Mars and Venus in the horoscope, Professor Curry is perhaps overly subtle psychologically; he tries to preserve

[21] For example, see Ptolemy, *Tetrabiblos*, p. 355; Ptolemy, *Centiloquium*, sig. G_3^v; Albohali, *De iudiciis natiuitatem*, sig. M_3^r; Bartomeu de Tresbéns, *Tractat d'Astrologia* (Barcelona, 1957-58), I, 161.

[22] See Robinson's notes and my article "Chaucer's *The Wife of Bath's Prologue*, D. 576 and 583," *The Explicator*, XXIII (1965), 73.

[23] Although Curry says that the Wife's dominant planet is Venus on p. 24, he later states that Mars rules in oppression over Venus in the horoscope (*Mediaeval Sciences*, p. 168).

for the Wife some characteristics of people influenced by Venus in good positions and to an extent ignores his own evidence about the unfortunate things that happen when Mars is in Taurus. Thus, instead of emphasizing the very unpleasant things he has cited from the astrologers about Mars in Taurus (the person born will be "criminal," "a fornicator," "will cuckold her husband"), Professor Curry places his concern with what the Wife might have been if her horoscope had been somewhat different:

> The key to her character, however, lies in the fact, as I have already indicated, that the fineness and delicacy which achieves expression in the story is but the resurging, as it were, of the artistic Venerean impulse, an outcropping of the poetic temperament which somehow has been kept, subconsciously no doubt, pure and untainted from the blasting and warping influence of Mars and circumstance. Or perhaps she has guarded faithfully as a kind of sacred possession this love of the beautiful, which no one about her could understand; it may be that in moments of world-weariness she sought the fairy realm of the imagination given to her by her mistress, and found refuge for a time from the coarseness inflicted upon her by the War-star. The unsatisfied yearning for that gentility and nobility of character which might and should have been hers, but for the power of an evil planet, is pathetic; the struggle which has kept unmarred a bit of her original nature in the midst of sordid conditions of life and in the face of adverse circumstances is heroic. The poet may, after all, have considered her his most tragic figure because—as is certainly the case—she is the most nearly completely human.[24]

The problem is that Professor Curry wants it both ways: on the one hand, the character formed by Venus "might" have been hers; on the other, the Wife maintains some of her "original nature"— an original nature that she never had. While Venus figures undeniably in the Wife of Bath's horoscope, to assume that she gave the Wife artistic impulses which were then overcome by the coarseness given by Mars is to be too generous to Venus astrologically and too

---

[24] Curry, *Mediaeval Sciences*, p. 115.

complicated psychologically. Since almost any mention of both Mars and Venus in the same astrological breath invariably brings forth references to adultery and fornication, Professor Curry is perhaps too scrupulous in bolstering the benevolent Venus; his analysis of Venus' influence toward artistry seems to stem more from his beliefs about the Wife's character as revealed in the *Tales* than from any strictly astrological viewpoint. Finally, literary characters who waver between their impulses toward the beautiful and the vulgar are common enough in modern fiction, but are relatively rare in mediaeval poetry. As Professor Robertson has put it, the Wife is not a character in the modern literary sense at all, but is rather "an elaborate iconographic figure designed to show the manifold implications of an attitude."[25] Certainly an important detail of the poetic iconography here is her horoscope.

If we grant that the Wife's horoscope was created by Chaucer to be emblematic of the Wife's lechery, which is surely attested to by her five husbands "withouten oother compaignye in youthe," we may then ponder the implications of her own astrological analysis. Her fatalism would be judged reprehensible by Chaucer's audience, but if she is resigned to following her "inclination" and her "appetite," why does she cry out, "Allas! allas! that evere love was synne!"?

Again Professor Curry's analysis must be taken into account. He sees much of the Wife's outward gaiety as but a mask to cover the bitterness that "has been forced upon her by an unholy constellation." From this viewpoint the Wife's plangent outburst is an indication that she at least knows better and has the grace to cry "alas."[26] It would seem, however, that if the Wife is repentant, she is not very repentant. If she is indeed bitter, as Professor Curry would have it, then she covers up her bitterness remarkably well, and aside from this one expression it would be hard to point to any indications of regret on her part. On the other hand, it is not at all difficult to find the Wife being shamelessly *un*repentant; in addition to the generally self-satisfied and thoroughly vindicatory tone of the whole Prologue, she goes out of her way to tell us that she has no regrets about her life:

[25] Robertson, *Preface*, p. 330.
[26] Curry, *Mediaeval Sciences*, p. 113.

> But, Lord Crist! whan that it remembreth me
> Upon my yowthe, and on my jolitee,
> It tikleth me aboute myn herte roote.
> Unto this day it dooth myn herte boote
> That I have had my world as in my tyme.
>
> *(WB Prol,* 469-73)

The evidence indicates that the Wife's cry of "alas" should be interpreted more as an expression of annoyance than of regret. Indeed, one of Chaucer's contemporaries, Thomas Usk, commented upon this very lack of regret among "Veneriens" like the Wife when he contrasted them with servants of Mercury. Veneriens, he said, "so lusty ben and so leude in thier wittes, that in such thinges right litel or naught don they fele; and wryten and cryen to their felawes: 'here is blisse, here is joye. . . .' "[27] When the Wife of Bath tells us that she is "al Venerien / In feelynge," she is not trying to apologize for what she is but rather to boast of it. Her cry of "alas" is not to be interpreted as an expression of repentance but as a comment on inconvenience. For the pragmatic Wife, for whom experience is "right ynogh," astrology offered a chance to justify her ways, as did Biblical texts and traditional anti-feminist literature. The Wife's knowledge of astrology and concern for her horoscope set her off against the clerks (like Chaucer himself), whom she disparages, and put her in the camp of those believers in divinatory astrology in whom Chaucer said he had "no feith, ne knowing of her *horoscopum.*"

3. TROILUS AMONG THE SPHERES:
A SURVEY AND A SUGGESTION

THE EXAMINATION of this particular crux in Chaucer's poetry must necessarily devote more space to a survey of opinion and argument than to the advancement of new material, for the problems at hand are sufficiently difficult to interpret that it is doubtful that any position taken now will be convincing unless contrary ideas can be shown to be wide of the mark. Reduced to the essentials there are two problems at the end of *Troilus and Criseyde*: to which sphere does Troilus

---

[27] Thomas Usk, *The Testament of Love*, in *Chaucerian and Other Pieces*, ed. Walter W. Skeat (Oxford, 1894), p. 100.

go, and what does that signify? The difficulty of the second question
is increased by that of the first, for while the majority of manuscripts
say that Troilus went to the seventh sphere, most editors have changed
it to the eighth, for reasons that will be examined presently. More-
over, when we have decided whether to discover Troilus in the
seventh or eighth sphere there remains the problem of which way
we are counting, for in the Middle Ages the spheres were regularly
numbered from the inside out and from the outside in. The passage
itself, then, is not as straightforward in close analysis as it first ap-
pears:

> And whan that he was slayn in this manere,
> His lighte goost ful blisfully is went
> Up to the holughnesse of the eighthe spere,
> In convers letyng everich element;
> And ther he saugh, with ful avysement,
> The erratik sterres, herkenyng armonye
> With sownes ful of hevenyssh melodie.
>
> And down from thennes faste he gan avyse
> This litel spot of erthe, that with the se
> Embraced is, and fully gan despise
> This wrecched world, and held al vanite
> To respect of the pleyn felicite
> That is in hevene above. . . .
>
> (*T&C*, v, 1807-19)

When Skeat grappled with this passage he claimed that the obvious
source was Boccaccio's *Teseida*, a work which Chaucer had already
used for the *Knight's Tale*, and he noted that Boccaccio referred not
to the seventh but to the eighth sphere. Assuming that Boccaccio
had in mind the system of numbering the spheres from the moon out-
ward to the fixed stars, Skeat argued that Boccaccio intended to have
Arcita look back from the eighth sphere of the fixed stars, from
which he would see both the erratic stars (*le stelle ratiche*) or planets,
and the elements that had been left behind. Skeat did not, however,
change the reading "seventh" that occurred in all the manuscripts
available to him.[28]

[28] Skeat, *Works*, v, 504-505.

In Root's edition of the *Troilus and Criseyde* there are two changes from Skeat. Root's examination of a large body of manuscripts led him to the conclusion that the reading "seventh" was an error introduced very early into a whole series of manuscripts, and although more common in extant manuscripts, was nevertheless an error. As is commonly known, the numbers in manuscripts were invariably written *vij* and *viij* and were very subject to error. Root also thought that the clear reading of "eighth" in Boccaccio gave more credence to the manuscript reading "eighth" in the *Troilus*, but he departed from Skeat in actually emending the wording to "eighth." He departed even more sharply in his interpretation of the numbering of the spheres, reversing Skeat's computations. Root argues that Boccaccio's source is Cicero's *Somnium Scipionis*, and in that work the spheres are numbered from the outside, beginning with the fixed stars and proceeding to the earth in the ninth position. Thus, Root argues, Boccaccio meant that Arcita ascended only to the sphere of the moon, the eighth sphere from the outside. As evidence that Chaucer intended this too, Root argues that he names the planetary gods in this order in Book III, that Troilus is close enough to earth to see the spot where he was slain, and that the reference to leaving the elements behind suggests a position close to the earth.[29]

Root anticipated possible objections to his interpretation and admitted that by the same wording Boccaccio might have meant one thing and Chaucer another. He also noted that although the spheres are numbered from the outside inward in the presumed source for Boccaccio's *Teseida*, the *Somnium Scipionis*, its hero takes up his stand in the Milky Way—i.e., in the sphere of the fixed stars. Troilus' ability to see the spot where he was slain might be set down to poetic license, and the naming of the pagan gods in descending order elsewhere in the *Troilus* needs more study.

The most important point to be made in this regard is that in Book III, 715-35, with the exception of Venus, the gods, not the planets, are considered, and while they are invoked roughly on the basis of proceeding from the outside inward, Venus is mentioned first

[29] *The Book of Troilus and Criseyde*, ed. Robert Kilburn Root (Princeton, 1926), pp. 559-62.

and Saturn is omitted. In short, it is difficult to see very much in this passage that bears on the ascent through the heavens in Book v, for here we are not concerned with the spheres, and the order, such as it is, seems to be insignificant. In conclusion, Root's arguments for emending the text to read "eighth" seem very good, although his interpretation of the eighth sphere as the sphere of the moon seems to be somewhat more warranted, but still not compelling, in Boccaccio than in Chaucer. Both Root's emendation and his interpretation of the numbering of the spheres are adopted by Robinson, although Robinson also directs the reader to another interpretation of the numbering of the spheres.

Professor Dobson countered Root's interpretation of the numbering of the spheres in Boccaccio and consequently in Chaucer with the claim that the correct source of the passage in the *Teseida* is not the *Somnium Scipionis* but rather Dante's *Paradiso*, xxii, 100-54. If this is so, then Boccaccio would no doubt have had in mind Dante's, not Cicero's, numbering of the spheres, and the eighth sphere would refer to the fixed stars. As further evidence Dobson notes that the sequence of vision for Boccaccio's hero, Arcita, is exactly like that found in Dante: the hero first sees the erratic stars and only subsequently the little earth, thus suggesting a position beyond all the spheres of the planets.[30]

Certainly Dante is as likely a source for the passage in the *Teseida* as the *Somnium Scipionis*, but even if he were accepted as such not everyone would be convinced that the numbering of the spheres used in Dante ought to be transferred to reading Boccaccio. For example, Professor Clark believes that Boccaccio had in mind the eighth sphere of the moon, and that Chaucer in turn was deliberately ambiguous in order to gloss over the differences between the two Italian poets. Clark's argument about the position in the spheres depends, like Dobson's, on the hero's sequence of vision; but whereas Dobson remarked that both Dante the pilgrim and Arcita first saw the stars and then the earth, indicating a position outside the spheres of the planets, Clark argues that in Boccaccio's *Teseida* the hero first looks up at

[30] E. J. Dobson, "Some Notes on Middle English Texts," *English and Germanic Studies*, I (1947-48), 56-62. N.B., title varies: *English Philological Studies*.

the erratic stars and then down at the earth, indicating a midway position on the moon.[31]

> quivi le stelle ratiche ammirava,
> l'ordine loro e la somma bellezza,
> suoni ascoltando pien d'ogni dolcezza.
>
> Quindi si volse *in giú* a rimirare
> le cose abandonate, e vide il poco
> globo terreno, a cui intorno il mare
> girava e l'aere e di sopra il foco,
> e ogni cosa da nulla stimare
> a rispetto del ciel.[32]

A possible exception to this view is the improbability of its assumption that Boccaccio would expect the earth to look small (*il poco globo terreno*) from the moon rather than large. There is also the problem that while Boccaccio says that Arcita looks down (*in giú*) at the earth, he does not say that his hero looks up at the erratic stars. Rather, Professor Clark deduces this from the hero's looking first at the stars and then turning to look down at the earth. This does not, however, necessarily mean that the hero turns from looking in one direction to looking in another. The reflexive form of the verb is used here (*volgersi*), and Dante, Boccaccio's idol, often uses the nonreflexive form of the verb to signify turning the eyes, but the reflexive form for turning the thoughts or the attention.[33] Thus while the phrasing could mean that the hero looked up and then turned to look down, it is equally possible that he looked down at the erratic stars and then turned his attention to the little earth, which was also below.

[31] John W. Clark, "Dante and the Epilogue of *Troilus*," *JEGP*, L (1951), 1-10.

[32] Boccaccio, *Teseida*, XI, 1-2; p. 316.

[33] Cf., *Inferno*, I, 25-27, where Dante uses the reflexive *volgersi* with the same secondary verb, *rimirare*, as Boccaccio. In this passage there is no physical turning implied:

> Così l' animo mio, ch' ancor fuggiva,
> Si volse a retro a rimirar lo passo,
> Che non lasciò già mai persona viva.

It must be emphasized that Dante does sometimes use the reflexive form for turning the body, as in *Inferno*, I, 22-25.

Somewhat more satisfying than the approaches to Chaucer via the source of Boccaccio is the approach used by Professor Cope, who looks closely at Chaucer's numbering of the spheres elsewhere in the *Troilus* itself, and notes that Chaucer commits himself to the method of computation from the inside out by calling Venus the ruler of the third heaven in the Prohemium to Book III. Professor Cope, basing his arguments more on an analysis of the symbolic value of Chaucer's source materials than on the sources themselves, also suggests that the manuscript reading "seventh" should be retained. Although he agrees with those who see Chaucer following Boccaccio and Boccaccio following Dante, Cope bases his interpretation of Chaucer's seventh sphere on an inquiry into which of Dante's spheres, the seventh or the eighth, would be more appropriate for Troilus. Because in Dante the eighth sphere of the fixed stars is the abiding place of the Christian Mystics, he believes that Troilus would more properly be assigned to the seventh sphere, that of Saturn, "where those spirits dwell whose lives have been given wholly to divine devotion, and where he would learn from Benedict of the current corruption in holy orders. Troilus has certainly become a devoted member of the order of earthly lovers, and through his devotion he has, no less certainly, learned of this order's corruption."[34]

Not every Chaucerian critic will feel altogether comfortable envisioning Troilus chatting with St. Benedict, but the major objection to Cope's interpretation here is that it overburdens the passage. Moreover, Cope assumes that "Chaucer has altered Boccaccio's cynical tale so as to make Troilus' mundane passion the first rung on a ladder to Paradise." Now of course love could be an ennobling thing in the Middle Ages, and one needs to look no further than Dante's love for Beatrice for an example, but it seems rash to compare Dante's love of Beatrice with the "blynde lust, the which that may nat laste" (*T&C*, v, 1824), that Troilus condemns from his sphere. The blind lust he condemns was presumably the nature of his own love, else why comment on it? It is hard to agree that the suicidal Troilus, who concludes his earthly speeches vowing his own destruction and whining to the absent Criseyde, "That ye thus doon, I have it nat

---

[34] Jackson I. Cope, "Chaucer, Venus, and the 'Seventh Spere,'" *MLN*, LXVII (1952), 245-46.

deserved" (*T&C*, v, 1722), is so ennobled by love that he is beginning the ascent to Paradise.

In spite of Cope's telling argument about Chaucer's numbering of the spheres from the innermost outward elsewhere in the same poem, several critics have persevered with arguments for discovering Troilus in an inner rather than an outer sphere. For example, Professor Scott believes that Troilus should be discovered in the seventh sphere of Mercury because it is Mercury who comes to guide him, and Professor Kellogg has suggested that Boccaccio's emphasis is on the discrepancy between earthly mutability and celestial stability and that the optimum place for the observation of this would be the eighth sphere of the moon.[35] This latter assumption is somewhat arbitrary, since the contrast could presumably be observed from outside all the spheres about as well as from the sphere of the moon. Kellogg's theory has the disadvantage of associating all the spheres above the moon with eternity, while it is quite easy to show that they were often associated with mutability—hence their appellation "erratic stars."

In opposition to Scott's theory that Troilus should be discovered in the seventh sphere (counting inwards) of Mercury because it is Mercury who comes to guide him, Professor Bloomfield has noted that Mercury is the traditional psychopomp, so it is not necessary for Troilus to be in his sphere to encounter him as a guide. Bloomfield also makes a very valuable contribution to the discussion by calling attention to the concept of the ogdoad, the eighth sphere to which the soul possessing gnosis returns at death. This concept, also found in Servius, Hermes Trismegistus, and the writings of the Neoplatonists, has the distinct virtue of accounting for an ascent to the fixed stars by the pagan Troilus without recourse to analogies with Dante's *Paradiso*, with or without Boccaccio as a middle source.[36]

The placement of pagans after death was always a tricky business in the Middle Ages, and Bloomfield's adduction of the eighth sphere

[35] Forrest S. Scott, "The Seventh Sphere: A Note on 'Troilus and Criseyde,'" *MLR*, LI (1956), 2-5; Alfred L. Kellogg, "On the Tradition of Troilus' Vision of the Little Earth," *MS*, XXII (1960), 204-13. Kellogg's article also advances valuable parallels from the *Somme le roi* to those things shown brought to nought at the close of the *Troilus*: "estat real," "worthynesse," and "noblesse."

[36] Morton W. Bloomfield, "The Eighth Sphere: A Note on Chaucer's 'Troilus and Criseyde' v, 1809," *MLR*, LII (1958), 408-10.

of the fixed stars as a traditional place for dead pagans offers us a way of understanding where both Boccaccio's Arcita and Chaucer's Troilus were positioned, providing we are willing to grant them at least some degree of gnosis. This seems advisable, for whatever we may think of Troilus as hero or heroic lover, certainly the whole metaphor of the ascent to the heavens is meant to indicate the acquisition of wisdom. Thus, whether or not we wish to think that Troilus possesses virtue and wisdom throughout the course of the poem, his ascent through the spheres is a signal to the reader of either an improvement or a change, and we need look no further than Boethius for the basic image:

> Whanne the swifte thoght hath clothid itself in tho fetheris, it despiseth the hateful erthes, and surmounteth the rowndnesse of the gret ayr; and it seth the clowdes byhynde his bak, and passeth the heighte of the regioun of the fir, that eschaufeth by the swifte moevynge of the firmament, til that he areyseth hym into the houses that beren the sterres, and joyneth his weies with the sonne, Phebus, and felawschipeth the weie of the olde colde Saturnus; and he, imaked a knyght of the clere sterre. . . .[37]

This concept would be ideal for Chaucer's purposes, for it would lead very smoothly into his moral for the poem with an image that is literally pagan, but bearing obvious Christian implications. Chaucer's gloss to the passage shows how this works: "*That is to seyn, whan the thought is makid Godis knyght by the sekynge of cleer trouthe to comen to the verray knowleche of God.*" Thus, with the image of the ascent Chaucer can lead into his Christian epilogue without doing too

---

[37] Bk. IV, m. I. It is just possible that the mention of Saturn here gave Chaucer the idea of describing Troilus' position in terms of the seventh sphere (the sphere of Saturn in the order of numbering used elsewhere in the *Troilus*), which is the reading encountered in most of the manuscripts. Chaucer may have been imitating Boccaccio's eighth sphere in a very circuitous manner by having Troilus ascend to the seventh sphere of Saturn, thence to be led forth by Mercury to the next sphere: the eighth sphere of the fixed stars: "And *forth* he wente, shortly for to telle,/ Ther as Mercurye sorted hym to dwelle" (*T&C*, v, 1826-27). There are two very real objections to this tentatively advanced reading: Root has argued quite convincingly for an early error in the manuscript, and Mercury could as easily lead Troilus "forth" from one specific location in the eighth sphere to another as from the seventh to the eighth.

much violence to the demands of the poem thus far. Certainly this is a more advantageous approach than one that would relate Troilus directly to the pilgrim Dante, for the two are very dissimilar as literary figures in general, and the treatments of their ascents through the spheres are markedly different. As Professor Robertson observes, it is Mercury, not Beatrice, who appears to guide Troilus, and in view of the circumstances it seems unlikely that he will lead Troilus up Jacob's Ladder as Beatrice does Dante.[38]

It also seems doubtful that Troilus' love for Criseyde is the cause for his ascent, for as we have seen, his love ends with carping. Rather, death itself, by releasing him from bodily desires, frees his mind for the Boethian ascent. Troilus leaves the realms of Fortune for the higher spheres where, as Lady Philosophy observed, "jugement is more cleer, and wil nat icorrumped."[39] This whole Neoplatonic concept is made even clearer by Lady Philosophy in the same passage, when she outlines a kind of descent through the spheres in which man's freedom is continually abridged as he descends to earth, becomes man, and descends to vice:

> But the soules of men moten nedes be more fre whan thei loken hem in the speculacioun or lokynge of the devyne thought; and lasse fre whan thei slyden into the bodyes; and yit lasse fre whan thei ben gadrid togidre and comprehended in erthli membres. But the laste servage is whan that thei ben yeven to vices and han ifalle fro the possessioun of hir propre resoun. (Bk. v, pr. 2)

Troilus' enlightenment, then, should probably be viewed as the reverse of the process just described by Lady Philosophy, and is to be considered the consequence of his release from earth rather than the result of some particular virtue imputed to him—certainly it is not as the result of his fornication with Criseyde. The problem of his entrance into the ogdoad remains, for it is difficult to argue that he

---

[38] For observations of the similarity between the *Troilus* and the *Parlement* with explanations of its significance quite different from the interpretation to be offered here, see Bertrand H. Bronson "In Appreciation of Chaucer's *Parlement of Foules*," *University of California Publications in English*, III (1935), 199-202; Sanford B. Meech, *Design in Chaucer's Troilus* (Syracuse, 1959), pp. 135-37. Robertson's point was made in a personal letter.

[39] Bk. v, pr. 2; as pointed out by Professor Robertson, *Preface*, p. 501.

attains gnosis while on earth. There is, however, an explanation that runs parallel to the ogdoad concept but which places the weak rather than the virtuous in the eighth sphere of the fixed stars, and it is a concept Chaucer knew.

In Chaucer's *Parlement of Foules* there is a retelling of the *Somnium Scipionis*, and here we find an appropriate place for Troilus. In the dream as Chaucer recounts it, Scipio is taken to "a sterry place" (*PF*, 43), which is presumably outside of all the movable spheres, for from it he is shown the galaxy, the nine spheres, and the little earth (*PF*, 55-61). Scipio is then told that the earth is little and full of torment, so he should not delight in it, but hope to come to heaven (*PF*, 64-72). It is then made very clear that the virtuous arise to heaven, which is beyond the spheres, but the un-virtuous are condemned to dwell for a long time within the moving spheres before they are permitted to enter the realm of stability:

> "... Know thyself first immortal,
> And loke ay besyly thow werche and wysse
> To commune profit, and thow shalt not mysse
> To comen swiftly to that place deere
> That ful of blysse is and of soules cleere.
>
> But brekers of the lawe, soth to seyne,
> *And likerous folk*, after that they ben dede,
> Shul whirle aboute th'erthe alwey in peyne,
> Tyl many a world be passed, out of drede,
> And than, foryeven al hir wikked dede,
> Than shul they come into this blysful place,
> To which to comen God the sende his grace."
>
> (*PF*, 73-84)

Troilus may be justly accused of being one of the "likerous folk," and it would be quite appropriate to the tone of the poem if Chaucer sent him to a place more like the Christian purgatory than either the Christian hell or the Christian heaven.[40] We may hypothesize, then,

[40] Were we to consider the possibility that Troilus was to be sent to a place of punishment rather than purgation, a case might be made for discovering him in the eighth sphere of the moon, rather than the eighth sphere of the fixed stars. In a letter Professor Robertson has called my attention to this passage in Remigius' com-

that Mercury does not lead Troilus away from the eighth sphere of the fixed stars into some other realm, but merely leads him to some spot within the eighth sphere. The remaining problem is to demonstrate that if Chaucer meant to assign Troilus to the realm of the moving spheres, it was the eighth and not the seventh or the second that he had in mind. For this we may once more go to Boethius who said that the soul ascending to wisdom ascends to the "houses that bear the stars," which seems to mean the fixed stars. He then specifies that the soul remains in the "circle of the stars," which is surely a reference to the sphere of the fixed stars, until it leaves the "last heaven" and, passing through the Primum Mobile, arises to the light of God. The reference to the "last heaven" seems to clinch the matter:

> . . . he areyseth hym into *the houses that beren the sterres*, and joyneth his weies with the sonne, Phebus, and felawschipeth the weie of the olde colde Saturnus . . . and thilke soule *renneth by the cercle of the sterres* in alle the places there as the schynynge nyght is ypainted. . . . And whan the thought hath don there inogh, he schal *forleten the laste hevene*, and he schal pressen and wenden on the bak of the swifte firmament, and he schal be makid parfit of the worschipful lyght of God. There halt the lord of kynges the septre of his myght and atemprith the governementz of the world, and the schynynge juge of thinges, stable in hymself, governeth the swifte wayn. (Bk. IV, m. I)

Thus we see that even the wise man must spend time "inogh" in the eighth sphere of the fixed stars, and only after that time can he go to the "back" of the next sphere to arise to that realm where all is stable. In remanding Troilus to the eighth sphere of the fixed stars, Chaucer sends him as one who is "likerous" to a place where the wise pause for some time and the lecherous must remain "Tyl many

---

mentary on Martianus: "Poetae enim fingunt animas post corpora inter septem planetarum circulos vel puniri vel purgari secundum merita prioris vitae, et infernum quidem dicunt esse infra circulum lunae, cuius fluvium Pyrflegetonta, id est igneum Flegetontem, in Martis circulo dicunt oriri. Elisios autem campos ubi purgatae animae requiescunt confingunt esse infra Iovialem circulum" (*Remigii Autissiodorensis comentum in Martianum Capellam*, ed. Cora E. Lutz [Leiden, 1962-65], pp. 91-92). This is mentioned only as a possibility, since Chaucer's use of the other method of counting the spheres elsewhere in the *Troilus* probably precludes it.

a world be passed" (*PF*, 81). For both the wise and the not-so-wise, the eighth sphere in the Neoplatonic concept is a place of purification or penance. Chaucer could not do any more than this for his hero, for to depict him leaving the eighth sphere would be to write a comedy, and Chaucer advises us that his comedy is yet to be written:

> Go, litel bok, go, litel myn tragedye,
> Ther God thi makere yet, er that he dye,
> So sende myght to make in som comedye!
>
> (*T&C*, v, 1786-88)

CHAPTER V

Astrology in the *Man of Law's Tale*

I. THE NARRATOR, PROVIDENCE,
AND ROMANCE

THE SEVERAL astrological passages in the *Man of Law's Tale*, especially the narrator's apostrophes "O firste moevyng! crueel firmament" and "In sterres, many a wynter therbiforn, / Was writen the deeth of Ector, Achilles" (*MLT*, 295 and 197-98), are rather complex in themselves and even more difficult to understand in relationship to the tale as a whole. This is because of the curious relationship of the Man of Law to the materials of his story. The Man of Law, as narrator, uses astrology to gloss the tale of Custance; therefore, the astrology cannot be fully understood until we understand what the Man of Law (not Chaucer) thinks about both astrology and devotional narratives. We know that the appropriate mediaeval response to a devotional tale, particularly to a saint's life or the life of a saintly person, was to ignore the individual and concentrate on the moral thesis involved. This the Man of Law does not do, and yet, as Professor Robertson has pointed out, the Man of Law's reiterated concern for the "fruyt" of his story as opposed to its "chaf" is a clear invitation to the audience both to seek the "sentence" of the story and to judge whether or not the Man of Law is successful in the interpretation of his own material.[1]

Indeed, the Man of Law stands high among the Canterbury pilgrims in the degree of his involvement with his story, and he is presented to us as one who cannot simply tell a tale, but who feels obliged to react to it sympathetically, to comment on it, and even to interpret it for us. Thus, he selects the story of Custance, whose

---

[1] Roberston, *Preface*, p. 366. For "fruyt" and "chaf" as literary terms, see the *Preface*, pp. 315-17. The terms occur in the *Man of Law's Tale*, lines 411 and 701-06. On devotional narrative see Jean Leclercq: "Hagiographical legend advances a moral thesis and a religious idea. No interest is taken in the individual as such, in the memory he has left behind him and which history will record. Not the things he did, only the ideal he illustrated will be remembered" (Jean Leclercq, O.S.B., *The Love of Learning and the Desire for God*, trans. Catharine Misrahi [New York: Mentor Omega Books, 1961], p. 164).

humble faith in God's providence is rewarded by numerous deliverances from death and from fates-worse-than-death, and, lest we miss the terror of impending doom or the moral of Custance's deliverances, the Man of Law intrudes repeatedly in order to emphasize and interpret. These interpretations and emphases are scarcely the serene summations of "sentence" we might expect this providential tale to elicit from an educated man; rather, they are a commentary on the narrator's and not the heroine's emotional reactions to the vicissitudes of the story. The Man of Law's specific and general interpretations of the story, as a consequence, become interesting both for their relevance, or lack of it, to the tale, and for their ability to disclose by their degree of pertinence much about the Man of Law's understanding of things providential.

In contrast to Custance, who is sometimes sad but always patient, continuously but confidently suffering, the Man of Law is intense both emotionally and intellectually about her sufferings. Whether bemoaning poverty, bewailing astrological determinism, or beseeching divine intervention for Custance's deliverance, he is no disembodied narrative voice but has more to say about the horrors of Custance's perils and the joys of her deliverances than does she. It is almost as though he feels obliged to color more brightly a somewhat pallid heroine. Indeed, by any standards of dramatic propriety it would seem that Custance's diverse adventures would call forth from her a greater volatility than is in fact the case, for her terrors and triumphs are extreme even by mediaeval standards.

In the course of the story Custance is affianced to a pagan sultan, married to King Alla, whom she converts to Christianity, and is twice set adrift at sea through the machinations of her enemies—a varied set of experiences to say the least. The adventures begin with Custance's leaving the court of her father, the Emperor of Rome, to journey across the seas to be married to the Sultan of Syria. However, the Sultan's mother thwarts the marriage because she objects to the Sultan's planned conversion to Christianity. The Sultan is slain by the Sultaness, who then sets Custance adrift, but Custance washes up on a friendly shore and promptly converts to Christianity the first person she meets there: Hermengyld, the wife of the Constable. Through the efforts of the wife, the Constable himself is converted,

but then a young knight threatens Custance's virtue and, being re-buffed, slays Hermengyld and attempts to affix the blame on Custance. She is brought to trial before Alla, the king of the land, but at her trial a hand miraculously appears out of nowhere to strike down her accuser, and so impressed is Alla that he converts to Christianity and marries Custance, who bears him a son. Unhappily, Alla's mother, Donegild, arranges for Custance to be set adrift again through an involved ruse. Ultimately, however, Custance is picked up at sea by a ship bound for Rome, in which city she is re-united first with Alla, who had gone there on a pilgrimage, and then with her father.

The many uses of "however" in recounting the tale of Custance bear witness to the numerous opportunities for a narrator to interject comments on the fickleness of fate, and the Man of Law lets none go by. He condemns the Emperor's failure to consult astrologers about Custance's marriage; he excoriates the evil mothers-in-law, Donegild and the Sultaness; he even introduces some astrological speculation of his own. On the other hand, he rejoices when Custance becomes a queen and treats us to a lengthy explanation of both why God chooses to "shewe his wonderful myracle" (*MLT*, 470-504) to the world in general and why Custance in particular is saved from death. The Man of Law, then, is more than just another story teller among the Canterbury pilgrims: he is an interpreter, an interpreter of both his story and of the world around him. Furthermore, the disparity between the reactions of Custance and the Man of Law to her vicissitudes points up Custance as a paradigm of Constancy whereas the Man of Law is shown to be a less constant figure. His analyses of the story are as much a gloss on his own character and the events of his world as they are a commentary on Custance and the phenomena of her environment. Because of the importance of the Man of Law as interpreter it will be argued here that he is best approached through a study of his interpretations, which, by mediae-val standards, are mainly misinterpretations. The confounding of im-mediate pleasure with ultimate satisfaction puts the Man of Law at variance with the personification of Constancy and leads him to take a materialistic, legalistic view of astrology, religion, literature, and everything else. It is this confusion, for example, that prompts his romantic, dramatic coloring of the Custance story—a story in a vein

uncongenial to him but very popular in the Middle Ages. It seems scarcely credible that the Man of Law's anti-Boethian, anti-humanistic, anti-religious approach to life should be credited to Chaucer, so it will be further argued here that the *Man of Law's Tale* as a whole is a satire—not on Custance but on the Man of Law. Finally, the consistency of characterization that emerges when this approach to the problems of the tale is taken leads to the conclusion that the *Man of Law's Tale* was indeed written to be told by the Man of Law, despite extant arguments to the contrary.

It is, perhaps, this complication in the relationship of the story of Custance's trials and its frame that has led many critics to puzzle over the tone of this particular tale and over its genre. However, an approach to the *Man of Law's Tale* that admits the possibility that the Man of Law's and Chaucer's views may not be the same could account for the co-existence of the seemingly irreconcilable elements of the saint's legend and the romance within this tale.[2] Such an approach is proposed here in order to distinguish the basic story of Custance from its immediate frame as a tale told by the Man of Law, and in order to distinguish that matrix in turn from the audience's perspective on a poem written by Chaucer in which the

[2] In recent years one critic has spoken of the "incongruous" romantic manner coupled with a "sentimental" tale; another has styled the tone as midway between "low seriousness and levity"; a third has seen Chaucer exposing himself to the charge of "poor art" in having an "irreconcilable dualism of purpose"; and another has called the tale a "drama of Providence." See Bernard I. Duffey, "The Intention and Art of the *Man of Law's Tale*," *ELH*, XIV (1947), 192-93; Paull F. Baum, "*The Man of Law's Tale*," *MLN*, LXIV (1949), 13; Edward A. Block, "Originality, Controlling Purpose, and Craftsmanship in Chaucer's *Man of Law's Tale*," *PMLA*, LXVIII (1953), 616; John A. Yunck, "Religious Elements in Chaucer's *Man of Law's Tale*," *ELH*, XXVII (1960), 256-57. In a very valuable article which appeared after this essay was written, Professor David happily offered confirmation of several (though not all) of the judgments advanced here. For Professor David, the Man of Law is one who insists that "art be serious, dignified, and moral. But what he actually appreciates in art is not morality but respectability." Furthermore David argues, Chaucer writes a tale that is a "straightforward tale of 'moralitee and hoolynesse' framed by links in which the point of view of those who insist that poetry deal exclusively with such subjects is deftly satirized." The point made in the present essay is that the tale is not entirely "straightforward" in its treatment of morality and holiness, and that Chaucer has satirized the Man of Law in the text of the tale as well as in the Prologue and Headlink to it. See Alfred David, "The Man of Law vs. Chaucer: A Case in Poetics," *PMLA*, LXXXII (1967), 217-25.

Man of Law plays a part. If we should argue that it is the Man of Law and not Chaucer who tries to turn the pious, unworldly tale of Custance into something resembling a romance, we should not only gain a better insight into this version of her story, but also into Chaucer's treatment of the character of the teller. In this way the *Man of Law's Tale* could be added to the *Franklin's Tale* and the *Squire's Tale*, both of which have recently been described as tales that exceed their ostensible teller's capacity to understand them.[3] Whether or not the Man of Law's attitudes are to be identified with those of Chaucer, there is no doubt that the Man of Law differs from his heroine in his reactions to her vicissitudes. We have already glanced at some of the broad differences between Custance and the Man of Law; it is even more instructive to examine the areas of their divergence in some detail.

Custance, who may be called Constance, is larger than life in her capacity for patient acceptance of God's will, as are her Chaucerian sisters Griselda and Cecilia. However, her constancy through both adversity and prosperity is not to be found in the Man of Law, who substitutes for her acceptance of both trial and deliverance some plangent praises of God, Christ, and the Virgin Mary for their ability to change adversity into prosperity. It is Custance's single attitude toward both faces of Fortune that most sharply separates her from the Man of Law. Custance has clear ideas about duty in this world. When going off to the "Barbre nacioun" (281) she characteristically asks Christ for "grace his heestes to fulfille" (284), even though it is clear that she is not eager for marriage to an unknown Barbarian. Even more illustrative of her equanimity is the similarity of her prayers to God when she is cast adrift on the sea and when she is safely set ashore: in both cases she welcomes God's "sonde" (523 and 826). In other words, she accepts what God sends, either good Fortune or bad, as good because it comes from God.

---

[3] See Alan T. Gaylord, "The Promises in *The Franklin's Tale*," *ELH*, XXI (1964), 332; and Haller, "Chaucer's *Squire's Tale*." Professor Robertson has suggested that many of the characters on the pilgrimage are blind to the implications of their own tales in such a way that the tales themselves become subtle comments on their narrators (*Preface*, p. 275). For other studies of this kind of interplay between tale and teller see Huppé, *Reading of the Canterbury Tales*, and recent articles by Paul A. Olson.

Custance's prayers for deliverance are equally instructive, for she does not pray for worldly or temporal satisfaction. When set adrift by the Sultaness, Custance does not pray for rescue, but rather for salvation should she drown (454-55), and the strength to amend her life should she live (462). It is not that Custance is unfeeling. She is sad at the thought of her departure to be married; she asks for death as a release from her miseries (516-17); she asks for divine intervention to justify her innocence (639-44); she asks that her son's life be spared (851-54); and she asks, at the end of her journeys, that her father not send her again into "noon hethenesse" (1112). If Custance is not above asking for life or death she is assuredly above arguing with the answers to her prayers and requests, and at the very end of her adventures, even though her husband dies, she returns home and praises God "an hundred thousand sithe" (1155). While Custance may pray for an avoidance of or an end to suffering, she nevertheless accepts whatever God sends with thanks, and certainly does not seek any worldly gain.

The Man of Law has different ideas about good and bad Fortune. For him there are value judgments to be made about Fortune: God is to be thanked and praised not for strengthening us by trial, but for accomplishing our deliverance; not for the promise of heavenly joy, but for the arrangement of our temporal satisfaction. As he says admiringly, "Thus kan Oure Lady bryngen out of wo / Woful Custance, and many another mo" (977-78). Similarly, we are not reminded by the Man of Law of the Christ who said "Si quis vult me sequi, deneget semetipsum: et tollat crucem suam" (Mark 8:34). Rather, we find Christ invoked as "Crist, which that is to every harm triacle" (479), and in the final lines of the story Christ is saluted by the Man of Law as one who can bring good Fortune in this life: "Jhesu Crist, that of his myght may sende / Joye after wo" (1160-61). We may remark, then, that the Man of Law differs from the heroine of his story both in the degree of his dislike of adversity and in the degree of his satisfaction with temporal prosperity.

The Man of Law can interject narrative comments about providential deliverance, but it is Custance who voices these expressions when things go badly as well as when they go to her advantage. Where Custance might ask to be spared suffering, the Man of Law

rejoices in divine intervention of the most dramatic kind, and is tellingly silent about the accomplishment of God's will when it involves his heroine's discomfort and danger. It is this fascination with God as a miraculous, dramatic bringer of good Fortune that impels the Man of Law to interject a thirty-line outburst of admiration for a God who saved Daniel from the lions, preserved Jonah in the whale, kept back the Red Sea, and fed the five thousand with two fishes and five loaves (470-504). This, to him, is the kind of unexpected bounty for which God is most to be praised; we hear nothing from him of the trials of the Hebrew people, of Moses, of Job, of Christ himself.

What the Man of Law forgets, in his enthusiasm for deliverance, is the necessity of trial, and his endorsement of the one to the neglect of the other could not have passed unnoticed in a society in which there were both secular and religious writings insisting that God sends adversity in order to exercise, try, and purify the good as well as to punish the wicked. Chaucer's Clerk calls our attention to an important Biblical *locus* on this very issue, and in Chaucer's translation of Boethius' *Consolation of Philosophy* the idea of "bad" Fortune is rejected on the grounds that such Fortune is, in truth, for the exercise of the good or for the punishment of the wicked.[4] Moreover, earlier in the same work, attention is called to the fact that "debonaire" Fortune is more dangerous than "contrary" Fortune, for while the former is deceptive, the latter is instructive (Bk. ii, pr. 8). This is particularly important to note, for it not only suggests that we may be able to distinguish between the attitudes of Custance and the Man of Law toward the uses of this world, but also that we may be able to judge them. The Man of Law does not hesitate to interpret his materials; we should not hesitate to judge both them and him, and to use his interpretations as a basis for judgment. Certainly the Man of Law falls short of his heroine in spirituality, and his particular kind of worldliness may be demonstrated in other ways as well.

For example, when the Man of Law and Harry Bailly are banter-

---

[4] Bk. iv, pr. 7. Also, Chaucer shows his knowledge of Biblical statements about testing when he has the Clerk refer us to the Epistle of James 1:12-13 (*ClT*, 1153-55). Other examples may be found widely, particularly in the didactic books of the Vulgate. For an important reference in the Fathers, see St. Augustine, *On Christian Doctrine*, i, xvi; 15.

ing legalisms before the tale-telling begins, the Man of Law says that whatever law a man sets for another he should use himself (Headlink, 43-44), which is an amusing analogue of the golden rule, twisted to a materialistic lawyer's viewpoint. It stands, moreover, in silent contrast to Chaucer's highly sympathetic Parson, who first follows Christ's "loore" and only then teaches it to others (*Gen Prol,* 527-28). The difference between law and lore, between making regulations for others and setting an example for others, emphasizes the distance between the worldly Man of Law and the spiritually oriented Parson. This, in turn, is analogous to the differences between the Man of Law and Custance, for the Parson is like Custance, Griselda, and Cecilia in being "in adversitee ful pacient" (*Gen Prol,* 484). The more we separate Custance and the Man of Law the more we see that Chaucer intended that her vision and not his should be our vision. Indeed, upon reflection we should be astonished if the literal-minded lawyer, who knew every statute "pleyn by rote" (*Gen Prol,* 327), should be possessed of much spiritual insight. In order to demonstrate this convincingly, however, we should consider the Man of Law as an interpreter of all the separate elements of his story as well as the whole, and as interpreter of all elements of the world around him as well as of Fortune and providence.

2. ATTITUDES IN THE HEADLINK AND THE PROLOGUE

THE PREVIOUS discussion of the Man of Law's concern to interpret his tale operates on the assumption that the tale is indeed his. Because this assumption has been challenged, and because the teller's relationship to his tale underlines some facets of the Man of Law's philosophy of temporal satisfaction, the situation demands further assessment.

Although the *Man of Law's Tale* is today thought regularly to be a tale that should be told by a different pilgrim, the grounds for removing it from the Man of Law are weak, and there exist compelling reasons for assuming that Chaucer intended it for him. Not the least of these is that rearrangement of the Tales should be avoided unless absolutely necessary. The only substantial reason for removing the tale from the Man of Law is that while the tale is in verse, the Man of Law himself says that he speaks in prose (Headlink, 96). Skeat attempted to account for this difference by arguing that the

Man of Law's statement meant that he usually or customarily spoke in prose in the law courts, so his tale would be "prosy." Robinson rejected this reading as "wholly unlikely," albeit without argument, but Skeat's interpretation is attractive in that it clears up the disparity without altering the attribution to the Man of Law that exists in all manuscripts.[5] An even more encompassing explanation may, however, be possible.

If we put the Man of Law's remark about speaking prose into context, it may be seen as part of an elaborate joke concerning ownership, stewardship, and poetry, in which the Man of Law contrasts his "prosy" tale to the more "poetic" tales told by one Geoffrey Chaucer. The Man of Law's desire to own the material things of this world is in marked contrast with traditional Christian ideas of stewardship, and Chaucer points up the fatuity of a philosophy of ownership as opposed to guardianship. He does this by setting forth the Man of Law as one interested in outright ownership, and then has him carry this philosophy over into the realm of poetry, where "owning" a story is impossible. In the General Prologue Chaucer presents the Man of Law as one to whom "Al was fee symple . . ." (*Gen Prol*, 319), or outright ownership in matters of real estate. However, when it comes time for the Man of Law to tell a story, he protests that he cannot tell one that he owns outright because a certain Geoffrey Chaucer has already told all the good stories, albeit he hasn't done much of a job with them:

> But nathelees, certeyn,
> I kan right now no thrifty tale seyn
> That Chaucer, thogh he kan but lewedly
> On metres and on rymyng craftily,
> Hath seyd hem in swich Englissh as he kan
> Of olde tyme, as knoweth many a man;

[5] Skeat, *Works*, III, 141. The *Second Nun's Tale* is an instructive case where a seeming discrepancy between the character, a nun, and her self-description as an "unworthy sone of Eve" (*SecNT*, 62) has been satisfactorily reconciled. See Robinson's notes. Robinson's remark that the Man of Law's statement is analogous to the Prologues to the *Tale of Melibee*, the *Monk's Tale*, and the *Parson's Tale* does not consider the fact that in none of the suggested analogues does anyone say he speaks in prose.

And if he have noght seyd hem, leve brother,
In o book, he hath seyd hem in another.
For he hath toold of loveris up and doun
Mo than Ovide made of mencioun
In his Episteles, that been ful olde.
What sholde I tellen hem, syn they been tolde?
(Headlink, 45-56)

In mediaeval literary art, as *The Canterbury Tales* themselves illustrate, the important thing is not the originality of the basic story, but rather the artist's execution of it. Thus the Man of Law's concern that another's "ownership" precludes his telling another's story is clearly a joke, emphasized by his ultimate need to borrow in spite of his theory. Moreover, there is perhaps a hint here that he will be concerned with prose for the same reason he is concerned with certain kinds of stories, i.e., that Chaucer's precedence has left him no alternative.

Chaucer has already undercut the Man of Law's amusing brand of literary materialism, and he goes on to have him blunder as a literary critic. The Man of Law argues that Chaucer has told all the tales of "noble wyves and thise loveris eke" (Headlink, 59) while refraining from the shocking alternative of wicked stories of incestuous love, such has those of Canace and Appolonius of Tyre. That sort of thing, he remarks, will not sully his lips either: "Ne I wol noon reherce, if that I may" (Headlink, 89). This is a peculiarly egregious attitude, for the Man of Law finds only a certain nastiness in the stories told by the man Chaucer himself called the "moral Gower."[6]

The Man of Law's dilemma of ownership continues with his choice of a different genre. If Chaucer has told all the tales of noble love, and if one should not tell tales of incestuous love, the Man of Law thinks he will be like the Pierian sisters in their unequal contest with the Muses if he tries to tell a tale in the same genre. He argues that he is forced to depart from the sort of story of noble love that

[6] This has been argued by William L. Sullivan, "Chaucer's Man of Law as a Literary Critic," *MLN*, LXVIII (1953), 7. Sullivan also remarks upon the Man of Law's concern for wealth (p. 3). For the contrary argument, that the references to Canace, etc., are not in fact to Gower, see Robert O. Bowen, "Chaucer, The Man of Law's Introduction and Tale," *MLN*, LXXI (1956), 165.

he most admires to something less romantic—indeed to a tale learned not from Ovid but from a merchant (*ML Prol*, 132-33). In short, he will have to tell something plain, unromantic, and prosaic:

"But of my tale how shal I doon this day?
Me were looth be likned, doutelees,
To Muses that men clepe Pierides—
Methamorphosios woot what I mene;
But nathelees, I recche noght a bene
Though I come after hym with hawebake.
I speke in prose, and lat him rymes make."
And with that word he, with a sobre cheere,
Bigan his tale, as ye shal after heere.   (Headlink, 90-98)

In comparison to Chaucer's tales of "loveris up and doun," the Man of Law's baked haw or plain fare is like water to wine or prose to poetry. However, it is what he must tell if he is to have his stories, like his land, in fee simple.[7] Part of the humor here is that he ends by borrowing anyway, and part is in the fact that Chaucer, the translator of Boethius who styled himself as an author of "othere bookes of legendes of seintes, and omelies, and moralitee, and devocioun" (Retraction), here has the Man of Law refer to him as a writer of love stories exclusively. Since the Man of Law will not tell stories of incest and cannot tell stories of romantic love, there remain only stories of spiritual love, such as the story of Custance, and yet there is the clear implication that he thinks this kind of story is somehow intrinsically inferior to stories of romantic love. Of course, in the Middle Ages stories such as the tale of Custance were held in high

---

[7] It may be that the Man of Law's desire not to be likened to the Pierian sisters, who lost their contest with the Muses, is also intended by Chaucer to be a slur on the Man of Law's powers of interpretation. The Man of Law has remarked just previously that Chaucer has told all the love stories and left him with only second-rate alternatives, and in the *Metamorphoses* there is a marked analogy to the situation here. The Pierian sisters lose a literary contest having told a tale of strife, while the Muses win with a tale depending heavily on Cupid's arrows: "illa, quibus superas omnes, cape tela, Cupido." In the Muses' story Love incites Dis to capture Proserpina, and it is Love that impels Alpheus to give chase to Arethusa in the second major incident of the story (*Metamorphoses*, Bk. V, 294-678). Thus, Chaucer may be underlining the Man of Law's curious idea that love stories are intrinsically superior to stories of other kinds, regardless of the execution of them.

esteem, and the story that Chaucer himself tells as a pilgrim, the *Melibee,* is in the same genre. Thus, the story of Custance clearly fits the character and circumstances of its pilgrim narrator, and that the Man of Law says in rhyme that he speaks in prose should be no barrier to our assigning the tale to him. Chaucer, the renowned poet of love whose metrical skill the Man of Law disparages, takes his "revenge" by writing the *Man of Law's Tale* in the difficult and elaborate Rhyme Royal. This was probably the antithesis of Chaucer's joke of having the pilgrim Chaucer make bad rhymes but good prose in the *Thopas* and *Melibee.* Finally, the irony is further complicated by the fact that we are prepared to find that the Man of Law not only misjudges Chaucer's metrical ability ("thogh he kan but lewedly / On metres") and Gower's moral tone, but also apologizes for his own tale, which turns out to be similar in content and identical in rhyme scheme to the tale told by the highly sympathetic Clerk. Clearly the Man of Law is a failure at interpreting literature in all aspects.

That the Man of Law borrows his tale from a merchant may perhaps soften the blow to his pride in ownership, for whatever he may think of Chaucer's skill and Gower's taste, the Man of Law admires merchants, particularly rich ones.[8] Indeed, the Man of Law's tale is preceded by what is virtually a dedication to rich merchants, and this encomium of mercantile riches is incongruously attached to a long quotation from the *De contemptu mundi* of Innocent III on the evils of poverty. Thus the story of the long-suffering Custance, who is never concerned with wealth or revelry, who travels about to fulfill God's will, and who refuses even to disclose her own origin (524-25)

---

[8] This is undoubtedly an aspersion not only on the Man of Law but on lawyers generally, based on the prevalent mediaeval view that lawyers had material ambitions in excess of their legal goals. In *Piers Plowman* B, VII, 39 "Men of lawe lest pardoun hadde • that pleteden for mede." In an English carol it is said of Truth that "With men of lawe he haght non spas" (*Early English Carols,* ed. Richard Leighton Greene [Oxford, 1935], #385). See further Maurice Hussey, A. C. Spearing, and James Winny, *An Introduction to Chaucer* (Cambridge, 1965), p. 43; and Bowden, *Commentary on the General Prologue,* pp. 168-71. The relationships between the Merchant and the Man of Law and between their tales deserve further study. In addition to the fact that the Man of Law admires merchants it should be remarked that the two men are similarly dressed, one wearing "mottelee" and the other "medlee" (*Gen Prol,* 271 and 328).

is inharmoniously introduced by a laudatory apostrophe to merchants who are rich, who dance merrily at Christmas, who travel for material gain, and who are noted for their bearing of news and stories:[9]

> O riche marchauntz, ful of wele been yee,
> O noble, o prudent folk, as in this cas!
> Youre bagges been nat fild with ambes as,
> But with sys cynk, that renneth for youre chaunce;
> At Cristemasse myrie may ye daunce!
>
> Ye seken lond and see for yowre wynnynges;
> As wise folk ye knowen al th'estaat
> Of regnes; ye been fadres of tidynges
> And tales, bothe of pees and of debaat.
> I were right now of tales desolaat,
> Nere that a marchant, goon is many a yeere,
> Me taughte a tale, which that ye shal heere.
>
> *(ML Prol, 122-33)*

It is indeed ironic that the Man of Law has learned the tale of the unworldly Custance from a worldly merchant, but it is even more ironic that he thinks Innocent's attack on poverty somehow implies a praise of wealth, and that it is in turn a fitting introduction to the tale of Custance. In an admirable phrase, Professor Huppé has described Innocent's *De contemptu mundi,* or *De miseria humane conditionis,* as "a most distressingly edifying work of immense popularity," and has tried to account for the inclusion of a part of it here on the grounds of its irony.[10] Because the work was immensely pop-

---

[9] Cf. Huppé, *Reading,* p. 96, where the merchants' dependence on Fortune, the throw of the dice, and their travelling without a spiritual goal is contrasted with the Custance story.

[10] Cf. Huppé, *Reading,* pp. 94 and 96. Huppé is assuredly right in remarking that Innocent's anathematization of poverty, which Christ praised, is not intended as a condemnation of poverty per se, but as a condemnation of poverty as it may be misused to lead to envy and malice. However, Huppé's ascription of irony to Innocent's apostrophe to the bliss of merchants is wide of the mark. The irony is Chaucer's for the paraphrase of Innocent does not include the apostrophe to merchants, which is an addition to Innocent, and we are supposed to see in it the Man of Law's error in interpreting Innocent's attack on poverty as though it implied praise of wealth. In an article that appeared after the present essay was written, Professor Lewis offered confirmation of the view that Chaucer has had the Man of Law

ular in the Middle Ages, and presumably closely known as a consequence, we may assume rather that Chaucer has given us an ironic interpretation of a straightforward passage than that he has given us an ironic passage.[11] The simple structure of the *De contemptu mundi,* which employs many pairings of opposites, would lead the audience to expect Innocent's condemnation of poverty to be followed by a condemnation of its opposite, wealth, and indeed that is what follows in the original. Certainly we should ascribe the misleading citation of it to the Man of Law and not to Chaucer, who must have known the work well since he translated it (*LGW* [G], 414-15). The conclusion must be that the Man of Law is once again interpreting, and interpreting badly.

Innocent's *De contemptu mundi* is a relentless diatribe against the situations and phenomena of this world that can turn one away from the path to God, which, of course, includes just about everything. A brief examination of the work's structure and content will show that any acquaintance with the essay sufficient to recognize a quotation from it would be more than adequate to uncover the Man of Law's curious conclusions as his and not Innocent's. For Innocent, man can gain spiritually by contemplating his lowliness on the one hand, and by despising all the things of this world on the other.[12] Consequently, Innocent divides the work into three sections, treating successively our "Ingressus," "Progressus," and "Egressus," which provides him with an opportunity to denigrate every conceivable facet of human life. All the chapters in the first section show the futility of finding a way out of the dilemmas of this world while still in it; and chap-

---

reverse the tone of the passage from Innocent as a device of characterization. See Robert Enzer Lewis, "Chaucer's Artistic Use of Pope Innocent III's *De Miseria Humane Conditionis* in the Man of Law's Prologue and Tale," *PMLA,* LXXXI (1966), 487.

[11] This work was extremely popular. There are more MSS extant of it than of the *Consolation of Philosophy,* and quite a few MSS have been turned up in recent years, suggesting that even more may be found. See Lotharii Cardinalis (Innocent III), *De miseria humane conditionis,* ed. Michele Maccarone (Lugano, Switzerland, 1955), p. x and n. 1; and Donald R. Howard, "Thirty New Manuscripts of Pope Innocent III's *De Miseria humanae conditionis* 'De Contemptu Mundi,'" *Manuscripta,* VII (1963), 31-35.

[12] The idea, of course, was widely known in many contexts, one of the more important of which is in St. Augustine, *On Christian Doctrine,* I, iii-iv.

ter fifteen, whence comes the passage in question here, is actually on the misery of both poverty and wealth. This is followed by other chapters that expose the miseries of other paired opposites: servants and masters, marriage and continence, and so forth. Not only does the paragraph following the passage cited by the Man of Law condemn wealth, not only does the work as a whole condemn misdirected involvement with this world, but also the longest sustained passage in the work is a fifteen-chapter excoriation of riches and cupidity.[13]

It is also instructive that Innocent's objections to wealth, which follow the passage quoted by the Man of Law, begin with a remark about the rich man's admiration of Fortune.[14] This is certainly pertinent in light of what we have already seen of the Man of Law's concern for the improvement of earthly Fortune as opposed to Custance's trust in providence, and indicates a distinction that underlies much of the tale. If the Man of Law was concerned for the "fruyt" of Innocent's *De miseria*, his employment of the work in the Prologue clearly suggests that he not only misinterprets Innocent, but misinterprets him with what can now be called his characteristically worldly bias.

Innocent's *De miseria* is typical of a whole genus of mediaeval documents condemning the misuse of wealth, which makes the Man of Law's misuse of Innocent's remarks on poverty the more glaringly obtuse. The *Dives* of Luke 16:19 who would not feed Lazarus and who consequently suffered in hell, found a literary place in *Piers*

---

[13] There are some other citations of Innocent III by the Man of Law that deserve brief mention. Of the four quotations from Innocent III in the story proper, three seem present simply for emphasis on the evils of the world. Chaucer, however, is careful not to let the Man of Law step out of character, and as a consequence his concern for wealth is maintained by the excision of "ardor avaritie" from an otherwise complete list of emotions that impel one to destroy the peace of a day (1135-38). See Innocent, *De miseria*, I, 21, p. 29.

[14] "Proh pudor! secundum fortunam existimatur persona, cum potius secundum personam sit estimanda fortuna. Tam bonus reputatur ut dives, tam malus ut pauper, cum potius tam dives sit reputandus ut bonus, tam pauper ut malus. Dives autem superfluitate resolvitur et iactantia effrenatur, currit ad libitum et corruit ad illicitum, et fiunt instrumenta penarum que fuerant oblectamenta culparum. Labor in acquirendo, timor in possidendo, dolor in amitendo, mentem eius semper fatigat, sollicitat et affligat: 'Ubi est thesaurus tuus, ibi est et cor tuum'" (Innocent, *De miseria*, I, xv, p. 21).

Plowman B, xiv, 122, as did the famous image from Matthew 19:23 on the impossibility of a rich man's entering the kingdom of heaven (B, xiv, 212). As Innocent pointed out, it is the misuse of wealth that makes us devotees of Fortune, and there was, therefore, a large body of commonplace material which urged that our watchword be "stewardship" rather than the Man of Law's "fee simple." The whole issue of the use and abuse of *temporalia* was of political and social as well as religious importance in the latter half of the fourteenth century, as the sections of *Piers Plowman* dealing with Lady Meed attest. Wimbledon's famous sermon at Paul's Cross, best known today for its social comment, takes as its motto the injunction of Luke 16:2 to give an account of one's stewardship: *"Redde racionem villicacionis tue."*[15] Wimbledon argues strongly in an anti-materialistic vein that the fear of Judgment should make a man despise this world.[16]

Thus, the Man of Law's concern for "fee simple" and his seeming busier than he was (*Gen Prol,* 322) are consonant with his seeming rather than being of great "reverence" (*Gen Prol,* 312-13).[17] In view of the mediaeval concern for the use rather than the enjoyment of worldly riches, the several elements of the Man of Law's character appear together in an easily recognizable whole; these aspects of the Man of Law are in turn harmonious with his praise of wealth and his concern for the temporal welfare of Custance. There is a consistency of characterization from the General Prologue all the way through the Headlink and Prologue to the *Man of Law's Tale* and the tale itself. When we accept the Man of Law as Chaucer drew him we may then see that he does not look beyond Fortune to providence, that he looks to the letter rather than the spirit of things, and that this short-sightedness is a characteristic which causes him to misinterpret the materials of his story. Thus, Chaucer can be daringly

---

[15] T. Wimbledon, *A Famous Middle English Sermon* (MS. Hatton 57, Bod. Lib.) *Preached at Paul's Cross, London, on Quinquagesima Sunday, 1388,* ed. K. F. Sundén, *Göteborgs Hogskolas Årsskrift,* xxxi (1925), Pt. 2, Section 5; p. 5.

[16] For an analysis of the problems related to the use of *temporalia* as set forth in another fourteenth-century poem, *Piers Plowman,* see D. W. Robertson, Jr. and Bernard F. Huppé, *Piers Plowman and Scriptural Tradition* (Princeton, 1951), p. 48.

[17] Cf. Sullivan, "The Man of Law as Literary Critic," pp. 2-3.

ironic by having the Man of Law say, when Custance is set adrift, "He that is lord of Fortune be thy steere!" (448). For Custance this phrase would express her submission to God's will, but from the Man of Law's lips it is a plea for good Fortune.[18]

3. THE NARRATOR, BERNARD SILVESTRIS, AND ASTRAL DETERMINISM

ANOTHER instance of the Man of Law's lack of acuity in interpretation occurs immediately after the Sultan has fallen in love with Custance from the reports about her. At this juncture the Man of Law, thinking of the Sultan's death, which happens later in the story, interjects a long passage on the unhappy fact that the death of every man is written in the stars, and the passage includes material from Bernard Silvestris:

> Paraventure in thilke large book
> Which that men clepe the hevene ywriten was
> With sterres, whan that he his birthe took,
> That he for love sholde han his deeth, allas!
> For in the sterres, clerer than is glas,
> Is writen, God woot, whoso koude it rede,
> The deeth of every man, withouten drede.
>
> In sterres, many a wynter therbiforn,
> Was writen the deeth of Ector, Achilles,
> Of Pompei, Julius, er they were born;
> The strif of Thebes; and of Ercules,
> Of Sampson, Turnus, and of Socrates
> The deeth; but mennes wittes ben so dulle
> That no wight kan wel rede it atte fulle. (190-203)

---

[18] This process of undercutting is often carried out very subtly. For example, the Man of Law is concerned about the monetary arrangement for Custance's proposed marriage to the Sultan, while Custance herself never alludes to the subject. "And he shal han Custance in mariage, / And certein gold, I noot what quantitee; / And heer-to founden sufficient suretee" (241-43). The Man of Law's distress when this financially satisfactory marriage does not take place is not dissimilar from the anguish of the women who carry on at Arcite's untimely death in the *Knight's Tale*, crying, " 'Why woldestow be deed, . . . / And haddest gold ynough, and Emelye?' " (*KnT*, 2835-36). There is neither bride-payment nor dowry when Custance later marries Alla.

The second part of this lugubrious passage is drawn from the *De mundi universitate* of Bernard Silvestris, but it cannot be called a translation or even a paraphrase. Rather, what Chaucer has done is to furnish the Man of Law with a passage that is partly a translation and partly a mistranslation: one which at the same time both echoes and falsifies its model. Chaucer's plan, it would seem, is to give the speaker a passage close enough to the original to permit identification, yet sufficiently changed, wrenched from context, or misplaced to underline the Man of Law's weaknesses as an interpreter of both letters and life. In this particular case we have something of all these sins of commission, and they are compounded, as they were with the citation of Innocent, by sins of omission. To be sure, Bernard Silvestris' work was not as well-known as was Innocent's, but it was quite familiar, and the passage cited by the Man of Law is a very quotable quote. Consequently it does not seem unreasonable that Chaucer might expect his audience to recognize the model and also the deviations from it; it was sufficiently well-known to be parodied in a rhetorical manual.[19]

It is more difficult to determine Chaucer's intentions in having the Man of Law echo Bernard Silvestris than in determining his goal for the translation of Innocent, for where Innocent's meaning is unmistakable, Bernard's work has been the subject of some debate. In this century the *De mundi universitate* has been called a work of "pagan Humanism" by Curtius and a philosophic commentary on Genesis by Gilson, while the author's precise position on astrology has occasioned even wider differences in analysis. However, few scholars have analyzed Bernard in depth, and, significantly, the only intensive study of Bernard's *De mundi universitate* to appear since Gilson's 1928 article is an illuminating piece by Professor Silverstein, who is in essential agreement with Gilson in emphasizing

---

[19] For the parody, which is on the horoscope of a teacher, see Évrard the German's *Laborintus*, in Faral, *Arts poétiques*, pp. 338-39. The parody is really quite good: "Scribitur in stellis paupertas, copia rerum, / Vitae commoditas, acre laboris onus; / Scribitur in stellis famae discrimen, honoris / Culmen, livoris flamma, favoris amor. . . ." For the work's citation by Boccaccio and its general popularity see Curtius, *European Literature*, p. 111, n. 17; and J. de Ghellinck, S.J., *L'essor de la littérature Latine au XII*ᵉ *siècle* (Brussels and Paris, 1955), p. 64.

Bernard's orthodoxy and in downgrading any supposed paganism.[20] Bernard's attitude about astrological determinism, however, is particularly vexatious to the critic of Chaucer, for the passage in his work that occasions the most debate is the very one the Man of Law misquotes, so before we can study the lines in their Chaucerian context we must examine them in their original setting.

The context of Bernard's astrological passage, according to Gilson and Silverstein, is similar to the productions of the school of Chartres in its attempt to deal with the nature of the world as revealed in the Bible with the Neoplatonic language and concepts of Chalcidius, Boethius, and Bernard himself. What needs more emphasis is that this attempt to deal with the providential order of creation with as little appeal to revelation and as much to philosophy as possible, coupled with a style that alternates prose and poetry in a *satura*, suggests that the author is making an overt attempt to signal his Boethian design. Some idea, then, of the place of astrology in Bernard's difficult work may be obtained by a consideration of Boethius' more transparent handling of the same issues.

If there is a single, supersalient theme in Boethius' *Consolation of Philosophy*, it is that providence is superior to Fortune, and it is worth remembering a point already made: the figure Boethius chooses to represent the wise man is an astronomer, who comprehends the motions of the heavens (Bk. I, m. 2). For Boethius, then, the study of the stars is a step upward toward providence and is not to be confused with judicial astrology, which studies the stars' influence on earthly things. Boethius argued that the stars, the planets, even devils, are all agents of the divine will (Bk. IV, pr. 6), and that we can only understand this world by looking beyond Fortune or destiny to providence, which is precisely what Custance does and the Man

---

[20] Curtius, *European Literature*, p. 112; Étienne Gilson, "La Cosmogonie de Bernardus Silvestris," *Archives d'histoire doctrinale et littéraire du moyen age*, III (1928), 5-24; Theodore Silverstein, "The Fabulous Cosmogony of Bernardus Silvestris," *MP*, XLVI (1948), 92-116. On Bernard's supposed determinism see Thorndike, *Magic and Science*, II, 102. Both Gregory and Garin assume Bernard's determinism without much argument: Tullio Gregory, *Anima Mundi* (Florence, 1955), pp. 216-18; and Eugenio Garin, *Studi sul Platonismo Medievale* (Florence, 1958), p. 21. There has also been a debate about the meaning of Bernard's *Mathematicus*, which traditionally has been seen as an attack on astrology, but which Thorndike believes to be otherwise (*Magic and Science*, II, 108).

of Law does not do. It is because of distinctions like this between destiny and providence, between immediate and final goals, that discussions of mediaeval "determinism" often lack precision and speak of fate as determining the courses of things, whereas in the Middle Ages it was felt that it was determined that things would fulfill their proper courses. As Professor Sherman Hawkins has brilliantly phrased it, there is a difference between our own age and a former one that may be seen in the analogy of a physics of push and a metaphysics of pull.[21] Consequently we should expect that in Bernard Silvestris, as in Boethius, whatever is said about the stars and their power over earthly events should be related to a chain of "causality" that reaches beyond them and extends beneath them; we should not expect, with Professor Thorndike, that in Bernard Silvestris fate, free will, and Fortune will "co-exist," but rather that they will appear in a hierarchical relationship in which each plays a part "determined" by providence.[22] In short, because of Bernard Silvestris' obvious debts to Boethius in many areas, we may argue for an indebtedness for his ideas of the stellar functions in the providential scheme. The Man of Law's worldly orientation, however, clearly leads him to be concerned with the immediate effects of the heavenly workings. Thus, we may expect that Bernard Silvestris and the Man of Law will be at loggerheads about celestial influence just as Innocent and the Man of Law were about riches; and if the Man of Law cites Bernard he will corrupt his sense, not promulgate it, as with the example of Innocent.

[21] Sherman Hawkins, "Mutabilitie and the Cycle of the Months," in *Form and Convention in the Poetry of Edmund Spenser*, ed. William Nelson (New York and London, 1961), p. 78. There is an excellent introduction to the nature and importance of Boethius' arguments on fate and free will in the translation by Professor Green. See *The Consolation of Philosophy*, trans. Richard Green, Library of Liberal Arts (Indianapolis and New York, 1962), pp. xiv-xix.

[22] Professor Thorndike further argues that this admission of co-existence is merely an instance of perversity in a writer who otherwise regularly believed in astral determinism (*Magic and Science*, II, 104-106). It is perhaps the use of the word "co-existence" that is confusing here, for in Boethius (whom Thorndike himself cites as a clear parallel of Bernard Silvestris) there is not so much a paradoxical, antagonistic co-existence of fate, free will, and providence, as there is a submission of fate to a providential order that takes into account the will. See Chapter I for a discussion of Thorndike's theory of co-existence in Boethius.

That the passage in Bernard Silvestris under discussion is Boethian in its treatment of astral importance may indeed be argued from its similarity to the Boethian concept of the stars as sometime ministers of the providential order. Although the passage has been cited to demonstrate Bernard's propensity toward a kind of pagan fatalism, its occurrence early on in the narrative, where it treats of the stars as a bridge between heaven and earth, suggests different conclusions. In Bernard's story of the creation, Noys, or providence, has been petitioned by Nature to create something beautiful out of the extant chaos. There are two important points to be made here: first, Noys is clearly equated with providence; second, Nature's petition is that Noys create something beautiful.[23] In short, because it is providence that creates, and because the created world is made beautiful we may assume that we are dealing here with something other than a "pure" philosophical account of creation; there are marked analogies to the creation and the created world as discussed in scripture. The tone of this account of creation indicates that, as in Genesis, there is the assumption (here tacit) that what is being created is good, and it is from this premise that mediaeval thinkers were able to reconcile the appearance of "good" and "bad" Fortune in this world. By subordinating all apparent vicissitudes in time to an eternal order that was stable and good, Boethius and others were able to discover God's plan throughout creation while leaving the will free, and to account for apparent victories of evil through the concept of an eternal good. As Bernard Silvestris puts it, Noys is able to weave patterns into the fabric of time without tearing it, and can create an order that is at once eternally derived yet temporal. This, of course, is related to the central antinomy of providence, fate, and free will that Boethius explained with recourse to the terms "simple" and "conditional" necessity (Bk. v, pr. 6). Bernard, like Boethius, takes pains to demonstrate that there is a place for everything and that everything is in its place,

---

[23] "In huius operis primo libro qui Megacosmus dicitur, id est maior mundus, Natura ad Noym, id est Dei providentiam, de primae materiae, id est hyles, confusione querimoniam quasi cum lacrimis agit et ut mundus pulcrius expoliatur petit" (Bernard Silvestris, *De mundi universitate*, ed. C. S. Barach and J. Wrobel [Innsbruck, 1876], "Brevarium"). For further remarks on the concept of beautification see Gilson, "Cosmogonie," p. 7 and n. 4.

including war, suffering, poverty, and what the Man of Law was to call "the deeth of every man."[24]

Having established the relationships of different temporal levels, and having established that everything is linked in an essentially good hierarchy, Bernard proceeds, in very Boethian terminology, to designate the stars as agents or ministers of the providential order and continues with a description of all created nature as a series of subcreations and a series of obediences.[25] That is, his account begins with a personified providence, and then moves downward through the ranks of angels—cherubim, seraphim, thrones, etc.—all of whom are obedient to Michael.[26] As providence has ordered the angels, so it ordered earthly things. As the angels are grouped in a chain of command, so the senses of man are subservient to his reason and the stars subservient to providence. In other words, the function of the forces creating and making beautiful the earth is to create not one but many relationships of control, of which the stars' influence over man is merely one, unexceptionable instance. When we appreciate that it is order which underlies the creation and that "fate" plays a part in that order which differs in prominence although not in kind from other relationships of influence in the scheme, then the grandiloquent oration on the ordering of earthly events under the stars that follows, the source of the Man of Law's excerpt, may be seen as a praise of the providential order rather than as an apostrophe to fate:

[24] "Ea igitur noys summi et exsuperantissimi Dei est intellectus et ex eius divinitate nata natura. In qua vitae viventis imagines, notiones aeternae, mundus intelligibilis, rerum cognitio praefinita. Erat igitur videre velut in speculo tersiore quicquid generationi, quicquid operi Dei secretior destinarat affectus. Illic in genere, in specie, in individuali singularitate conscripta, quicquid hyle, quicquid mundus, quicquid parturiunt elementa. Illic exarata supremi digito dispunctoris textus temporis, fatalis series, dispositio saeculorum. illic lacrimae pauperum fortunaeque regum. illic potentia militaris, illic philosophorum felicior disciplina. illic quicquid angelus, quicquid ratio conprehendit humana. illic quicquid caelum sua conplectitur curvatura. Quod igitur tale est, illud aeternitati congruum, idem natura cum Deo nec substantia disparatum. Huiusce igitur sive vitae sive lucis origine vita, iubar et rerum endelechia quadam velut emanatione defluxit" (*De mundi universitate*, I, 2, ll. 152-169).

[25] "In caelo divina manus caelique ministris / Omne creaturae primitiavit opus" (*De mundi universitate*, I, 3, ll. 3-4).

[26] "Caelestis pars militiae numerosus ad astra / Angelus obsequitur sub michaele suo. / Angelus inferior gradus est ordire priores. / In hierarchias concidit ordo novem" (*De mundi universitate*, I, 3, ll. 27-30).

Terrenis excepta super substantia caeli
Ut melior cultu sic meliore fuit.
Scribit enim caelum stellis totumque figurat.
Quod de fatali lege venire potest,
Praesignat qualique modo qualique tenore
Omnia sidereus saecula motus agat.
Praeiacet in stellis series, quam longior aetas
Explicet et spatiis temporis ordo suis.
Sceptra Phoronei, fratrum discordia Thebae,
Flammae Phaethontis, Deucalionis aquae.
In stellis Codri paupertas, copia Croesi,
Incestus Paridis Hippolytique pudor.
In stellis Priami species, audacia Turni,
Sensus Ulixeus Herculeusque vigor.
In stellis pugil est Pollux et navita Tiphys
Et Cicero rhetor et geometra Thales.
In stellis lepidum dictat Maro, Myro figurat,
Fulgurat in Latia nobilitate Nero.
Astra notat Persis, Aegyptus parturit artes,
Graecia docta legit, proelia Roma gerit.
In causas rerum sentit Plato, pugnat Achilles,
Et praelarga Titi dextera spargit opes.
Exemplar specimenque Dei virguncula Christum
Parturit et verum saecula numen habent.[27]

The stars do their part in the execution of the providential plan, but the stars are blind and the sublunary events reflect purpose. As in Genesis the creation was crowned and justified by the creation of man, so in this philosophical account of creation the vicissitudes of mankind throughout history are crowned and justified by the birth of Christ. This quotable passage is nothing more or less than an account of world history up to the time of the Incarnation that emphasizes the apparent vagaries of this world in order to show the ultimate propriety of all of these events when they are consummated by the birth of Christ. In keeping with the author's stylistic concerns this account depends upon both historical and mythological figures. Yet

[27] *De mundi universitate,* I, 3, ll. 31-56.

it also overtly speaks of Christ, in whom a link is provided between this world and one beyond the "fatal law," so that Bernard can say with confidence that this world is a continuation of Heaven in its perfection.[28]

This plangent unfolding of terrestrial affairs leading up to the birth of Christ has undergone an astonishing metamorphosis at the hands of the Man of Law. He has changed the tone of the whole by altering the nature of the parts and has made the passage into a gloomy prediction of the death of every man. Where the original passage remarks upon the strength of Hercules, the audacity of Turnus, and Plato's understanding, in the Man of Law's echo we hear only of the deaths of Hercules, Turnus, and Socrates. Similarly the death of Hector is modeled on the striking appearance of Priam in the original. Only Achilles seems correctly derived, and even then a difference in tone is evident, for his death is remarked upon by the Man of Law whereas only his battles are recounted by Bernard Silvestris. That Chaucer hoped his audience would recognize both the quotation and the misquotation may seem far-fetched in a day when

---

[28] "In Deo, in noy scientia est, in caelo ratio, in sideribus intellectus. In magno vero animali cognitio viget, viget et sensus causarum praecedentium fomitibus enutritus. Ex mente enim caelum, de caelo sidera, de sideribus mundus. unde viveret, unde discerneret, linea continuationis excepit. Mundus enim quiddam continuum, et in ea catena nihil vel dissipabile vel abruptum. Unde illum rotunditas forma perfectior circumscribit" (*De mundi universitate,* I, 4, ll. 74-81). Bernard takes his hierarchies rather far, and extends them, in Book II, to man. However, in man the right order has been overthrown by the Fall: "Et gravis in nostra carne tyrannus amor" [II, 14, l. 152]. Thus, although the sense of touch properly comes last in the hierarchy of the senses, it is not entirely under the control of the reason: "Militat in thalamis, tenero deservit amori / Tactus, et argute saepe probare solet. / Aut castigato planum sub pectore ventrem, / Aut in virgineo corpore molle femur" (II, 14, ll. 105-108). Cf. St. Paul's statement about a law in his members at war with the law in his mind (Romans 7:23). We are scarcely dealing here with a "touch of pagan sensuality," M. Gilson's argument to the contrary notwithstanding (Gilson, "Cosmogonie," p. 6, n. 3). Curtius points out that the work closes with a remark on the fitting use of the male organs when that use accords with what is needful, and then makes the astonishing statement that the entire book is "bathed in the atmosphere of a fertility cult, in which religion and sexuality mingle" (Curtius, *European Literature,* pp. 111-12). On the use of pagan language with these Christian themes see Richard McKeon, "Poetry and Philosophy in The Twelfth Century: The Renaissance of Rhetoric," *Critics and Criticism: Ancient and Modern,* ed. R. S. Crane (Chicago, 1952), p. 305.

Bernard Silvestris is not much read even by scholars, but this is exactly what happened with an early commentator who, in a marginal gloss, gave excerpts from Bernard Silvestris, which, unlike those of the Man of Law, are accurate in tone.[29]

Thus, the Man of Law selects only some figures from Bernard and changes what is said about them. The result is the falsification of the tenor of the whole passage, because while the Man of Law is citing these sad forecasts in order to underscore his fear that the stars may predestine that the Sultan die for love, the original phrases are intended to exhibit, in spite of superficial strife, an underlying order in harmony with a kind of predetermination that rules the stars. While Bernard tells of times of apparent chaos, such as the quarrels of Eteocles and Polynices at Thebes, Achilles' struggles at Troy, and the ancient days when Phaeton and Deucalion almost destroyed the world with fire and flood, there is, nevertheless, a growing sense of order as he moves chronologically toward the birth of Christ. The paired opposites of the imagery—fire and water, chastity and incest— at first suggest a purposeless vacillation or perturbation, but in the long view there is ordered progress from Phoroneus, who was renowned as a lawgiver and the pagan equivalent of Adam, to Christ, the second Adam who fulfilled the Law.[30]

As we move chronologically and sequentially closer to the birth of Christ, the figures Bernard introduces are figures of order: Thales the geometrician, Cicero the rhetorician, Virgil the poet, and Myron the sculptor. Similarly one may assume that the Roman wars, coming where they do in the sequence, after Egyptian arts and Greek philosophy, are to be distinguished from the disruptive wars of Thebes and Troy and are to be thought of as wars that spread the *Pax Romana*. Although much of this analysis must be tentative, the con-

---

[29] "Ceptra Phorenei fratrum discordia Thebe fflamam Phetontis Deucalionis Aque In stellis Priami species Audacia Turni Sensus Vlixeus Herculeusque vigor" (Manly and Rickert, *Text*, III, 493).

[30] For Phoroneus as a lawgiver, see St. Augustine, *Civitas Dei*, XVIII, 3. For Phoroneus as the "first man," see *Timaeus* 22. This is scarcely a novel concept. Boethius was only one of many who argued that an apparent contrariety in things was in truth harmony due to "love" (Bk. II, m. 8). On the concepts of the harmony of this world and its relationship with heaven, see Leo Spitzer, *Classical and Christian Ideas of World Harmony* (Baltimore, 1963), passim.

struction placed upon Bernard's words here would not set him apart from the Middle Ages, for the idea that providence prepared for Christ in history figures importantly elsewhere in mediaeval writings. Drawing upon St. Paul's suggestion that Christ came in the fullness of time, Dante wrote, both in the *Convivio* and in the *De monarchia*, of God's great design in history preparing the way for Advent. This design brought the historical world to "justice" under Roman rule, and one of the reasons for Dante's choice of Virgil as guide is that Virgil's statements in the famous Fourth Eclogue about a Golden Age were interpreted as signs of the birth of Christ. "Iam redit et Virgo, redeunt Saturnia regna."[31]

If this is Bernard's idea too, then we have in Chaucer a most challenging play on the ideas of justice, for we are dealing with more than historical justice. In the Middle Ages the process of the creation and ordering of the world described by writers from Plato down to Bernard Silvestris and beyond was known as "natural justice."[32] Thus, on the first level we find in Bernard a relationship between natural justice and historical justice. When we look at the Man of Law's reduction of this relationship to a simple rule or law that the stars often prefigure death, we have discovered another level of ideas. For the final level of perception we should not forget that the hero here is Chaucer's major figure from the fourteenth-century world of secular justice, and he says of him significantly, "Justice he was ful often in assise" (*Gen Prol*, 314). All of this suggests that the Man of Law is no paradigm of justice, and we may wonder if Chaucer was as dissatisfied with the secular justice administered by the Man of Law through patent and plain commission as he was with canonical justice as corrupted by the Summoner.

In any event, there can be no doubt that the Man of Law has changed both the parts and the whole of the passage he cites. The joy at the beauty of creation that marks Bernard's work is turned to

[31] For a brilliant exposition of this theme see Charles S. Singleton, *Dante Studies 2: Journey to Beatrice* (Cambridge, Mass., 1958), pp. 86-99.

[32] Cf. Guillaume de Conches' commentary on the *Timaeus* (J. M. Parent, *La doctrine de la création dans l'école de Chartres* [Paris and Ottawa, 1938], p. 142). This is not to be confused with the "natural justice" given to human nature in Adam. For further remarks on the several kinds of justice, see John Freccero, "Dante's Pilgrim in a Gyre," *PMLA*, LXXVI (1961), 177, n. 48.

despondency at the inevitability of astral determinism by the Man of Law. A passage on birth has been changed to one on death. The order of creation has been turned into a law of fatality. As Noys, or providence says, quoting Boethius, the different elements of the world are bound together and unified by love.[33] It follows that when Noys looks over his handiwork and exclaims over its beauty, it is its former chaos to which it is contrasted.[34] The imposition of order is here and elsewhere perceived as a good in the Middle Ages, and we may not only differentiate the Man of Law's ideas from those of Bernard Silvestris, but also compare them to what Chaucer's may have been. It seems inconceivable that the poet who translated Boethius would not have understood that Bernard Silvestris was concerned here and elsewhere with an order that overreaches "fate" and "Fortune"; in one particularly transparent passage Noys points out that he himself ascribed to the stars their laws of motion and to the planets their courses in such a way that the *Parcae* themselves are ruled in turn by providence.[35] If it seems unlikely that Chaucer is here misinterpreting Bernard, we are left with only the Man of Law as interpreter, or rather misinterpreter, and we may argue safely that the Man of Law's misinterpretations are sufficiently glaring that Chaucer intended them as devices to undercut.

In the last analysis the major change is from birth and joy to death and sorrow. We should not forget that the birth of Christ was a more famous event foretold by a stellar phenomenon than any death at all. Chalcidius' commentary on the *Timaeus*, the probable source of

[33] "Quae membris animam numeri proportio iungat, / Ut res dissimiles uniat unus amor" (*De mundi universitate*, II, 8, ll. 27-28). Cf. Boethius, Bk. II, m. 8.

[34] "Ecce, inquit, *mundus, o natura, quem de antiquo seminario, quem de tumultu veteri, quem de massa confusionis excepi.* Ecce mundus, operis mei excogitata subtilitas, gloriosa constructio, rerum specimen praedecorum, quem creavi, quem formavi sedula, quem ad aeternam ideam ingeniosa circumtuli mentem meam propiore vestigio subsecuta" (*De mundi universitate*, II, 1, ll. 4-10).

[35] "Induxi rebus formas, elementa ligavi / Concordem numero conciliante fidem. / Ascripsi legem stellis iussique planetas / Indeclinatum currere semper iter. . . . Unde Atropos, Clotho, Lachesis, iurata Providentiae Fatoque germanitas, similem sed dissimili loco mundanae administrationis diligentiam curamque sortitae. Orto sphaeram firmamenti Atropos, planetarum erraticam Clotho, Lachesis terrena disponit" (*De mundi universitate*, II, 2, ll. 9-12 and II, 11, ll. 51-56).

Bernard's passage on the stars, reminds us of the larger tradition by contrasting in a very precise way those stars that prefigured death to the star of Bethlehem.[36] In light of these arguments it seems quite likely that Chaucer's audience would not only have perceived the Man of Law's misquotations but would also have censured his morbid determinism, which is given the lie by the very passage he misquotes and misinterprets.

4. THE HOROSCOPE

THE PASSAGE of astrological description, usually called the horoscope, in the *Man of Law's Tale* is another occasion of interpretation by the story-teller and is another difficult passage to work into the fabric of the whole. Before we can consider how the passage functions poetically, we must first concern ourselves with what the astrological situation is, then with what it means astrologically, and only at the last with what this has to do with the Man of Law's and Chaucer's handling of the Custance story.

The situation at this juncture in the story is straightforward enough: Custance has agreed to the marriage her father has arranged, preparations have been made, and the day of departure for the foreign land has come. At this point the Man of Law interjects an apostrophe to the heavens. He would like a "happy" story in which Custance would marry the Sultan, but he knows that she not only does not marry him, but barely escapes with her life from the slaughter at the marriage feast. Consequently, he condemns the First Moving for having caused at the time of departure the astral configuration that forestalls the marriage; he describes that astrological situation in some detail; then he excoriates the Emperor, Custance's father, for not having taken an astrological "election" to mitigate or overcome the astral forces by the choice of a more propitious moment for the departure:

[36] "Est quoque alia sanctior et uenerabilior historia, quae perhibet ortu stellae cuiusdam non morbos mortesque denuntias sed descensum dei uenerabilis ad humanae conseruationis rerumque mortalium gratiam" (*Timaeus: a Calcidio translatus commentarioque instructus*, ed. J. H. Waszink, in *Corpus Platonicum medii aevi, Plato Latinus*, ed. Raymond Klibansky (London and Leyden, 1962), IV, cxxvi; pp. 169-70).

O firste moevyng! crueel firmament,
With thy diurnal sweigh that crowdest ay
And hurlest al from est til occident
That naturelly wolde holde another way,
Thy crowdyng set the hevene in swich array
At the bigynnyng of this fiers viage,
That crueel Mars hath slayn this mariage.

Infortunat ascendent tortuous,
Of which the lord is helplees falle, allas,
Out of his angle into the derkeste hous!
O Mars, o atazir, as in this cas!
O fieble moone, unhappy been thy paas!
Thou knyttest thee ther thou art nat receyved;
Ther thou were weel, fro thennes artow weyved.

Imprudent Emperour of Rome, allas!
Was ther no philosophre in al thy toun?
Is no tyme bet than oother in swich cas?
Of viage is ther noon eleccioun,
Namely to folk of heigh condicioun?
Noght whan a roote is of a burthe yknowe?
Allas, we been to lewed or to slowe! (295-315)

The Man of Law is once again being lugubrious in the face of astral
determinism—yet the marriage of Custance and the Sultan might
not have been an unmitigated blessing.

In the technical matters that abound in this passage we may, as
usual, follow Skeat with safety. While there have been several ob-
jections to his interpretations, the objections do not offer superior
or even equal alternatives, and we are back at the beginning. While
we cannot hope to determine the precise meaning of the passage be-
cause of a certain latitude in the terminology of the astrologers and
because of the necessity of reading parts of the passage inferentially,
we may nevertheless gain a good idea of its basic meaning. To begin
with, there are direct and tortuous signs of the zodiac; here we are
dealing with a tortuous one, which is also said to be the ascending
sign, meaning the sign ascending on the eastern horizon at the crucial

moment.[37] This tortuous ascendant is further characterized as "infortunate," for which understand "malevolent" or "unlucky." The Lord of the Ascendant has fallen from his angle into the darkest house, and because Mars is in the next line styled as the "atazir," or planet with influence, Skeat argues that Mars is to be identified as the Lord of the Ascendant. This is inferential, to be sure, but necessary if we are to make any sense out of the passage; and however devious Chaucer may be at times, it seems doubtful that he would be willfully opaque.

The "angle" out of which Mars, Lord of the Ascendant, has fallen, is part of a system for the study of stellar influence. This system divides the heavens into twelve equal or unequal parts (more commonly unequal) which arbitrarily receive the names "angle," "succedent," and "cadent," starting with the division on the eastern horizon and proceeding counterclockwise or against the daily motion of the sun through the heavens. These divisions or "houses," as they were known, were numbered sequentially, and each had a peculiar province such as love, death, or travel, which was arbitrarily assigned to it. It should be remarked that these houses inevitably are confused with another kind of house—the houses that planets have in the two signs where they are most powerful.[38]

[37] Some of the confusion about this passage stems from a misunderstanding of the word "ascendant." In modern times our simplified astrological materials are usually represented in terms of the month of one's birth and in terms of the sign of the zodiac that the sun is in during the appropriate portion of that month. In the Middle Ages, however, both horoscopes and elections had as their most important feature the sign that was ascending in the east at a particular moment in the daily, not yearly, course of the heavens. Thus, while the sun is in the sign Aries for about a month at the beginning of spring, the sign Aries is in the ascendant position for about two hours every day. This is the "ascendant" referred to in the poem, and all other computations must proceed from this. For Skeat's remarks on the passage see the notes to his edition, v, 148-52. For Alchabitius, one of the few astrologers named by Chaucer, on the "sex tortuose ascendentia," see *Alcabitii ad magisterium iudicorum astrorum isagoge: commentario Ioannis Saxonij declarata* (Paris, 1521), sig. a₂ʳ. Other references abound.

[38] Professor Curry has argued that the planets move into the divisional houses successively, from the first to the twelfth, in the same way that they move through the signs (and associated houses) of the zodiac (Curry, *Mediaeval Sciences*, pp. 172-75). However, Robertus Anglicus, commenting on Sacrobosco's *De sphaera*, says that a sign "which at its rising was in the first house begins after its rising to be in the twelfth house . . ." (Lynn Thorndike, *The Sphere of Sacrobosco and its*

If we assume that Mars is indeed the Lord of the Ascendant, as we must if the passage is to be comprehensible, then we can be sure that the ascendant sign is Aries, one of the two houses of Mars and the only tortuous one. We can also know with certainty why it is "infortunate," for Chaucer tells us himself. The term "Lord of the Ascendant" has been a trouble-maker with regard to critical commentary on this passage, which is not surprising in light of the fact that even the *NED*, citing Chaucer himself as an authority, mistranslates the phrase. The *NED* definition is that the Lord of the Ascendant is a planet in the ascendant sign, while properly it means the planet with the most power when in that sign, regardless of where the planet may be while the sign is in the ascendant.[39] Thus, Mars

---

Commentators [Chicago, 1949], p. 220). Similarly in Chaucer, the sun is said to have left the "angle meridional" (*SqT*, 263) while Leo continues to rise. If the sun is in an angle called the meridian angle it certainly seems that the planets move through the angles, cadents, and succedents in their daily, not annual motion, which would mean that, like the signs discussed by Robert Anglicus, they would travel through the divisional houses from the first to the twelfth to the eleventh. The whole matter of "equal" and "unequal" houses is vexing semantically, since the houses of the zodiac can be considered "equal" houses in one sense, while the divisional houses are "equal" in one sense and "unequal" in another. Al-Biruni says that they are equal divisions of the visible heavens formed by great circles passing through the prime vertical. Because the zodiac is not in the same plane, these equal divisions of the heavens are unequal divisions along the course of the zodiac. See Al-Biruni, *The Book of Instruction in the Elements of Astrology* . . . , trans. R. Ramsey Wright (London, 1934), p. 149, n. 2. For mediaeval confounding of the two kinds of houses, see *The Astronomical Works of Thabit B. Qurra*, ed. Francis J. Carmody (Berkeley and Los Angeles, 1960), p. 175.

[39] "Any planet within the house of the ascendant" (*NED*, s.v. "ascendant," B, 1, 1). Chaucer quite clearly says that an ascendant is fortunate when no unfortunate planet is in it or is in aspect to it. The Lord of the Ascendant is fortunate or unfortunate depending upon where he is in aspect to the ascendant sign and in relation to the angles and the other planets. Thus, the Lord of the Ascendant need not be in the ascending sign if he can be Lord of the Ascendant while in aspect to the ascendant. Mars can be both Lord of the tortuous, ascendant sign Aries (one of his two houses) and yet be located elsewhere, perhaps in Scorpio (his other house), which may coincide with the cadent eighth house (a house of the other kind), the house of death. "A 'fortunat ascendent' clepen they whan that no wicked planete, as Saturne or Mars or elles the Tayl of the Dragoun, is in the hous of the ascendent, ne that no wicked planete have noon aspect of enemyte upon the ascendent. . . . The lord of the ascendent, sey thei that he is fortunat *whan he is in god place fro the ascendent*, as in an angle, or in a succident where as he is in hys dignite

can be the Lord of the Ascendant sign Aries, and yet be located else-where, specifically in the darkest house where he has fallen from an angle. Because he has so fallen he must, by Chaucer's definition, be unfortunately situated, and because Chaucer calls him a "wicked planet" in the *Treatise on the Astrolabe*, we may deduce that it is Mars' aspect toward the ascending sign Aries that makes Aries "infortunate."[40]

The exact meaning of the "darkest house" is not altogether clear, but Skeat argued convincingly that if "house" refers to one of Mars' two houses, then Scorpio, which is often associated with death and travail, would figuratively be the darker of the two; and if "house" refers to one of the unequal or divisional houses, then the eighth house, the house of death and a cadent, would be the one implied. The darkness in either case would have to be figurative, as no literal sense has been discovered and Scorpio is Mars' "day" house as opposed to his "night" house in Aries. Since the ascendant in Aries would demand that Scorpio be located at least partly in the eighth divisional house, it seems most likely that Chaucer intended that Scorpio be discovered coincident with the eighth divisional house for emphasis on the idea of death.[41]

---

and comfortid with frendly aspectes of planetes and wel resceyved; and *eke that he may seen the ascendent . . .*" (*A Treatise on the Astrolabe*, II, 4).

[40] Professor Curtiss has argued against the supposition that Mars is the Lord of the Ascendant on the grounds that (a) Mars is said to have "slain this marriage" in l. 301, and (b) the Lord of the Ascendant is said to have fallen helpless in l. 303, so the weak Lord of the Ascendant should not be identified with the power-ful Mars (Joseph T. Curtiss, "The Horoscope in Chaucer's *Man of Law's Tale*," *JEGP*, XXVI [1927], 28). The sense of the passage, however, is that the diurnal rotation of the First Moving has forced the planets into their present positions, and we should therefore read l. 303 to mean that Mars has fallen helplessly rather than that he has fallen into a state of helplessness. Professor Browne has argued that Mars cannot be the Lord of the Ascendant because the Lord of the Ascendant is the "celestial guardian," while Mars is at the same time the atazir, which means "evil genius" (William Hand Browne, "Notes on Chaucer's Astrology," *MLN*, XXIII [1908], 53). Professor Browne adduces no evidence in support of his defini-tion, which is in conflict with Chaucer's declaration that the Lord of the Ascendant can be either malevolent or benevolent.

[41] Skeat, *Works*, III, 150. Professor Curtiss objected to identifying the darkest of the twelve houses of the zodiac with the darker of the two houses of Mars (Cur-tiss, "The Horoscope," p. 29). There does not seem to be any objection to Skeat's

The word "atazir" has also come in for its share of interpretation, and each subsequent refinement of meaning has carried us further away from the most useful understanding of the term. Skeat confines himself to understanding atazir as "influence," while Professor Curry insists that atazir cannot be understood without reference to hyleg and alchochoden. Professor Manly cites Alchabitius to prove that atazir refers to the process of obtaining a celestial distance, and Haly to prove that it is the "significator nativitatis," whatever that may mean.[42] The root of the problem is the inability of the astrologers themselves to agree upon the meaning of the word "atazir"; the arguments were so extensive that one of the encyclopedists, Albohazen Haly, takes about 300 lines just to recount the history of opinion.[43] In view of all this, the most we can say with assurance about the atazir is that it emphasizes the importance of Mars in the stellar configuration but does not tell us what kind of importance is involved. Thus, we do best to return to Skeat's interpretation and understand no more than that Mars is the most influential planet here.

The final element in this astrological situation is the moon, which has occasioned virtually no disagreement. The moon has been forced, "weyved," from a good position to one less fortunate and is now

---

reading "darkest" as "darker," which is not overly bold; and there is in fact some manuscript authority for understanding "the" darkest house as "his" darkest house, the variant occurring in several MSS (Manly & Rickert, *Text*, V, 468). Professor Browne's objection that Scorpio cannot be Mars' darkest house because it is one of his own houses, in which he is powerful, neglects the fact that Mars is a "wicked planet" in Chaucer's phrase, and where powerful will be powerful to do evil, which would make either of his houses "dark" because of and not in spite of his power there (Browne, "Notes on Astrology," 53).

[42] Skeat, *Works*, III, 150-51. Curry, *Mediaeval Sciences*, 182-87. *The Canterbury Tales*, ed. John Matthews Manly (New York, 1928), p. 587. See n. 43, below, for an illustration of the confusion over "significator nativitatis."

[43] "Athazir est significator natiuitatis, deferens significationem nati ad quodlibet signum, eundo per signa & domus. Discordes sunt similiter in cognoscendo significatorem: quia Ptolemaeus dicit quod significator est planeta habens maiorem potentiam in gradu ascendentis, qui est nominatus almutez . . ." (Albohazen Haly, *De judiciis astrorum* [Basle, 1551], sig. B₃ʳ). Pico della Mirandola makes fun of the astrologers' inability to define the sometimes complementary term "alchochoden." See Pico della Mirandola, *Disputationes adversus astrologiam divinatricem*, ed. Eugenio Garin (Florence, 1946-52), I, 148.

"knyt" to another planet, which can mean either "in conjunction with" or "in aspect to" it.[44] Because Mars is the only other planet named in this passage, we may assume that the moon is "knyt" to him and, since he is never benevolent, she is not "receyved" where she is.

If we grant that Mars, Lord of the Ascendant, is located in Scorpio and in the eighth house, the house of death, and that he is cadent from an angle and possibly in conjunction with the moon, we must still inquire what this has to do with the marriage of Custance and the Sultan. It is clear enough what the Man of Law thinks: he says specifically that the First Moving forced the planets into a certain configuration "at the bigynnyng of this fiers viage." Then, having described that configuration, he laments the fact that no astrologer was consulted to take an election to find a more favorable moment for departure. Indignantly he asks if there was no "philosophre" available to elect a more favorable time for the journey, which is once again referred to as a "fierce" voyage.

It is this particular adjective, twice used, that provides a clue both to the astrology and to its poetic uses here. Had there been an astrologer present to take an election before this voyage, he would have emphatically suggested that a different time be chosen, for if the lord of the eighth house (here Mars) "infortunes" the Lord of the Ascendant (here also Mars, who may, presumably, "infortune" himself), particularly if the Lord of the Ascendant is in the eighth house (as Mars is here), the astrologers say that a shipwreck is in the offing.[45] This is not too surprising in light of the emphasis on dark houses, cruel Mars, and the like; but has the Man of Law really done a good job as interpreter of the situation? Has all been lost because no astrologer was called upon? It would seem not, for in spite of the Man of Law's concern for astral determinism, in spite of the prognostication of the heavens, there is no shipwreck, no drowning, no "fiers viage" at all. It is true that the wedding does not take

[44] For "knyt" as descriptive of a relationship other than conjunction see *The Complaint of Mars*, ll. 50-51.

[45] "Porro si dominus octauae infortunauerit dominum ascendentis, maxime ipsomet in octaua existente, accidet naui impedimentum & destructio, quod erit secundum naturam infortunij illius" (Albohazen Haly, *De judiciis*, sig. K₄ᵛ).

place, but the passage states that it is because of the stellar situation at the start of the voyage that "cruel Mars has slain this marriage." This, in turn, implies that it is the timing of Custance's departure which brings about the disaster, when in fact the actual disaster is in no way related to Custance. It would appear that once again the Man of Law has interpolated into the story material that is not appropriate to the situation in spite of his interpretation of it. The astrological imagery does have significance, however, and does describe a pattern that is astrologically capable of forestalling the marriage, not by shipwrecking Custance, however, but by signalling the death of the Sultan to "whoso koude it rede." The Man of Law's concern for determinism is short-range and short-sighted and he mistakes a providential decree about marriage for an astrological decree about shipwreck. In his enthusiasm for the marriage and regret that it does not occur he neglects to examine either the astrological situation or the import of the marriage very closely. This action is in keeping with the character that we have now come to know.

While the Man of Law is most concerned with the astral impact on the marriage of Custance and the Sultan, any astrological imagery that prominently involves Mars leads us to think of death rather than marriage, so we may expect that Mars will indirectly and not directly avert the marriage. While today we ordinarily think of Mars in terms of warfare and the violence of war, in the Middle Ages Mars was associated with all kinds of death, as we may observe in the *Knight's Tale*, where Mars is prominently associated with secret murder, open slaughter, and suicide (*KnT*, 1995-2050). Moreover, while the particular situation of Mars at the start of Custance's voyage can be a prognostication of shipwreck, he is regularly associated with death of a more violent species. Again, Chaucer himself is the best glossator: in the *Knight's Tale* he tells us that those of "Mars' division" are the barber, the butcher, and the smith, all iron-wielders, while death in the same passage comes from a nail, a knife, and the embrace of a bear. One might expect, then, that the Man of Law's description of the astrological situation would prefigure a violent death by steel rather than the blocking of a marriage because of shipwreck. Finally, while Mars is associated with death, and with death by steel, he is also associated with death for a specific cause: one not asso-

ciated with him today. In the only passage in Chaucer outside of the
Man of Law's Tale in which Mars as a planet is involved in astrolog-
ical foreshadowing, the "menacing of Mars" is the sign of death for
love:

> Yet was hir deth depeynted ther-biforn
> By manasynge of Mars, right by figure.
> So was it shewed in that portreiture,
> As is depeynted in the sterres above
> Who shal be slayn or elles deed for love.
>
> (*KnT*, 2034-38)

In light of these remarks on Mars as astrological harbinger within
Chaucer's writings, it seems likely that Chaucer would have expected
his audience to discover in the description of Mars in the darkest
house a sign that someone will die of the sword for love. The irony
would then be that the astrological configuration remarked upon by
the Man of Law is indeed significant and, in fact, "cruel Mars has
slain this marriage" with the death of the Sultan, who dies "tohewe
and stiked" (l. 430) at the wedding in an appropriately Martian
fashion. The Sultan's hypocritical mother, who engineers the murder,
is a typically Martian "smylere with the knyf under the cloke"
(*KnT*, 1999). The Man of Law's suggestion earlier in the story that
perhaps the stars had decreed that the Sultan should die for love,
makes his subsequent concern for Custance's rather than the Sultan's
safety even more ironic. Once again the Man of Law seems to have
misinterpreted his own observations, for while it is possible to dem-
onstrate, with reference to the astrologers, that Mars in the situation
described could cause shipwreck, the astrological evidence for a death
by steel is more convincing.[46]

---

[46] "Continet autem haec domus mortem, eius conditiones, causas, infirmitates,
morbos varios, & casus nunquam satis praeuisos: etiam si natus sit moriturus in
opulentia & divitijs, uel in indigentia & labore: etiam si morietur in terra sua uel
extra . . . uel si fuerit Luna cum Marte in octaua, maxime in natiuitate nocturna . . .
significant quod natus interficietur ferro, uel truncabitur ei caput, aut morietur mala
morte & turpi. . . . Praeterea si quando Luna in natiuitate nocturna iuncta fuerit . . .
uel fuerit in coniunctione Martis. . . . mors erit propter ignem: sed si quando Mars
fuerit in octaua domo damnificans dominum octaue domus, mors nati erit ex ferro"
(Albohazen Haly, *De judiciis*, sig. S₄ᵛ and S₅ᵛ). "Quando Aries fuerit ascendens,
Mars qui est dominus eius, erit significator mortis, eo quod Scorpio erit in octaua

There is an alternative reading of the passage that yields a very similar tone. We have assumed thus far that "fiers viage" refers to the voyage Custance takes to the Sultan's homeland, but there is an ambiguity about the voyage that permits it to be identified with another, larger voyage, the figurative voyage of life. In this sense we would understand the Man of Law's statement that at the beginning of this fierce voyage the First Moving had set the heavens in such array that "Mars has slain the marriage" to mean that the marriage was foredoomed because of the astrological situation at the time of Custance's birth. This would, in turn, be consonant with the Man of Law's upbraiding of her father for not taking an election to mitigate the adverse prognostication of her "root," or horoscope, which he says was known. The question so often raised by critics—whether the passage in question describes the astrological situation at the time of Custance's birth and is thus a horoscope, or whether it describes the situation at the time of her departure and is thus the first step in taking an election and discovering a better time—is really not to the point. In either case, the Man of Law argues that the situation threatens the marriage by threatening Custance, but the marriage is thwarted by the death of the Sultan, and the astrological situation would fit him perfectly and Custance not at all.

If the Man of Law is once again being undercut in his interpretation of things, we should be alert to the possibility that not only his astrological ideas but also his matrimonial views may be in doubt. We have come to expect the Man of Law's short-sightedness to be belied by the longer view, and it would follow here that the marriage of Custance and the Sultan, which the Man of Law so desires and which he says is blocked by Mars, is perhaps undesirable and prevented by providence. Professor Beichner has pointed out that the Christian Custance's marriage to the pagan Sultan would have been

---

domo, cuius etiam Mars est dominus . . . Quando Mars in octaua domo fuerit, aut octauam domum impedierit, natus ferro morietur" (Albubatur, *De natiuitatibus* [Nuremberg, 1540], sig. r₃ᵛ and s₁ᵛ). Alchabitius overtly quotes Albohazen Haly (Alchabitius Abdylaziz, *Libellus Ysagogicus* [Venice, 1511/12], sig. f₅ᵛ). The association of Mars with death was so widespread that Pico della Mirandola felt obliged to deny that Mars in the house of death in Christ's horoscope brought about his death (*Disputationes*, I, 606).

invalid without the latter's baptism, but we should perhaps inquire after the marriage's desirability as well as its validity.[47] While marriage with a pagan could serve a very real function "in encrees of Cristes lawe deere" (237), as the Man of Law points out, we may nevertheless question whether or not this is what actually happens. The Sultan's "conversion" is certainly a cynical one, for, like many another Chaucerian lover, he rather bluntly wants to "have" Custance and is willing first to be baptized and then to marry her in order to implement this desire.

> . . . but he myghte have grace
> To han Custance withinne a litel space,
> He nas but deed. . . .   (207-209)

We may further remark that marriage as a solution to the Sultan's physical and emotional problems is quite cynically arrived at only after deceit and rape ("magyk and abusioun" [214]) have been rejected not as unsuitable but as impractical alternatives: "But finally, as in conclusioun, / They kan nat seen in that noon avantage" (215-16). Perhaps it was the danger of a superficial conversion coupled with Christian ideas about duty in marriage that led St. Paul to warn Christians against being yoked with unbelievers in II Corinthians 6:14 and Ephesians 5:7. In any event there can be no doubt that this particular marriage between a pagan and a Christian will not increase Christ's law. Custance goes dutifully but not joyfully to her marriage with a stranger in a pagan land. " 'Allas! unto the Barbre nacioun / I moste anoon, syn that it is youre wille' " (281-82). Her reluctance to be married to the Sultan is in marked contrast to the Man of Law's eagerness that the marriage take place, and the Man of Law's protestation against the forces that he believes conspire to prevent the marriage is consequently discordant.

The Sultan of Syria, to whom the Man of Law is so desirous of marrying Custance, may be instructively contrasted with King Alla, whom she actually marries. Where the Sultan wanted to have Custance physically, Alla has "compassioun" (659) on her at her trial; where the Sultan agreed to be baptized in order to accomplish

---

[47] Paul F. Beichner, C.S.C., "Chaucer's Man of Law and *Disparitas Cultus*," *Speculum*, XXIII (1948), 72-73.

his desires, Alla is converted by the miracle that occurs at Custance's trial. We may argue, then, that the Man of Law's concern over the "woe" of the thwarted marriage between the Sultan and Custance is at the least premature, for Custance ultimately makes a marriage that is more promising both emotionally and spiritually, and which would even measure up on the Man of Law's financial yardstick.

If we continue in this vein of analysis, we may find in the Sultan's mother a summation of all that is unchristian. She is worried that her son will leave his "olde sacrifices" (325) for "this newe lawe" (337), and she herself is not disadvantageously compared to the "serpent depe in helle ybounde" (361). Chaucer's choice of words here emphasizes the symbolic force of a contrast between the "new law" and the "old law" in traditional Christian writings about the new dispensation, all of which draw heavily from St. Paul. If the Sultaness stands for the old law, then certainly the Emperor of Rome would stand for the new, whatever we may think of his actions in the poem. The characters in question do not, of course, function as personifications of the two ideas in question, but their associations are there for the purpose of suggesting that the marriage of Custance and the Sultan would be more than undesirable, it would be impossible. Thus, if the marriage is blocked by some power beyond that of the principals, it is a power which is also beyond that of the stars. Consequently the Man of Law's attempts to turn a pious legend into a romance are not only unsuccessful and self-revelatory but also "foredoomed" to be so. As interpreter of his tale he has misapplied his astrological information and mourned the thwarting of a marriage that both could not and should not be; he has compounded these errors by ascribing the whole situation, which he thinks is bad, to the "cruel" First Moving, which he considers the very epitome of deterministic nastiness.

While the exact intention of Chaucer's use of a planetary situation is obscured by the inexact nature of the terminology, the Man of Law's egregious comments on the role of the planets in relation to the First Moving give us a firm ground for interpreting the tone of what follows. As we have now seen with regard to worldly and spiritual wealth in a variety of contexts, the Man of Law's immediate concern for the one blinds him to the possibilities of the other. This blindness,

moreover, is particularly marked in those passages where he evinces a concern for the effects of the planets on worldly affairs to the neglect of any concern for the powers beyond the stars that made them part of God's providential plan. These powers, of course, are represented traditionally in the First Moving, the very force the Man of Law chooses to "blame" for what he considers to be the tragedy of the forestalled marriage of Custance and the Sultan. In so doing he is characteristically short-sighted, for in a tradition as old as Plato and Aristotle, the east to west, daily motion of the Primum Mobile or First Moving has been contrasted with the west to east, annual motion of the planets, much to the detriment of the latter. The motion that the Man of Law scorns, the motion of the First Moving, is regularly associated with rationality.[48]

Although no adequate survey of this tradition is possible here, we may review some of its outstanding features. The Pythagoreans had equated the left with evil and the right with good, and Aristotle, while revising part of the Pythagorean orientation, retained some of this value association. Aristotle argued that the right hand is where motion properly begins and ends, and that the daily east to west motion of the sun and other stars should begin and end at the right

[48] I have been anticipated in much of my research here in studies of Donne and Dante. Professor A. B. Chambers, in a brilliant study of Donne's "Goodfriday, Riding Westward," has shown that Donne plays upon two spiritual orientations: first the east to west rational movement is opposed to the west to east irrational movement, and then this whole idea is contrasted with an overly "passionate" desire to move east toward the rising Sun of Justice. See A. B. Chambers, "Goodfriday, 1613. Riding Westward: The Poem and the Tradition," *ELH*, XXVIII (1961), 31-53. Chambers' article has a wealth of documentation ranging from the *Timaeus* through Plutarch, Philo, Proclus, and Chalcidius down to a variety of late mediaeval figures. Professor John Freccero, in an equally learned and impressive study, has analyzed many of these and some other materials and has related them to the directions in Dante's *Commedia*. See John Freccero, "Dante's Pilgrim in a Gyre," *PMLA*, LXXVI (1961), 168-81. Also see the same author's "Donne's 'Valediction Forbidding Mourning,'" *ELH*, XXX (1963), 335-76. In addition to these discoveries I have found a commentary in Pierre Bersuire, and can add a passage in Arnulph of Orleans, for which I am indebted to Professor D. W. Robertson, Jr. Similar material has been pointed out by Professor Garin, and there is no doubt that much more will be found. For a rare instance in which the Primum Mobile is seen as hindering the planets in their attempt to return to the east of their origin, see John Lydgate, *The Pilgrimage of the Life of Man*, EETS, Extra Series 77, 83, 92 (London, 1899-1904), 12, 205-440.

hand of the earth's presumed anthropomorphic structure. Thus, if we imagine a human figure stretched through the earth from pole to pole and if we arrange this figure so that the sun will rise on his right hand, pass before his face, and set at his left, his feet must be at the arctic and his head at the antarctic pole.[49] The south pole, then, is properly "up"; and "proper" motion is the motion of the Primum Mobile, which carries everything on a daily course from east to west. Plato had already discussed something quite similar in the *Timaeus*, but he put more emphasis on the difference between the east to west, daily motion of the stars and planets, and the annual, irregular, west to east motion of the planets only. In the *Timaeus* a piece of soul-stuff is cut in two and made into circles of the "same" and the "other," which cross in a Greek *chi* (X) and revolve in opposite directions, representing the two motions of the heavens. Chalcidius, commenting on the passage, remarked upon the analogy of this macrocosm to the microcosm of man, and said that the motion of the Primum Mobile (here represented as the circle of the fixed stars and the motion of the "same") is reason, while the contrary motions of the planets are *iracundia* and *cupiditas*.[50]

This Chalcidian commentary sets the form for most of the mediaeval remarks on the two motions, which see the one as rational and the other as irrational, but which change Chalcidius' *cupiditas* (that term having been pre-empted by the theologians) and *iracundia* to *sensualitas*.[51] There is not, however, any great change in meaning, for *sensualitas* is a synecdoche for all the passions, as is *iracundia*.

[49] Aristotle, *On the Heavens*, trans. W. K. C. Guthrie, Loeb Classical Library (Cambridge, Mass., and London, 1939), II, 2; pp. 139-47. Because of this dictum artists represented the world with the antarctic pole at the top of the picture and the arctic pole at the bottom well into the Renaissance. See Fig. 30.

[50] See Waszink, ed., *Timaeus*, IV, 28 (for *Timaeus*, Bk. I); and IV, 148 (for Chalcidius' *Commentary*).

[51] "Duo sunt motus in anima unus rationalis alter irrationalis: rationalis est qui imitatur motum firmamenti, qui fit ab oriente in occidentem, et e contrario irrationalis est qui imitatur motum planetarum qui moventur contra firmamentum. Dedit enim deus anime rationem per quam reprimeret sensualitatem, sicut motus irrationalis VII planetarum per motum firmamenti reprimitur. . . . Vel intencio sua sit nos ab amore temporalium immoderato revocare et adhortari ad unicum cultum nostri creatoris, ostendendo stabilitatem celestium et varietatem temporalium" (Arnulph of Orleans, *Commentary on the Metamorphoses*, in "Arnolfo D'Orleans un Cultore di Ovidio nel Secolo XII," ed. F. Ghisalberti, *Memorie del R. Istituto Lombardo di*

Thus, in Pierre Bersuire the motion of the Crystalline Sphere (which he uses instead of the Primum Mobile, as does Dante) is compared to the desire in some men for justice, and the contrary motion of the planets, to the carnal appetites.[52] In his *Commentary on the Metamorphoses*, Arnulph of Orleans remarks that the two motions of the firmament were established by God expressly to call us back from the love of *temporalia* by showing us the contrast between the perturbation of *temporalia* and the stability of heaven. This contrast reminds us of the Man of Law, who is notably concerned with vicissitudes and all too little with the serenity of heaven. The Man of Law's complaint against the First Moving is as much as a complaint against God himself, as Professor Huppé has pointed out. More specifically, this is another instance of the Man of Law's reprimanding the providential order for not bringing about material happiness.[53] By accus-

---

Scienze e lettere, XXIV [1932], 181). For similar terminology see Alanus de Insulis and Pseudo-John the Scot: Alanus de Insulis, *Liber de planctu naturae, PL,* 210, col. 443; Pseudo-John the Scot in *Saecvli noni avctores in Boetii consolationem philosophiae commentarivs,* ed. E. T. Silk, *Papers and Monographs of the American Academy in Rome,* IX (1935), 34-35. Sacrobosco uses the terms "rational," "irrational," and "sensual" in his discussion of astronomy, which was very widely used as a text, and which has been suggested as one of Chaucer's sources for the *Treatise on the Astrolabe.* See Thorndike, *The Sphere of Sacrobosco and its Commentators,* p. 123; and Walter B. Veazie, "Chaucer's Text-book of Astronomy; Johannes de Sacrobosco," *Colorado Univ. Studies,* Series B, Studies in the Humanities, I (1939-41), 169-82. Pseudo-Bede refers to the "rational motion of the firmament" with reference to Chalcidius' commentary, and Guillaume de Conches talks of the rational and sensual movements of the soul and compares the human soul to the Anima Mundi when commenting on Book III, m. 2 and m. 3 of Boethius' *Consolation*: Pseudo-Bede, *De mundi coelestis terrestrisque constitutione liber, PL,* 90, col. 900. Also see Guillaume de Conches' *Commentary* in Charles Jourdain, "Des Commentaires Inédits de Guillaume de Conches et de Nicolas Triveth sur la Consolation de Philosophie de Boèce," *Notices et extraits des manuscrits de la Bibliothèque Impériale,* XX, 2 (1865), 75ff; and Eugenio Garin, *Studi sul Platonismo Medievale* (Florence, 1958), p. 41, and n. 1.

[52] "Vel dic moraliter, quod caelestes viri ad reprimendum ardorem & zelum justiciae, rebellionem inferiorum orbium, i.e. carnalium appetituum, in seipsis sentiunt, ac per crystallinam sapientiam, ardorem istum prudenter compescunt" (Pierre Bersuire, *Reductorium morale in Opera omnia* [Cologne, 1730-31], I, 105, col. 1).

[53] The First Moving is God's primary agent in the providential order, and only an Aristotelian distinction separates the First Moving from the First Mover, apostrophized in the *Knight's Tale* (2987 ff.), which is in turn modeled upon the

ing the First Moving of forcing the planets to bring about a situation that he will judge only from the material standpoint, the Man of Law is expostulating with the symbol of Wisdom and endorsing the symbol of sensuality. In this perverse maneuver he is being "contrary" in the most literal sense of the word, and he renounces the Boethian concept of philosophical astronomy for the shorter and narrower vision of the judicial astrologer.

5. CHAUCER, THE MAN OF LAW, AND THE TREATMENT OF THE SOURCES

THE MAN OF LAW has not been a good interpreter of his literary forerunners, and his clumsy handling of passages from Innocent III and from Bernard Silvestris leads us to expect that for all his emphasis on the "fruyt" of his matter, not only elements of his tale but also the main themes will be wrongly interpreted. Like such disparate fellow pilgrims as the Miller and the Parson, the Man of Law will tell a tale appropriate to his character; and since he is notably fond of love stories, the tale of Custance, so different from a romantic love story in tone, is changed to suit the pilgrim Man of Law, not the poet Chaucer. This change and the reasons for it are evident from a study of the differences between the Man of Law's version and the source or sources of the story.

Of course Chaucer himself made all the changes from the source, but we may legitimately inquire whether he would have made precisely the same changes from the source if he had written the tale for such a sympathetic pilgrim as the Clerk. Certainly the interjected astrological material from Bernard Silvestris and the judicial astrologers is an addition to the source, and it seems very dubious that Chaucer would have made the same sort of change if he had intended the tale for the Franklin, who, although intrigued by astrology, nevertheless maintains that the church has circumscribed the practice. Thus, in changing the story for his own purposes Chaucer adapts his original to the nominal teller and in that way ultimately to his own purposes. In this case, since the Man of Law is temperamentally dif-

---

famous eighth meter of Book II of Boethius, on the stability of heaven. Cf. Huppé, *Reading of the Canterbury Tales,* p. 99.

ferent from his heroine, the basically austere story of a saintly, patient, suffering Christian is told with a sense of personal involvement, for the Man of Law's true literary interest is in love stories, and we may hazard the guess that a saint's legend would show insufficient sentimentality to satisfy him. Indeed the changes from the source indicate that Chaucer attempted to do two things; to underline the story's moral more markedly, and to charge the narrative with suspense. The two, it may be added, are not very compatible, for the moral is to be patient in adversity and not to fear the future. The changes, therefore, suggest that Chaucer is making a deliberate attempt to undercut the Man of Law by adapting the tale to a poor tale-teller and emphasizing a moral incompatible with the treatment of the theme.

The basic story of Custance was available in versions by Nicholas Trivet, in his Anglo-Norman *Chronicle*, and by Gower, in his *Confessio Amantis*.[54] In the first instance the story is the record of the patience and good works of Custance, written for a nun; in the second it is a diatribe against envy in particular and "this worldes faierie" (l. 1593) in general.[55] That a story so clearly otherworldly in its orientation could be construed by the Man of Law as evidence of God's ability to send worldly prosperity is a certain indication of his perversity as an interpreter, and his introductory remarks to the effect that rich people are spiritually superior to poor people constitute a staggering prologue to the story of Custance. Trivet's Anglo-Norman *Chronicle* was presented to Princess Marie, the daughter

[54] The priority of Gower's version to Chaucer's seems to be agreed upon today, but Chaucer's story is probably directly descended from Trivet's version. The Man of Law's violence to the source can be demonstrated, however, by reference to either version. For the history of opinion on these matters see Margaret Schlauch, *Chaucer's Custance and Accused Queens* (New York, 1927), pp. 132-34, and her chapter on the *Man of Law's Tale* in *Sources and Analogues of Chaucer's Canterbury Tales*, ed. W. F. Bryan and Germaine Dempster (Chicago, 1941), pp. 155-206. For convenience the *Sources and Analogues* texts of Trivet and Gower are used here and are cited in the text by page and line reference respectively.

[55] Miss Schlauch's characterization of the story as a "romantic digression" in Trivet's *Chronicle* is not convincing. The story of Custance would undoubtedly have been considered excellent reading for a nun, and neither romantic nor a digression. The story of St. Cecilia, told by Chaucer's second nun, is similar in many ways.

of Edward I, after her entry into the convent, and it seems most
unlikely that Chaucer's audience, which included members of the
same royal line, could hear without amusement a story thought to
be appropriate to a royal rejection of the world interpreted as an
indictment of poverty. There is nothing suspenseful nor romantic
in the Custance story as we have it in the sources, yet in the *Man
of Law's Tale* this story of steadfast trust in providence is overlaid
with inharmonious elements of suspense, tension, and drama.[56] Ulti-
mately, however, the irreconcilability of the religious tale and the
romance should be laid at the Man of Law's and not at Chaucer's
door.

Given the difference between Custance's patience in the face of
adversity and the Man of Law's alternating fear and delight, it
would seem that Chaucer intended to point up the disparity between
the Man of Law and his characters, especially since he has changed
the character Alla and made him more like Custance. While
Custance's " 'Lord, ay welcome be thy sonde!' " (826) has an exact
source in the model, Alla's identical statement in line 760 represents
a marked change from the source, where he is not nearly so Job-
like.[57] Thus, in Chaucer's version, the Man of Law's attitudes are
in contrast to two, not merely one, of the characters in his story.
Another technique used by Chaucer to point up the Man of Law's
distance from the material with which he works is prompting the
audience to see what the Man of Law does not see. In Trivet the
meaning of patience in adversity is assumed to be understood, but
in Chaucer's adaptation a character (the Constable) steps forward
to ask some questions about God's justice toward the innocent in
very Boethian terms, which are surely intended to point toward the

[56] Cf. John A. Yunck, "Religious Elements in Chaucer's *Man of Law's Tale*,"
ELH, XXVII (1960), 249-61. Professor Yunck's conclusions about the tone of the
Man of Law's version seem wide of the mark. While the story is indeed about
providence, the term "drama of providence" is misleading, for the idea that God's
providence is the protagonist and that "the antagonists are the stars and the devil
. . ." is to come dangerously near the Man of Law's worldly perspective.

[57] "Mes [la] lettre ly fist retourner a dolour, e ly fist noun creable; quar le roys,
quant auoit lez lettres regarde, hastiuement suppris de grant dolour e parfond
pensee, defendi al messager, a grantz manaces de peine, que riens de sa femme ne
del enfaunt parlat . . ." (Trivet, p. 173). The king has no outward reaction in
Gower.

familiar Boethian answers to these questions—familiar, that is, to all but the Man of Law:

> "O myghty God, if that it be thy wille,
> Sith thou art rightful juge, how may it be
> That thou wolt suffren innocentz to spille,
> And wikked folk regne in prosperitee?"[58]

Because the Man of Law so admires prosperity, he gives no sign that he is acquainted with the customary answers here, and his failure to think as does his heroine is once again pointed up by a change from the source.

In addition to remarking about impending calamity and man's helplessness, the Man of Law delights in Custance's occasional good fortune, and his remarks on this subject also bring about a change in tone from the original. For example, although the source for the trial scene is quite flat in tone, the Man of Law's narration of events is such that a feeling of suspense is introduced. Moreover, while in the original the miraculous intervention of God causes Alla to convert to Christianity, in the Man of Law's version the emphasis has been shifted from the spiritual reward of Alla to the temporal reward of Custance; in accordance with the Man of Law's concern for temporal success, it is Custance's elevation to queenhood that becomes the climax of the incident, while Alla's conversion is sharply subordinated:

> And after this Jhesus, of his mercy,
> Made Alla wedden ful solempnely
> This hooly mayden, that is so bright and sheene;
> And thus hath Crist ymaad Custance a queene.[59]

Having already investigated the degree of desirability of Custance's proposed marriage with the Sultan, we may now add that the attitudes of the characters in the Man of Law's story toward this mar-

---

[58] *MLT*, 813-16. Cf. Boethius, *Consolation*, Bk. 1, m. 5. There is no similar utterance in either Trivet or Gower.

[59] *MLT*, 690-93. The difference in tone in Trivet is quite marked: "Puis le rey— pur le grant amour qil auoit a la pucele, e pur lez miracles par dieux moustrez—le rey Alle se fist baptizer del euesqe Lucius, auant nome: et esposa la pucele, qe conseut del rey [vn] enfaunt madle" (Trivet, p. 172). There is no comment on Custance's queenship in Gower.

riage are significantly different from those in the original. It is the forestalling of the marriage that prompts much of the Man of Law's interjected lamentation, while the possible barrier of religion is ignored by both the teller of the story and his characters. It is proclaimed ". . . thurghout the toun / That every wight, with greet devocioun, / Sholde preyen Crist that he this mariage / Receyve in gree, and spede this viage" (256-59). Contrastingly, Custance's departure for a barbarian land is mourned by the entire city in Trivet.[60] The change seems to indicate that Chaucer wished to show the Man of Law as overly optimistic as well as overly pessimistic. Changing the reaction of the townspeople reinforces Chaucer's previous manipulation of the sources to give the effect that the Man of Law has vainly tried to turn the story of Custance into a simple love story.

Another departure from the source, again adapting the tale to the Man of Law but falsifying the tone of the original, is in the works and deeds of Custance. Custance's stature is diminished in Chaucer's redaction for the Man of Law, presumably to make her appear more the innocent, helpless pawn of those destinal forces the Man of Law is so concerned with. While she is an active preacher of God's word in Trivet's version of the story, she is virtually without volition in the Man of Law's tale. She has ceased to be a person who exerts influence on others and has become an object moved about by forces which she has no control over and little understanding of. Of course, this change makes her a less exciting heroine in a religious tale, and it does not really enhance her appeal as a romantic heroine either. We can only conclude that Chaucer has indeed changed things so as to diminish the appearance of the Man of Law as raconteur. Gone is the educated young woman, trained in "les sept sciences" and in "diuerses langages," who in Trivet's version converts the Syrian merchants and later Hermengyld through rational argument.[61]

---

[60] "E pur lour conunes sur cest maundement tous se acorderent e en temps maunderent la pucele hors de la mesoun son piere e hors de sa conisaunce, entre estraunges barbaryns a grant doel e lermes e crie e noise e pleinte de toute la citee de Rome" (Trivet, p. 166). Gower omits the incident.

[61] "Mes puis qil aueyent suffisauntment defendu la ley Iesu Crist encountre les paens qi ne sauoient plus countredire, comenserent de preiser la pucele Constaunce qui les auoyt conuertu, de trop haute e noble sen e sapience e de graunde merueilouse biaute e gentirise e noblesce de saunc. . . . E Hermingild homblement e deuoutement

In the Man of Law's version Custance remains a paradigm of morality, but her intellectual attainments are not mentioned, nor is her conversion of the merchants. Similarly, the conversion of Hermengyld is present in the Man of Law's version, but has been subtly altered in tone, for where it was Custance's teachings that converted Hermengyld in the original, here it is her prayers and tears to God: "Til Jhesu hath converted thurgh his grace / Dame Hermengyld, constablesse of that place" (538-39). Chaucer permits Custance to go so far as to be instrumental in the conversion of Hermengyld's husband through declaration of "oure lay" (572), but again alters the tone, placing less emphasis on Custance's hard work than in the original, where she and Hermengyld preached incessantly to bring about the conversion.[62] Thus Chaucer has made the heroine show less self-determination, as though the Man of Law's determinism had caused him to weaken some aspects of the emphasis on spiritual strength found in the original.

Still another example of change is the incident in which Custance is attacked on shipboard. In Trivet's version it is Custance's own ingenuity in devising a ruse that salvages her honor, while in this version Custance receives "myght and vigour" (945) from Christ which enables her to fend off her would-be attacker.[63] The differences are small but clear. In each case Chaucer has reduced Custance from a person who acts to a person acted upon, and yet this reduction

---

escota la doctrine de la fei par la bouche Constaunce, que lui aprist la puissaunce dieu en la fesaunce de tut le mound . . ." (Trivet, pp. 165 and 169). Gower refers to Custance's "wordes wise" (1. 606) in the conversion of the merchants, and says that Hermengyld's conversion comes about because Custance "tawhte the creance / Vnto this wif so parfitly" (ll. 754-55). This change and several others discussed here have been noticed by Professor Duffey in his article "Intention and Art." For an opposing view of Custance's character, which, however, adduces only one example in evidence of Custance's "vitalization," see Claude E. Jones, "Chaucer's Custance," *Neuphilologische Mitteilungen*, LXIV (1963), 175-80.

[62] Trivet, p. 170; Gower, ll. 775-78.

[63] "Mes Dieux, a qi ele auoit done son qoer denfaunce, ne la voleit suffrir assentir a tiel mal. Douant quant cist Theolous par dures manaces la voleit aforcer, *ele refreynt sa folye par resoun* . . ." (Trivet, p. 175; italics mine). Custance then goes on to trick her adversary into losing his balance. Gower also says that she employs a ruse, and he adds the comment that God gives her the strength to accomplish her plan (ll. 1107-25).

should be charged to the Man of Law, whose concern for the "fruyt" of his tale is given the lie overtly by his comments and tacitly by "his" changes in what may have been a well-known source.

The final and probably the most telling change from the source is in the handling of the ending of the tale. Here, in spite of the Man of Law's now customary lament over the transitoriness of earthly bliss, we find a rather happy ending—an ending that is incompatible both with the ending in the source and with the tale as the Man of Law has told it. The various threads of plot are drawn together: Alla and Custance who had been separated after their marriage are here re-united, as are Custance and her father, the Emperor. Having told us of these relatively happy occurrences, the Man of Law prepares us for a final picture of misery by quoting Innocent III (for the second time) on the evanescence of the joy of this world, and then tells us how Alla dies:

> I ne seye but for this ende this sentence,
> That litel while in joye or in plesance
> Lasteth the blisse of Alla with Custance.
>
> For deeth, that taketh of heigh and logh his rente,
> Whan passed was a yeer, evene as I gesse,
> Out of this world this kyng Alla he hente,
> For whom Custance hath ful greet hevynesse.
>
> (1139-45)

We might expect that the story would end here in order to underline the Man of Law's moral concerning transitory worldly bliss, but instead it continues, and the succession of events discredits the Man of Law's interpretation. Custance returns home to her father, and they determine to live in Rome for the rest of their days:

> To Rome is come this hooly creature,
> And fyndeth hire freendes hoole and sounde;
> Now is she scaped al hire aventure.
> And whan that she hir fader hath yfounde,
> Doun on hir knees falleth she to grounde;
> Wepynge for tendrenesse in herte blithe,
> She heryeth God an hundred thousand sithe.

> In vertu and in hooly almus-dede
> They lyven alle, and nevere asonder wende;
> Til deeth departeth hem, this lyf they lede.
> And fareth now weel! my tale is at an ende.
>
> (1149-59)

Custance's blithe heart, her safe and sound friends, her end to adventure and the promise of a future life close to her father all combine to paint an unmistakably happy picture, which is in marked contrast to the original, where it is explicitly stated that Custance's father dies six months after Alla, and she herself one year after that.[64] Like most of the changes from the source, this one's purpose seems to be to put words into the mouth of the Man of Law that expose his errors without his knowledge. Thus, the story of Custance, which in Trivet's version terminates with the deaths of all concerned, here is brought to a close on an incongruously happy note and is followed in the text by the Man of Law's remarkable invocation of Christ as the bringer of good Fortune:

> Now Jhesu Crist, that of his myght may sende
> Joye after wo, governe us in his grace,
> And kepe us alle that been in this place! Amen[65]

6. PROVIDENCE, MEANS, AND ENDS

THE CHANGE in the conclusion of the story is a typical and characteristic device by which Chaucer undercuts the Man of Law, here as

---

[64] "E apoy apres vn demi aan, Constaunce, que en grant honur e amur estoit a tute la terre, returna a Rome pur la nouele qe ele oy de la maladie son piere; le tressime jour apres sa venue, morust Tyberie seintement deyns lez bras sa fille, e rendi lalme a dieu" (Trivet, p. 181). In Gower she "was noght there bot a throwe" before her father died, and she herself died the next year (ll. 1580-94).

[65] *MLT*, 1160-62. A contrary opinion is presented by Professor Lewis, who sees the happy conclusion of Custance's life as introducing the "moral" of the story: that "joye after wo" in this life comes to him who believes in Christ through all misfortunes ("Chaucer's Artistic Use of Pope Innocent," p. 492). Since Custance herself is equally happy with material joy or woe—either bringing her spiritual joy—perhaps it would be more precise to say that joy after woe in this life sometimes comes to those who, unlike the Man of Law, welcome "wo after gladnesse." If the happy conclusion of the story is not at odds with the rest of the events, surely the Man of Law's praise of Christ only for bringing "joye after wo" at the end of the tale is inharmonious with the overall message to be constant in adversity.

elsewhere giving him enough rope with which to ensnare himself. Chaucer has created a character who is constant in his perversity, one whose misinterpretations of literature, moral essays, astral influence, and the spiritual welfare of merchants are logical and easily antici- pated developments of his central concern for worldly prosperity. That he should be such a character is not especially remarkable, for if we forget the well-known biographical suppositions that have been constructed on his being a Sergeant of the law and consider him only as an example of the class of men at law from which the Sergeants were drawn, his credentials are quite in order. We have already re- marked that lawyers were widely thought of as materialistic; indeed, to the author of *Piers Plowman* the avaricious lawyers come in for the harshest treatment in the whole society: "Men of lawe lest par- doun hadde · that pleteden for mede" (B, vii, 39).

This concern for material prosperity, so marked in Chaucer's Man of Law, both explains and comments on his concern for astrology to the neglect of providence, an attitude that has characterized him throughout the tale. Like most adherents of judicial astrology, the Man of Law is concerned with the "immutable" decrees of the stars only in order to modify and to mitigate them, as is illustrated by his concern that no election was taken for Custance's voyage. In a master- ful stroke of poetic economy Chaucer joins the Man of Law's infatu- ation with the wealthy and his concern to avoid those very unavoid- able destinal forces he fears in Custance's horoscope. The irony of The Man of Law's complaint is that his outcry is simultaneously against Lady Fortune and for her; not only is he vexed that someone has not carefully guarded against the future the stars foretell, but he is particularly annoyed at the idea that people of "heigh condicioun" (313) should do such a thing, for they have the money to spend on horoscopes and owe it to themselves to supplement these with elec- tions. Typically, the Man of Law makes the same mistake that the literary character "Boethius" made in forgetting that when Fortune ceases to be variable she ceases to be Fortune. Thus, by admiring her one face and fearing her other, he puts himself under her domination.

With this in mind, the Man of Law's praise of Mary and Christ rings hollow indeed, for it sounds dismayingly similar to his praise of astrologers. His praise of astrologers is for their ability to know

both what the future will be and how we may avoid it, while his praise of divine figures is for their ability to know the future and to be able to change it for our pleasure. When the Man of Law says that no man can read the messages of the heavens "atte fulle," he clearly implies that some of it can be read; and it is not surprising that the astrologer who can both determine a horoscope and take an election to mitigate some part of the prognostication therein is called a "philosophre" (310). In the same fashion, he argues, we are ignorant of God's designs, and although "philosophers" may understand astrology, not even "clerks" understand the ways of God. This remarkable statement about our understanding of God's ways should not be left without comment, for it is the Man of Law's most basic and ultimate confounding of means and ends. When faced with a miracle of salvation, the Man of Law's thoughts are that Christ is to be praised for bringing good Fortune and that while we may observe the means we cannot know the end of God's workings. This is because "purveiance" (unlike astrology) is something we cannot understand at all:

> God liste to shewe his wonderful myracle
> In hire, for we sholde seen his myghty werkis;
> Crist, which that is to every harm triacle,
> By certeine meenes ofte, as knowen clerkis,
> Dooth thyng for certein ende that ful derk is
> To mannes wit, that for oure ignorance
> Ne konne noght knowe his prudent purveiance.
>
> (477-483)

Christ, then, is a kind of super-astrologer, who not only knows the future, but can change it for our immediate pleasure. The Man of Law's remarks about "purveiance," "meenes," and "ende" are also examples of misinterpretation of standard material, for "purveiance" is the word Chaucer uses for "providence" in his translation of Boethius. We can and do know the "ende" of providence—it is the good; the "meenes," however, are sometimes opaque.

> . . . no thing is leveful to folye in the reaume of the devyne purveaunce . . . syn that the ryght strong God governeth alle thinges in this world. For it nis nat leveful to man to comprehenden by

wit, ne unfolden by word, alle the subtil ordenaunces and dis-
posiciounis of the devyne entente. For oonly it owghte suffise to
han lokid that God hymself, makere of alle natures, ordeineth
and dresseth alle thingis to gode. (Bk. IV, pr. 6)

The Man of Law, who prefers the irrational motion of the planets
to the rational motion of the Primum Mobile, characteristically
argues that we are ignorant where in fact we may be wise. By con-
cerning himself with "ordenaunces and disposiciounis" of things
rather than with the end of things, he commits the same blunder
of short-sightedness that led him to prefer the planets to the First
Moving and the knowledge of the astrologers to the wisdom of the
Boethian astronomer who measures the ends of things. This in-
sufficient distinction between the levels of providence and destiny,
a distinction on which much of the *Consolation* rests, is the source of
the Man of Law's misinterpretation of the proper use of worldly
goods and the purpose of heavenly signs.

If this treatment of the Man of Law seems harsh in comparison
with customary interpretations of his character, the harshness would
seem to have been contrived by Chaucer and to have been rather
tirelessly pursued. Indeed, that the Man of Law is treated harshly
should be no great surprise, for with the exception of Harry Bailly
he is the only pilgrim to criticize Chaucer's rhyming.

CHAPTER VI

Time and Tide in the *Franklin's Tale*

I. MEDIAEVAL TIDAL THEORY AND THE DISAPPEARANCE OF THE ROCKS

No STUDY OF the *Franklin's Tale* could fail to mention the incident of the disappearance of the rocks along the coast, but few studies have focused carefully upon the incident itself before going on to discuss the impact of the vanished rocks on the rest of the tale. The disappearance of the rocks has usually been accepted at face value for the sound reasons that magic is a common feature of the Breton lays after which the *Franklin's Tale* is patterned, and that the impossible is common enough elsewhere in the *Tales*. Thus, when Tatlock wrote his pioneer study of astrology and magic in the tale, he accepted the surface demands of the poem without question and directed his efforts toward explaining why the date was propitious for magic. Indeed, Tatlock suggested that Chaucer removed the action from England to ancient Brittany in order to be able to endorse astrological magic safely.[1] There exist, however, warning signals in the poem that make one reluctant to charge up the disappearance of the rocks to the realm of the supernatural or the arcane, and these have led Professor Owen to deny that the rocks are actually removed, and Professor Robertson to go even further and say that the rocks are covered over by a high tide that the Orleans clerk predicts.[2] Both of these suggestions are provocative, and this essay, which adduces evidence for Robertson's tidal hypothesis, owes much to the original

[1] John S. P. Tatlock, "Astrology and Magic in Chaucer's *Franklin's Tale*," in *Anniversary Papers by Colleagues and Pupils of George Lyman Kittredge* (Boston and London, 1913), pp. 339-50. For Professor Tatlock's beliefs on Chaucer's removal of the action see his book *The Scene of the Franklin's Tale Visited*, Chaucer Society, 2nd Ser., No. 51 (London, 1914), pp. 35-37.

[2] Charles A. Owen, Jr., "The Crucial Passages in Five of the *Canterbury Tales*: A Study in Irony and Symbol," *JEGP*, LII (1953), 296. Robertson, *Preface*, p. 276. In the latter work the remark about the tides is peripheral to the matter at hand, and so Professor Robertson makes his statement without documentation or demonstration. I am indebted to Professor Robertson for ideas about tone in the *Franklin's Tale*.

concern for the true status of the rocks shown by these critics and by Phyllis Hodgson.[3]

The bluntest of the warnings not to accept the disappearance of the rocks without question is in the language used to describe the event. The rocks are not said to be gone but merely to seem to be away: ". . . thurgh his magik, for a wyke or tweye, / It *semed* that alle the rokkes were aweye" (*FranklT*, 1295-96). Suggestive too is the fact that neither Aurelius nor his brother thinks for a moment of fulfilling the actual conditions of Dorigen's rash behest that the rocks be removed stone by stone, but both turn their thoughts to ways of bringing about the appearance of vanished rocks. Now there are two ways of effecting this appearance alluded to in the poem: first is Aurelius' method, which is to wish for a tide so strong that it would cover up the rocks, and second is his brother's technique, which is to employ a conjurer of sorts who would create the appearance that the rocks were gone. First Aurelius says:

> Wherfore, lord Phebus, this is my requeste—
> Do this miracle, or do myn herte breste—
> That now next at this opposicion
> Which in the signe shal be of the Leon,
> As preieth hire [the moon] so greet a flood to brynge
> That fyve fadme at the leeste it oversprynge
> The hyeste rokke in Armorik Briteyne.[4]

[3] Phyllis Hodgson has been less bold than Owen or Robertson but has inserted an intermediate step in the course of events. She would attribute the vanished rocks to "natural forces" and these in turn to some occult influence. It may be that by this she means that the clerk causes a high tide or a high sea through magic. She does, however, believe that "there is no question of charlatanism." See her edition of *The Franklin's Tale* (London, 1960), p. 132.

[4] *FranklT*, 1055-61. There has been some confusion about what and where the opposition is. We know from line 906 that Aurelius first encounters Dorigen on May 6, and we can assume that he prayed to the sun shortly thereafter. When Skeat first wrote about Aurelius' prayer he interpreted it as follows: the date is May 6, therefore the sun is in the 23rd degree of Taurus and the "next opposition" will occur when the moon arrives at the 23rd degree of Leo, the sign mentioned by Aurelius. See the *Treatise on the Astrolabe*, ed. Walter W. Skeat for the Chaucer Society, 1st Ser., No. 29; and for EETS, Extra Ser., No. 16 (London, 1872), p. lviii. In trying to account for everything mentioned in the passage, Skeat confused opposition with quartile aspect. When the sun is in Taurus and the moon is in

Aurelius' brother is equally devious, because whether he believes in the "moon mansions" or not, he clearly expects that the magician will not do more than frame some kind of illusion:

> Now thanne conclude I thus, that if I myghte
> At Orliens som oold felawe yfynde
> That hadde thise moones mansions in mynde,
> Or oother magyk natureel above,
> He sholde wel make my brother han his love.
> For with an apparence a clerk may make,
> To mannes sighte, that alle the rokkes blake
> Of Britaigne weren yvoyded everichon. (1152-59)

Two ideas, then, are advanced about means by which the rocks might be made to disappear, and they do not necessarily preclude one another, because an obvious way for the Orleans clerk to bring about the appearance of vanished rocks would be to cause some sort of magical occurrence that would create a very high tide. Surely Chaucer put the idea of a high tide in our minds for a purpose— but for what purpose? Because Aurelius insists on a supernatural cause for a natural phenomenon, it may be that Chaucer is hinting that the natural forces alone might suffice, albeit not for two years. The passage suggests that a tide could cover the rocks, and although magic is needed to prolong their disappearance, no time limit was set in Dorigen's behest. Aurelius' prayer, then, is a mixture of the pertinent and the impertinent, and magic seems to fall into the latter category. He asks for a "spring flood," the markedly high tides that

---

Leo they are not diametrically opposed but rather occupy positions 90 degrees apart. Years later, when Skeat wrote his notes to the *Tales*, he silently corrected his previous error and supplied the interpretation used here. That is, when the sun is in Taurus, in May, the full or opposed moon must be located in Scorpio. Therefore, Aurelius' mention of the next opposition that will occur in Leo must mean the opposition that will occur in a few months time when the sun, not the moon, is in Leo. In Chaucer's time the sun was in Leo from mid-July to mid-August. (See Skeat, *Works*, v, 390-91.) Skeat's analysis may seem to tax the reader's ingenuity, but the phrasing itself would suggest the same conclusion. Since the moon passes through all the signs every month it is not a helpful referent, and the phrasing "in the sign of the Lion" would probably suggest to most people the time when the sun, not the moon, was in the sign. Whatever the month, the hoped-for tide is to come in the summer, which is the most important factor.

come with the full and the new moon; he specifies that it should come at the next opposition of sun and moon, which is to say at the next full moon; finally he requests that the tide be five fathoms over the rocks, which is perhaps enough to keep the rocks covered during the variation between high and low tide in that part of France.[5] Dorigen's original request would undoubtedly have made people think in terms of normal tidal possibilities simply because the coast of Brittany is famous for its tides, such as the impressive daily ones at Mont-Saint-Michel, which were known in the Middle Ages.[6] In view of all this we might wish to think that the Orleans clerk did not cause a tide but only predicted one. This, if true would reveal the Orleans clerk as markedly lacking in "gentilesse," and the two brothers as distinctly lacking in worldly wisdom.

All theories about the meaning of the action must rest on whether or not we can predict a markedly high tide ourselves with the information that we are given in the tale. The fact of the matter is that we are not really given much information about the conditions at the time of the magician's operations, but what we have is sufficient for our purposes. Professor Tatlock went so far as to pin down the date as January 3-4, when the full moon would be in the fourth term of Cancer and in its own face or decan, but he deduces these things more from his assumption that the conditions must be propitious for magic than from the information in the poem.[7] Indeed, although Aurelius talked about the positions of particular planets in particular configurations in the zodiac, we are not given any such information at the time of the disappearance of the rocks. The famous passage about the Toledan Tables, the moon mansions, and the moon's face and term (1273-91), tells us what things the clerk was

---

[5] Hodgson, *Franklin's Tale*, p. 92.

[6] Roberto Almagià, "La Dottrina della Marea nell'Antichità Classica e nel Medio Evo. Contributo alla Storia della Geografia Scientifica," *Atti della Reale Accademia dei Lincei, Memorie della Classe di Scienze Fisiche, Matematiche e Naturali*, 5th Ser., No. 5 (1904), p. 428. Moreover, there were tidal powered grain mills in operation on the coast of Brittany in the Middle Ages, particularly in the Rance River estuary. See Jacques Duport, et al., "Power from the Tides," *International Science and Technology*, May, 1965, p. 34.

[7] Tatlock, "Astrology and Magic," pp. 343-44. In the poem, indeed, there is not even a reference to the moon's phase, let alone to its position in regard to the decans or even the signs.

concerned with and what aids he used to find them out, but it does not tell us what situation he discovered. The only specific information that we are granted in regard to the clerk's arrival and his subsequent operations is that they occur at a broadly limited time in the winter:

> And this was, as thise bookes me remembre,
> The colde, frosty seson of Decembre.
>   Phebus wax old, and hewed lyk laton,
> That in his hoote declynacion
> Shoon as the burned gold with stremes brighte;
> But now in Capricorn adoun he lighte,
> Where as he shoon ful pale, I dar wel seyn.
> The bittre frostes, with the sleet and reyn,
> Destroyed hath the grene in every yerd.
> Janus sit by the fyr, with double berd,
> And drynketh of his bugle horn the wyn;
> Biforn hym stant brawen of the tusked swyn,
> And "Nowel" crieth every lusty man. (1243-55)

A modern author who wished to make use of the tides in his writing might well consult an encyclopedia such as the *Encyclopaedia Britannica*, in which he would read that there are two high and two low tides each day, and that there are two periods each month when the tides are particularly marked—the spring tides that occur at the new and the full moon.[8] We do not encounter anything here that is at variance with Aurelius' remarks about the tides, but the poem suggests something that the *Britannica* does not, namely an annual as well as a monthly period of the tides. Aurelius, it will be remembered, specifies a time of year for the great tide that he desires, and the time of year stands out in our minds because it is a few months off in July or August, and he will have to wait for it. The tide, however, does not come that summer. When the rocks seem to disappear, whatever the cause, there is a particular time of year mentioned, a period in the middle of winter which is almost diametrically opposed to the time in the middle of summer that Aurelius thought would

[8] *Encyclopaedia Britannica,* 11th ed. (Cambridge and New York, 1911), s.v. "tide."

be appropriate. There seems to be a possibility that Chaucer was playing upon a theory that the highest tides came in the winter rather than the summer, which would in turn imply that he was poking gentle fun at Aurelius' impatience, or even his ignorance. Though perhaps less well known than the monthly period of the tides there is indeed an annual period, but as it is known today it does not fit the requirements of our hypothetical theory for the *Franklin's Tale*. As known today the annual period brings about particularly marked high tides at the new or full moon near the vernal and autumnal equinoxes, which are the "equinoctial springs" of sailors. Mediaeval theories of the annual period, however, were as much concerned with the solstices, or at least with winter and summer, as they were with the equinoxes.

In general the mediaeval beliefs about the causes of the tides were remarkably similar to our present ideas, but in the later Middle Ages the time of the monthly spring tides was not always agreed upon because some writers held that there was only one spring tide a month, while the time of the annual reinforcement of the monthly springs was thought in the Middle Ages to come in the winter (or in both winter and summer) rather than at the equinoxes in spring and fall, as is today known to be the case.

Today we know that it is the changing relationship of the sun and moon that is primarily responsible for causing both the tides themselves and their inequalities. Thus, the moon's daily rotation around the earth causes two daily highs and two daily lows, the high tides coming shortly after the moon is directly over a place, and again when it is on the opposite side of the earth. When the moon's attractive force is aided by the sun, when the two are either in opposition or conjunction (that is, at both the new and the full moon), the high tides are higher and the lows lower than usual, while the quarter moon pulls at a right angle to the sun and results in weaker highs and weaker lows than at other times. In addition to these basic causes of the tides, the moon's apogee and perigee (its changing distance from the earth each month) has an effect on the strength of the tides. The moon's declination, that is, its changing northern or southern distance from the celestial equator, also causes a marked difference in successive daily tides when the moon is far away from

the celestial equator. Finally, the sun's declination can combine with the moon's phase and declination to cause the equinoctial springs we have already discussed, while the sun's changing distance from the earth, the extremes being aphelion and perihelion, can combine with the moon's phase and distance from the earth to strengthen or weaken the tides.

Despite a lack of unanimity about tidal phenomena in the Middle Ages, one of the later authorities mentions all of the causes known to-day save for the sun's distance, although he expresses them in a somewhat different way because of the different cosmology. Furthermore, certain "special days" of the moon were thought to play a part in things. Thus, there was a truly impressive tidal theory extant in the later Middle Ages. It should, however, be emphasized that not even Newton's equilibrium theory solved all the problems of these very complicated motions, and even the best theory of the causes will not serve to predict with complete accuracy all actual tides in specific places, which depend upon coastal irregularities, basin resonances, and even winds and barometric pressures.[9] So, having established the great similarity between mediaeval and modern beliefs about the causes of the tides, let us return to the problem of the difference between mediaeval and modern beliefs about the time of year when the greatest tides occur.

The proper starting place for mediaeval beliefs about the periods of the tides is the works of Bede. In his *De temporum ratione* Bede makes three observations about the annual period of the tides: the

[9] For a good introduction to current tidal beliefs see Albert Defant, *Ebb and Flow* (Ann Arbor, 1958), pp. 9-16; and for a more technical account see the same author's *Physical Oceanography* (Oxford, London, New York, and Paris, 1961), II, 245-48. The mediaeval authority is Albumasar's *Introductorium in astronomiam* . . . (Venice, 1506), III, Chapters 4-8. The sun's annual influence at aphelion and perihelion is ignored by Defant and by some other contemporary oceanographers, perhaps because it must coincide with appropriate lunar phenomena in order to be effective, and this does not happen every year. For an account of this particular period see *Collier's Encyclopedia*, ed. William D. Halsey, et al. (n.p., 1963), s.v. "tide"; and Nathaniel Bowditch, *American Practical Navigator*, Publication of the United States Hydrographic Office, No. 9 (Washington, 1933), p. 247. Paul Schureman remarks that the sun's distance is usually unimportant, but can be important in shallow water tides. See his *Manual of Harmonic Analysis and Prediction of Tides*, United States Coast and Geodetic Survey Special Publication, No. 98 (Washington, 1941), pp. 40, and 46-47.

tides are strongest at the equinoxes, they are weak at the winter solstice, and they are strong at the summer solstice.[10] While this runs counter to our hypothesis about the *Franklin's Tale*, it is worth noting that this theory was not commonly put forth. Elsewhere, in the *De natura rerum*, Bede ignores any difference between the winter and summer tides.[11] The four seasons, represented by the sun at the equinoxes and solstices, all come in for their share of attention. This is a feature of much of the later mediaeval writing on the annual period of the tides, as is a lack of unanimity about the relationships of the different tides to one another.

Isidore of Seville ignores the annual period of the tides in his *De natura rerum*, but in his *De ordine creaturarum* he has a few lines saying that the tides are strongest at both the equinoxes and the solstices.[12] Apart from Bede and Isidore, however, the encyclopedic corpus, so often so valuable, is not helpful here. The *De universo* of Rabanus Maurus and the *De universo* of William of Auvergne both ignore the annual period completely, while Honorius of Autun and Vincent of Beauvais talk about markedly strong tides when the moon is in the equinoctial points, which is a monthly and not an annual phenomenon.[13] Finally, Pierre Bersuire, writing in the fourteenth

[10] "Ergo malinam quinque fere ante novam sive plenam lunam diebus, ledonem totidem ante dividuam saepius incipere comperimus, et circa aequinoctia duo majores solito aestus adsurgere, inanes vero bruma, et magis solstitio, semperque luna in Aquilonia et a terris longius recedente, mitiores, quam cum in Austro digressa propriore nisu vim suam exercet, aestus adfluere, naturalis ratio cogit" (Bede, *De temporum ratione*, PL, 90, col. 426). Roberto Almagià says that most of Bede's comments on the tides in the *De temporum ratione* are taken from Pliny, including ". . . l'osservazione che i flussi sono massimi all'equinozio e minimi al solstizio . . ." ("La Dottrina della Marea," p. 424). Bede, however, does not say precisely the same thing. Almagià's article and several sections in Pierre Duhem's *Système du monde* are valuable for studies of the periods of the tides. It should be pointed out, however, that both authors are primarily interested in theories of tidal causation, and neither one generalizes about mediaeval beliefs about the annual period.

[11] Bede, *De natura rerum*, PL, 90, col. 259.

[12] ". . . duae scilicet aequinoctiales malinae, et aliae duae, cum aut dies aut nox incrementi et decrementi sui finem faciunt, solito validiores, sicut oculis probare licet . . ." (Isidore of Seville, *De ordine creaturarum*, PL, 83, col. 937).

[13] Honorius of Autun, *De imagine mundi*, PL, 172, col. 133: "Cum luna est in aequinoctio, majores Oceani fluctus surgunt, ob vicinitatem lunae; cum in solstitio, minores, ob longinquitatem ejus." Vincent of Beauvais, *Speculum Quadrvplex* (Paris, 1624), I, 318: "Cum luna est in equinoctio maiores fluctus Oceani surgunt, ob

century, extracts ingenious allegories from the actions of the sea, but refers only to a monthly period of the tides and bases his writings upon the very brief account in Macrobius.[14] Thus, a sampling of encyclopedists spanning the five hundred years from Rabanus to Bersuire bears no fruit whatsoever insofar as statements about the anual period of the tides are concerned. In view of the fact that both Isidore and Bede commented on the annual period it is puzzling that the later encyclopedists, with their genius for derivation, ignore it; but it is much stranger that the annual period is ignored by the most detailed and important study of the tides to appear in the later Middle Ages, the essay appearing in the *Introductorium in astronomiam* of Albumasar. This essay, which was translated into Latin in the twelfth century, has a wealth of description of the tides and an extensive and carefully worked out tidal theory. Yet, in spite of the fact that Albumasar goes so far as to discuss eight causes of the inequality between the day tide and the night tide, the annual period is not mentioned.[15]

---

vicinitatem lunae." Almagià claims that Honorius says that the tides are greater at the equinoxes, but this is not so ("La Dottrina della Marea," pp. 428-29). The phrase "at the equinoxes" must mean when the sun is at the equinoxes. What Honorius is talking about is a monthly period dependent upon the moon's passage through the zodiac.

[14] ". . . Luna est anima. Mare corpus, utrumque fluit & refluit, scilicet anima per diversa desideria & affectiones . . . Macrobius dicit, quod mare in principio lunationis minuitur septem diebus, iterum aliis septem augetur . . ." (Pierre Bersuire, *Reductorium morale*, in *Opera omnia* (Cologne, 1730-31), I, 244-45.

[15] Albumasar, *Introductorium*, III, Chapters 4-8. Albumasar does say that the relationship between day tides and night tides (the diurnal inequality of succession) is affected by the sun's passage through the zodiac, but this is quite a different thing from the annual period. Almagià uses the phrase "periodo annuo della marea" rather too broadly when he applies it to this phenomenon ("La Dottrina della Marea," p. 440). There were two translations made of Albumasar's work, one by John of Seville and one by Hermann of Carinthia. Almagià realized that the published translation, which he wrongly thought was by John of Seville, was an abridgement, and he therefore tried to fill in possible gaps by reference to Albertus Magnus and Vincent of Beauvais (p. 438, n. 6). More recently Richard Lemay has also pointed out the inadequacies of Hermann's translation. Unfortunately John of Seville's more literal rendition, of which the extant MSS outnumber those of Hermann by almost three to one, has never been published. See Richard Lemay, *Abu Ma'Shar and Latin Aristotelianism in the Twelfth Century* (Beirut, 1962), p. xvii and n. 1. Professor Lemay is presently working on an edition of the two

The encyclopedias are wanting, Albumasar is not helpful, and the early statements by Bede and Isidore are contradictory, so we must look elsewhere for a consistent body of opinion. Such a body of opinion exists—consistent at least in some aspects—largely in commentaries on Aristotle, many of which were dependent for their beliefs on an anonymous English or perhaps French treatise on the tides. This treatise, the *Tractatus de fluxu et refluxu maris*, has been attributed to Roger Bacon and to Walter Burley, among others, but all we can say of its provenience is that its author claims to have observed the tides all around England and around a large part of France, which suggests English or French authorship.[16] This anonymous *Tractatus* appeared sometime in the second half of the thirteenth century and introduced a comment on the annual period of the tides that had been lacking in western thought for hundreds of years. The comment, with variations, was picked up by a number of writers in the thirteenth

---

translations that will be of great value, but until its appearance we shall have to be content with Hermann's translation, which does not mention an annual period. Almagià's attempt to broaden the available translation by reference to Albertus Magnus and Vincent of Beauvais is probably unsound. Albert, for example, believed in a single rather than a double monthly period, and other such inconsistencies are almost a certainty. Hermann's use of Latin sometimes creates difficulties for the reader so it is worth noting that there is a French translation of most of the section on tides in Duhem, *Système du monde*, II, 369-86.

16 *Tractatus de fluxu et refluxu maris*, Bibl. nat., Lat. Ser. MS 16089, folio 257, col. c. The MS has never been published, so citations are from Duhem's selections in translation (Duhem, IX, 41-53). Duhem points out that the anonymous *Tractatus* follows the exposition of Albertus Magnus, and was known to Egidio Colonna. This would point to a date in the second half of the thirteenth century, unless we should ascribe it to Walter Burley. The author's nationality cannot, of course, be determined with any certainty from his remarks about the areas of his observations. Further along in the MS he refers to himself as a resident of Paris (Duhem, IX, 45), and we know that Burley was for a time associated with the Sorbonne (Duhem, VI, 673), so the ascription to Burley remains tempting. The MS Duhem uses differs in *incipit* from that described by Jebb, who removed the work from the Bacon canon. See the Preface to Jebb's edition of Roger Bacon's *Opus majus* (London, 1733); and Duhem, IX, 41. Walter Burley did write a treatise on the English tides, the *De fluxu et refluxu maris anglicani*, but the work has not been published, and the only known MS has had this section ripped out *per plagiarios* (*Catalogus codicum mss qui in collegiis aulisque Oxoniensibus hodie adservantur*, ed. Henricus O. Coxe [Oxford, 1852], I, p. 5 of the Oriel College listings). Of course, insofar as Chaucer is concerned a possible influence is more easily argued from the widespread influence of this anonymous *Tractatus* than from its possible English origin.

and fourteenth centuries, and the annual period of the tides is almost as regularly discovered in later commentaries on Aristotle as it is consistently absent in the encyclopedists.[17] What the *Tractatus* says is important, for here we discover the thesis that the highest tides occur in the winter as opposed to the summer.[18] This theory would help to account for the mid-winter disappearance of the rocks in the *Franklin's Tale* and would run counter to Aurelius' hope for a high tide in the summer.

There are four commentators on Aristotle's *Meteorologica* who are indebted to the anonymous *Tractatus*: John Buridan, Thimonus Judei, the pseudo-Duns Scotus, and Paulus Venetus.[19] The statements of John Buridan and Thimonus Judei, in the versions available, are very brief and to the point. Both say simply that the tides are higher in the winter than in the summer, with a slight variation when Thimo-

[17] That a fourteenth-century encyclopedist like Bersuire did not make use of what must have been a reasonably accessible body of information about the tides indicates either that he was ignorant of what we might call scientific as opposed to encyclopedic writings, or that he chose not to consult them.

[18] The *Tractatus* says that the tides are greater in winter than summer because of the sun's weakness, and in the *Franklin's Tale* the sun's dull, coppery color in Capricorn is contrasted to its gold hue in the summer declination (1245-49). Another interesting point of correspondence is in the "sleet and rayn" of winter in Chaucer (1250), and the *Tractatus'* statement that the sun's weakness produces rains in the winter as well as high tides: "Demandera-t-on, par example, pourquoi, dans le Nord, les marées sont régulièrement plus fortes en hiver qu'en été? On peut répondre . . . que le Soleil, en produisant la chaleur et repoussant le froid, est, pour l'eau, cause d'évaporation et non de génération; plus donc il est éloigné du pôle septentrional, mieux et plus vite le froid qui y règne pourra condenser et disposer la matière afin qu'à l'aide de la Lune, elle se transforme en eau; or, du tropique du Cancer, qu'il atteint en été, le Soleil, en hiver, recule jusqu'au tropique du Capricorne, où il se trouve à sa plus grande distance du Septentrion; on peut donc dire raisonnablement que les flux et reflux seront, par là, plus grands en hiver qu'en été. . . . Cette augmentation du flux et du reflux trouve encore grand secours dans les eaux pluviales, qui sont plus abondantes à cette époque" (as translated by Duhem, IX, 51-52).

[19] Duhem analyzes Buridan's debt to the *Tractatus* in some detail (IX, 68-72), and Thimonus refers to it by name. The apocryphal commentary attributed to Duns Scotus was written by a faithful disciple of Buridan, according to Duhem, which is to say that it was written by a direct or indirect follower of the *Tractatus* (Duhem, IX, 76). Paulus Venetus may or may not be imitating the *Tractatus*, but at the least his statements about the annual period are coincident. Duhem has also demonstrated the indebtedness of Egidio Colonna to the *Tractatus*, but insofar as can be determined Colonna does not mention the annual period (Duhem, IX, 53-56).

nus includes the fall season with the winter.[20] The pseudo-Duns Scotus, on the other hand, mentions the equinoctial springs and says that the highest tides occur at the equinox. He does not say which equinox, but he is probably following a linguistic convention that an unspecified equinox refers to the one in the spring. However, he also says, along with the other writers on Aristotle, that the winter tides are higher than the summer ones.[21] A very similar thesis is found in the collection of comments made by Paulus Venetus, where it is said that the winter tides are higher than the summer ones, and also that the spring tides are higher than the autumnal ones.[22] It is doubtful that Paulus Venetus' collection would have been available to Chaucer, but his *Summa* is valuable because it shows what a near contemporary of Chaucer chose to select from the commentaries before him. Like most mediaeval synthesizers Paulus wants to have the best of both worlds.

[20] Johannes Buridan: "La sixième expérience, c'est que les flux sont plus grands en hiver qu'en été" (*Quaestiones super tres primos libros metheororum* . . . , Bibl. nat., Lat. Ser., MS 14.723, fol. 205, col. c; cited by Duhem, IX, 63). Thimonus Judei: ". . . quare in autumne et in hyeme sunt maiores fluxus quam in aestate" (*Quaestiones super quatuor libros metheororum compilate per doctissimum philosophie professorem Thimonem*, bound with Caietanus de Thienis, *Gaietanus super metheo* . . . [Venice, 1522], no page given; cited by Almagià, p. 471). Almagià refers to Thimonus as "Timone Anglo" and since we know that Thimonus was thrice Procurator of England in the mid-fourteenth century, we may be reasonably confident that Almagià is indeed referring to Thimonus Judei. For Thimonus' English career see Duhem, VIII, 436-37.

[21] "Quinto sciendum est de augmentatione, et diminutione istius fluxus, quod in hyeme fluxus iste est major quam in aestate, et adhuc major circa Aequinoctium, quam in hyeme, vel in aestate" (Duns Scotus, *Meteorologicorum libri quatuor*, in *Opera omnia* [Paris, 1891-95], IV, 134). Duhem has adduced several arguments to the effect that the work is apocryphal (IX, 73-75).

[22] ". . . fluxus et refluxus maris maiores fiunt in hyeme quam in estate et vere quam in autumno postquam fluuij currentes ad mare sunt maiores in hyeme quam in estate. et in vere quam in autumno ideo maiores fiunt fluxus maiores autem fiunt refluxus . . ." (Paulus Venetus, *Liber methaurorum*, Colophon: Explicit sexta et vltima pars summe naturalium acta et compilata per . . . Paulum de Venetijs . . . [Venice, 1476], sig. l$_1$^{r}). Almagià thinks that Paulus was born in 1429, but this is the date of his death (Almagià, p. 488). Errors of this sort are easy to make about a man who is known by at least four different names. Paulus was born at Udine of the Nicoletti family and was given the sobriquet "Venetus" in order to distinguish him from Paolo called "Fiorentino." See the enthusiastic account of him, which calls him the foremost philosopher of his day, in *Biographie universelle, ancienne et moderne* (Paris and Leipzig, n.d.), s.v. "Paulus."

In the later Middle Ages, then, an annual period of the tides was indeed known, and the five documents that have been adduced, while offering a variety of opinions about equinoctial tides ranging from silence to the statement that they are even higher than the winter tides, all agree that winter tides are higher than summer tides.[23] A writer in the fourteenth century would certainly feel that he was on the surest ground if he made use of the belief that winter tides were higher than summer ones, whatever he might think of the contradictory theories about the relative strengths of equinoctial and solstitial tides. Specifically insofar as Chaucer is concerned, we really do not know anything one way or another about his possible readings in these Aristotelian commentaries. The commentaries and the anonymous *Tractatus* were extant and presumably available; and while Chaucer's writings are not colored by Aristotle in the way that Dante's are, nevertheless Chaucer's highly sympathetic clerk ". . . was levere have at his beddes heed / Twenty bookes, clad in blak or reed, / Of Aristotle and his philosophie, / Than robes riche . . ." (*Gen Prol*, 293-96). Certainly, if there was any area in which we might expect Chaucer to be conversant with Aristotle or Aristotelian commentaries it would be the natural sciences, the field in which it has been argued Aristotle made his greatest impression on the Middle Ages, and in which Chaucer, himself the author of a treatise on the use of a scientific instrument, would probably be *au courant*. When Hoccleve says that Chaucer was the heir to Aristotle in philosophy, perhaps we should pay more attention than has been our wont.[24]

While Bede and Isidore mentioned the solstices by name, the later writers avoid the specific dates of the solstices and speak instead of the winter and the summer. This may be of some significance, for as was pointed out above, Chaucer tells us the time of year in rather broad terms, mentioning the solstice, the crying abroad of "Noel,"

[23] Surely not a source, but important as an analogue, is the Icelandic *Rymbegla*, composed about 1375, which follows generally the materials surveyed here, saying that the tides are weakest at the summer solstice and strongest at the equinoxes (Almagià, pp. 483-84).

[24] That Aristotle made his first impact on the Middle Ages as a writer on natural science is the thesis of Lemay's book already mentioned. We should never underestimate Chaucer's knowledge. Cf. Chapter IV, Section 1, where it is argued that Chaucer is up-to-date on a matter of Biblical exegesis.

and the picture of Janus, who gives January its name. He seems to be concerned to set the event at some time after the solstice and clearly not at it. When John Buridan said that high tides come in the winter rather than the summer, and that he knew this from his own experience, he was taken to task by Pierre Duhem, who said that every sailor, indeed every fisherman, knows that the most powerful tides come at the equinoxes and that the weakest tides come at the solstices.[25] Duhem has made the unwarranted assumption that Buridan was talking about solstitial tides, when Buridan said no such thing. Had Duhem been more generous he might have inquired why Buridan thought as he did, and he might have discovered that shortly after the winter solstice there exists a period of very high tides, and that there is a corresponding period of lower tides than usual after the summer solstice. When the sun is at perihelion, its position closest to the earth, which occurs today about January 2, there is a period of increased tides, and the corresponding low tides of mid-summer come when the sun is at aphelion.[26] That some writers in the Middle Ages spoke of high tides in the winter as well as at the equinoxes can be credited to their sophistication and not to their naiveté or guile.

Chaucer's rather broad definition of the time of year is perhaps the direct result of his knowledge of the details of the tides, whether or not he is undercutting the Franklin's skill at astronomical periphrasis. If Chaucer was acquainted with mediaeval theories of the tides, he would have believed that there was a high tide in the winter, and he might have known firsthand or from some essay unknown to us that the winter high tides come after the solstice. Today perihelion occurs on about January 2, or about ten days after the winter solstice. In Chaucer's day the sun reached the solstitial point on the twelfth of December, and so ten days later would take us to December 22, a time close to Christmas and the end of the month. It would be going too far to suggest that Chaucer actually knew any more details than are given in the authorities, but it is worth remarking that there

---

25 Duhem, IX, 63. Almagià similarly accuses Paulus Venetus of distorting the truth (p. 489).

26 This phenomenon also depends upon the moon's perigee and apogee, which, when coincident with perihelion and aphelion cause increased and reduced tides respectively. The phenomenon is known as the solar parallactic inequality. See *Collier's Encyclopedia*, s.v. "tides," and note 9 above.

is nothing in the tidal theories of his day or ours that is at variance with this aspect of the situation in the *Franklin's Tale*.

2. SCIENCE, MAGIC, AND "GENTILESSE"

WHATEVER the details of Chaucer's beliefs about the annual time of the tides, he is definitely concerned with time in the *Franklin's Tale*. In addition to the absent tide of the summer and the presumed high tide after the winter solstice, Chaucer calls our attention to the fact that the Orleans clerk chooses his moment with care:

> So atte laste he hath his tyme yfounde
> To maken his japes and his wrecchednesse. (1270-71)

We can say that the clerk is waiting for a good time for magic, or we can think that he has calculated the period of the tides and is waiting for nature to take its course. This, however, is as far as we can go, because there is a deliberate ambiguity in the situation. We have already remarked upon the fact that the rocks only seemed to be away at the climax of the poem, but that same line includes the fact that the rocks seemed to be away "for a wyke or tweye" (1295), which would be too long a period to be accounted for by any tide. Even if we were to grant that the range of the tide would be such that the daily alternation of highs and lows would not destroy the concealment of the rocks, there is no doubt that a two-week period would change the phase of the moon sufficiently to bring a return to normalcy. The alternative to a tidal explanation of the phenomenon, however, is magic or illusion, and it too is unsatisfactory from the point of view of time, for there seems to be no reason for the magic to last only two weeks instead of the two years Aurelius asked for, if we are to grant that it can work at all. Since neither a tide nor magic seems to suit all of the demands of the situation we are perhaps best advised to assume that Chaucer intended not that we should deny the magic, as the Franklin does, but rather that we should question it, which the Franklin does not. In order to do this we must take a longer view of the problems of the tale with careful regard for both tone and characterization. If Chaucer has arranged things so that "magic" is compromised, if not denied, then we should properly expect that "gentilesse" may also be presented in such a way

that the events do not logically compel us to interpret them as the Franklin does. From this vantage point it can be argued that what passes at first glance for "gentilesse" is in fact somewhat tawdry, and the Franklin's admiration for the world of the romances can be construed as leading to an overvaluation of both the behavior of his characters and the natural and supernatural circumstances surrounding them.

If we entertain the hypothesis that the Orleans clerk only predicted a high tide, then Aurelius was gulled and the clerk was deceitful. Moreover, if the clerk did not cause the tide, then not only is his thousand pound fee unearned, but his remission of it is hypocritical. Thus, if the clerk has not in fact given up something he has earned, then he is not only not "gentil" but actually the opposite, for he trades upon Aurelius' trust in order to swell his own reputation. If, then, the clerk's gentility may be called in doubt, it is tempting to inquire further into the behavior of the other characters in the tale.

Almost half a century ago Professor Hinckley observed that Arveragus could scarcely be called "gentil," because he threatened Dorigen's life if she should expose his conduct. More recently Professor Gaylord has noted that "Arveragus gives up his honor in order to save its appearance."[27] If Aurelius is self-seeking and prodigal, the clerk deceitful, and Arveragus bluntly hypocritical, then only Dorigen is left as a possible figure in whom to discover "gentilesse," but as so many critics have pointed out, it is difficult to generate whole-hearted admiration for a woman who is as single-mindedly literal as Dorigen. Thus, if at the end of the tale no one can be said to be particularly "gentil," we should then assuredly undertake a reconsideration of the Franklin's ideas of what constitutes gentility.

Because the Franklin clearly admires the people in his tale, even though their conduct is open to question at the least, it would seem that his vision is colored. Putting to one side the vexed issue of the Franklin's own social standing, it is clear that he admires the people

[27] Henry Barrett Hinckley, "Chauceriana," *MP*, XVI (1918-19), 44. Alan Theodore Gaylord, *Seed of Felicity*, unpublished dissertation (Princeton, 1958), p. 538. For a very different and challenging view that considers two levels of "gentilesse," see Gerhard Joseph, "*The Franklin's Tale*: Chaucer's Theodicy," *The Chaucer Review*, I (1966), 20-32.

in his tale not because they are higher than he on a social scale but because they live in a bright, intense world of romance and adventure, located somewhere long ago and far away, and born out of the Franklin's imagination: "Thise olde gentil Britouns in hir dayes / Of diverse aventures maden layes" (709-10). The Franklin's concept of "gentilesse" involves a former time, a different country, and the poetry of "aventures." Indeed the actual provenience of the *Franklin's Tale* could not be as important as the one with which he provides us. To a degree we are reminded of Don Quixote, who was inebriated by the world of romantic adventure; with the *Franklin's Tale*, as with the *Don Quixote*, this infatuation is satirized by showing the romantic world in such a state of excess that it becomes grotesque in its lack of proportion.[28] Chaucer's own attitude toward the romances is well illustrated by the satirical excesses in the *Thopas*, which are specifically aimed at the chivalric romances, and some elements of the *Thopas* turn up in *Franklin's Tale*.[29]

The *Franklin's Tale* opens with the hyperbolic introduction of Dorigen as the fairest woman under the sun, and then proceeds to her marriage to Arveragus. The "noble" gentleman agrees to serve his wife in marriage, but to maintain "the name of soveraynetee, / That wolde he have for shame of his degree" (751-52). A nominal sovereignty for the sake of appearances connected with social standing is a sovereignty that swells large and rings hollow, and its suggests that here social status must be achieved regardless of cost. After Arveragus' departure to the wars, the Franklin turns eagerly to the

---

[28] This lack of proportion may be seen in the Franklin's curious rhetoric. Professor Harrison's remarks on rhetoric show that the Franklin is inconsistent, because he claims not to know the Latin "colors" and yet uses some seventy of them in his tale. See Benjamin S. Harrison, "The Rhetorical Inconsistency of Chaucer's Franklin," *SP*, XXXII (1935), 55-61. Whether or not one would agree with all of Professor Harrison's identifications, the tale is highly "colored" rhetorically, in the broader sense of the word.

[29] Professor Robinson, in his notes to *Sir Thopas*, comments that while Chaucer himself wrote romances, the absurdities of the genre were obvious targets for burlesque. The particular nature of these "absurdities" is important too, because of its relationship to the *Franklin's Tale*. A. T. Byles says that the romances were extravagant and gave a sense of unreality and also placed an emphasis on "enchantment and faery" ("Medieval Courtesy Books and the Prose Romances of Chivalry," in *Chivalry*, ed. Edgar Prestage [New York, 1928], p. 185).

description of Dorigen's mourning, which is of passionate intensity, and which, he assures us, is peculiar to noble wives, who presumably suffer more exquisitely than we burel folk:

> For his absence wepeth she and siketh,
> As doon thise noble wyves whan hem liketh.
> She moorneth, waketh, wayleth, fasteth, pleyneth;
> Desir of his presence hire so destreyneth
> That al this wyde world she sette at noght. (817-21)

Aurelius, in his turn, will also offer all the world for love. "This wyde world, which that men seye is round, / I wolde it yeve . . ." (1228-29).

The actions of the principals are exaggerated, and the descriptions of them are overdone. As Dorigen was the fairest woman under the sun, so Aurelius sings and dances "passynge any man / That is, or was, sith that the world bigan" (929-30), and it follows unsurprisingly that the meeting of two such singular beings occurs in a spot so favored "That nevere was ther gardyn of swich prys, / But if it were the verray paradys" (911-12). The emphasis on singularity undercuts the very common situation dealt with here, and this is far from being the only use of this technique in the *Tales*. Chaucer does not always use such terms humorously, but they lend themselves to comedy very well.

Still, we know these people best by their actions, and after Dorigen refuses Aurelius and makes her tasteless joke about the rocks, he goes home and proves himself her equal in sensibility by matching her hysteria:

> Up to the hevene his handes he gan holde,
> And on his knowes bare he sette hym doun,
> And in his ravyng seyde his orisoun.
> For verray wo out of his wit he breyde.
> He nyste what he spak. . . .   (1024-28)

Aurelius is indeed raving, but there is some method in his madness. He appeals to the sun three different times, twice asking that the sun enlist the moon to cause a high tide and once asking the sun simply to sink the rocks into hell. He also requests that the tide be achieved

and maintained by an opposition of sun and moon that will last for two years.[30] While Aurelius' repetitiveness and inconsistency are signs of his disturbed emotional state, he is nevertheless on the right track when he asks that the high tide be brought about by an opposition of sun and moon, but he is confused when he hopes that the high tide will come in the summer.[31] In view of mediaeval theories of the tides, this is of a piece with his request that the moon keep pace with the sun for the next two years, a clear case of wishful thinking.[32]

When the wished-for tide does not appear that summer, Aurelius takes to his bed for two years, which presumably completes his credentials as a sensitive person. It is at this point that Aurelius'

[30] William Hunter points out that it behooves Aurelius to pray to Apollo, the sun, to intercede with the moon, here styled as Lucina, because Lucina is the goddess of chastity and would therefore not be the goddess to approach directly when one is interested in adultery, as is Aurelius (William B. Hunter, Jr., "*Canterbury Tales* V, 1031ff.," *MLN*, LXVIII [1953], 174). Perhaps the point to be made is that even the indirect approach does not work.

[31] A widespread editorial comment at this point is that the high tides come at the new and the full moon and that the full moon is arbitrarily chosen by Chaucer. The fact of the matter is that we do not know what Chaucer thought about the monthly period of the tides. The most cursory examination of the writings on the annual period finds disagreement when they speak of the monthly period. The anonymous *Tractatus* says that there are high tides at both the new and the full moon, while John Buridan, the pseudo-Duns Scotus, and Paulus Venetus all say that the tides are higher at the full moon than at the new. Albumasar also says that the tides are higher at the full than at the new moon, and Duhem twits him for this, saying that the opposite was true. The points to be made are, first, that not all twentieth-century writers can agree on all tidal phenomena; second, that Chaucer may not be being arbitrary at all; and third, that it may even be that further study would show a possibility of Chaucer's having believed that the higher tides were at the new moon and consequently would prove Aurelius' concern for the full moon as wrong-headed as his hope for a high tide in the summer. This last, of course, is doubtful, but remains as a warning to us not to interpret mediaeval poems with modern science.

[32] It has been suggested that Aurelius wants to wait until the opposition with the sun in Leo, the sun's own house, because it is powerful there and because the moon in opposition would consequently be in Aquarius, which would be an appropriate sign for the "watery miracle" (Hodgson, *Franklin's Tale*, p. 92). Even though Chaucer's audience was more familiar with the signs of the zodiac than we are, one wonders whether they could visualize the situation so clearly that they could discover the sign of the moon's opposition. As for the sun, there is no evidence that its discovery in Leo has anything to do with high seas or high tides.

brother takes charge and decides that they should go to Orleans and arrange for a clerk to make a kind of stage illusion of vanished rocks. The brother has heard that at feasts, in large halls, the "tregetoures" have caused rivers to flow and barges to move up and down on the water, and this, along with other impressive feats, has made him devoted to magic and magicians. Once again, the feasts, the halls, and the elaborate entertainments remind us of the Franklin's insatiable thirst for the exciting life of glamorous people, while his abrupt dismissal of magic as "nat worth a flye" (1132), warns us not to be overly credulous about the possible relationships between moon mansions and floating barges. The moon mansions are mentioned, along with "oother magyk natureel above" (1155), as potential agents for the creation of the appearance of vanished rocks, and Professor Robinson has argued that natural magic was a legitimate science in the Middle Ages. However, whether or not this is so we should not "conclude" (1152) with Aurelius' brother that the parlor tricks are effective because of moon mansions, when the Franklin himself has no use for them and when it has been shown by Laura Hibbard Loomis that these events were mechanical rather than magical.[33] Indeed, the incident of the barge floating on the water actually took place at a royal feast in Paris, created by accomplished artisans who made

[33] Laura Hibbard Loomis, "Secular Dramatics in the Royal Palace, Paris, 1378, 1389, and Chaucer's 'Tregetoures,'" *Speculum*, XXXIII (1958), 242-44. For Robinson's remarks on natural magic see his note to *Gen Prol*, 416. Professor Benjamin has perhaps granted too much of the supernatural to the clerk's entertainment, but he is surely right in his interpretation of the import of all these illusions for the moral fabric of the tale: "We can recognize Satan when he squats by our head in the form of a toad, as in Milton, or when he howls in the storm, as in Blake; it is less easy to spot him in more homely and familiar forms—in the neurotic fancies of a pretty woman, or in the pleasant illusions that come to us while we are waiting for our dinner" (Edwin B. Benjamin, "The Concept of Order in the *Franklin's Tale*," PQ, XXXVIII [1959], 123-24). Professor Lumiansky has noted that magical effects, which were regular features of the Breton lays, constitute the kind of romance material that the Franklin thinks proper for people of breeding (R. M. Lumiansky, "The Character and Performance of Chaucer's Franklin," UTQ, XX [1950-51], 353). One could add that not only the magic but other elements of the tale as well are products of the Franklin's version of what is "right." Professor McAlindon has observed that magic is generally a diabolical feature in mediaeval narratives and that the *Franklin's Tale* can be located in the genre in which a man enlists magic to win the body of a woman, usually a Christian ("Magic, Fate, and Providence," p. 126 and n. 5).

automata, and was a well-known occurrence. In view of this evidence
of the existence of mechanical explanations for the phenomena that
have impressed Aurelius' brother, we should be well advised to dis-
cover in his fascination with magic, moon mansions, and subtle clerks,
a kind of naïveté in regard to human nature as well as to stage illu-
sions. When Aurelius and his brother are treated to some illusions
in the clerk's study, they are illusions of the very kind that the brother
admires: completely courtly, for it is no less a courtly personage
than Sir Thopas who excels in the first two illusions, deer hunting
and hawking, while jousting and dancing speak for themselves. It
would seem that the brother's interests were known in advance.

All this has been a prologue to the episode of the rocks, which
will be the measure of magic just as the characters' reactions to the
rocks' disappearance will be the Franklin's test of "gentilesse." If
we accept the theory that the Orleans clerk only predicts a tide, then
his preparations for the disappearance of the rocks may be understood
as an elaborate series of actions designed to impress his victims; the
description of this technical display is in keeping with the highly
colored state of the whole tale. The Franklin's disclaimer of knowl-
edge of the terms of astrology is, of course, on a par with his dis-
claimer of knowledge of the colors of rhetoric. He seems to know
enough technical terms of astrology, but he does not see through the
clerk's maneuverings:

> His tables Tolletanes forth he brought,
> Ful wel corrected, ne ther lakked nought,
> Neither his collect ne his expans yeeris,
> Ne his rootes, ne his othere geeris,
> As been his centris and his argumentz
> And his proporcioneles convenientz
> For his equacions in every thyng.
> And by his eighte speere in his wirkyng
> He knew ful wel how fer Alnath was shove
> Fro the heed of thilke fixe Aries above,
> That in the ninthe speere considered is;
> Ful subtilly he kalkuled al this.

Whan he hadde founde his firste mansioun,
He knew the remenaunt by proporcioun,
And knew the arisyng of his moone weel,
And in whos face, and terme, and everydeel;
And knew ful weel the moones mansioun
Acordaunt to his operacioun. (1273-90)

In spite of the elaborateness of this passage, there are actually only
a few basic considerations, and none of them is complex. The collect
years, centers, etc., are all things used in connection with the Toledan
tables in order to determine the positions in the zodiac of the various
planets; the face, term, and mansion of the moon are all arbitrary
(and overlapping) places on the zodiac; while the distance of Alnath
from the equinoctial point of Aries is a way of measuring the amount
of precession of the equinoxes that has taken place.[34] What have
these things to do with the matter at hand? Certainly the precession
of the equinoxes has nothing to do with tides, high seas, magic, or
anything else that might be pertinent, and is clearly included for the
sake of impressive ornamentation.[35] As for the Toledan tables and
their attendant paraphernalia, they are of use in computing the posi-
tions of the various planets, but the question at hand, whether the
moon is full, new, or at quarter, is much too readily observable to
require calculation. The faces and terms can have something to do
with the power of the moon, as Tatlock has pointed out, but these
situations are of no moment in regard to the tides. Professor Tatlock
has also confessed his inability to understand why the clerk is con-
cerned about a particular mansion of the moon, and it may be that
the mansions are just not pertinent to the situation.[36]

[34] Professor Robinson, in his note to line 1277, follows Skeat in making the
"centris" an exception to the list. Skeat thought that the centers were parts of an
astrolabe, but in fact both centers and arguments have to do with the angular rela-
tionship of a planet to the center of its sphere or its eccentric. Cf. Skeat, *Works*, v,
394; and *Middle English Dictionary*, ed. Kurath, s.v. "centre," 7c.

[35] Alpetragius once argued that the movement of the tides was related to the
movement of the Primum Mobile, but here we are concerned with precession, which
was usually thought to be a function of the Crystalline sphere or of the sphere of
the fixed stars. In addition, we should not confuse the movement of the tides with
the period of the tides. Also, Alpetragius' ideas were not popular in the West. See
Almagià, "La Dottrina della Marea," pp. 449-50.

[36] Tatlock, "Astrology and Magic," pp. 342-48.

The solution to the clerk's concern for the mansions of the moon, which are thought to be silly by even the Franklin, is to be found in Aurelius' brother's concern for them. It is he who introduces the moon mansions into the tale when he reminisces about Orleans, and it is he who muses that some "oold felawe" might be able to create the desired illusion by means of the moon mansions. When, following this, Aurelius and his brother are met at the city's edge by a young messenger who knows their purpose without having to inquire, we may assume that their specific interest in moon mansions could also be known. When the Orleans clerk puts on a display of astrological and magical knowledge in order to impress his victims, he is careful, like many a confidence man before him, to give his victims just the sort of display that they want. Once again, the *Franklin's Tale* is very much concerned with appearance and reality. Aurelius will do anything to obtain what he wants, and this kind of blind devotion to one's personal satisfaction creates the perfect victim for a confidence man. There is a strong similarity between the situation here and the situation in the *Miller's Tale*, where old John is noted for self-interest, indeed for a kind of miserliness (*MillT*, 3851), and he too is taken in by the smooth words of a self-styled astrologer. There is also, of course, some satire here on both avarice and generosity, for when Chaucer sets the "miracle" of the rocks at about Christmas time, he takes advantage not only of the scientific suitability of the time, but also of its artistic appropriateness. As we remarked earlier, Chaucer uses the successive images of the sun in Capricorn, Janus at the fire, and the crying of "Noel" to tell us the time of the year, and the images are no doubt pertinent. The sun, which in the summer had been like gold, is now debased to copper (1245-47), while in like manner Christmas, the time of giving and generosity, is the time for the tale's characters to hold one another to their real or fancied vows and to give away "generously" one's wife, one's honor, one's adulterous claims, or one's suspect fees. Janus, then, appropriately links the images of the debased sun and Christmas, for he is not only the source of January, but is also the familiar, two-faced symbol of hypocrisy and double-dealing.

While we chide Aurelius and his brother for their overly trusting belief in magic, we should not praise the Franklin overly much for

his dismissal of it. Professor Lumiansky has rightly argued that the Franklin's practical sense prevents his acceptance of magic, even though it appeals to him.[37] The Franklin loves the mysterious. Certainly the Franklin's interjection about the eight and twenty mansions "That longen to the moone, and swich folye / As in oure dayes is nat worth a flye—" (1131-32), is a very flip statement from the man who so glowingly describes the conjured illusions at the magician's house. However, there is more naïveté than practicality in the Franklin's subsequent statement "For hooly chirches feith in oure bileve / Ne suffreth noon illusioun us to greve" (1133-34). Holy Church does not prevent men from deceiving themselves and thus subjecting themselves to illusion. In some respects the Franklin's inability to see very deeply into the characters of the people in his story represents a kind of willingness to be gulled not entirely dissimilar from that encountered in Aurelius and his brother.

Indeed, here the whole matter of illusion, reality, and delusion must be faced, and we must inquire to what extent the Franklin's unconcern about the illusions in his tale represents self-delusion. The Franklin's casual dismissal of magic is given the lie by his enthusiasm for its effects, and we can consequently argue that the tale is set in the long ago and far away so that the Franklin, not Chaucer, can indulge his obvious fondness for magic. As Professor Gaylord has put it, we must "separate the *persona* of the Franklin from his Maker, attributing to Chaucer the finesse of stroke capable of creating a Tale exceeding its ostensible teller's capacity to understand."[38] This is a very helpful approach to the problems here, for the way in which possible alternatives to magic such as tides, gossip, and automata are woven into the fabric of the story without any insistence on their employment as alternatives presents us with a fascinating ambiguity in which the Franklin may be misunderstanding the sentence of his

[37] Lumiansky, "Character and Performance," p. 353. Professor Huppé has recently compared the Wife of Bath's disclaimer of belief in elves to the Franklin's disclaimer of belief in magic and has argued that both are the victims of illusion. See Huppé, *Reading of the Canterbury Tales*, p. 167.

[38] Alan T. Gaylord, "The Promises in *The Franklin's Tale*," ELH, XXI (1964), 332. This learned and perceptive article appeared after this essay had been written or even more use would have been made of it.

tale and misconstruing its surface elements as well. Indeed, Chaucer's changes from his source indicate that this is the case, for as Professor Gaylord has pointed out, the purpose of the changes is clearly to emphasize the absurdity of an attempt to make an abstract dilemma into an *exemplum* of "gentilesse."[89] Thus, in the *Filocolo* the clerk's promise is fulfilled in fact, while in Chaucer the promise is fulfilled, at best, in appearance and may be to the discredit rather than the credit of the clerk. Further, in Boccaccio the wife plucks fruit in the garden, while in the *Franklin's Tale* no one even goes to look at the rocks; we have only the Franklin's word for both the length of time they are gone and for their complete disappearance.[40] Thus, while Boccaccio insisted that the lady have tangible satisfaction that the magic had worked, Chaucer gives us both trusting characters and a trusting narrator. Where Boccaccio's heroine, *non credendolo*, could say, " 'Assai mi piace; faretelomi vedere domani,' " not only do Chaucer's characters not inspect the coast, but also his narrator only vaguely says that it seemed (we might inquire to whom) that the rocks were away for a rather indefinite "week or two."[41] Since the narrator is given to exaggeration throughout, we may properly question to what degree this statement is "reportorial" and whether or not it obviates a tidal explanation. The insistent reality, then, is the Franklin's self-delusion about appearance and reality, illusion and truth.

As Professor Bloomfield has recently observed, it is in the framework of the *Tales* that we must look for realism, not in the tales themselves, but even in the framework there is a strong element of artistic strategy by which the author urges the examination of narrative intention in order to accomplish his purpose. Thus, as Professor Bloomfield remarks, if we are unaware of this, we may fall into the error of saying that Marie de France believed in the magic and supernatural so common in her *lais* merely because she says that these

[89] *Ibid.*, p. 364.

[40] Bryan and Dempster, *Sources and Analogues*, pp. 380-81; and Gaylord, "Promises," pp. 357-65. Chaucer also changes the date from January to late December. Tatlock, however, thinks not ("Astrology and Magic," pp. 343-44).

[41] *FranklT*, 1295-96. Also see Bryan and Dempster, *Sources and Analogues*, p. 381.

things happened.[42] Much the same situation obtains in the *Franklin's Tale*, for that gentleman's blindness to the rather obvious shortcomings of the Squire makes us suspicious of his authority on "gentilesse"; and his unquestioning acceptance of the effects of the supernatural, accompanied by denials of the principles of magic, should lead us to be suspicious of his authority there too. Chaucer does not manipulate his materials so that we reject magic out of hand, which is what the Franklin claims to do, but rather he organizes both frame and story so that the Franklin is undercut. We should not forget that, for Chaucer, the teller of the story is best known by what he tells and how he tells it.

In the General Prologue the Franklin is presented as "Epicurus owene sone" (*Gen Prol,* 336), and in Chaucer's translation of the *Consolation of Philosophy* we are told that Epicurus considered delight to be the sovereign good (Bk. III, pr. 2). In the Middle Ages, it was considered natural to seek the true good, or God, and this is so basic a belief that squarely in the middle of the *Divine Comedy* Virgil discourses on the subject.[43] Thus, to turn away from the true good, whether toward delight, like Epicurus and the Franklin, or towards any other lesser thing, was not considered admirable or even natural. To turn away from the true good is to follow error, and one follows error because one has dwelt overmuch on transient, earthly things.[44] Therefore, the Franklin's preoccupation with "gentilesse," closely related to his dreams of another, distant and better world, may be seen as something more than an inconsequential affectation. It is a kind of mental Epicureanism that complements the

[42] Morton W. Bloomfield, "Authenticating Realism and the Realism of Chaucer," *Thought,* XXXIV (1964), 341 and n. 11. Cf. McAlindon, "Magic, Fate, and Providence," passim.

[43] Professor Fergusson has commented on the literal and figurative centrality of this passage: Francis Fergusson, *Dante's Drama of the Mind* (Princeton, 1953), p. 230.

[44] Typically, the Boethian vocabulary is very much to the point: "forasmoche as thi syghte is ocupyed and destourbed by imagynacioun of erthly thynges, thow mayst nat yit seen thilke selve welefulnesse. . . . Forwhy the covetise of verray good is naturely iplauntyd in the hertes of men, but the myswandrynge errour mysledeth hem into false goodes" (Bk. III, pr. 1 and 2). Epicureans were abused for their denial of Plato by one of Chaucer's favorite authors, Macrobius, in his *Commentary on the Dream of Scipio,* trans. William Harris Stahl (New York, 1952), p. 83.

Franklin's physical Epicureanism. It is a basic self-deception that closes the eye of understanding, as Boethius says, and subjects one to false goods.[45] The Franklin does not notice the limitations of his characters because he himself is subject to the same limitations; he does not see deceit because he himself is deceived. His careless dismissal of heathen illusion, which he does not think the church will permit to vex him, is Chaucer's way of underscoring the Franklin's own illusions. The Franklin's vague denial of astrological magic is proper, but unenlightened, for while Chaucer denied that faces and ascendants had any meaning and would have scoffed with the Franklin at moon mansions, he would have believed, as we do, that the tides were caused by celestial influence. Thus is the last change rung on appearance and reality. The Franklin's love of romantic tales comes from what Boethius called a "disturbed vision" of the world, and the exaggerated elements of the story reflect what the Franklin likes. If we know the mediaeval theory of the annual period of the tides and make a bold application of it to the *Franklin's Tale*, we can discount the "magic" in the tale for "disturbed vision," and we can contrast the Franklin's vision with Chaucer's own.

---

[45] January's blindness in the *Merchant's Tale* and Chauntecleer's closing his eyes in the *Nun's Priest's Tale* are outward manifestations of this.

CHAPTER VII

The Parson's Prologue

I. THE TIME OF DAY AND THE
SIGN OF LIBRA

As THE CANTERBURY pilgrims prepare to hear the last of the tales, signaled by Harry Bailly's remark that "Now lakketh us no tales mo than oon" (*Pars Prol*, 16), Chaucer first calls attention to the time of day and then to the sign of the zodiac rising in the east. The time-telling completes a motif that was begun in the Headlink to the *Man of Law's Tale*, where the Host told the time by reference to the date and the proportion of a shadow to the body casting it:

> Oure Hooste saugh wel that the brighte sonne
> The ark of his artificial day hath ronne
> The ferthe part, and half an houre and moore,
> And though he were nat depe ystert in loore,
> He wiste it was the eightetethe day
> Of Aprill, that is messager to May;
> And saugh wel that the shadwe of every tree
> Was as in lengthe the same quantitee
> That was the body erect that caused it.
> And therfor by the shadwe he took his wit
> That Phebus, which that shoon so clere and brighte,
> Degrees was fyve and fourty clombe on highte;
> And for that day, as in that latitude,
> It was ten of the clokke, he gan conclude,
> And sodeynly he plighte his hors aboute.
> "Lordynges," quod he, "I warne yow, al this route,
> The fourthe party of this day is gon."[1]

[1] *ML* Headlink, 1-17. There is some question here with regard to the Host's time-telling ability. If the "arc of the artificial day" is understood as Chaucer uses it in the *Treatise on the Astrolabe*, that is, as the sun's diurnal journey, then the Host has miscalculated the time. If the fourth part of a day beginning at 4:43 A.M. and lasting fourteen and one-half hours of daylight has passed, then the time must be about 8:30 plus the "half an hour and more" mentioned, bringing the time to about 9:00 A.M.—a full hour short of the time the Host calculates. However, as Brae long ago observed, Chaucer confused the hour angle with the azimuthal arc—

Harry Bailly is in a hurry here, and will be in a hurry again at the beginning of the *Parson's Tale*; his haste underscores the characteristic immediacy of his philosophy.

The second instance of time-telling by the height of the sun is performed by Chauntecleer in the *Nun's Priest's Tale*, and it is possible that the Nun's Priest has Chauntecleer do this as a riposte to Harry Bailly's use of the technique. In the Bradshaw order the *Nun's Priest's Tale* comes only five tales after the Man of Law's, and the Nun's Priest and the audience might be expected to remember Harry's time-telling. Wheeling his horse about to tell the time, he does so with a flourish even though it is not much of a trick, since Harry can do it and he is not "depe ystert in loore." When Harry calls upon the Nun's Priest for a tale it is with some fairly good natured banter about the Nun's Priest's "foul and lene" horse (*NP Prol*, 2813), and we might expect that the Nun's Priest might wish to take a return shot at Harry in the course of the tale. Since Harry is described as the "rooster" of the flock of pilgrims ("Up roos oure Hoost, and was oure aller cok, / And gadrede us togidre alle in a flok" [*Gen Prol*, 823-24]), the comparison of him with Chauntecleer is almost inevitable. However, Chauntecleer's time-telling ability, which parallels Harry's in technique, is a natural and not an intellectual phenomenon and so undercuts whatever self-

---

an error also found in his source for the *Astrolabe*. That is, Chaucer confused the sun's distance from the meridian measured along the horizon (the azimuth) with its distance from the meridian measured along the celestial equator (the hour angle). Because the celestial equator is inclined to the visible horizon, the sun's course along the celestial equator is at an uneven speed. Thus, in spring when the sun has accomplished one fourth of its temporal journey it has not covered one fourth of the distance from its point of rising to the south point measured along the horizon. Brae calculated this distance and found that the sun covered it at 9:20 A.M. on the 18th of April in Chaucer's era. With the addition of the "half an hour and more" we discover the time to be 10:00 A.M. as the Host calculates. As a check on this Skeat and Brae calculated the time from the Host's other observation: that the sun's altitude was 45 degrees because objects were casting shadows equal to their heights. The check gives confirmation of the confusion of azimuthal arc and hour angle. Consequently we may judge that Chaucer may have wished to play down the Host's intellectual abilities by noting that "he were nat depe ystert in loore" (*ML* Headlink, 4), but he does not make him so incompetent as to miscalculate the actual time. See *The Treatise on the Astrolabe of Geoffrey Chaucer*, ed. Andrew Edmund Brae (London, 1870), pp. 68-71; and Skeat's notes to the passage in question.

satisfaction Harry may have in his ability to measure the sun's altitude.[2] Chauntecleer measures the sun's height by nature:

> By nature he knew ech ascencioun
> Of the equynoxial in thilke toun.
>
> *(NPT, 2855-56)*

This is reinforced by a second passage in the *Nun's Priest's Tale*, especially similar to the Host's time-telling in the Headlink to the *Man of Law's Tale*. Chauntecleer takes note of the date, calculates the height of the sun, and then determines the time of day. Note that he does it by "kynde" not by reason:

> Bifel that Chauntecleer *in al his pryde*,
> His sevene wyves walkynge by his syde,
> Caste up his eyen to the brighte sonne,
> That in the signe of Taurus hadde yronne
> Twenty degrees and oon, and somwhat moore,
> *And knew by kynde*, and by noon oother loore,
> That it was pryme, and crew with blisful stevene.
>
> *(NPT, 3191-97)*

If these two ventures into time-telling by means of the height of the sun have been more for humor than substance, we may properly inquire why Chaucer uses the same form in the Prologue to the *Parson's Tale*, where he even goes so far as to perform the calculations himself, that is, in the poet's voice and not Harry Bailly's. Surely there is no attempt on Chaucer's part to undercut the Parson, but there may be an attempt to link him with time-telling. Certainly the passage itself is so similar to the preceding ones as to recall them without fail:

> By that the Maunciple hadde his tale al ended,
> The sonne fro the south lyne was descended
> So lowe that he nas nat, to my sighte,
> Degreës nyne and twenty as in highte.
> Foure of the clokke it was tho, as I gesse,

---

[2] The similarity between Chauntecleer and Harry Bailly has been noted by Huppé, *Reading of the Canterbury Tales*, p. 226.

> For ellevene foot, or litel moore or lesse,
> My shadwe was at thilke tyme, as there,
> Of swiche feet as my lengthe parted were
> In sixe feet equal of proporcioun.
>
> (*Pars Prol*, 1-9)

If these lines are intended to remind us of Chauntecleer—a rooster who does not have control over himself, much less over his flock—and of Harry Bailly—a figurative rooster who governs his flock of pilgrims with indifferent success—perhaps we should see here the introduction of another figurative rooster, the Parson. This rooster is a better one than Harry and is to be the true, spiritual leader of the flock. He is linked with the other metaphorical roosters by the device of time-telling in order to demonstrate his categorical similarity and his individual difference. In the General Prologue the Parson was several times described as a shepherd with a flock of sheep, and it surely requires no stretching of the imagination to perceive the obvious similarities between a shepherd of a flock and a rooster of a flock. Moreover, there is a Latin poem from about 1300 comparing priests to the roosters on weather vanes.[3]

This device of linking several rooster figures does not mean that the time of day itself, or the elements of its description are without meaning. One of these, the sign Libra, seems to be an extremely important symbol:

> Therwith the moones exaltacioun,
> I meene Libra, alwey gan ascende,
> As we were entryng at a thropes ende.
>
> (*Pars Prol*, 10-12)

Chaucer has chosen to preface the last of *The Canterbury Tales* with an astrological image that balances the image which opened the *Tales* in the General Prologue. Because of the strategic position of this image we should certainly make an attempt to determine its meaning, yet most Chaucerian scholars have ignored it altogether or treated it as just another instance of Chaucer's "realism." Indeed, even Professor Robertson, in a rare departure from his customary

---

[3] See *The Oxford Book of Medieval Latin Verse*, ed. F.J.E. Raby (Oxford, 1959), pp. 437-39.

analytical frame of mind, has called the appearance of Libra here a "curious but irrelevant echo of Homer. . . ."[4] That Chaucer should close *The Canterbury Tales* with a reference to the zodiacal sign Libra is no more curious than his opening the *Tales* with a reference to Aries; and it may be argued that the scales which appear in Homer are remote from but not entirely irrelevant to a discussion of the occurrence of Libra at this juncture in *The Canterbury Tales*.

Before discussing general and particular meanings of either the astrological sign Libra or the scales, it is necessary to turn our attention to the details of the temporal and astrological situation, for not all scholars are in agreement that Libra was to be found ascending in the east at this time. The disagreement has its source in a palpable error in the text. Chaucer says that Libra, the moon's exaltation, is ascending, but the fact of the matter, agreed on in all the manuals of astrology, is that Libra is the place of exaltation of Saturn, not the moon. Something is clearly awry here, but the efforts to account for the discrepancy have themselves been at odds. Happily no one has suggested that the word "Libra" ought to be cancelled in favor of the word "Taurus," which is the sign in which the moon has its exaltation, because in order to discover Taurus rising in the east at 4:00 P.M., the action would have to occur in the wintertime, which would do violence to the April date of the departure, which has been clearly and repeatedly indicated. An alternate solution *has* been proposed by Andrew Edmund Brae, who seized upon the reading "in mena Libra," which occurs in some MSS rather than the more common "I meene Libra," and from this made some bold emendations in order to find one of the mansions of the moon rising in the sign Libra. This is ingenious but not much to the point, for Brae makes no suggestion as to why the moon mansions should play any part in the scheme of things.[5] Skeat's explanation of the difficulties, on

[4] Robertson, *Preface*, p. 373.

[5] Brae's emendations are as ingenious as they are unconvincing: they involve the transposition of two words, the dropping of a letter, and the adding of a letter. They result in a complete change of the sense of the entire passage. In the system wherein the heavens are divided into 28 mansions of the moon, the thirteenth is called "Min al auwa," which is identified by the star al auwa. With this in mind, Brae emends the reading found in some MSS as follows:

the other hand, leaves the error as an error but emphasizes the simplicity of the basic situation, which is that at 4:00 P.M. in late April in the 1380's the sign Libra was rising in the east, and since the situation in the Parson's Prologue fits the facts, it is best to leave things as they are.[6]

Furthermore, while it is possible through some calculations to determine the position of the heavens on a given day some 600 years ago, and to determine whether or not Libra was indeed rising, the astrological situation would not have seemed as opaque to Chaucer's audience as it does to us today. In order to calculate the exact time at which a sign arose on a given day in the distant past requires a fair amount of data that is not given in Chaucer's poem, but a rough-and-ready calculation could have been made easily by those in his audience. Two items are given us before the information about Libra: the time of day and the height, in degrees, of the sun:

> The sonne fro the south lyne was descended
> So lowe that he nas nat, to my sighte,
> Degreës nyne and twenty as in highte.
> Foure of the clokke it was. . . .
>
> (*Pars Prol*, 2-5)

Chaucer had carefully established the fact, both in an astrological and a straightforward fashion, that the date was in the latter part of April, when the sun was in the sign Taurus. It would be claiming too much to argue that Chaucer's audience might reasonably be expected to know the order of all the signs of the zodiac, but we may assume that they would know that the sun entered the equinoxes in the signs of Aries and Libra and that those two signs are necessarily diametrically opposed to one another. Thus, at sunset in the beginning of springtime the sun would set in Aries just as Libra arose, while later in the spring more and more of Libra and less and less

---

In mena Libra, alway gan ascende
In Libra men al awai gan ascende.

Even as emended it is not clear what the moon's exaltation has to do with the mansion of the moon. See Brae's comments in full in "The Star Min-al-auwa," in his edition of the *Astrolabe*, pp. 88-89.

[6] Skeat, *Astrolabe*, p. lxiii.

of Aries would be above the horizon at sunset until the sun moved into Taurus, at which time the sun would set in the first degree of Taurus at about the time that the last degree of Libra and the first of Scorpio would be arising. Now let us return to the poetic situation. Chaucer has established that the sun is in one of the first few degrees of the sign Taurus, where it must set, and also that some 29 degrees still separate the sun from the horizon. Because the space between the sun and the horizon cannot be filled by Taurus, for the sun is in the western part of that sign in the low degrees, it must be occupied by the preceding sign, Aries, most of which would still be above the horizon, since there are only 30 degrees in each of the signs and only a few of the sun's 29 degrees of height could be in Taurus. Thus, since Aries is just sinking, Libra must be just rising, which is exactly what Chaucer tells us, the business about the moon really being nothing more than one of the not unfamiliar rhetorical flourishes in which Chaucer seemed to delight when employing astrology in poetry. Just as he talked about the "second half-course" of Aries in order to discuss Taurus and made us calculate May 3 from the fact that 32 days had passed since March began and ended, so he first erroneously calls Libra the moon's exaltation, and then gives us the name of the sign straightforwardly. It is worth pointing out that Chaucer uses the same form when he speaks of "Cancer, Jovis exaltacion" (*MerchT*, 2224). There, however, he is accurate about the sign of the planet's exaltation.

If we accept the theory that Chaucer's principal emphasis here is on the sign of Libra and that the business about the moon is an inexplicable but certain error, we have still to inquire why Chaucer should choose to emphasize Libra rather than some other sign, and 4:00 P.M. rather than some other hour. The emphasis is not on what sign the sun is in, so we are not concerned with the time of year, and there is no question at all of a horoscope. Astrologically, that we are concerned with the sign ascending, or "in the ascendant," suggests that if no horoscope is involved perhaps an election is. However, the common astrological practice of electing appropriate times of the day and the year to depart on journeys, get married, declare war, and the like, probably does not apply here. Unfortunately for this hypothesis the elections of the first house, the ascendant, which Libra is in when

just arising, are the elections of propitious moments for taking baths, getting haircuts, letting blood, and paring one's nails, all of which seem to have little to do with the *Parson's Tale*.[7] If there is not much to be found in the astrological meaning of Libra, or in the zodiacal calendar, we must look at the time of day and the sign itself for possible significance.

Chaucer does, we must remember, commonly use the planetary deities by themselves without any astrological or calendarial involvement. Mercury, for example, is found in an astrological "tower" in the *Complaint of Mars*, but is also referred to as the spouse of Philology in the *Merchant's Tale*, and as conductor of souls in *Troilus*. Similarly Chaucer uses the Ram, Aries, as part of a calendar image in the General Prologue, but also uses the "fixe Aries," the original constellation rather than the astrological sign, as part of the magician's calculation of the precession of the equinoxes in the *Franklin's Tale*. A much more striking illustration of the principle, however, is afforded by a passage in the *House of Fame*, wherein Scorpio is used both in relation to a classical myth and as a sign of the zodiac—proof that Chaucer could use a sign of the zodiac in his poetry with connotations extrinsic of astrology or the calendar. The passage, which concerns Phaeton's uncontrolled ride through the heavens on his father's sun-chariot, is worth looking at firsthand:

> The carte-hors gonne wel espye
> That he [Phaeton] koude no governaunce,
> And gonne for to lepe and launce,
> And beren hym now up, now doun,
> Til that he sey the Scorpioun,
> *Which that in heven a sygne is yit.*
> And he, for ferde, loste hys wyt
> Of that, and let the reynes gon.
>
> (*HF*, 944-951)

There exists, then, in Chaucer's poetry a clear-cut instance in which a sign of the zodiac is linked directly with classical legend rather than with any astrological phenomenon, which is not surprising when we remember that much astrology depends upon presumed planetary

---

[7] Albohazen Haly, *De judiciis*, sig. Cc₂ᵛ.

malevolence and benevolence, which in turn derives from mythological accounts. It would seem to follow that Chaucer could use Libra in tacit connection with its classical and other cultural associations rather than with any specifically astrological intention. If we turn to these associations, starting with the reference in Homer already mentioned, we find that there is evidence that the scales of Jove's judgment are the same as the scales of the zodiac.

2. THE SYMBOLISM OF LIBRA

BECAUSE OF Libra's very late entrance into the zodiac, the scales are not equated with Libra in as many classical texts as one might expect. As late as the time of Hipparchus (160-126 B.C.) there were only eleven symbols in the zodiac, Scorpio extending from its present eighth position through the space now occupied by Libra. It was not until the middle of the first century B.C. that Libra obtained an official place in the Julian calendar, but as late as 30 B.C. Virgil, in the *Georgics*, left the space supposedly filled by Libra vacant, in order that it might be ready for the apotheosis of Augustus.[8] Because of the absence of classical descriptions of the catasteration or translation to the heavens of Libra, such as may be found for the other signs, it has been argued that the scales were chosen for their suitability to the equinox, when day and night are, as it were, balanced. While the appropriateness of the scales to this time of year no doubt played a role in their selection for the autumnal equinoctial position in the zodiac, it should be remembered that none of the other signs of the zodiac is particularly suited to its position, while all of them have some source in classical myth.

Undoubtedly the mythological legend that contributed to the selection of the scales to fill the gap in the zodiac is the event in the twenty-second book of the *Iliad* in which Zeus holds up his golden scales, one assigned to Hector and one to Achilles, both weighted with death. The one assigned to Hector sinks down, and with it Hector. The incident is omitted from the mediaeval *Ilias Latina*, so there can be no direct link between Chaucer and Homer on this point, but Virgil availed himself of the same scales in imitation of Homer, and they appear in the twelfth book of the *Aeneid*, held by Jupiter. A much more proximate example of the scales of Zeus or

---

[8] *Encyclopaedia Brittannica*, ninth ed. (New York, 1888), s.v. "zodiac."

Jupiter, however, is afforded by the twelfth-century account of the third Vatican Mythographer, who not only retells the story, albeit with yet another set of characters being judged, but also specifically states that the scales of Jupiter's judgment are translated to the heavens to become the sign Libra:

> In bello Thebano Pallas cum quibusdam aliis diis favebat Graecis; Bacchus, quia Thebanus erat, cum quibusdam aliis diis favebat Thebanis. Unde inter deos orta est discordia, quinam deberent victoriam obtinere. Juppiter hoc videns sedit in Parnasso monte, qui est juxta Thebas, auream libram tenens in manu, ut de utraque deliberaret parte. Ad exitum autem belli ipse vidit aequale esse judicium. Sed mox ad Thebanam destructionem Graecos habere victoriam percipiens, Thebanos dejudicavit, Graecos exaltavit. Unde ad memoriam istius rei libra delata est in caelum, et ex ea factum signum caeleste.[9]

From this we can see that a mediaeval poet could use Libra as a symbol of judgment by the chief of gods, Jupiter, or, by a simple extension, as a symbol of God's judgment. Thus, at the end of the *Iliad* and the *Aeneid* the scales of God's justice appear, and it may well be that Chaucer's use of Libra at the end of *The Canterbury Tales* was intended to represent his God's justice, which, of course, is of a somewhat different sort. Some bolstering of this view may be found in the writings of Pierre Bersuire, the fourteenth-century encyclopedist and exegete, who, in his discussion of Libra, mentions not Jupiter but rather Christ as judge:

> Quando Sol, i.e. Christus ascendet signum librae, i.e. thronum judicii, ubi facta omnium librabit, & ponderabit, tunc vere aequinoctium faciet, i.e. judicii aequitatem, quia & noctem & diem, i.e. peccatorem & justum secundum normam justitiae aedaequabit, reddens unicuique, quod suum est; malis paenam, justis gloriam.[10]

[9] *Scriptores rerum mythicarum*, p. 255. One would expect that this incident would be found in Statius' *Thebaid*, but such is not the case, also it is not to be discovered in the thirteenth-century *Roman de Thèbes*, although the lacunae in that work are well known. No doubt the source of this passage is one of the numerous mediaeval accretions on the Thebes legend.

[10] Bersuire, *Reductorium morale*, in *Opera*, I, 108. Bersuire also discusses the scales as merchants' scales.

While this passage is concerned with the sun in the sign of Libra, rather than with the sun in Taurus when Libra is ascending, as in Chaucer, Bersuire's words are nonetheless significant. We are not searching for a source for the complete image as used by Chaucer—indeed Chaucer probably combined several different kinds of general and specific materials—but we are attempting an assessment of the connotations the adducement of Libra could carry. Christ's judgment of the just and the unjust, whether the sun is actually in Libra or only associated with it, is surely one of these.

There are several iconographic representations of Libra and other, unspecified scales that add to our understanding of the mediaeval conception of the sign. The first of these is a depiction of the scales of God's justice in a thirteenth-century missal that simply shows a hand descending from above holding a pair of scales. While not in itself of great importance to our present purposes, this picture nevertheless establishes that a balance can stand for God's justice in iconography. This is important for a more pertinent figure in Herrade de Landsberg's *Hortus Deliciarum*,[11] a twelfth- or thirteenth-century work illustrating the signs of the zodiac with fairly usual drawings of animals and people (for the twins and Virgo). Here, however, the illustration of Libra does not show merely a pair of scales; rather, the scales are held by a hand descending from a cloud, a traditional iconographic method of illustrating the hand of God. The association of Libra and Christ in Judgment made by Bersuire is broadened and reinforced by this iconographic representation of Libra as the scales of God's judgment.

In addition to associations of Libra with God's or Christ's judgment of man, there exist two fascinating iconographic motifs that elaborate on and change the classical conception of the theme of judgment. The first motif relates a balance to the crucifixion, and the second specifically identifies Libra with the crucifixion. Of course, because the Latin words "statera" and "trutina" translate "scales" as

---

[11] For the missal see Eric George Millar, *The Library of A. Chester Beatty; A Descriptive Catalogue of the Western Manuscripts* (Oxford, 1927-30), II, Plate CXIII (i). That the motif is indeed that of the hand of God is attested by the Princeton Index of Christian Art. For the other picture, see Herrade de Landsberg, *Hortus Deliciarum*, ed. Joseph Walter (Strasbourg and Paris, 1952), Plate V.

well as "libra," almost any scales found in mediaeval art could legiti-
mately be related to the zodiacal sign Libra, but it is always more
satisfying to discover positive instances of these relationships.

The relationship of the balance to the crucifixion in mediaeval art
was first remarked upon by Professor Francis Wormald, who noted
that while the balance is not unusual in connection with judgment,
it is both rare and interesting to discover the balance in conjunction
with the crucifixion.[12] Professor Wormald discusses two fifteenth-
century miniatures of the crucifix, both of which share certain basic
features. Both portray the crucifix with a pair of scales dependent
from one arm of the cross, and in both pictures one pan of the scales
is labelled "peccata," and a small devil tries unsuccessfully to drag
it down, while the other pan, which outweighs the sins, is labelled
"Passio Christi" and shows the cross, the nails, and the thorns. The
idea is a simple one, powerfully expressed: it is only through the
agency of Christ's sacrifice that man's sins can be expiated. (See Figs.
25 and 26.)

Professor Wormald has noted that this iconographic motif springs
from writings that sometimes envision Christ hanging on the cross
the way something hangs in a balance, and sometimes see Christ him-
self as a balance.[13] This latter concept is to be found in exegetical
commentaries on the famous lines in the sixth chapter of Job, in
which Job wishes that his sins and his subsequent sufferings might
be weighed against one another in a balance, for his sufferings would

[12] Francis Wormald, "The Crucifix and the Balance," *JWCI*, I (1937-38),
276-80.

[13] For instances in which Christ is spoken of as suspended from the cross as though
in a balance, Professor Wormald cites two passages in Fortunatus, the first from his
Expositio Symboli, the second from the famous hymn, "Vexilla Regis Prodeunt":
(a) "Aut ideo quia ante gravis latro in cruce configebatur, ergo ad hoc elegit
Christus principale supplicium, ut hominem absolveret originali peccato quod erat
principale tormentum, aut ideo dominus in cruce suspenditur, ut pro captivitate nostra
pretium sui corporis mercator in statera pensaret."
>   (b)   Beata cuius brachiis
>   Pretium pependit saeculi
>   Statera facta est corporis
>   Praedamque tulit Tartari.
Venantius Fortunatus, *Venanti Honori Clementiani Fortunati Presbyteri Italici
Opera Poetica*, ed. Fredericvs Leo for *MGH*, Auctores Antiquissimi (Berlin, 1879),
IV, 34 and 256; cited by Wormald, pp. 277-78.

appear heavier than the sands of the sea. In a seminal commentary on this passage in his *Moralia in Job*, which is cited by Professor Wormald, Gregory the Great says that Christ is a balance in which what we deserve and what Christ suffered for us are weighed together. Christ as mediator between man and God is not only raised up as the balance, but also comes to the judgment bringing with him justice and mercy, the balance pan of the latter outweighing that of the former.[14]

What is pertinent to Chaucer in these variations on an artistic theme is that in the Middle Ages various people at various times saw the scales as more than the scales of God's judgment; by associating the scales with the crucifixion, they regarded them in a twofold light as representative of the Old Law of retribution and the New Law of mercy. This is why commentators on Job chose to talk about the crucifixion and about Christ or the cross as a balance, whereas Job had spoken of a balance of a somewhat simpler sort.[15] This point, which is not mentioned by Professor Wormald, is very important for literary considerations of the connotations of Libra: the scales have, in addition to their classical connotations of arbitrary judgment based on *de facto* considerations, connotations of the Old Testament view that a man's calamities should balance his sins, and connotations of the New Testament view that God's justice is not retributive but merciful. Through the agency of the cross, Christ's sacrifice makes the "just" verdict the merciful one. For Chaucer's purposes the scales provided a symbol of the crucifixion and its role in God's judgment.

[14] "*Christus libra est in qua et quod meremur, et quod pro nobis passus est, pensantur. Poenae nostrae gravitatem nobis notam fecit.—*Quis alius staterae nomine, nisi Dei et hominum mediator exprimitur? qui ad pensandum vitae nostrae meritum venit, ad secum justitiam simul et misericordiam detulit; sed misericordiae lance praeponderans, culpas nostras parcendo levigavit" (Gregory the Great, *Moralia in Job*, PL, 75, col. 767; cited by Wormald, p. 278). Later commentaries adduced by Professor Wormald show a variety of minor changes. For example, one says that the cross (rather than Christ) is a balance weighing retribution for sins against mercy for mankind, while another argues that the cross is a scale balancing Christ's innocence and sacrifice against man's sins and just desserts.

[15] The association of Job's scales with the crucifixion extended from exegetical writings into Biblical illuminations, and one of Wormald's figures shows two medallions from a thirteenth-century moralized Bible with Job in one and the crucifixion in the other.

In Chaucer, however, it is Libra in particular and not just any pair of scales that is referred to, so it is fortunate for our purposes that there exist two iconographic representations of the zodiac that show the cross of the crucifixion in the position of Libra. Both of these are to be found in the *Atlas* of the fourteenth-century political writer and artist, Opicinus de Canistris. (See Figs. 27 and 28.) This interesting figure, who is better known to students of Italian literature than to students of Chaucer, was perhaps acquainted with the great fourteenth-century encyclopedist and commentator on Ovid, Pierre Bersuire, who was in turn a friend of Petrarch. While the question of Bersuire's direct or indirect influence on Opicinus has been debated, there is no question that both associate Libra with Christ; Bersuire speaks of Christ's ascent to the throne of judgment in the sign Libra (in the passage we have cited already), and Opicinus uses the cross to depict Libra.[16]

Opicinus' two representations of Libra by means of the cross occur in pictures that Professor Salomon, following Ghisalberti, has called "cartes moralisées." In the first of these we see a circle with an ellipse superimposed on the left (Fig. 27). Closer inspection of the figures around the circle shows that the top one is labelled "Aries," and that the circle is in fact a zodiac. It is somewhat less obvious but equally ascertainable that the ellipse to the left also represents a zodiac. Looking at the figures on the right hand side of the ellipse, just above the

---

[16] Professor Salomon, in his discussion of the possible acquaintance with and influence of Bersuire on Opicinus, says that the major difference between the two is that Bersuire was an objective encyclopedist, while Opicinus was entirely subjective. See Richard Georg Salomon, *Opicinus de Canistris* (London, 1936), pp. 79–80. Those who know Bersuire's encyclopedia know that his objectivity is not to be thought of in the modern sense, and while Opicinus may indeed be more "subjective" than Bersuire, the modern association of subjectivity in art with a fruitful imagination is not to be made here. We should not think that the psychological element in Opicinus meant that his drawings were necessarily capricious and without traditional motifs. Professor Salomon has emphasized the psychological element here perhaps at the cost of downgrading the learned element. At one juncture he says of Opicinus that "Die Welt der Erscheinungen wird ihm zum Symbol seiner persönlichen Gefühle und Befürchtungen" (Salomon, *Opicinus*, p. 37). Be that as it may, the expression of these feelings will nevertheless be in terms of mediaeval artistic conventions, and not in anything like contemporary art. In short, there is no reason to think that Opicinus' conception of Libra as a cross was the result of an unprecedented whim.

halfway mark, we see a stylized lion, representing Leo; above it a very clearly drawn girl, representing Virgo; and, at the very top of the ellipse, on the inner part of the track where we would expect the scales of Libra, a small cross.

Figure 28 is somewhat more distinct and the relative clarity of the signs of the zodiac is great. Here again Opicinus has presented two zodiacs and a rather hazy map, but this time the ellipse is on the outside and the circle is inscribed within it. If we look at the top of the circle, we see two figures on each side of the vertical axis: to the right is a maiden representing Virgo, and to the left a cross representing Libra. As a check on our identification we can easily trace the signs around from the vernal to the autumnal equinox. Directly across the circle from the cross illustrating Libra we see, upside down but quite distinguishable, a ram representing the first of the zodiacal signs, Aries, the sign of the spring equinox. The signs proceeding to the right are a bull for Taurus and a pair of look-alike youths for Gemini, the twins. Next there is a blank medallion where the crab should be, then a very bovine lion for Leo.[17]

What emerges from this discussion is the conclusion that if the sign Libra was meant to convey anything at all, it was freighted with ideas of judgment, and the evidence is quite strong for believing that the connotations of Libra would include not only judgments in general but particularly God's judgment of man under the new dispensation, made possible by Christ's sacrifice on the cross. This concept of a new justice for mankind, different from both Hebraic and classical ideas of the relationship of God and Man, is seldom used elsewhere with specific reference to Libra; but the concept of the New Law expressed in terms of the crucifixion and scales was com-

---

[17] There is a possibility that the equation of Libra with the cross may owe something to a minor tradition, mainly known in Greek writings, that saw in both equinoctial signs the cross of Christ, without reference to either scales or judgment. St. Justin Martyr, writing in the second century, equated Plato's World Soul with Christ, and the Greek Chi (X), formed by the intersection of the circles of the Same and the Other (later the equinoctial and the ecliptic), with the cross of Christ. Thus, from a very early period in Western thought, either of the equinoctial signs, Aries or Libra, could be thought of in terms of the cross. Irenaeus also identified the Chi with the Christian cross. For a study of the whole problem, see W. Bousset, "Platons Weltseele und das Kreuz Christi," *Zeitschrift für die Neutestamentliche Wissenschaft*, XIV (1913), 273-85.

mon in the Fathers, and became a popular poetic image in the Renaissance. As Rosemond Tuve put it, "the basic concept is the weighing by the just Father of man's sins in one dish against the sufferings of Christ as Man—so that when the Crucifixion took place the sufferings in their dish completely outweighed the sins, and the *just* verdict can be in favour of man's salvation."[18] Perhaps it is some measure of Chaucer's genius that he chose Libra as a symbol, for its classical connotations and associations with the crucifixion would make God's justice tempered with mercy stand out the more brightly for its contrast.

3. THE SIGNIFICANCE OF THE SCALES
AND THE CRUCIFIXION

WE MAY legitimately ask what this has to do with the *Parson's Tale*, to which it serves as prologue. While one might initially think that an image of the Last Judgment is not wholly pertinent to a prose sermon on the Seven Deadly Sins, further reflection reminds us that while the Parson speaks much of sin, his true theme is not sin itself but rather the eradication of its stain through confession and penance. For this theme an image that combines talionic justice and justice as tempered by Christ's sacrifice on the cross is quite suitable. The world offered the mediaeval man more in the way of hope than it had offered his pre-Christian ancestor, but as a consequence it put a very immediate burden of sacramental as well as ethical practice upon him. Phrased another way, we might say that Christ's freeing man from his sins gave man the possibility of salvation, but as Christ made possible the way to salvation, so he commanded man to imitate his actions in this world and to take up a cross too. In a very general way we might say that penance represents that cross.

For the mediaeval Christian there was not just one judgment of

[18] Rosemond Tuve, *A Reading of George Herbert* (London, 1951), p. 165. Miss Tuve also points out that Libra is specifically linked with the scales of God's justice in a woodcut in Guillaume de Deguileville's *Pilgrimage of the Soul* (pp. 166-67). It is important to note that the cross in connection with judgment conveys the theology of the atonement: As Dorothy Sayers says, commenting on *Paradiso* VII, "He did not simply remit the debt, but by becoming Man, gave man the means to satisfy justice" (*Introductory Papers on Dante* [London, 1954], p. 82). Cf. *On Christian Doctrine*, Bk. I, xi.

God about which to be concerned, but three, all of which were rather closely related. The first of these is the common judgment pronounced on all mankind as a result of the Fall, and we saw, in one of the citations from Fortunatus adduced previously, that Christ's hanging on the cross was for the purpose of freeing man from *originali peccato*. This is carried out through the sacrament of baptism. With the exception of those few harrowed out of hell by Christ, all who lived before Christ's time are in hell because of original sin, so that Virgil says to Dante, "E vo' che sappi che, dinanzi ad essi, / Spiriti umani non eran salvati" (*Inferno* IV, 62-63). There is a second, particular judgment awaiting each man at the moment of his death, then a third. In this last or general judgment Christ will judge all nations and all individuals, those in heaven and hell as well as those on earth, and will make a final disposition of mankind as a whole as well as each individual. In the previously examined passages from both Gregory the Great and Pierre Bersuire, Christ's coming to the judgment bringing both mercy and justice suggests that both writers had in mind the general judgment, and we have seen how in that judgment all men's sins would be very damaging if Christ's suffering on the cross did not outweigh the sins. The general judgment depends upon the particular, and with regard to the more proximate particular judgment there is much that man can do: he can erase the effect of the sins he has committed after baptism through the sacrament of penance, the efficaciousness of which was brought about by Christ's crucifixion. Thus, in a famous phrase, which is quoted down to the present day, the *Glossa ordinaria* held that "from the side of Christ dying on the cross flowed the sacraments by which the Church was saved."[19]

In the sign of Libra, with its associations with the judgment and the cross, Chaucer has chosen an excellent image with which to introduce the Parson's sermon on penance. The *Tales* opened with an image of Noah's flood, often understood as a type of baptism, and they fittingly close with an emphasis on the sacrament of penance,

---

[19] *Glossa ordinaria*, PL, 114, col. 486. The phrase is quoted in *The Catholic Encyclopedia*, ed. Charles G. Herbermann, et al. (New York, 1910), s.v. "judgment." For a striking mediaeval iconographic representation of the stream from Christ's side flowing into the chalice of the sacraments, see the *Hortus Deliciarum*, Plate XXVIII.

which takes up the cleansing of sin after baptism. Indeed, in medi-
aeval iconography the scenes of the general judgment often involve
elements of confessional scenes, because while some theologians hold
that at the general judgment all sins, both forgiven and unforgiven,
will be publicly reviewed, only the unforgiven sins will determine
the final separation of sheep and goats. Thus, through confession and
penance the Christian can best prepare himself not only for the par-
ticular but also for the general judgment, as Chaucer's Parson attests.[20]
After death there is nothing that can be done about the disposition
of one's soul, which is why the Parson is concerned to show us here
on earth the way of the pilgrimage to the celestial Jerusalem.[21]

The Parson then proceeds with his metaphor of a journey by quot-
ing from Jeremiah, and in order to be sure that no one mistakes his
intentions, Chaucer has the Parson give the passage in both Latin
and English; he has him identify its source; and in spite of the
Parson's protestations that he will not gloss things literary, he glosses
a line of this Biblical passage:

> *Jer. 6°. State super vias, et videte, et interrogate de viis antiquis
> que sit via bona, et ambulate in ea; et inuenietis refrigerium anima-
> bus vestris, etc.*
>
> Oure sweete Lord God of hevene, that no man wole perisse, but
> wole that we comen alle to the knoweleche of hym, and to the
> blisful lif that is perdurable, / amonesteth us by the prophete
> Jeremie, that seith in thys wyse: / Stondeth upon the weyes, and
> seeth and axeth of olde pathes (that is to seyn, of olde sentences)
> which is the goode wey, / and walketh in that wey, and ye shal
> fynde refresshynge for youre soules, etc. / Manye been the weyes
> espirituels that leden folk to oure Lord Jhesu Crist, and to the

---

[20] Émile Mâle, for example, refers to a window at Bourges depicting the last
judgment; it has, at its base—almost as the base—a Christian kneeling before a priest
in the sacrament of penance (Mâle, *Gothic Image*, p. 383). Similarly in some
thirteenth-century moralized Bibles there are illuminations of the Apocalypse that
show Christ and the Elect above in the clouds while below are confession scenes or
scenes of extreme unction (Alexandre de Laborde, *La Bible moralisée* [Paris and
London, 1921], IV, the second medallions in Plates 619, 620, and 669). Chaucer's
Parson clearly says that penance is a worthwhile preparation for the general as well
as the particular judgment: *ParsT*, 157-75.

[21] See the Parson's Prologue, lines 48-51.

regne of glorie. / Of whiche weyes, ther is a ful noble wey and a ful covenable, which may nat fayle to man ne to womman that thurgh synne hath mysgoon fro the righte wey of Jerusalem celestial; / and this wey is cleped Penitence. . . . (*ParsT*, 75-81)

The emphasis on the crossroads, the choice of the right way that one must (like Hercules) make, the reference to those who have lost the way, and the quotation from Jeremiah certainly remind us of some elements of the opening of Dante's *Commedia*; but because of the poetic matrix here, the mood is a good deal different. Here Chaucer picks up the theme of pilgrimage that has provided him with so much for so long, and, for the first time, explicitly compares the "wandrynge by the weye" of some with a consciously directed pilgrimage toward the correct goal—a pilgrimage that is not the norm of *The Canterbury Tales*, but which is normative for the true pilgrim.

In addition, there are hints here of the kind of antinomy that characterized the connotations of Libra. There we saw that both the idea of judgment and that of the crucifixion involved Christ, with the result that Christ is both judge and, in a sense, advocate, providing the only defense man has against his record of sin. In a similar fashion the opening lines of the *Parson's Tale* involve Christ in a seeming paradox, for he is clearly said to be the goal of the "weyes espirituels that leden folk to oure Lord Jhesus Crist," but it may be argued that he is also the way to the goal. In the *Glossa ordinaria* on the passage from Jeremiah that the Parson cites we read:

State super vias. Legamus Evangelicam parabolam, in qua negotiator bonus omnes vendidit margaritas, ut unam emat pretiosam: ut scilicet per patriarchas et prophetas veniamus ad eum qui dicit: *Ego sum via, veritas et vita* (*Joan.* xiv), unde, *State super vias*, etc.[22]

In other words, the right way to Christ is to be found in Christ who said "I am the way," so Christ is both the goal and the way to that goal. This is a popular Christian rhetorical device which dates as far back as the time of St. Augustine, a device long used by poets and

---

[22] *Glossa ordinaria, PL*, 114, col. 19.

noted by critics. When Boccaccio comments on the opening lines of Dante's *Inferno*, he says that the "way" which Dante had lost in the dark wood was Christ who said "I am the way."[23] From this we begin to see how a sermon on penance can be appropriately introduced by an image of judgment and the crucifixion, for in order to face Christ the judge with any hope, we need Christ the way. In order to follow that way we must imitate Christ to some degree, and that part of his life which we are to imitate is the crucifixion, while the way in which we imitate it is by doing penance. As the Parson says fairly early in his tale, "Penaunce is the tree of lyf" (127); or, as he says at the very end of his sermon, by means of penance we purchase "lyf by deeth" (1080). The right "way" is the way of the cross.

The fact that Libra is associated with judgment and the crucifixion, with all its implications, brings us to yet another possible connotation of the sign; Libra can also be connected with the individual Christian's free choice of how he will face judgment. At the very end of *The Canterbury Tales*, Chaucer takes a last chance to strike a blow for the individual's freedom of choice against those who try to rationalize their actions by reference to the stars. That great rationalizer the Wife of Bath said that she followed her "inclinacioun / By vertu of my constellacioun" (*WB Prol*, 615-16), but Chaucer's choice of a sermon on penance to close the *Tales* strongly suggests that he intended to deny any shred of astrological determinism. This observation is bolstered by the fact that the image of Libra can also concern judgment in the sense of "good judgment." There exists, in fact, in the work of Marbod an instance in which Libra is adduced as a symbol of not only the freedom to judge rightly, but specifically the freedom to do so in spite of the astrologers' opinions to the contrary. Marbod, the Bishop of Rennes who died in 1123, wrote one work that Chaucer knew, and it is possible that Chaucer also knew of his fascinating poem "De fato et genesi," in which he uses astrological images to undercut astrology and features Libra prominently among them:

---

[23] St. Augustine, *On Christian Doctrine*, XI, 11; p. 13. Giovanni Boccaccio, *Il Comento sopra la Commedia di Dante Alighieri*, ed. A. Penna (Florence, 1831), I, 80.

Esse meum fatum summi Patris assero Verbum,
A quo cuncta regi debent quicunque fateri,
Ingenitamque mihi dico genesis rationem,
Et libertatem qua quo volo tendere possum,
Sponte bonum, vel sponte malum sine sidere patrans.
Ergo si fuerit rationi juncta voluntas
In signo Librae, Christo me respiciente,
Prospera cuncta mihi contingent hic et ubique.
Haec est cunctorum genesis bona Christicolarum.[24]

Marbod argues that when reason and will properly complement each other, that is to say are in "balance"—in the Balance or Libra—then a man can choose his own destiny, for better or for worse, so that whatever we perform in the way of evil is to our personal discredit and cannot be shunted off as astral influence.[25] Using a slightly different set of concepts, Chaucer's Parson said much the same thing: "God sholde have lordshipe over resoun, and resoun over sensualitee, and sensualitee over the body of man" (*ParsT*, 262). This harmony of man's inner self was known in the Middle Ages by the term "justice," and when Marbod talks about Christ's "good aspect" permitting reason and will to function together properly, he is using Libra as a symbol of more than judgment or even "good judgment," he is using it as a symbol of justice or right order in the soul of the individual, in the Platonic sense.[26]

[24] Marbod, "De fato et genesi," in *Liber decem capitulorum, PL*, 171, col. 1707. Chaucer refers to Marbod's *Lapidarium* in *HF*, 1352. Of course, it does not necessarily follow that Chaucer knew any of the Bishop's other works.

[25] Of course Marbod knew that it was exceedingly difficult to have a proper harmony of the intellectual and volitional faculties because of the Fall, which afflicted man's will in such a way that St. Paul says, "Non enim quod volo bonum, hoc facio: sed quod nolo malum, hoc ago" (Romans 7:19). In the *Commedia* Dante is told that "Libero, dritto e sano è tuo arbitrio" (*Purgatorio* XXVII, 140) only when he has ascended to the top of the mountain of Purgatory, while the final harmonization of "disiro" and "velle" occurs only in the closing lines of the poem. Professor John Freccero has argued convincingly that Dante limps at the outset of the journey because of a tradition that saw the intellectual and volitional faculties as two "feet" of the soul, the latter of which drags because it was wounded in the Fall. See John Freccero, "Dante's Firm Foot and the Journey Without a Guide," *Harvard Theological Review*, LII (1959), 245-81.

[26] See Charles S. Singleton, *Dante Studies 2: Journey to Beatrice* (Cambridge, Mass. 1958), p. 60: "If justice means right order in the soul and right order before

Is it possible that Chaucer had in mind connotations of individual justice in the soul as well as the particular and general judgments when he seized upon Libra in the Parson's Prologue? It would seem so, for it has been observed that in the Middle Ages the three advents of Christ were spoken of together: his advent in the flesh, his second coming at the last judgment, and his invisible and mystical coming to each soul that attains justice.[27] Thus, Libra, which is easily associated with the last judgment, might be related to justice in the soul as well, since Christ has an "advent" with both. In the *Parson's Tale* Christ's crucifixion is related specifically to man's difficulty in maintaining justice or proper order in the soul. Following the passage on the proper order of reason and sensuality that we have already cited, the Parson goes on to say that "whan man synneth, al this ordre or ordinaunce is turned up-so-doun" (*ParsT*, 263). He then concludes that "this disordinaunce and this rebellioun oure Lord Jhesu Crist aboghte upon his precious body ful deere" (*ParsT*, 267). As in the *Parson's Tale* individual justice is linked with the crucifixion, so in the Parson's Prologue Libra no doubt links the crucifixion, individual justice, and God's justice.

In surveying the many associations of Libra, we find that in perspective they are really mutually complementary, however much divisiveness there may have seemed in the course of tracing the various strains. Libra served Chaucer as a symbol of God's judgment under the New Law, tempered with mercy, made possible by Christ's balancing of man's sin on the cross, looking forward to Christ's coming again with the scales of judgment, and standing for that justice in the soul that would aid a man to refrain from many sins and to do penance for those he committed. This is a heavy, but not impossible burden for the image to bear, and the other aspects of the image tend to bear out its far-reaching but harmonious series of suggestions.

For example, in the Parson's Prologue the sign of Libra was rising in the east while the sun was beginning to sink in the west at 4:00 P.M. While in modern terminology this would scarcely

---

God, then we shall see that such indeed is Dante's conception in the poem; such is, in fact, the 'end' of his journey."

[27] Singleton refers us to St. Bernard and to St. Thomas in his *Studies 2*, pp. 74-78.

constitute "evening" for the corresponding date at the end of April in our century, the fact remains that to the mediaeval mind 4:00 P.M. indicated the evening, and the evening has connotations that are significant here.[28] For reasons that are not entirely clear to liturgical historians, a practice sometimes encountered in the mediaeval church is to arrange the various offices of the day, Lauds, Nones, Vespers and the like, around the hour of noon in such a way that the offices of the first two quarters of the day were celebrated at the ends of their respective periods, in order to be closer to noon, and the offices of the latter part of the day were celebrated at the beginning of their respective quarters. Dante says this is because Christ was crucified at noon, but it would be difficult to find many other mediaeval examples of such a theory. While the hours of celebration of the morning services are not well known, there does seem to be some evidence that Vespers, at least, was frequently celebrated at the tenth hour of the liturgical day, which would be 3:00 P.M. at the equinoxes and a little after 3:30 P.M. in the latter part of April.[29] This is not to suggest that Chaucer intended the time of the day to remind us of Vespers, but rather that he intended the time of the day to be evening, which is *vesper* in Latin.

[28] Chaucer cannot resist one more joke on Harry Bailly, even this late in the day, as it were. Harry is always concerned with the practical as opposed to the spiritual side of things, and in the Headlink to the *Man of Law's Tale*, he worries that a fourth of the day has already passed and that the pilgrims and the story-tellers must hurry up. Then, in the last few lines of the Parson's Prologue, which constitutes the last bit of conversation in the entire *Tales*, Harry introduces the Parson's sermon on things of deep spiritual significance by warning him to hurry up! "But hasteth yow, the sonne wole adoun; / Beth fructuous, and that in litel space" (*Pars Prol*, 70-71). This is amusing enough as it stands, but is made even funnier when we learn that in Chaucer's age, at this time of the year, the sun was not due to set for over three hours! (See Skeat, *Astrolabe*, 1-li.) Harry, however, will seize on any sort of excuse to avoid having to listen to a sermon, or perhaps he fears that the Parson will speak for three hours.

[29] Dante discusses the arrangement of the offices around the hour of noon in *Convivio*, IV, 23. For the celebration of Vespers at the tenth hour, and perhaps even earlier in the winter, see F. Cabrol and H. Leclercq, *Dictionnaire, d'archéologie chrétienne et de liturgie* (Paris, 1907-53), s.v. "vêpres." It should be emphasized that liutrgical practice varied from time to time and from place to place. The calculation that the tenth liturgical hour would occur at a little after 3:30 P.M. in late April in Chaucer's time is based on figures for sunrise and sunset given by Skeat, *Astrolabe*, 1-li.

Peter Lombard, commenting on Psalm 54:19, says that Christ arose into heaven at noonday, was resurrected in the morning, but was crucified in the evening.[30] Thus it is appropriate for the poet to introduce an image associated with the crucifixion in the evening rather than at some other time. It is perhaps because of this association of Christ's crucifixion with the "evening" (although the scriptural accounts suggest a time during what we would call the "afternoon"), that prompted St. Bonaventura to say that the journey of the soul in its ascent to God begins in the evening and is carried on in the morning and at noonday.[31]

When we remember that the Parson insists that penance is a way to the celestial city, and that he has emphasized one's choice of ways very emphatically, the time element in Chaucer's Parson's Prologue makes good sense. We have been "on the way" on a pilgrimage to Canterbury, which in the best sense, for some of the pilgrims, would be an analogy of the way of penance leading to the celestial Jersualem. For those who have been wanderers by the way, like the Wife of Bath, Chaucer starts the poem in the morning (*Gen Prol*, 33-34) and finishes at eventide to suggest that it is time to set out on the true pilgrimage. By the same token, the *Tales* open with a complicated astrological image telling us that the sun is in Taurus, but doing so with reference to the Ram. This was perhaps arranged so that Chaucer could mention the sign of one equinox at the opening of the *Tales* and the sign of the other, Libra, at the close. Boccaccio had done something much like this in one of his notes to the *Teseida*: he said that Aries is the sign in which the world renews its beauty with foliage, flowers, and grasses, while Libra is the one in which not only does the foliage dry up, but also the leaves fall from all the trees, and that it is as though Libra takes from the world the beauty that Aries has given it.[32] (Cf. Figs. 6, 7 and 8.) Christ himself com-

---

[30] "Vespere enim fuit Dominus in cruce; mane, in resurrectione; meridie, in ascencione . . ." Peter Lombard, *Commentarium in psalmos*, PL, 191, col. 514.

[31] St. Bonaventura, *The Mind's Road to God*, trans. George Boas, Library of Liberal Arts (Indianapolis and New York, 1953), Chapter I, 3; p. 8.

[32] "Ariete è uno de'XII segni del sole e Libra è uno altro. Sta in Ariete il sole da mezo marzo infino a mezo aprile, e in questo tempo tutto il mondo si rifá bello di frondi, di fiori e d'erbe. In Libra sta da mezo settembre infino a mezo ottobre: in questo tempo non solamente si seccano tutte le frondi, ma caggiono tutte degli alberi, sí che Libra

pared his crucifixion to a baptism (Mark 19:38), and if Chaucer's references to April showers and the seventeenth of April are indeed intended to conjure up an image of Noah's flood, which in turn was commonly glossed as a type of baptism, then it might be said that the *Tales* move from a baptism by water to one by blood, from Taurus to Libra, from morning to evening, from a suburb of London to a suggestively unspecified "thropes ende" (*Pars Prol*, 12), and from the beginning of one pilgrimage to the beginning of another.[33]

We have seen that the evening is appropriate for Chaucer's purposes here, as is Libra, and it remains only to inquire why he should set the time at precisely 4:00 P.M. The question is not an easy one to answer with assurance because of the variations in the canonical hours from time to time and place to place. These were sometimes divisions of the daylight hours into twelve equal parts so that an "hour" would be longer than sixty minutes in the summer and shorter in the winter, and they were sometimes divisions of the day based on a conventional sunrise and sunset at 6:00 A.M. and 6:00 P.M. The issue is also complicated by the fact that in the later Middle Ages the canonical hours seem to have lapsed into desuetude so that even a professional astronomer like Johannes de Sacrobosco could err in his description of them. Moreover, relating them to secular times or to offices of the day is further obscured by the practice begun in Roman times of using Latin ordinal numbers in a cardinal sense.[34] Thus, while Chaucer knew about the canonical or unequal hours in theory, and could employ them in the *Knight's Tale* without any adjustment to the clock-time of the season (by using only inequal hours), it seems very doubtful that he would have had them in mind when using the various times of day referred to in *The Canterbury*

---

toglie al mondo quella bellezza che Ariete gli aveva data" (Boccaccio, *Teseida*, "Chiose," p. 386). Benvenuto da Imola, commenting on the opening of the *Divine Comedy*, observes that spring is always followed by winter, therefore in the spring we should castigate the flesh. See his *Comentum super Dantis Comoediam*, ed. J. P. Lacaita (Florence, 1888), I, 39.

[33] Noah's Flood was used in the Easter liturgy because of its baptismal associations. See Singleton, *Studies 2*, pp. 225-27. Singleton cites Guglielmus Durandus.

[34] Much of this information comes from an excellent and often overlooked essay, "On the Meaning of Chaucer's Prime," by Andrew Edmund Brae in his edition of *The Treatise on the Astrolabe*, pp. 90-101.

Tales. On the other hand, it seems unlikely that Chaucer would use specific references to the time of day with no purpose whatsoever, so we might speculate that he had in mind some reference to the conventionalized church hours, or to conventionalized scriptural hours.

In scripture things are always described as happening at the third or the seventh hour of the day and so forth, and while this probably referred to a flexible time system like the mediaeval canonical hours, most mediaeval readers of the Bible probably related these times to a conventional day of sunrise at 6:00 A.M. and sunset twelve hours later. If this is the case, Chaucer might be associating 4:00 P.M. with the eleventh hour, which is one of the few scriptural times that has become proverbial.[35] In the story of the laborers in the vineyard who are hired early in the day, in the middle of the day, and late in the day at the eleventh hour, we are told that those who were hired last were paid first, and Christ himself interpreted the parable (Matthew 20:1-16) saying, "Sic erunt novissimi primi, et primi novissimi. Multi enim sunt vocati, pauci vero electi."[36] Chaucer may have set the *Parson's Tale* at the end of *The Canterbury Tales* in order "To knytte up al this feeste, and make an ende" (*Pars Prol*, 47), as he says, and he may have arranged for it to be told at the eleventh hour so that that which was last in order might be pointed out as first in value for any pilgrimage.

[35] Even in English the ordinal numbers can occasion disagreement: Skeat thought that 4:00 P.M. would be the tenth hour reckoning from 6:00 A.M., but this would require that we count 7:00 A.M. as the beginning of the first hour (*Astrolabe*, lxiii). This would require that the twelfth hour conclude at 7:00 P.M., whereas it seems that the point of the system is to count twelve hours between 6:00 A.M. and 6:00 P.M. If we assume that the twelfth hour ends at 6:00 P.M., then it begins at 5:00 P.M., and the eleventh hour begins at 4:00 P.M.

[36] Professor Peck in his analysis of the symbolic numbers used to calculate the time of day in the Parson's Prologue offers support for many of the conclusions about Libra advanced here. According to Peck the numbers "focus the reader's attention on the themes of penance and fulfillment . . ." (Russell A. Peck, "Number Symbolism in the Prologue to Chaucer's *Parson's Tale*," *ES*, XLVIII [1967], 206).

APPENDIX

The Workings of Astrology
"Brede and Milke for Childeren"

FEW SCHOLARS who use this book will require instruction in the basic elements of mediaeval astrology and astronomy, and the more complicated issues I have attempted to deal with as they arose in discussions of particular passages. However, some people may not know the basic concepts behind the astrology and astronomy discussed here, while others may wish to refresh their memories without reference to other books.[1] Consequently there is here presented a brief sketch of mediaeval astronomy and astrology that is deliberately intended to be simple and straightforward for the benefit of those who are unfamiliar with the concepts involved. Some indulgence toward the repetitious style used here is therefore asked of the *cognoscenti*, for this section is not written for them. As Chaucer wrote in his *Treatise on the Astrolabe*, "me semith better to writen unto a child twyes a god sentence, than he forgete it onys."

THERE ARE three concepts fundamental to an understanding of the old cosmology: the universe is composed of a series of spheres, one within another; the earth is at the center of these; the planets have two basic motions in opposite directions, one a daily motion and the other an annual motion. Strictly speaking only the sun has both a daily and an annual motion, since only the sun runs its course through the zodiac in a year's time, the moon taking only a month and Saturn taking about 30 years. However, the concept of the two motions is best discussed with reference to the sun, and thus the terms daily and annual motion are convenient. That the universe was conceived of as a series of concentric spheres with the earth at the center in

---

[1] There are very good introductions to mediaeval astronomy and astrology in the following: Florence Marie Grimm, "Astronomical Lore in Chaucer," *University of Nebraska Studies in Language, Literature, and Criticism*, II (1919), 1-96; M. A. Orr (Mrs. John Evershed), *Dante and the Early Astronomers* (London, 1956), pp. 22-28. There is a good account of the precession of the equinoxes in Edward Moore, *Studies in Dante* (Oxford, 1903), III, 6-18. A very sophisticated account of fully developed late mediaeval astronomy is to be found in *The Equatorie of the Planetis*, ed. Derek J. Price (Cambridge, 1955), pp. 93-118.

mediaeval cosmology is rather well known today. Just what those spheres and the planets they carry are doing, however, is rather more complex, yet if not understood leaves one in confusion about the simplest astrological phenomena. Using the sun (which was considered to be a planet in the Middle Ages) as an example, let us investigate the two motions.

The sun rises in the east every day, crosses the sky, sets in the west, and—if we grant that it revolves around the earth—continues around the earth to rise again the next morning in the east. Were we to watch the stars and planets at night we would note that they too have an east to west motion on this same daily basis, so that any star or constellation discovered in the east at evening will move to the western sky by dawn. The stars, unlike the planets, remain fixed in their relationships to one another, and so were known as the fixed stars. To phrase this another way, we might say that the stars have only a daily motion. This is not strictly accurate, but sufficient for the present. The fixed stars constituted the eighth sphere, the seven planets making up the inner spheres. (See Fig. 29.) Ptolemy numbered the spheres at only eight, but in the Middle Ages this was commonly modified by the addition of a ninth sphere, the Primum Mobile, which accounted for the daily motion. Another sphere that was sometimes posited in the later Middle Ages is the Crystalline. There is a discussion of theories regarding the Crystalline sphere in Chapter II.

The sun in its daily course appears to circle the earth in twenty-four hours to rise again in the east. Upon closer inspection, however, it does not quite complete a full circle but falls short by about one degree out of the 360 in a circle. Thus, if we noted what constellation was on the eastern horizon just before the sun rose, we should find that after a month the same constellation would be somewhat elevated above the eastern horizon just before sunrise. After six months that star group would be on the western horizon just before sunrise, and after a year it would once again be immediately above the eastern horizon just before dawn.

There are two ways in which we might express this relationship. We could say that both the sun and the entire heaven moved daily from east to west, but that the sun moved a little more slowly; or

we could say that the sun and the other stars all moved on a daily basis from east to west, but that the sun and the other planets also had a contrary, annual motion in the opposite direction from west to east. In the Middle Ages the usual way of explaining the two motions was to consider them as motions in opposite directions, although it should be pointed out that al-Bitrûjî, or Alpetragius, wrote a treatise arguing that all the motions of the heavens were in the same direction but that some were slower than others.[2] Indeed, it should be remembered that while we refer to the "Ptolemaic" cosmology quite freely for any geocentric world view, Ptolemy's theories received several important modifications at the hands of the Arab astronomers, and competing theories for various parts of the whole scheme appeared from time to time.

The sun, then, moves daily from east to west across the sky, but during the course of a year moves in the opposite direction across the heavens. The backdrop of constellations through which the sun moves constitutes the zodiac. The zodiac was imagined as a sort of belt draped at an angle across the heavens and measuring 16 degrees in width. It is bisected by an ecliptic, which is the annual path of the sun. Figure 30 shows a representation of the zodiac, divided into 12 equal parts of 30 degrees each, each part constituting a sign of the zodiac.[3] It should be remarked here that the constellations which originally gave the signs their names no longer correspond to the signs themselves because of a phenomenon called precession which will be discussed below. The zodiac's being at an angle to the celestial equator—which is a projection of the earth's equator—explains the varying declination or altitude of the sun from the equator. The

---

[2] See al-Bitrûjî: *De motibus celorum*, ed. Francis J. Carmody (Berkeley and Los Angeles, 1952), pp. 11-38. For histories of cosmology in antiquity and the Middle Ages see the following: Pierre Duhem, *Le système du monde* (Paris, 1913-59), II, 59-259; J. L. E. Dreyer, *A History of Astronomy from Thales to Kepler*, rev. W. H. Stahl (Dover Publications, 1953), pp. 1-280; M. A. Orr, *Dante and the Early Astronomers*, pp. 29-148; A. C. Crombie, *Medieval and Early Modern Science*, rev. ed. (Garden City, N.Y., 1959), pp. 75-98; A. Pannekoek, *A History of Astronomy* (London, 1961), pp. 19-177.

[3] In this representation the "Antarctic Pole" is located at the top of the picture in order that the sun's daily motion from east to west would correspond with Aristotelian ideas of "correct" motion "from the right." The whole phenomenon is discussed in Chapter V.

sun's daily path across the sky is low in winter and high in summer because its annual path takes it above and below the celestial equator. Figure 31a shows the sun "in" Aquarius—that is, rising and setting with Aquarius as a backdrop, which it does in late winter. Note that in Aquarius the sun both rises and sets below the celestial equator. In Figure 31b, showing the sun halfway around in its daily journey, it is only outlined to suggest that it is on the far side of the sphere. Here Aquarius and the signs contiguous with it are no longer visible, because the other side of the zodiac intervenes. Notice that because the zodiac is inclined to the celestial equator at an angle of 23½ degrees, it does not turn on its own axis, but swivels around on the axis of the celestial equator. The planets, however, move through it, and by summer the sun will rise and set in the signs above the celestial equator. The resolution of the two motions of the sun, the daily and annual, gives a spiral. Dante compared this spiral motion of the sun to the turning of the screw of a great press, and another famous metaphor describes the sun as like a fly crawling on the rim of a wheel while the wheel daily swivelled around in the opposite direction, carrying the fly with it.

Once the sun's two motions are understood, the other apparent motions of the heavens are easy to comprehend. Like the sun, the other planets revolve daily around the vertical axis of the earth and move through the zodiac. However, they move at very different rates of speed. The moon, for example, manages to traverse the whole zodiac in about a month, while Mars takes about 2½ years, and Saturn about 30 years. Moreover, planets other than the sun sometimes reverse their course along the zodiac and run in the opposite direction, a phenomenon called retrograde motion. To account for these more complicated motions the Ptolemaic system uses a series of eccentrics, equants, and epicycles. While these are rarely brought up by poets like Chaucer and Dante, it is worth knowing how the Ptolemaic system answered the difficult problems of celestial phenomena as well as the relatively straightforward problem of the sun's annual motion.

Aristotle had taught that the various spheres were concentric, having the earth in the exact center, but it was soon found that concentric spheres were not adequate for explaining the observed phe-

nomena, so a system of eccentric spheres was evolved. Eccentric spheres revolve around centers located near but not exactly at the earth. The sun, for example, takes longer to travel from the vernal to the autumnal equinox than it does to travel from the autumnal to the vernal, and this inequality could be accounted for by supposing that the center of the sun's path was at some distance from the earth, that is, on an eccentric point. The circle (to keep the discussion in two dimensions) drawn around this eccentric point was called the deferent, and the eccentric point itself was called the center deferent. (See Fig. 32.) This was sufficient for dealing with the motion of the sun, but for other planets further modifications were required.

For Venus, Mars, Jupiter, and Saturn it was necessary to consider an epicycle and an equant in addition to the deferent. The equant is simply an elaboration of the deferent. Instead of supposing that a point on the circumference of the deferent moved at a constant speed when viewed from the center deferent, the constant speed was thought to be observed from a different point called the equant, located twice the distance from the earth as the center deferent. The line connecting these three points—the center of the earth, the center deferent, and the equant—was called the line of the aux. When one deals with the moon and Mercury these modifications are further complicated by positing for Mercury a center deferent revolving in a circle, and for the moon both a revolving center deferent and a revolving equant. The epicycle is much better known than any of these other devices and consists of a circular path, with its center on the circumference of the deferent, along which the planet was supposed to move. Figure 32 shows these constructs. For further discussion of this aspect of the Ptolemaic theory, with much more elaborate diagrams, see Price's edition of *The Equatorie of the Planetis.*

By the end of the Middle Ages several additional spheres had been added to Ptolemy's original eight. An outermost sphere, the Primum Mobile, was universally used to account for the daily movement of all the underlying heavens from east to west; and a Crystalline sphere was posited by some to account for calendrical precession—that slow decrease in the date of the vernal equinox that we allow for in our calendars by omitting leap year once every century

except when the year is evenly divisible by 400. Leap year is necessary because the sun's annual course in a complete circle (the sidereal year) is a little more than 365 days—about ¼ day more—but its course from one vernal equinox to the next (the equinoctial or tropical year) is twenty minutes of time less than that. This is not much, to be sure, but it mounts up over the centuries. Another, later addition to the original Ptolemaic theory gave the sphere of the fixed stars a small annual motion to account for the precession of the equinoxes. Because of calendrical precession the sun crosses the vernal equinox some twenty minutes of time earlier every year, which means that it arrives at this point in the zodiac in fifty seconds less space every year. Thus, if the sun entered the imagined band of the zodiac against a backdrop of stars in any given year, the following year it would cross the same point on the zodiac against a backdrop very slightly to the west of the first point. Because of this phenomenon the signs of the zodiac no longer correspond to the constellations they were originally named for. A theory that never gained universal acceptance in the Middle Ages was that this motion of the fixed stars did not proceed in one direction but oscillated back and forth. This motion was called trepidation.

In addition to astronomical matters it is necessary to have some knowledge of astrological practice. The basis of all astrology is the horoscope, which involves calculating first what positions the planets were in at the moment of a person's birth, and second, what the configuration means in terms of the native's personality, fortune, and so forth. No one believed in complete astral determinism, however, so in addition to the casting of horoscopes, astrologers sought various ways to mitigate possible adverse forecasts through elections, the choosing of propitious times for doing things, based on the horoscope whenever possible. Finally there was the practice of questions, a formal attempt to determine future happenings.

The calculation of a horoscope is a much more complicated affair than one might think. Contemporary horoscopes depend upon the sign the sun is in during the month of one's birth, while mediaeval horoscopes were based upon the sign ascending in the east at the moment of a person's birth. Determining this usually required some rather careful computation, for all twelve signs move across the east-

ern horizon every day in the daily rotation of the heavens. After this it was necessary to determine exactly where every planet was in the zodiac at the moment of birth, and then the meaning of it all had to be determined. First of all each planet was located in a sign of the zodiac, that is, rising and setting in one sign or another, and then its degree of power in that sign was determined. Figure 33 is a chart of the signs of the zodiac and the planetary powers therein, the power decreasing from top to bottom. Secondly there were three-fold divisions of the signs called decans or faces, each of which was a place of power of one of the planets, and five-fold divisions of the signs called terms, which were also places of power for the different planets. The planets were also measured in relation to one another across the zodiac—whether they were in conjunction (present in the same degree of the same sign), opposition, triune, quartile or sextile aspect.

In addition to the planet's position in the zodiac it was important to know its position among the astrological houses. These houses are to be distinguished from the houses or mansions of the planets, which are appellations of power in certain signs. The astrological or divisional or computational houses are arbitrary divisions of the whole heavens into twelve parts—sometimes equal parts, but more often unequal.[4] The latter method divided the heavens with great circles beginning with one on the poles of daily rotation. From that point the zodiac appears as an ellipse, so equal divisions of the heavens result in unequal divisions of the zodiac. These divisional houses were arbitrarily numbered counterclockwise from the ascendant, and each was assigned a peculiar province, such as love, death, marriage, and fortune. They were oftentimes charted in a square in drawing up a horoscope, and thus four of the twelve were in corners. Perhaps because of this the first, fourth, seventh, and tenth houses were called "angles," while the remaining houses were known as suc-

---

[4] Pico della Mirandola satirizes the astrologers for not being able to agree on how to form these houses. See G. Pico della Mirandola, *Disputationes adversus astrologiam divinatricem*, ed. Eugenio Garin (Florence, 1946-52), II, 314ff. One should note that it is not always possible to determine which kind of house the astrologers are concerned with. See *The Astronomical Works of Thabit B. Qurra*, ed. Francis J. Carmody (Berkeley and Los Angeles, 1960), p. 115.

cedents and cadents. The lines demarcating the houses were known as cusps.

It is readily apparent from this discussion that Chaucer never uses genuine horoscopes, for the simple reason that they are far too cumbersome. No one can imagine the Wife of Bath saying that her ascendant was Taurus, with Mars therein, and then proceeding to each of the six remaining planets, telling their signs, houses, degrees of power, and aspect to other planets. On the other hand, some knowledge of the details of astrology is assumed by Chaucer, and when he describes Mars in the *Man of Law's Tale* as having fallen from an angle into the darkest house, he did not mean to be obscure. This introduction to the subject is intended to mitigate some of Chaucer's seeming opacity.

Yif thou, wys, wilt demen in thi pure thought the ryghtes or the lawes of the heye thondrere (*that is to seyn, of God*), loke thou and byhoold the heightes of the sovereyn hevene. Ther kepin the sterres, be ryghtful alliaunce of thinges, hir oolde pees.

(Boethius, Bk. IV, m. 6)

Index

1. Horoscope of Agostino Chigi for December 1, 1466
Palazzo Farnesina (Baldassare Peruzzi)

2. God and the Planets
Santa Maria del Popolo
(Raphael)

3. Night Sky of Florence,
July 8-9, 1422
San Lorenzo

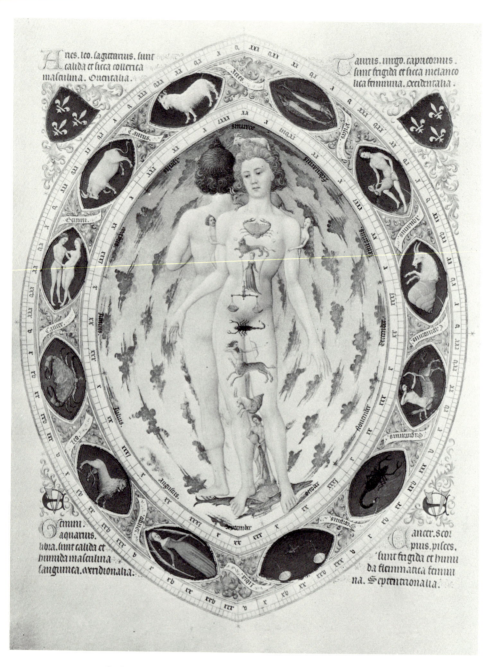

4. Influence of the Zodiac on the Body (Pol de Limbourg)

5b. The Zodiac and the Labors of the Months: Scorpio/October and Sagittarius/November. Amiens

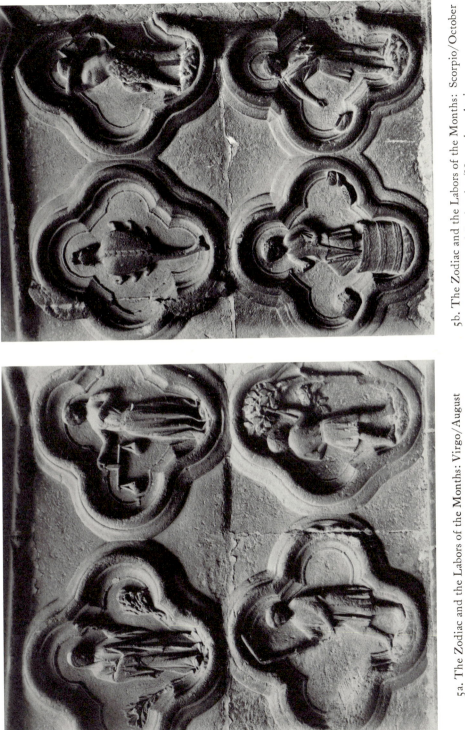

5a. The Zodiac and the Labors of the Months: Virgo/August and Libra/September. Amiens

6. The Zodiac and the Labors of the Months: Taurus/April
(Pol de Limbourg)

7. The Zodiac and the Labors of the Months: Libra/September
(Pol de Limbourg)

8. The Zodiac and the Labors of the Months: Scorpio/October
(Pol de Limbourg)

9. The Zodiac and the Labors of the Months. Chartres

10. The Zodiac and the Labors of the Months. *Vézelay*

11. The Planets and the Seven Liberal Arts. Santa Maria Novella

12. Jupiter as Monk (Andrea Pisano). Santa Maria del Fiore

·SATVRNVS·

Saturno huomini tardi er rei produce
Rubbaduri er buriardi er assasini
Villani er uili er senza alchuna luce
Pastori er zoppi er simili meschini ··

13a. The "Children" of Saturn, *De sphaera*, folio 4[v]

13b. The "Children" of Saturn, *De sphaera*, folio 5ʳ

14. Mars, Venus, and Jupiter, *Complaint of Mars*, folio 14ᵛ

15. Mars and Venus (Boucher)

16. Mars and Venus (Botticelli)

17. Mars and Venus (Piero di Cosimo)

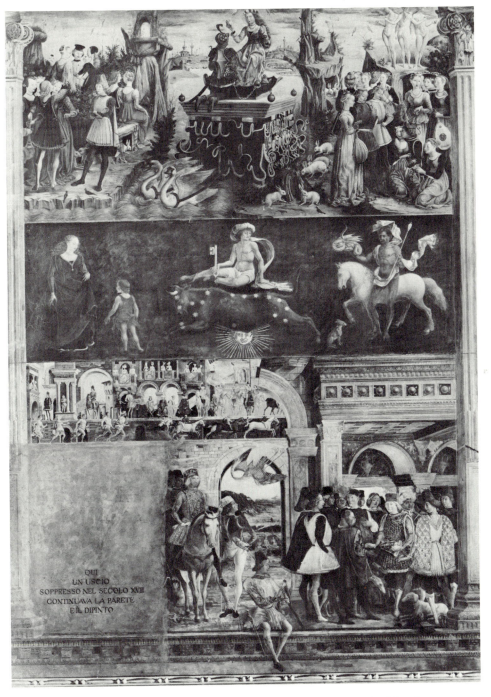

18a. Mars and Venus, Taurus, and Aristocratic Labors of the Months
(Francesco Cossa)

18b. Mars and Venus, Taurus, and Aristocratic Labors of the Months
(Francesco Cossa). Detail

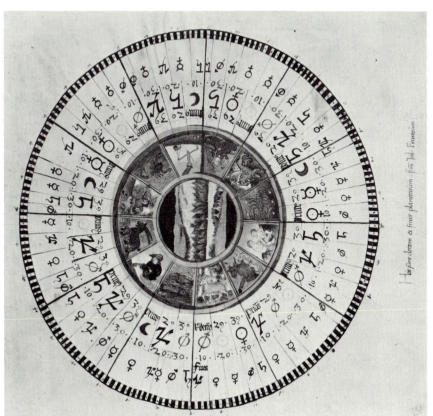

20. The Decans of Scorpio

19. Signs, Decans, and Termini according to Firmicus Maternus

21. Signs and Towers

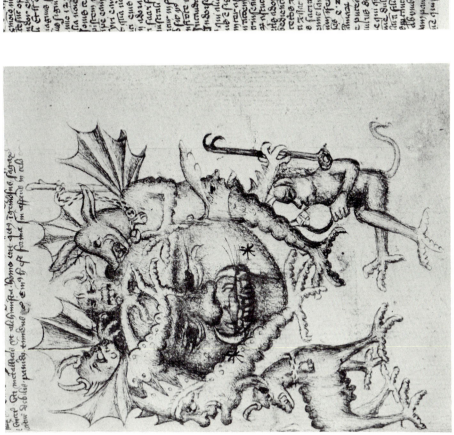

22. Puteus

23. Galaxy, Piscis Magnus,
Piscis Parvus, and Puteus

24. Hellmouth, *Book of Hours of Catherine of Cleves*, folio 168ᵛ

25. The Crucifix and the Balance, *Ars moriendi*, folio 62^v

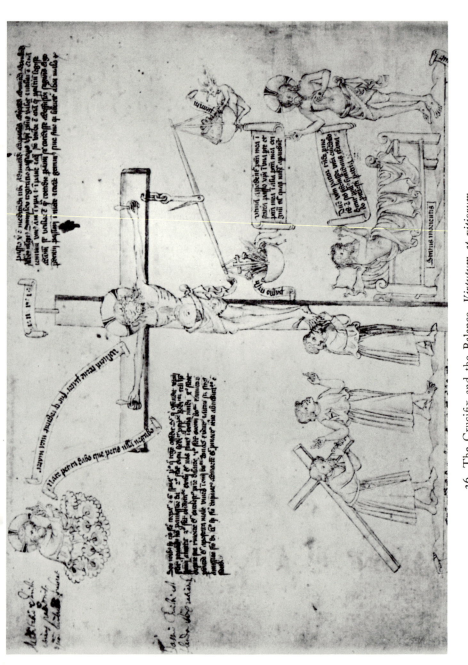

26. The Crucifix and the Balance, *Virtutum et vitiorum omnium delineatio*, folio 37ᵛ

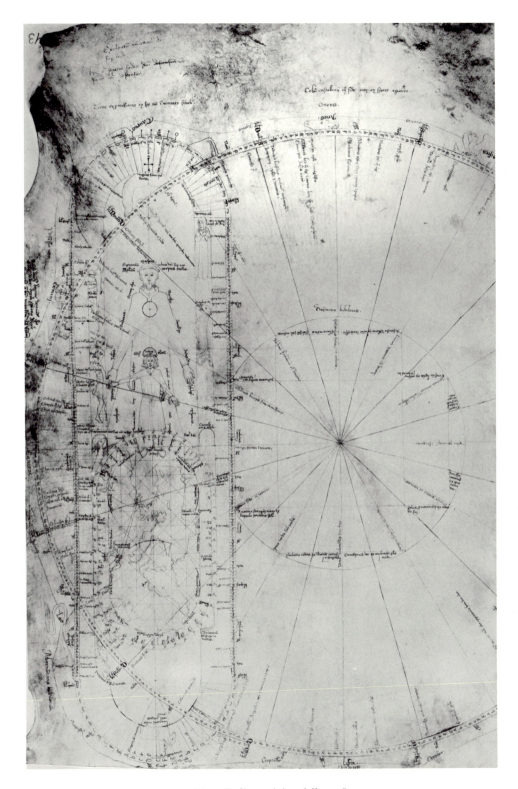

27. Two Zodiacs, *Atlas*, folio 13ʳ

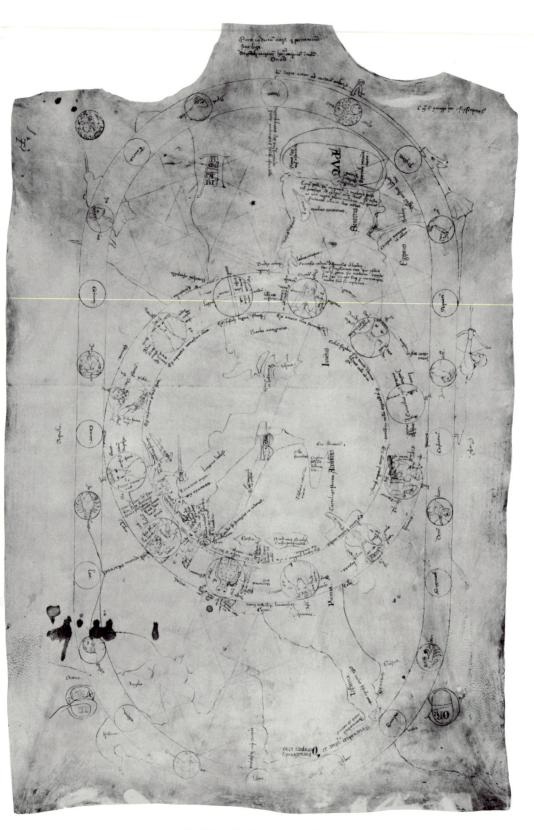

28. Two Zodiacs, *Atlas*, folio 6ᵛ

29. Ptolemaic Planetarium (Rowley)

30. Armillary Sphere, *Textus de sphaera*, folio 3ᵛ

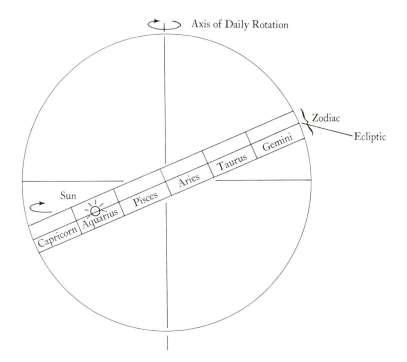

Axis of Daily Rotation

Zodiac

Ecliptic

Gemini

Taurus

Aries

Pisces

Sun

Capricorn Aquarius

31a. The Sun in Aquarius

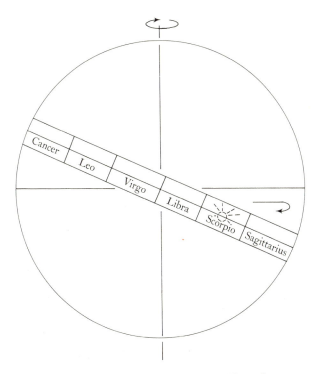

Cancer

Leo

Virgo

Libra

Scorpio Sagittarius

31b. The Sun in Aquarius Twelve Hours Later

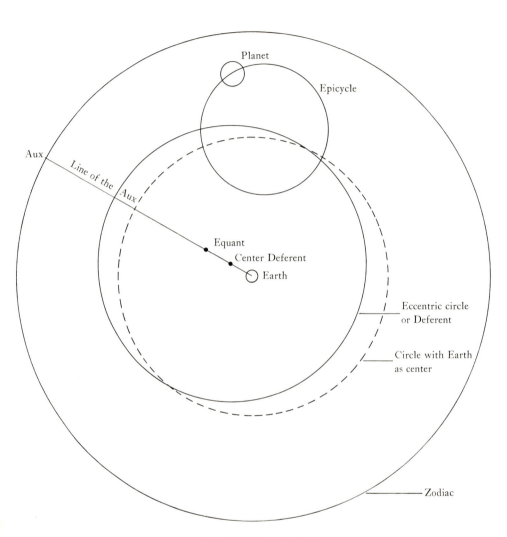

32. Deferent and Epicycle

Signs	Aries	Taurus	Gemini	Cancer	Leo	Virgo
House	Mars	Venus	Mercury	Moon	Sun	Mercury
Exaltation	Sun 19°	Moon 3°	Venus 3°	Jupiter 15°		Mercury 15°
Debility	Venus	Mars	Jupiter	Saturn	Saturn	Jupiter
Fall	Jupiter & Saturn			Mars		Venus

Signs	Libra	Scorpio	Sagittarius	Capricorn	Aquarius	Pisces
House	Venus	Mars	Jupiter	Saturn	Saturn	Jupiter
Exaltation	Saturn 21°			Mars 28°		Venus 27°
Debility	Mars	Venus	Mercury	Moon	Sun	Mercury
Fall	Sun	Moon		Jupiter		Mercury

33. The Powers and Debilities of the Planets
in the Signs of the Zodiac